THE ELECTRONIC ERA OF PUBLISHING

THE ELECTRONIC ERA OF PUBLISHING
An Overview of Concepts, Technologies and Methods

OLDRICH STANDERA
The University of Calgary
Calgary, Alberta
Canada

ELSEVIER
New York • Amsterdam • London

Elsevier Science Publishing Co., Inc.
52 Vanderbilt Avenue, New York, New York 10017

Distributors outside the United States and Canada:
Elsevier Science Publishers B.V.
P.O. Box 211, 1000 AE Amsterdam, the Netherlands

© 1987 by Elsevier Science Publishing Co., Inc.

This book has been registered with the Copyright Clearance Center, Inc., Salem, Massachusetts.

Library of Congress Cataloging in Publication Data

Standera, Oldrich, 1925–
  The electronic era of publishing.

  Bibliography: p.
  Includes index.
  1. Electronic publishing. I. Title.
Z286.E43S73 1987   070.5'028'5   87-8872
ISBN 0-444-01200-1

Current printing (last digit):
10 9 8 7 6 5 4 3 2 1

Manufactured in the United States of America

To My Family

Contents

List of Figures *xi*
List of Tables *xiii*
Foreword *xv*
Preface *xix*
Acknowledgments *xxi*

1 INTRODUCTION *1*
1.1 The Scope of the Discourse *3*
1.2 Terminology: Definitions *6*
1.3 About the Book *10*

2 TECHNOLOGY: THE BACKGROUND *15*
2.1 Sketch of Progress in Telematics *15*
2.2 Analog and Digital Information *34*

3 NON-PRINT-BASED ELECTRONIC PUBLISHING *43*
3.1 Offline (Batch) Retrieval *44*
3.2 Online Retrieval *45*
3.3 End User-oriented Online Services *51*
3.4 Online Public-access Library Catalog *54*
3.5 Videotex: Viewdata and Teletext *59*

- 3.6 Cable TV *67*
- 3.7 Optical Memory Media *73*
- 3.8 Electronic Mail *93*
- 3.9 Teleconferencing *97*
- 3.10 Electronic Journal *99*

4 PRINT-BASED ELECTRONIC PUBLISHING *105*
- 4.1 Data Entry Plus the Editorial Process *112*
- 4.2 Typesetters and Their Front-ends *126*
- 4.3 Complete Prepress Systems *138*
- 4.4 Assorted Prepress Subsystems *171*

5 ELECTRONIC DOCUMENT DELIVERY *189*
- 5.1 Delineation of the Concept *189*
- 5.2 The Rationale Behind the Electronic Document Delivery Efforts *190*
- 5.3 Background *191*
- 5.4 Modes of Operations *193*
- 5.5 Users: Problems and Help *195*
- 5.6 Examples of Electronic Document Delivery Systems *197*
- 5.7 Innovative Distribution Formats *206*
- 5.8 Electronic Document Management Systems and Electronic Publishing *208*
- 5.9 Concluding Remarks on Electronic Document Delivery *211*
- 5.10 Telefacsimile *213*

6 ARTIFICIAL INTELLIGENCE *217*
- 6.1 General Observations *217*
- 6.2 Expert Systems *218*
- 6.3 Other Artificial Intelligence Concepts Relevant to Electronic Publishing *226*

7 MICROCOMPUTERS IN ELECTRONIC PUBLISHING *229*
- 7.1 Applications *230*
- 7.2 Microcomputers and Current Trends *232*
- 7.3 Roles of Microcomputers in Prepress (1986 and Beyond) *235*
- 7.4 A Note on the Economics *237*
- 7.5 The Marketing Aspect *239*
- 7.6 Conclusion *240*

8 ELECTRONIC PRINTERS 243
8.1 Versatile Output Device 243
8.2 Technical Features and Performance Indicators of Page Printers 246
8.3 Page Description Languages 248
8.4 A Few Representatives of the Growing Printer Family 249

9 SOME IMPLICATIONS OF ELECTRONIC PUBLISHING 253
9.1 Authors 254
9.2 Publishers 255
9.3 Libraries 257
9.4 Changing Role of the Intermediary 259
9.5 Users 262

10 CONCLUSIONS 265
10.1 Non-print-based Electronic Publishing 266
10.2 Print-based Electronic Publishing 268
10.3 Electronic Document Delivery 272
10.4 Artificial Intelligence 273

REFERENCES 277

APPENDIX 289
  A.1 Casual Users and the Editorial Process 289
  A.2 Some Notes on Reader Response and Costs 311
  A.3 Human Performance and Information Processing in the Context of the Electronic Journal 326

GLOSSARY OF TERMS AND ACRONYMS 345

LIST OF ORGANIZATIONS 389

INDEX 399

List of Figures

1. The Position of Electronic Publishing *5*
2. Electronic Publishing and Electronic Delivery *9*
3. OCR—Device-facilitated Publishing *38*
4. An Outline of the Online Business *46*
5. Videotex: Viewdata *60*
6. Videotex: Teletext *62*
7. Hybrid "Online Text/Local Videodisc Graphics" Technology *85*
8. Publishing System Based on Optical Digital Disk *89*
9. Information Traffic Between the Originator and Typesetter *115*
10. Front-end-to-Typesetter Subsystem *131*
11. Authors, Publishers, Editors, Typesetters, and Printers *137*
12. Originator-to-Paper System *141*
13. Originator to Film (Monochrome) *144*
14. Originator to Film (Color) *145*
15. A Hypothetical Digital Color Prepress System *149*
16. Raster Image Processor Facilitated Subsystem *176*
17. Page Makeup In Broader Context *180*
18. Graphics Pasteup-to-Plate Subsystem *182*
19. Electronic Document Management Systems in the Electronic Delivery Role *209*
20. Expert System *219*
21. Evolution of Information Technology *223*

22. User Performance *303*
23. Comprehension Errors *330*
24. Random Errors *331*
25. Probability of Errors *332*
26. Model of Human Information Processing *337*

List of Tables

1. Indication of Trends in Integrated Circuits *17*
2. Examples of Storage Media Capacity *23*
3. User Characteristics *300*
4. Users A, B and C: Actions per Error *302*
5. Total Errors as Percentage of Actions *303*
6. Scores of Format Acceptance *317*
7. Significance of Criteria Applied to Acceptance Rating *318*
8. Actual Costs of Five Journal Formats *320*
9. Cost of Five Journal Formats *322*
10. Cost-Benefit of Five Journal Formats Based upon User Acceptance and Journal Cost on a Five-Point Scale *324*
11. Usage of the "Cut-and-Paste" Feature *335*

Foreword

This book appears at a particularly appropriate time. Information systems design and implementation may be usefully characterized as having passed through two distinct stages, and as beginning a third stage. John Rockart of the Harvard Business School has characterized these three stages as clerical, operational and managerial.[1] A complementary characterization, and one particularly appropriate to the subject matter of this book, is a stage hypothesis based on the fundamental technologies of information systems, computation, storage and communication.[2]

The most striking aspect of modern information systems technology, that which distinguishes it from all previous technologies, is its rate of growth. In the early 1960s Gordon Moore observed that the number of elements that could be integrated into one chip was growing with a sustained doubling period of not much more than 2 years.[3] "Moore's law" has become the token of that dramatic rate of growth. Hot metal printing technology by contrast had a doubling period of 24 years.[4]

---

[1] Rockart, J. (1986). Computer use enters third era. *IBM Innovation Digest*. p.3.
[2] Koenig, M.E.D. (1986). The convergence of computers and telecommunications: Information management implications. *Information Management Review*. Vol.1, No.3, pp.23–33, Winter.
[3] Noyce, R.N. (1977). Microelectronics. *Scientific American*. Vol.237, No.3, pp.62–69, September.
[4] Koenig, M.E.D. (1982). The information controllability explosion. *Library Journal*. Vol.107, No.19, pp.2052–54, 1 November.

xv

By combining the Moore's law concept of exponential growth with the three prime components of information systems technology, we are led rather neatly to three distinct stages in the growth of information systems.

The Three Stages of Information Systems Capability

Stage	Exponential Growth of
I (1950s to 1971)	1. Computational Capability
II (1971 to 1986?)	1. Computational Capability
	2. Storage Capability
III (1986 to 199?)	1. Computational Capability
	2. Storage Capability
	3. Communications Capability

Stage I was characterized from an operational perspective by rapid exponential growth in computational capacity. The ability to do mathematical operations, number crunching, was the central focus of the era. It was in stage I that Moore made his observation about circuit integration, whose effect initially was, of course, to foster computation.

While great progress was being made in stage I on computationally dependent applications such as payroll and accounting, in other areas stage I was a period of substantial disillusionment. Obviously the computer was an information-processing device of immense potential power, and the union of the computer with traditional information systems such as libraries and information centers should have been a marriage made in heaven, to be consummated as soon as possible. Unfortunately, such traditional information systems are far more dependent upon storage and communication capabilities than upon computational capabilities, and the technology of stage I was simply not yet very appropriate to such applications. The classic statement of that disillusionment was Mason's "The Great Gas Bubble Prick't, or Computers revealed by a Gentleman of Quality."[5]

---

[5]Mason, E. (1971). The great gas bubble prick't, or computers revealed by a gentleman of quality. *College and Research Libraries.* Vol.32, No.3, pp.183–196, May.

FOREWORD

Meanwhile behind the scenes in stage I, the framework was being built for stage II. The principal component of that framework was the development of direct access storage (disk) drives, relatively inexpensive mass storage. Stage II, which we entered approximately 15 years ago, and which we are about to leave for stage III, has been characterized by the continued explosive growth of computational capability and by similar growth in operational storage capability. The transition from stage I to stage II was, of course, a gradual, not an overnight affair, but it can be pegged with some confidence to the year 1971. That year saw the emergence of large-scale online commercial database services, specifically System Development Corporation's Orbit system offering Chemical Abstracts and other databases online. In the same year OCLC, the Online Computer Library Center (then the Ohio College Library Center) began offering what was in effect an online macro library catalog, and the US National Library of Medicine launched the Medline service.

Behind the scenes in stage II, the framework was being laid in similar fashion for stage III. In 1971 Robert Maurer and his team at Corning Glass developed a new type of glass for use in optical fibers that was of a purity hitherto unknown, with a half absorption distance of 150 meters, and communication technology began a new phase of exponential growth. Since that time the two principal operational parameters of fiber optics, the data rate of transmission, and the distance that a signal can be transmitted before it has to be extracted, amplified and retransmitted, have been doubling at a Moore's law rate of 1 1/2 years.[6]

During stage II, the capability per cost of telecommunications has largely remained plateaued. We are, however, nearly at the point in regard to telecommunications capabilities at which the exponential growth of the technological substrate will surpass the operational threshold, and we will begin to see an exponential growth of capability per cost. At that point, we will enter stage III, with all three parameters—computational, storage and communications capabilities—growing exponentially.

If we are indeed beginning stage III, then the effects on the communication of knowledge will be profound. We will have to cope with a new-found Moore's law rate of exponential growth of communications capability. Those stage III techniques that we will use are of

---

[6]Koenig, M.E.D. (1984). Fiber optics and Library Technology. *Library Hi-Tech*. Vol.2, No.1, pp.9–15.

course electronic publishing, and that is what this book is about: where we are, what technologies are available now and where we are likely to be going.

>Michael E. D. Koenig
>Director of Information Retrieval
>Trafinex Limited
>
>Adjunct Associate Professor
>School of Library Service
>Columbia University

Preface

In the four centuries since Johannes Gutenberg created the new world of publishing through his technological revolution, the process of recording the memory of our cultures has grown and developed in many directions. Each avenue has grown in complexity, dividing and redividing into new subspecialties, technologies and talents. In a world that honors the innovator and the explorer, recognition should also be given to the work of the chart maker. Oldrich Standera is such a chart maker. In the *Electronic Era of Publishing* he has attempted to create that most difficult of charts—the overview.

The effort to plot the convergence of the many elements of the publishing process in the era of electronic technology is a challenge that few would tackle. Boundaries are defined and redefined, appearing and disappearing. New alliances are identified and tracked. An attempt is made to offer a panoramic view of a churning, shifting world that has been in a state of constant, accelerating change throughout the last two decades.

The strength of this book must be its ultimate shortcoming, for like great panoramic photography, it attempts to freeze a wide, complex, multifaceted world at a particular point in time and then draw some conclusions from an examination of the many actions, reactions, movements, and interactions that are observed.

Using techniques similar to the genealogist, Standera pursues the growth of publishing from its roots through the migration and diaspora of its seemingly many unrelated parts, and then plots the reunification and reintegration of the many branches being brought about in this era of electronic technology.

As with an early map of a continent, the diverse users of this work should be able to bring new specific detail and updates to it, while still benefitting and being guided by the overview it provides.

Alan H. MacDonald
Director
University of Calgary Press
The University of Calgary Library

Acknowledgments

I wish to extend my thanks to Alan MacDonald, Director of the University of Calgary Libraries and University of Calgary Press, for his interest and financial support without which completion of the research project Electronic Publishing and work on this study would not have been possible.

The first inspiration and encouragement to write this book came from Louis G. Vagianos, Executive Director of the Institute for Research on Public Policy, even though at that time we did not contemplate a work of this wide scope; for this I would like to express my gratitude to him.

Finally, I would like to thank LuAnn Zahara of Technical Services in the University of Calgary Libraries for the able and efficient wordprocessing support.

O.L. Standera
September, 1986

THE ELECTRONIC ERA OF PUBLISHING

1

Introduction

In recent years electronic publishing has become a hot topic not only in science and technology publications, but in association with computers, communications, publishing and other related concepts, whose progress it has shared and interactively spurred, it has been highlighted in weekly news magazines and newspapers. It has been heralded as one of the portents of the impending information age which is expected to usher us into the lap of a postindustrial era. Because electronic publishing has come to be a bailiwick for an ever-increasing number of people in keeping with the general trend toward employment in information-related areas and in view of the ominously growing avalanche of pertinent literature, it was deemed useful to pause for a while in the midst of these developments and take stock of the concepts, facts, events, hardware, software, products, etc. in this subject "space" called electronic publishing with the aim of bringing it into some perspective and of answering questions such as: what is it and what does it mean to all of us. Perhaps it will bring us closer to the realization that electronic publishing is not going to launch us into the despair of an information pandemonium nor is it going to be the last milestone on the road to information paradise, that as with all marvels of technology, it will be left to us—individuals, corporations and the society at large—to make what we will of it, and according to this achievement, to incorporate into our lives and work the essence of its spirit and content.

In the following text we shall be probing various industries, technologies and methods germane to the information age. The term "postindustrial society" mentioned above appears to be a misnomer since contemporary society is, and will continue to be, vitally dependant on a vast array of industries both information-related (electronics, computers, communications, publishing, etc., to name a few) and otherwise. To say that in the information era material goods, typical for the industrial society, are being replaced by intangible commodity, i.e., information which is in infinite supply, is symptomatic for the hype that has accompanied so-called high technology; it ignores the fact that national economies that have been performing best are those with competitive and productive industries. Only such economies will be able to sustain a strong information industry with a progressive information technology of which electronic publishing industry is an indivisible part. It appears that information age is still very much an industrial age with many more people being hungry for "industrial" goods than for information goodies; yet information has a decisive role to play in boosting production of goods and services due to its dual nature as both an end-product for consumption and as a catalyst for further growth.

The lifeblood of electronic publishing is information which will be phased out to a large degree by knowledge as information technology grows gradually more sophisticated. Information has become both a commodity as well as an important societal and corporate asset which postulates, due to its idiosyncrasies, a different mechanism for its evaluation and management than other assets such as manpower, capital goods, etc. Information has a few peculiar characteristics: it can be easily transported along networks; it is a valuable renewable, updatable resource; it can be easily discarded; it is readily copied, modified and also abused; once produced it is not used up by increased consumption; it poses more problems, than conventional goods, when it comes to fairly rewarding the originator. Information exists in several representational forms (see under 2.2), on many kinds of vehicle (media) and serves many purposes (entertainment, education, business, administration, production, etc.).

We find ourselves in the information era where an increasing albeit still relatively small, portion of the gross national product is generated as a result of money changing hands in the information market. Whether information will justify the immense infrastructure, hardware, software and lifeware costs will depend on the value of content carried as well as suitability of the publishing format in each particular instance; this is ultimately tested in the information market under the laws of information economics; we do not understand these laws quite yet. Many people might be in for an unpleasant surprise if they believed that generating real wealth could be supplanted by peddling unsolicited information along expensive electronic highways as we have witnessed in some of the field trials.

Whereas traditional, conventional publishers were selling packages such as books, magazines, etc., electronic publishers are in the business of merchandising information (and later on, knowledge) in addition to packages: videotex, online information, software, expert advice, knowledge; in doing so they will have to contend for customers' time and a share of their financial resources. This will be their ultimate challenge as patrons have increasingly more opportunity to choose a given desired content (a specific book in print or on audiotape, news on paper or on videotex screen, etc.), in the preferred publishing format and they have even a choice between multiple services within a given publishing format (vehicle, medium, communication channel) as for instance different online providers and databases to meet a specific user need in a subject area. The possibility of mixing content with a variety of publishing formats in an environment characterized by competing information services, forces electronic publishers into studying human information gathering habits; these issues which are not our primary concern in this volume, involve in addition to economics, also disciplines such as psychology, ergonomics, human-machine interface, artificial intelligence, cognitive science. Nobody will acquire information, whether in the public or private domain, just because it is "electronic." In fact very often technology is transparent to the user: the changeover from conventional technical report to one which has been produced using an electronic desktop system will go unnoticed; users are driven in their search for information by information seeking patterns which vary for different individuals and groups depending on their education, social and cultural background, previous experience, habits, expectations, financial circumstances, and a variety of other psychological and physiological factors.

1.1 The Scope of Discourse

This volume is about various modes of communication of ideas in a formal, and as it turned out with respect to some new media, also an informal manner, following the path from an originator to a user, i.e., reader in the conventional terminology. More particularly, it is devoted to the modern methods of publishing that sprang up in the last two decades as a result of the inroads made by the ubiquitous computer into this area of human endeavor with such a longstanding tradition. The impact of this development has not been, of course, restricted to publishing: computers have made themselves felt in the communications technology and the office/library technology to name two fields, to an equal, i.e., revolutionary extent. Advancements in these areas, in their own turn, again appreciably affected electronic publishing (1), which may thus be located within a triangle, if we may adopt an iconographic approach to symbolize the relationships, formed by computer (2), communications (3) and office/library technologies (4), with two strong links binding to media (5) and the graphic arts/printing industry (6), respectively, which themselves have been heavily influenced by the ever-increasing power of computers (see Figure 1). The significance of the boundaries between the above disciplines has been diminishing constantly as the distinction between their characteristics has become increasingly blurred by the process of continuing mutual integration.

It is difficult at times to separate the events which belong clearly to the realm of publishing from the rest of activities in related fields of electronic communication. Greenberger (1985) for instance, recently edited a book entitled *Electronic Publishing Plus* which concept includes, in addition to the operations related to traditional publishing and broadcasting, also the software, transactions and communication functions of the new information industry.

This volume has set as its conceptual framework a field of study that transcends the borderlines of traditionally treated subject areas and of necessity deals with a broad spectrum of issues, technological and otherwise, in a less comprehensive manner instead of discussing any of its constituents in minute detail, thus presenting a large-area, multicolored mosaic with some focus on the component parts. The diverse modes of communication tackled in this study are not expected, by an overwhelming consensus of experts in the field, to be mutually exclusive but rather to coexist side by side in a variety of specific conditions and environments: e.g., it is perfectly possible for a larger organization to publish internal technical publications using electronic composition and an electronic printer, and at the same time to maintain a technical information unit conducting online searches of remote databases, to subscribe to a local or regional videotex service in order to obtain local information, and to purchase a videodisk with an encyclopedia or art collection to supplement the collection of audiotapes and videotapes for local replay in the library which contains books (some of them having been produced with the application of modern methods of electronic publishing). This example is not a far-fetched dream of the past but a reality of today and reminds us that we are perhaps closer to the ideal of an electronic communication system than many among us dare think. Coexistence of these varied electronic information systems is on the increase and assumes a new dimension, especially in view of the fact that we are concerned here

INTRODUCTION

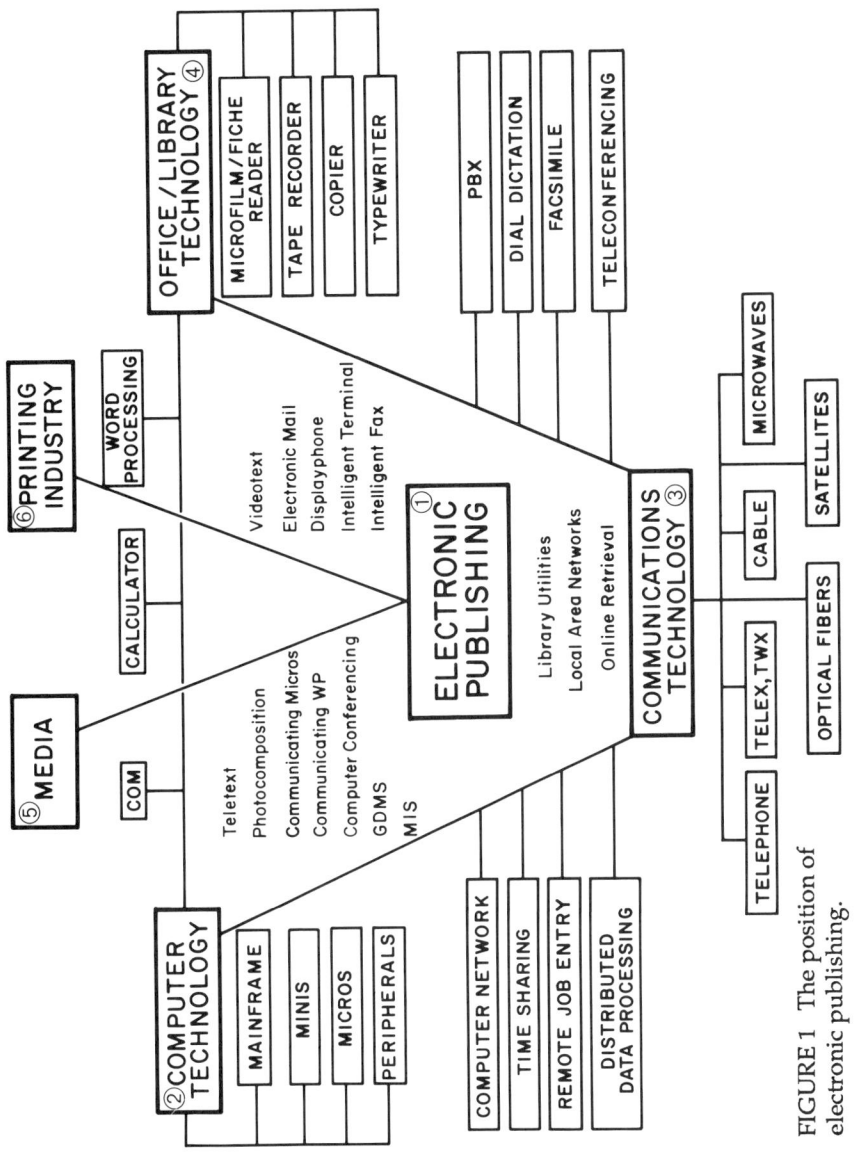

FIGURE 1 The position of electronic publishing.

not only with a symbiosis but rather with synergism of the individual publishing technologies; this might be exemplified by a videotex terminal and a microcomputer, serving several functions within a corporate environment—if the microcomputer is furnished with an appropriate software, it may be employed not only to receive in a passive manner but also to create videotex frames, thus saving the cost of a videotex input terminal and at the same time increasing its own value in more than one way through enhanced versatility.

1.2 Terminology: Definitions

Given the appearance on the scene of the recent modes of publishing, we can distinguish two broad categories in the subject area: the traditional means and electronic publishing. The former pertains generally to the state of the art up to the early 1960s marked by the advent of computer-assisted composition and database publishing; it covers publishing activities, methods and products other than those staked off as electronic publishing. This division is not based on the end product and does not coincide with the "print-based" and "non-print-based" or "paper-based" and "non-paper-based" dichotomy inasmuch as electronic publishing may produce a hard copy as its main product, as an alternative product or as a by-product. In contrast to "traditional" publishing, electronic publishing is also referred to as "nontraditional" and it has been also labeled as "screen-based" publishing with reference to its output media, but this term does not suit us well because it involves neither printed products nor sound. "New media publishing" is yet another synonym introduced for electronic publishing as is "computer-assisted publishing," but all names must be defined by the reader as to their meaning in any particular context.

In that electronic publishing is the central theme of our discussion, let us dwell awhile on its definition, both in general and as employed in the conception of this study, to preclude any possible misunderstanding and to do justice to Voltaire's demand that whoever talked to him had better define the terms used first.

Lerner (1978) defines electronic publishing in its broadest sense as "the use of electronic devices in all aspects of the production, management and distribution of primary and secondary information services." In a later review chapter (Lerner, Metaxas, Scott, Adams and Judd 1983) the same author notes that "the term 'electronic publishing' has been used to refer to the use of the computer in the production of publications and also in the sense of the electronic distribution of text via computer terminals."

Cuadra (1981) proposes similarly that "electronic publishing refers to the use of computers to facilitate the production process and the distribution of data to users at computer terminals through telecommunications networks"; the same author cautions that there are two major ways in which the term "electronic publishing" may be interpreted, either of them denoting a substantially different concept: (1) the first means "the use of computers to facilitate the production of a printed product" whereas the other (2) refers to electronic data distribution to users involving computers and telecommunication systems. The second concept could have taken off only after the first one had experienced an industry-wide acceptance. Thus the typesetting tape has become the vital link between these two vastly different notions implemented in the historical sequence.

Guernsey (1982), while in agreement with the two above definitions, goes on to distill the products and services in the area of data distribution into four main categories not encompassing the production of a conventional print product, viz. (1) broadcast, noninteractive services, (2) interactive services, (3) stand-alone products and (4) the electronic journal.

The Working Group on Electronic Publishing (1983), which is composed of members of varied interests, sees electronic publishing as "a form of publishing in which information is distributed using electronically encoded signals, stored for processing on computers or other means and displayed for viewing by users either on a screen or as a printout." The Working Group conceives of publishing, and by implication, of electronic publishing "as the systematic open communication of information and ideas through recognized channels in such a way as to permit retention and archiving for future use." Stress is put here on "open" and "retainable" publications but the Working Group acknowledges the existence of "less open or more ephemeral forms of communication between both individuals and organizations" which may gain more prominence as new forms of publishing spring up in the looming electronic era.

Look (1983) views electronic publishing as the storage and distribution of "information" using electronic media; as a distinguishing feature of electronic publishing he points out that information stored in it is in machine-readable form and must be made human-readable by an electronic device. The electronic publishing techniques dealt with in his book include online information retrieval, videotex, teletext and videodisk. Look also reminds us that we must differentiate between electronic document delivery and electronic publishing and notes that the boundary between these two concepts may be vague.

Collier (1981) adopts an even narrower definition and presents the concept of the access device, computer store and electronic communication as the three essential components of electronic publishing to be composed of online retrieval, videotex and teletext.

Lancaster (1978) offers his vision of an electronic information system for the year 2000, which implies and subsumes the notion of electronic scholarly publishing as part of a paperless system for scientific communication, and suggests that the publication of primary literature in the year 2000 may be an electronic parallel of the conventional publishing of today; the scientists of the future will have at their disposal a facility enabling them to compose, search for and receive text as well as obtain factual data, build information files and maintain conversations with others, and all this will make it possible for the scientist to act both as author and reader from the same terminal.

Nugent and Harding (1983) contend that electronic publishing becomes iconic publishing; they identify three forms or "waves" of electronic publishing in the historical perspective: the initial forms were database publishing characterized by a computer database of character-encoded text, which has offered significant benefits but has been unable to completely surmount the limitations with respect to graphics, tabular data, mathematical text and foreign languages. The next form of electronic publishing is represented by various videotex and teletext systems based on display of character-encoded text on television receivers accompanied by similarly encoded graphics. The optical disk technology is viewed as the third wave.

Butler (1986) uses electronic publishing as a general description of (1) electronic publishing of traditional printed publications, (2) electronic distribution of information in both electronic and print form and (3) true electronic publishing in electronic media.

Standera (1984) defines electronic publishing using the term as it has been recently coined with reference to a wide variety of processes in which the material to be published appears at one or more stages, or at all stages, transformed into and processed in the electronic form. At the earliest the material may assume electronic form at the moment when ideas to be communicated have been conceived, and it may remain in the electronic state all the way to the moment of delivery on the screen as in the case of an electronic journal or videotex pages. Alternatively, the final product may be delivered to the consumer (reader) as a hard copy, in microform, audio tape, videotape, videodisk, braille, sound, etc.

By adopting this definition for our present study we manage to accommodate electronic publishing as the generic term with electronic document delivery as its subcategory (see Figure 2), to include both the production and distribution aspects of the notion; this encompasses all

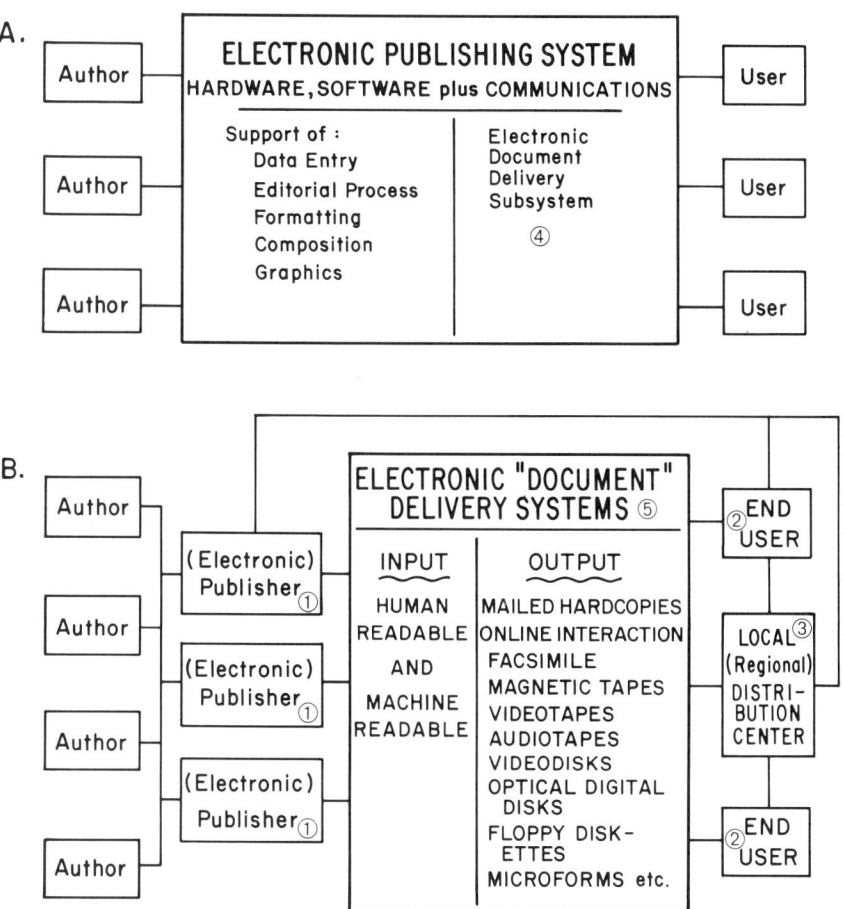

FIGURE 2 Electronic publishing and electronic delivery.

forms of product—electronic print product, frames on screen, microform, etc.—in human-perceivable (i.e., readable, audible, tactile) form if only it assumed electronic form at any stage in the course of its production. Figure 2 shows electronic delivery both (A) as a constituent part of the electronic publishing system itself (4) and (B) as a separate entity (5) positioned between the publisher (1) on the one hand and the end user (2) or a local distribution center (3) on the other hand; various modes of input/output are listed. Inasmuch as printed product is concerned, prepress technology is treated only by the inclusion of modern electronic printers that hold the potential to move printing from traditional printshops to the in-house technical publisher or to the automated office; text entry and editorial aspects have been also included to elucidate the involved relationships in this changing field.

1.3 About the Book

This book concerns itself with developments in all major categories of both print-based and nonprint-based publishing to some extent insofar as they contribute to the evolution of the new concept of electronic publishing: even though the primary focus was initially planned to be on scholarly publishing, developments in technical (in-house) publications, the newspaper industry, the magazine industry, software houses, commercial typesetters, CAD/CAM systems and office and microcomputer systems were added. The main criterion for inclusion was the novelty of hardware, software, product or service in the field of electronic publishing and the potential to become or contribute to a trend characteristic of this expanding area of human endeavor.

Although technology is the primary concern in the terms of reference of this study, it is realized that electronic publishing has more facets than that. The social, economic, legal, cognitive and ergonomic aspects of the discipline as well as acceptance of the new mode of communication all play a vital role in its genesis; they are discussed where applicable in the respective context but they do not represent the main thrust of this study.

By virtue of the above, this volume may prove useful to the practitioner in the publishing field, to the student and to the researcher, all who seek a broader frame of reference than the one in which they have been working or to which they have been exposed to date, in addition to the scholar who is involved in the process of publishing as a reader, author, reviewer or editor. At another level, because of the interdisciplinary nature of electronic publishing, the present study is of interest to those in the computer field, telecommunications, the office of the future, all aspects of publishing, media and communication in general, in that it increases the awareness of new developments in related areas and enables cross-fertilization to take place.

In the writing of this study we have described and made reference to some specific makes and manufacturers with regard to equipment, products, services and methods; this has been done solely with the objective of facilitating understanding of the subject matter and in no way implies that the author recommends or claims any superiority of the said equipment, products, etc. It also does not mean that the equipment referred to performs at any special level of efficiency in a particular situation. It is entirely possible, given the frantic pace of technology, that some products may no longer be available or may have been supplanted by new brands, models, etc.

In organizing this volume we thought it useful to preface the main body of text on electronic publishing proper by Chapter 2 entitled "Technology: The Background"; the rationale for this has been that all modes of electronic publishing described in later chapters have common roots and depend in their evolution on the feverish research, development and production activities in the computer and communications fields which in their turn draw heavily on the more fundamental scientific fields of mathematics, physics and so on. It is hoped that this chapter will provide a background on which the advancement of electronic publishing may be traced as a spin-off application of the unrelenting progress being realized in the computer area and communications, and that thereby the influence of the vast hinterland of relevant technology may be better appreciated; this will help put the subject field of electronic publishing in a broader context and will intimate the dimensions of impact that may be anticipated on our area of study.

Throughout this volume reference is made to information and data being generated, stored, processed, transmitted and produced in analog or digital form. Character coding as well as image (raster, facsimile) coding and vector coding are also frequently mentioned; the section "Analog and Digital Information" is designed to introduce the reader to these notions which are at the very heart of all modes of electronic publishing.

The electronic publishing technology dealt with in the subsequent text of this study has been divided into "non-print-based" (Chapter 3) and "print-based" (Chapter 4) methods of electronic publishing. These two fundamentally different groups of technology have been identified for the sake of convenience as either relying on print as the main output or not; "paper-based" and "non-paper-based" would be equally suitable. It is realized that "non-print-based" publishing often offers hard copy output as an alternative as well; nevertheless, these two groups have historically evolved as separate entities and despite their obvious links such as common databases, common publishers and intermediaries, and despite some similar components (such as workstations and displays), they are conveniently dealt with as two separate groups. It may be safely predicted that both technologies will integrate to a large degree in the future, a process which has been already started. Dealing with both print- and non-print-based publishing in one volume will allow us to take a much broader view of present events and better assess what is in the cards for the publishing of tomorrow; it is also the unique feature of this study.

Electronic document delivery as a specific topic is the subject of Chapter 5, including delineation of the concept, its historical evolution and examples that illustrate the magnitude of the challenge. Chapter 6 is about the promise of artificial intelligence as related to our theme. Chapter 7 summarizes the role of microcomputers in the area under scrutiny, and Chapter 8 is about the great potential that electronic printers possess in transforming our publication scene by moving from traditional to "electronic" readers. Chapter 9, entitled "Some Implications of Electronic Publishing," examines the likely impact of the present development on publishers, authors, libraries, intermediaries and users. Conclusions highlight the main trends in electronic publishing as detected in course of this study.

The main problem in laying out the conceptual framework for a study of this nature and width is the state of flux in which the component parts are found, but a solid frame for reporting on technologies that have not yet "solidified" must eventually be found. The most disquieting aspect of writing a book in the subject area of electronic publishing is the realization that whatever statement is made today may already have been overtaken by some new development yesterday and will appear as a "deja vu" tomorrow. But the subject is nevertheless an exciting one to report on because throughout the history of mankind the adaptation of humans to changing conditions of the environment in all its aspects and dimensions—physical, political, social, economic, technological, etc.—has been the salient feature of our species, and this adaptation has been founded on our ability to glean, analyze and synthesize information as well as distill knowledge from it as a higher-level product. Therefore, delving into information and knowledge processing may well bring us closer to understanding one of the cornerstones of our very existence. Reading on will make it clear that any fear of future shock is unwarranted; we are in the midst of the future right now.

Looking back, for a minute, there was type before Gutenberg. Gutenberg's contribution to human civilization was that he invented movable type; what we have today is manipulable, electronic type of an intangible nature. Until Gutenberg the communication bridging time was very restricted, unaccessible and unaffordable; most of mankind's progress remained unrecorded and was thus lost unless it was handed over to the next generation verbally. The very existence and far-reaching effect of the printing press was of course predicated on the previous development of the phonetic alphabet: this demonstrates once again that conceptual breakthroughs open the gates for further progress on a general front, and that technology is not working in isolation but rather hand in hand with other aspects of human civilization.

Elsewhere in this book are found references to the trends that are moving toward the broader inclusion of other forms of communication into the publication/communication process: joining text are data, voice, sounds and graphics; images and sound are already the modes of expression in mass media with whom electronic publishing shares one of its means of final output, namely, the video display. This similarity has been thus far superficial because text is still the prevailing form to carry the informational content. But with digital encoding being more widely adopted in information technology and with impending new telecommunications links, the impact of images and sound will with certainty be expected to rise. Multimedia electronic publishing is a new phenomenon now in the making, and it is by no means premature to include it in serious research considerations concerning its other aspects in addition to the technological one.

What we know is that written (or printed or displayed) text is an accountable, reproducible record of information in human-readable form that presupposes and in its turn, promotes literacy. If properly interpreted and assimilated, it may come to fruition in knowledge, which in its turn, may culminate in wisdom. Written or printed or displayed information may be objectively scrutinized, retrieved, browsed through or easily referred to. Writing and reading requires an interaction at the cognitive level that makes the reader a less passive recipient of information than, e.g., a habitual TV watcher. Well-applied images and sound as accompaniment to text will strengthen all the above positive attributes of text and prove themselves to be useful content enhancers in well-designed applications.

Indiscriminately applied imagery and sound on the other hand, appeal to senses rather than to reason, and it appears unrealistic that predominantly image-based information could ever supersede the proven means of linguistic-textual communication. In this respect a potential social and cultural gap could develop between passive media consumers and electronic publishing users, should such polarization occur because of differing predilections in navigating the "electronic seas."

2

Technology: The Background

2.1 A Sketch of Progress in Telematics

Electronic publishing is both a consequence of the waves of change on the existing publishing technology and some of the new technologies themselves in their publishing-related applications; ultimately, this means not only turning out old or customary products through new, more efficient means, but also introduction of totally or partially new products and services.

Along with the established ones, new modes and patterns of communication are competing for their place in the spectrum of the processes of creating, storing, retrieving, transmitting and distributing information. This is gradually affecting the entire cycle of communications from the originator to the ultimate user and results in profound changes in our society, which has been designated as an "information society" to denote the prominent part information is destined to play in this stage of its development. The concept of electronic publishing is central to the notion of an information society and, whether we like it or not, no member of our human community can escape the consequences of this technology, its products and ramifications. The purpose of this chapter is to outline some advances in telematics in general to provide a framework for the subsequent discourse of the more specific topic of electronic publishing, which is rather eclectic by its nature and cannot be studied without due regard to the disciplines that provide its footing and breeding ground. Concrete applications in electronic publishing may, in a way, be viewed as packages assembled from those "more basic" disciplines of communications, computer science, etc., as will be demonstrated in the course of the discussion. For example the prevailing trend toward converging technologies makes computing functions an indispensable part of packet-switching networks whereas communication functions are built into computer utilities. The general trend toward interdisciplinary science and technological applications may be exemplified in the human-machine interface area that embraces hardware and software aspects entangled with issues related to psychology, cognitive science, medicine, economics, linguistics, artificial intelligence, information science and communication.

We will cover first the computers and then a few salient points in communications. As Hall (1986) pointed out, computers and the international telecommunications network are the tools of the presently evolving service economy much the same as the tractor was the tool of the agricultural epoch and the assembly line the tool for the industrial age.

We shall deal with some aspects of computing that are indicative of the directions as well as dimensions of the change; the rest must be acquired by supplemental reading of which there is plenty. Our attention will focus on the building components, architecture, input/output, storage and fifth-generation computers; there will be bits and pieces on this and related topics strewn in other sections such as artificial intelligence and microcomputers.

2.1.1 Components and Architectures

The impact of microelectronics on contemporary society has been profound. Today microprocessors may be found in nearly every electrical appliance with an endless list of other applications. Despite their relatively recent debut (Intel Corporation developed the Intel 4004 in late 1971), microprocessors or miniaturized large-scale integrated circuits (LSI was further perfected into VLSI [very large-scale integration] and eventually into ULSI [ultralarge-scale integration]) led to miniaturization of circuit designs for large computers and also made possible the microcomputer, which is based on a single microprocessor ("chip") serving in the capacity of the central processing unit. Chips ushered in the exponential growth of density of electronic circuits in the coming years, without a need for corresponding increase in power supply; while reliable, fast and with rising capabilities, their relative size and cost have been declining constantly because they can be manufactured in large quantity. Single-chip microprocessors have evolved from 4- to 8-bit and then to 16- and 32-bit versions, but for a microcomputer a variety of other chips is needed; it is likely that in the next few years ahead, for several reasons beyond the scope of our study, the idea of a single-chip computer is not going to be realized. It is still too early to assess the practicality of using the information processing capabilities of carbon-based materials (organic molecules) in place of digital switching devices in what is called molecular computing; this is a result of convergence of computing, physics, chemistry and biotechnology (Conrad 1985).

In 1980 the largest-capacity chip in production was a 72-Kbit RAM chip (Eres 1983). The 1-megabit (Mbit) RAM memory chip has emerged in 1986 as possibly one of the main achievements of the semiconductor industry for the year. New techniques can now generate a variety of crystals by interleaving extremely thin layers of different materials to form multilevel laminates of compounds such as gallium arsenide and gallium aluminum arsenide; by controlling the thickness and composition of layers one can achieve electrical and optical properties with a precision not previously possible (Brody 1986). Devices based on these and similar principles are expected to multiply the speed of integrated circuits of the present that use silicon. As complexity of integrated circuits escalates, design engineers have been availing themselves of computer-aided design (CAD) methods (Daniel and Gwyn 1982), and management of the design data has required a database approach (Wiederhold, Beetem and Short 1982); thus computer-based systems become progenitors of new, more powerful generations. An outline of trends in integrated circuits is delineated in Table 1.

Because having efficient components is not enough, new architectures are needed to overcome the deficiencies of von Neuman's sequential computer architecture, which has been modified somewhat by vector instructions, cache memories and pipelining of instructions, but still

TABLE 1   Indication of Trends in Integrated Circuits

Year	Number of Transistors	Chip Size (mm)	Line Width (μm)	Instructions per Second
1960	10	1 × 1	30	
1970	10^3	2.5 × 2.5	10	10^4
1980	10^5	6 × 6	3–2	10^5
1985	10^6	8 × 8	1	10^6
1990 (est.)	10^7	10 × 10	0.5–0.1	10^7

supports essentially a sequential computer. Hwang (1983) distinguishes three configurations in his paper on image processing: pipeline computers, array processors and multiprocessors; hybrid structure combining both pipelining and array processing is also possible. Snyder (1984) recommends parallel processing for supercomputers involving many processing elements to perform complex functions and recognizes two architectural choices: (1) common-memory parallel architectures and (2) distributed-memory architectures, which most frequently are either the array or tree architecture. At any rate, we are near the limits of technologies developed around a single processor; the only approach left to us if we want to exceed 1 GFLOPS (1 giga floating-point operations per second) is parallel computation that allows partitioning into many segments (Denning 1985).

2.1.2 On the Road to the Fifth Generation

Whereas the first generation of computers was based on vacuum tubes and the second generation on transistors (1959-1963), the third generation was built around integrated circuits (1964 until early 1970s), leading to the fourth generation which is characterized by further escalated integration wherein microcircuits on a single silicon chip are designed on principles of LSI and VLSI. Most of our present hardware is anchored in the fourth generation but so-called supercomputers are now leaving manufacturers' plants and discussion goes on about the fifth generation. One of the supercomputers, the CRAY X-MP superseding the CRAY-1 first delivered in 1976, boasts a clock cycle time (time to perform an instruction) of 9.5 ns and can perform at the rate of up to 200 MIPS (million instructions per second), 400 MFLOPS while combined arithmetic/logical operations boast rates of 1 GIPS and above (one billion operations per second); the CRAY-2, which will succeed the CRAY X-MP, has a clock cycle time of 4 ns and the size of the total system is expected to be only one tenth of the CRAY-1 (Sumner 1983) while, at the same time, six to twelve times faster. Two methods enable supercomputers to surpass other computers with regard to speed: vector processing and pipelining. Vector processing on the one hand allows supercomputers to process arrays or multidimensional vectors rather than scalar processing which, on conventional computers, handles single-element variables one by one. Pipelines on the other hand afford performing of several operations within one cycle. High processing speeds require high-density packaging and this calls for new methods of cooling as well (e.g., CRAY has adopted immersion in pure fluorocarbon). CRAY-3 is expected to be based on gallium arsenide components and reach the speed of 7 GFLOPS (seven billion floating-

TECHNOLOGY: THE BACKGROUND

point operations per second). The CDC Cyber GF-10 supercomputer is expected to operate at 10 GFLOPS.

The fifth generation computer systems (FGCS), whose development has been conceived in Japan, have something special about them. They are the first generation to be touted years ahead, the first generation to have detailed specifications publicly discussed; already they have their admirers and disbelievers while still in the planning stage. These fifth-generation computers, dubbed knowledge information-processing systems, or KIPS for short are intended to be symbolic inference machines. They are being designed as machines that can learn, associate, make inferences, make decisions and otherwise behave as is common within human reasoning; the research includes understanding speech, text analysis and picture and image understanding (McCorduck 1983). The FGCS are predicated on the concepts of logic programming which have been elevated to the bridge between knowledge engineering and parallel computer technology. The target machine will perform 100 M to 1 G (100 million to one billion) LIPS (logical inferences per second) and involve 1,000 processing elements; the knowledge-based management system will have a capacity of 100 to 1000 GB (gigabytes); the intelligent interface system aims at a vocabulary of up to 10,000 words, 2000 grammar rules and 99% accuracy in syntactic analysis of written natural language; a speech recognition system capable of recognizing up to 50,000 words with 95% recognition; and a graphic system capable of storing and utilizing up to 10,000 images (Shapiro 1983). It must be stressed once again that the most important aspect of the FGCS is the predicate logic underlying all programming, data description and query languages as the suitable common formalism.

2.1.3 Microcomputers

The microcomputer revolution that started in late 1970s has never stopped. After having started with 8-bit word microprocessors they were able to exploit the benefits of the 16-bit and now even the 32-bit architectures. Main memory has been augmented from 16K to 64K and later to 128K, but machines with a memory as large as 512K and more are being distributed to make use of the kind of future software that is being alluded to in this study. In 1986, the 1-Mbyte Macintosh Plus was introduced expandable to 4 Mbytes when 1-Mbit RAM chips are installed. Auxiliary storage to match with this development has exploded from 5 Mbytes to nearly 400 Mbytes on rigid 5.25-inch magnetic minidisks. Conversely the size has shrunk and portable microcomputers have become a reality, which can benefit from the new display technology as evidenced in flat-panel displays. On the operating systems front, the miniaturization inherent in the VLSI technology has made it feasible to incorporate multiple operating systems in separate microprocessors into one microcomputer to increase the versatility of micros. The communications capabilities have been rightly perceived as bottlenecks to further proliferation, and intense effort has been undertaken to enable micros to talk to mainframes and eventually with each other in addition to their stand-alone tasks. Voice capabilities and image processing have been enhancing the functionality of micros considerably.

Amid all the frantic activity surrounding microcomputers, a new buzzword has emerged under the heading of supermicrocomputers—the net result of which may mean closing the gap between the top-end micros and low-end minis. Although there is no generally accepted definition, it generally connotes the new high-performance microcomputers which bring to the desk top the power once wielded by mainframe computers; they are based on 16-bit and even 32-bit chips which are becoming standard for this category. Other characteristics imputed to supermicros are those of multi-tasking, multiuser computers operating in the neighborhood of one MIPS (one million instructions per second), capabilities that are very desirable for graphics, parallel processing and realtime applications.

It looks as if 32-bit parts and architectures are to stay for an extended period simply because 16-bit systems do not have enough power for many applications and the 64-bit counterparts are too wide to be efficiently utilized except in some very specific applications (Hindin 1986).

On the software side of micros, one important innovation for electronic publishing is remote "sharing of the visual space," a principle which Lu (1986) calls interactive communication. This is software that allows two or more people such as author and editor, coauthors among themselves and eventually even a reader and author, to work on a common document, which is visible to parties involved at all times.

2.1.4 Storage

A relatively new development in storage hardware is videodisks and optical digital disks (ODD). Videodisk is based either on optical videodisk technology using laser reading devices distinguished by no contact with the disk, or on the capacitance technology employing a stylus to read from the videodisk on contact while the stylus is guided either by the grooves (grooved technology) or by additional tracking pits (grooveless technology). Whereas videodisks are captivating interest in the storage of photographs (art) for education, instruction, training, document management systems and information retrieval owing to their capability to store both analog and digitally encoded information on the same disk to represent, also in the interactive mode, text, images (still and animated) and sound, optical digital disks have their future cut out as a mass storage device.

The ever-increasing demand for more and more storage has been intensified by the inclusion of graphics in contemporary computerized publishing and has been multiplied by the emergence of color-processing systems. It has been found that the conventional magnetic disk could continue to be used as working disk but the archival function could be taken over by the optical digital disk to replace or supplement floppy disks and magnetic disks in that capacity. The ODD has the potential to become also a powerful store of information at a site where it is needed frequently and can thus save the communication costs that are now incurred in applications such as online information retrieval and document delivery.

To compare the optical digital disk with the magnetic disk let us consider three factors: capacity, mean retrieval time and erasability. First let us compare the storage capacity of an ODD (20-30 Gbits and more for a 30 cm ODD) with that of a magnetic disk (up to 450 Mbytes for a fixed Winchester disk) to see that an ODD may have considerably larger storage capacity. Comparisons of this kind can serve only to illustrate the order of magnitude because magnetic disks vary in capacity and so do optical digital disks both in use and on the drawing board. By contrast, magnetic disk has a definite edge in a faster access time (16-55 ms compared with ODD's 100-500 ms); also, information may be "written" on magnetic disk repeatedly whereas the erasable ODD is still only a subject of intense research. But the handicap of non-erasability may turn into a boon where this is a desirable quality as in archiving. ODD is removable and can be reproduced with all the information on it; not all magnetic disks can be removed from their disk drive and they have to be rewritten each time the information has to be duplicated.

Fox (1986) compares optical disk and magnetic disk storage in a rather graphic way: a large version of optical storage embracing 128 Gbytes in a single unit a little smaller than a compact car vs. 200 magnetic disk drives arrayed over half an acre of floor space.

Although Compact Disc serving as read-only memory (CD-ROM) disk has become first known to the public as a music medium, it has recently roused a great deal of interest as a means to store data. CD-ROM is a computer-based storage system capable of storing text, graphics, pictures, data and sound in digital, compressible form; this data may be repeatedly read on a reader: online databases, computer programs, online public-access library catalogs, corporate databases, inventories, museum and arts collections are but a few examples. This optic 4 3/4-inch (12 cm) disk can store over 700 Mbytes of data or 1000-1600 times more than a floppy disk even though it does not possess floppy's writing capability which undoubtedly will be the target of high priority for research. This storage capacity translates into 200,000-275,000 typed pages or roughly 700 bound volumes of 300 pages each, on a disk taking up 1/4 inch of shelf space. With the cost of $10 per disk this medium could become an economical means to store and distribute published information. The success of the CD-ROM carrying audio may well prove to be a psychological boost in marketing it as a database distribution medium.

But magnetic recording has bright prospects, too. A new, promising technology under research, so-called vertical recording, might push the linear bit density in both hard- and floppy disk drives and track density may be also considerably increased. Presently the largest magnetic storage device is the IBM 3850 mass storage system which encompasses 9440 data cartridges stored in a honeycomblike structure. Data cartridges contain magnetic tapes whose contents can be transferred at a read/write station on to a disk pack for online use. Each cartridge encloses 50 Mbytes amounting to 472 Gbytes for the entire device.

Magnetic bubble memory has been around for a number of years but its future is not certain. It is compatible with the semiconductor processing technology but semiconductor random access memory (RAM) has better access time, higher transfer rate and simpler interfacing, whereas magnetic bubble can claim to its credit more bits per chip and lower cost per bit; besides, it is not volatile. Charged-coupled devices (CCD) are volatile and cannot be accessed randomly; they are also slower than RAMs. CCDs are relevant to electronic publishing also through their application in scanners. Research is continuing in the field of laser-holographic memories as well, and in experimental developments high storage densities have been achieved as well as short random access time; cost per bit is low and recording is permanent.

So far, none of the new and not-so-new principles of data storage has been able to threaten the dominant position of magnetic memory and prevent the coming of optical digital memory.

Magnetic storage for microcomputers is also undergoing a change. Although the 5-inch rigid magnetic disks have been in use for microcomputers and associated applications with storage capabilities typically from 5 to 30 and more Mbytes, there is a move afoot to boost the storage capacity from twice to ten times up to almost 400 Mbytes by introduction of thin-film high-density recording surfaces and reading heads with future increases being made possible by the new

TECHNOLOGY: THE BACKGROUND

"vertical recording" technology. The 3 1/2-inch diameter high-density microdisks are also being promoted.

See Table 2 for a few examples of storage capacity; other factors to be considered are erasability, storage density, access time, data transfer rate, lifetime, possibility to write as well as read, system cost, media cost, cost per bit, error rate and backup.

2.1.5 Input/Output

Turning now to the peripheral side of computers, much has been reported lately about increasing capabilities of cathode-ray tubes (CRTs), which may be rightly viewed as the crucial line in the battle for user acceptance of electronic publishing. Typically up to 2000 characters are presented with line graphics and color with 125-400K addressable points in a horizontally positioned window. The advantages of CRTs so far have been relatively low cost, color capability, relatively good resolution, no moving parts; on the debit side is the lack of portability due to size, high power consumption and fragility, which along with other factors contribute to their low user popularity in electronic publishing. A great deal of research and development is being under-

TABLE 2 Examples of Storage Media Capacity

Storage Media	Capacities
Winchester disd RA81 (DEC) (fixed)	456 Mbytes per drive 1.368 Gbytes per cabinet (includes three drives)
Removable disk RA60 (DEC)	205 Mbytes per drive 615 Mbytes per cabinet
Floppy diskette RX50 (DEC)	409 Kbytes per diskette 818 Kbytes per drive
Magnetic tape drive TA78 (DEC)	140 Mbytes at 6250 bpi density; 2400 foot tape reel
Book	1 Mbyte; 4 Kbytes per page; 250 pages
Human brain	1,000 Tbits
IBM 3850 mass storage system	472 Gbytes
Optical digital disk	100 Gbits or 12.5 Gbytes Jukeboxes of 64 and 128 disks under development
Compact Disk—ROM	600 Mbytes

taken in the CRT field to stem the bourgeoning flat-panel displays' competition: e.g., Tektronix Inc. has developed a 19-inch monochrome CRT with a 1500 × 2000 picture element (pel) screen to be able to satisfy the requirements for higher resolution; CAD, CAM and electronic publishing are all parties to the trend toward image/text processing and integration calling for color and improved resolution; other trends are improving phosphor materials, the associated electronics of CRT displays and combining the virtues of CRTs and flat-panel displays, both in black and white as well as color (Bindra 1984).

Flat-panel displays have been the most serious threat to the CRTs' monopoly. Following the tradition customary in electronic publishing that nothing gets ever completely replaced by new developments but rather complements the existing options in specific applications, flat panels will not, in the short run anyway, supplant the CRT, yet their handy size (as their name suggests) will make it possible to add considerable storage and processing power to their display capability, thus elevating them to a qualitatively higher level as compared with a book or journal. Bindra (1984) distinguishes active and passive technologies. Active technologies are light-emitting which embrace (1) the electroluminiscent, (2) plasma-gas discharge and (3) vacuum fluorescent techniques; the plasma technology has produced real-world results already with over 700K addressable pels (IBM 581). The passive technology is represented by liquid crystal display (LCD) flat panels as most promising owing to their low power consumption and cost. The world market for flat panels is estimated at $4.5 billion in 1992 as compared with $5 million in 1982, with LCD popular in the office, business equipment and portable computers, whereas electroluminiscent and plasma techniques are still being somewhat limited by their more expensive driving circuitry (Alam Mahbub 1984).

Considerable amount of work is being done to improve touch screen technology which can make computer use much easier: acoustic, optical and capacitance sensing as well as resistive membranes are being employed.

What holds the brightest prospect in communication with computers is found in voice input based on voice recognition and voice output realized by voice synthesis. Both will add yet another dimension to electronic publishing on the input and output side, respectively, where line graphics, halftone pictures and continuous-tone images have already aligned themselves with text both on screen and in print.

Voice input promises to revolutionize the man-machine interface because it is the most natural one to humans. The problems are the multitude of constantly varying frequencies and amplitudes of acoustic waves composing any given sound, the number of sounds, the pronunciation differences between people and even for the same individual;

recognizing sounds is only a small portion of the total job—to figure out the meaning of words, phrases and sentences further complicates the task. The essence of recognition is comparing and finding optimum matches between digitally stored patterns in the computer's memory and the incoming analog signals which must be first converted to digital form. The processing power and computer storage required is enormous but large-scale integration and further advances in artificial intelligence are expected to bring about a breakthrough referred to in Section 2.1.2 in the discussion of FGCS (fifth-generation computer systems). Most systems today operate with disconnected (discrete) speech, some must be trained for a particular user and become largely speaker-dependent, but most have a very limited vocabulary. Noisy background requires special units. Research, however, is in progress to eliminate the present restrictions and make voice input a means for untrained public to obtain access to information (e.g., electronic journals). But speaker-independent products are getting ready to enter markets. This may make telephone the most common computer terminal in the future. Voice recognition systems are mostly encountered as add-on boards in microcomputers or as a front-end processor.

A significant contribution to the field of voice recognition is a device capable of producing documents on receiving voice input. IBM's Talkwriter and Voicewriter by Kurzweil Applied Intelligence are both the reverse of text-to-voice systems. The Talkwriter recognizes 5000 words and works at 95% accuracy; the potential of this kind of device for electronic publishing will probably be realized first in word processing and in assorted workstations which, by their nature, do not require other type of input.

Voice output is offering an alternative or supplement to totally visual output, whether it be on screen or paper, which may be a pleasant change to any user or a sheer necessity for visually and verbally handicapped people as well as in some particular situations. At present there are more speech synthesis systems on the market than voice recognition devices, which poses a more serious challenge. Receiving some information in printed form (such as factual data) and other information in verbal form (such as systems related, prompts, comments, warnings, etc.) and inclusion of color in the printout (for highlighting) will by itself improve efficiency of the human-machine communication. The speech synthesizer has been implemented both as a computer terminal and in stand-alone applications such as an optical character recognition (OCR) input of printed text plus a microcomputer with a voice synthesizer; the latter is the preferred choice for a blind person but has the potential of being attractive to some readers in general; verbally impaired people have a choice of using talking typewriters or a voice communicator with a store of words and phrases operated from a keypad. Other applications range from computer-assisted instruction to dispatching systems, entertainment, translation, telephone order-entry systems, telephone access systems, etc. The idea that computers listen and speak is an idea that is being actively pursued.

Besides voice recognition and speech synthesis, there are two more phenomena that may be identified in the new voice technology: voice mail and voice response. Voice mail is now a commercial reality; it works in a manner similar to electronic mail except the message input is in analog form as voice, which is digitized and stored in a "voice-mail box" until such time that it can be delivered to its destination. Voice response operates in applications of narrower scope and limited dictionary where "prepackaged" words or phrases respond to specific identifiable situations.

Voice technology is expected to grow from (U.S.) $40 million in 1983 to a forecast $500 million in 1988 according to Evans Research Corp., Toronto; sales of voicemail systems reached over $100 million and are expected to climb to $1 billion by 1990 (Chevreau 1986). Although there is no doubt that voice technology is advancing fast, there is a similar hype noticeable in this area that is typical of the entire high-technology field; pronouncements about qualitative aspects of products are often made ahead of time and pertain more to laboratory stage or to products at various stages of testing rather than to marketable units.

Our society probably will not be paperless but it most certainly will be one with less paper; a great deal of output will be directed to the display but electronic publishing had better heed the coming of voice.

In speculating on output alternatives in the context of the "paperless" society, one must not ignore the computer output microfilm and microfiche (COM) technique despite the tendency on the part of some users to dislike microforms on account of their being unreadable by plain eyes. COM has been embraced by some organizations as an efficient means to print and store data along or as an alternative to print on paper, magnetic media or videodisk. COM, which works on a principle similar to phototypesetter, prints at up to 27,000 lines per minute (impact printers up to 2000 lines per minute) and duplicating can be done at 300,000 lines per minute by automated equipment offline so that a 1000-page three-part report takes 8 minutes when prepared on COM compared with 49 minutes for paper; the COM device can be attached to a mainframe computer, thus becoming the fastest output device on the system (Stoate 1984). Additional advantages accrue from the lower storage and retrieval, distribution, medium and copying costs when compared with paper.

Hard copies may be obtained from a variety of printers either of the impact or nonimpact category. Nonimpact printers are available based on a variety of working principles that attest to the breadth of research and development in this area reflected in the vast array of products hitting the market and indicate that the "pure" electronic publishing and the heralded paperless society are not yet going to be upon us for a while. Techniques involved in nonimpact printers include those listed in Chapter 8.

In much the same way color hard copies may be also prepared as color display capability is becoming common. Computer users who want color hard copy graphics may choose from six basic technologies depending on their particular application (Dawes and Durno 1984): impact printer, pen plotter, film camera and film plotter, laser copier, inkjet and electrostatic; there are differences in resolution, number of colors, speed, image size, quality, versatility and cost.

To underscore the role terminals play as points of contact with users, in 1983 in the United States there were over 8 million computer terminals and the share of VDT's amounted approximately to 6.2 million; but 250 million telephone sets and some 100 million TV sets are potential candidates for becoming computer terminals in the future. Microcomputers often act as terminals as well; if the number of home computers in the United States reaches 55 million by 1990 as anticipated, then 58% of the 95 million U.S. households would be equipped with micros, two thirds of them rigged with modems.

2.1.6 Software

Although in this chapter hardware aspects have received a preponderant share of attention, it should be stressed that software has not been neglected as evidenced by numerous references to it throughout this study wherever appropriate. It is only logical that software development for a category of hardware follows in that order but unavailability of suitable quality application software for any hardware is a major brake imposed on computer acceptance in that particular area and in general inasmuch as people do not buy computers but applications (at least for the sake of argument). This has been witnessed, for instance, by the recent upsurge of activity in microcomputer composition software which adds to microcomputers' general utility. Software may be either developed in-house or purchased or leased. It may be acquired from computer hardware manufacturers, software developers, brokers, time-sharing companies and individual programmers or user groups. The growth of *The Software Catalog* (Elsevier Science Publishing Co, Inc., New York) may serve as one indicator of the burgeoning activities in the software field: the 1983 Fall Microcomputers edition carried 9470 programs representing 28,300 software packages, the Spring 1984 edition listed 10,757 program descriptions, and the Summer 1984 Update contained 1453 additional programs. Whereas ordinary high-level programming languages were designed with numeric operations in mind and of necessity deal with quantities only, the new symbolic or object-oriented languages have introduced logic programming capable of nonnumeric operations on words, sentences, geometric shapes, etc.; Lisp and Prolog are thus more suitable to perform artificial intelligence tasks. Prolog has been selected to play a significant role in the Japanese fifth-generation computer project.

Availability of software is the determining factor in buying computer hardware. Selection is not made any easier by the vast amount of hardware/software options: problems to watch out for are suitability for a given purpose and compatibility with other data formats involved in a given application; such problems often arise with disks received from authors that do not match editors' and reviewers' formats, or front-ends not being able to "talk" to typesetters, for instance. These problems can be rectified by special kinds of software called conversion software capable of reading hundreds of data formats received from disks, magnetic tapes or over the phone and translate them to other disk formats; conversion software thus alleviates one of the impediments on the road to going electronic all the way from the originator to final copy.

The hardware-software relationship takes a new twist in what has been described as "software chips" (Martin 1985); according to this concept the software engineers will have at their disposal precoded routines in a large library of standard modules from which to build application programs. Martin (1985) also opines that we need to build a type of computer "common sense" and that future language interpreters and dialogues will lead to "reasonableness in software" whereby the computer may adopt on its own initiative certain computational measures if and when they appear warranted.

As Valovic (1986) rightly points out, as the different types of hardware function more and more alike, it is the software that will eventually dominate. We can see that happen, e.g., in microcomputer-based workstations in publishing whereby various functions can be assigned to different keys; these functions can be programmed and reprogrammed as needed thus obviating the need of hardware acquisition. Software availability is the determining factor when it comes to chosing between similar micros for a specific purpose such as composition.

2.1.7 Telecommunications

Telecommunications are in the process of merging with information and data processing by computers. The present study clearly demonstrates this convergence in many concrete examples such as online systems, electronic document delivery, videotex, computer conferencing, etc. The process does not end there, and some members of the "communication" family of technologies bear on other phenomena such as "office of the future" and electronic publishing which in their turn, are conglomerates of diverse technologies. The need for computers communicating with each other may be seen from how users feel: modems rank first on the list of peripherals users buy after the acquisition of their microcomputer; for the end users, data communication is just another part of the total computer concept as they perceive it. At the corporate level, IBM and AT & T have more in common than they used to.

Telecommunications are designed around twisted wire-pairs, cables, optical fibers, microwaves, infrared and satellites for signal transmission. Coaxial cables offer freedom from interference by external signals and high transmission rates (over 100 Mbits per second). Coaxial cables are used for cable TV, closed-circuit TV which may be employed as a vehicle delivering information services to closed user groups, such as, for example, videotex services. Two-way digital communication over the cable is possible today and can support interactive information services.

Since the early 1960s telecommunications have been influenced by AT & T's so-called T-carrier technology which uses TDM (time division multiplexing) in order to accommodate 24 PCM-encoded telephone conversations on one pair of copper wires (PCM stands for pulse-code modulation; see Glossary). Based on this development is the ongoing quiet revolution called Integrated Services Digital Network (ISDN), which will provide digital operation and full-duplex 64 Kbits per second data transmission capability to each subscriber. In fact each subscriber will have access to two 64 Kbits per second channels plus one 16 Kbit per second channel for signaling and supervisory purposes. This transmission facility will further boost the germane developments in contiguous areas of electronic publishing in that it will serve end-user's needs with regard to voice, data and image either consecutively or simultaneously: this is an essential ingredient in text/image integration as well as in voice/text interchangeability. While ISDN is not something that will be upon us tomorrow but will increase its practical impact as a 1990's technology, many corporations already include it in their purchase specifications and some vendors claim ISDN compatibility in order to sharpen their competitive edge. The ultimate upshot of all this will be universal information services (UIS), at which stage the end-user will be provided with a universal socket serving as a common port for just about any kind of information technology (IT) device; allocation of the required bandwidth is going to be performed by intelligent switches working along the above mentioned 16 Kbits per second channel.

Optical fibers are extremely thin fibers made of high-purity glass that carry pulsed modulated light. Large bandwidth for a single fiber (up to 20 GHz) can carry hundreds of thousands of telephone conversations simultaneously; other advantages which will occasion fast implementation are improved security of transmission, small attenuation loss, no electromagnetic interference, low cost of material, small size and lower error rate; data rates are on the order of gigabits per second.

A direct impact on electronic publishing has also been reported (Koenig 1984): the Online Computer Library Center, Inc. (OCLC) has installed a fiber optic communication system, FOX (Fiber Optic Extension developed by Tandy Computers Incorporated) which links OCLC's mainframe computers at a rate of four million bytes per second and enables them to work virtually as one computer, thus obviating the need for acquisition of more powerful hardware; the impact of fiber optics on electronic document delivery, e.g., can be speculated upon from the transmission speed of 160 Mbytes per second which has been already achieved over a 40-km line. This translates into 40,000 printed pages with 4000 characters each and points to bottlenecks other than transmission.

Satellite communication is bound to have significant repercussions on electronic publishing in the capacity of information delivery medium (see Chapter 5). Satellites operate on frequencies of 4 to 6 GHz or 12 to 14 GHz and carry typically 24 transponders, each of them capable of carrying one video channel or 1200 voice channels or 50 Mbits per second. New satellites are designed to carry as many as 52 transponders. Although there has been some usage in electronic publishing (e.g., Dow Jones & Co. transmits complete editions of the *Wall Street Journal* to regional printers, much the same as *U.S. News and World Report* and *The Financial Times* send facsimile pages to printers in the United States), data account for only 3% of all satellite traffic. Project Apollo sponsored by the European Economic Community is designed as a pilot project for the storage, retrieval and dissemination of full-text computer-stored documents; use of a satellite has also been tested with a facsimile machine developed by Agfa Gevaert which transmitted an A4-size document in 4 seconds (Morris 1983). But the 50 Mbits per second would theoretically allow six to seven millions of bytes equal to characters to be transmitted in a second from a file via one transponder. Project Universe using a combination of local area data transmission networks with satellite transponders is described in Chapter 5 on electronic document delivery. It is interesting to note that the Satellite Business Systems (SBS) satellite system is digital. In listing electronic publishing applications of satellite transmission to date, we must not forget teletext which is broadcast along with the largest user of satellites—the television. Cost of satellite communication is distance independent and the cost of receiving dishes has been declining like their size; they are easier to install than cables.

Direct broadcast satellites (DBS for short) can broadcast TV programs and any other content, including video, audio and data, directly to homes. They appear to be a powerful channel of information delivery which can be utilized by any vendor in electronic publishing to deliver information to users spread over a wide area whose sets have been provided with a black box to decode the scrambled signal. High-power satellites will require a smaller-diameter antenna which will make them affordable for mass markets. DBS can offer some services not currently available on cable TV such as audio, computer downloading and information services (Surprenant 1984).

Satellites provide communication capability between many locations and can be rapidly deployed but the potential capacity is limited when compared with modern terrestrial links. Yet satellite transmission is an ideal link between the prepress production stage and remote printers. Technically, pasted up pages are read by a scanner and digitized data may be compressed to reduce transmission costs; at the receiving end film negatives are prepared from the transmitted stream of bits. Resulting films are stripped and offset plates are produced for local printing. The efficiency of satellite communications in publishing may be demonstrated on data transmitted daily from Los Angeles to Milan's newspapers *Corriere de la Sera* and *La Gazzeta Dello Sport* during the 1984 Olympic Games (Hayes 1985) via satellite by Modulation Associates 48,000 Data System (Modulation Associates Inc., of Mountain View, California). Olympic information was processed in Milan into made-up pages, retransmitted back to the United States Intelsat facility and from there (again by satellite) to the Ricoh Corporation in San Jose California where film negatives were imaged from received data. Newspapers were printed in a plant close to the San Francisco airport and shipped to Italian communities on the North American continent within a few hours of the production/transmission cycle.

Networks. Long-haul networks based on the X.25 standard protocol of the Consultative Committee on International Telephony and Telegraphy (CCITT) and on the packet-switching principle have been around for over a decade (Arpanet since 1971)—Arpanet, Uninet, Telenet, Tymnet in the United States, Datapac in Canada, Transpac in France, DDX in Japan. These networks have been widely reported in the world literature. Local area networks (LANs) are of more recent origin and unfortunately a satisfactory interconnection between the long-haul and the LANs is still missing.

Interest in LANs has continued, as evidenced by the number of vendors, spurred by the much faster decline of computation costs as compared with data transmission costs and hence the tendency toward distributed processing. Three topologies have become most prominent: star, ring and bus plus hybrid configurations. Two methods of traffic routing have gained wide acceptance: the so-called token passing as well as the carrier sense multiple access with collision detection (CSMA/CD) plus combinations of both methods. LANs are being installed with the aim of consolidating various functions within a limited area such as an office, building, corporate headquarters or campus. They are based on twisted pair or coaxial cable, with fiber optics holding out a promise of transmission speeds up to 200 Mbit per second over longer distances as compared with the typical LANs operating at 1-15 Mbits per second. For electronic publishing, as for other areas, LANs offer integration of a variety of input, output and storage devices including printers, displays (also microimages), modems, typesetters, scanners; if properly planned and implemented they enable files to be shared among workstations. LANs also may provide links to mainframes or minicomputers and may connect microcomputers among themselves as well as to make them benefit from peripherals on the network. Many expensive devices such as typesetters, electronic printers and scanners can often be cost justified only if their usage can be increased and the cost spread over a number of users; LANs provide a vehicle for achieving the necessary economy of scale in sharing of files, hardware and software.

Among the perceivable trends in local networking one can identify an enhanced variety of services available from these networks that will eventually be mutually interconnected and will be integrated through gateways into long-haul (wide area) networks; this will be made possible both by standardization in which all suppliers have common stake and by the wider availability of interface devices taking advantage, among other things, of the VLSI technology. LANs are already assuming and will continue to play an important role in electronic publishing both at the originator (author) level and at the user (reader) level as part of document delivery systems. If long-haul networks make it possible, some day in the future, for microcomputers not only to communicate with mainframes but also among themselves and do local processing, we will have achieved a LAN stretching across the continent which would afford users the benefits of both the long-haul networks and local LANs.

One alternative for local networking which has been recently tried out in an electronic publishing/delivery environment is the packet radio which, under circumstances, may prove to be an effective complement to the existing technologies (base band, broad band, twisted pair, fiber optics) (Brownrigg, Lynch and Pepper 1984). With its modest data rate of under 250 Kbytes per second it is not a panacea in resolving all the data transmission problems, but it may be a valuable part of a multiple local network in which laying cables may pose serious problems as may be the case with some libraries of the future engaging in public access services such as online catalogs and the ensuing electronic document delivery. Packet radio is a result of successful combination of two concepts: packet switching as known in the long-haul networks and radio transmission of data over broadcast channels as implemented in microwave point-to-point communications.

To document the variety of research and development in local networking, yet another option for wireless interconnection has been introduced (Takatoshi Minami, Kenjiro Yano, Takashi Touge, Hisashi Morikawa and Osamu Takahashi 1983), namely, optical wireless transmission in the infrared region which offers resistance to electromagnetic interference and to interference by similar systems; a typical application for the optical wireless modem enabling data transmission at rates up to 19.2 Kbits per second in full-duplex mode for the distance of 10 m might be interconnecting a cluster controller with a number of terminals in the same room; the advantage of optical transmission, while limited in scope, is the avoidance of recabling each time there is a need to change the position of terminals.

With the proliferation of networks, both long-haul and local, the need for gateways connecting these networks has become manifest. For example the iNET2000 Gateway developed by member companies of Telecom Canada can provide access to all connected hosts in Canada and through Datapac to packet-switched networks in the United States and in other countries, from a wide variety of American Standard Code for Information Interchange (ASCII) and Telidon videotex terminals from virtually any place where access via Datapac, dedicated circuit service or public switched telephone network can be obtained. The purpose is to facilitate for the user the selection of pertinent databases through directories, and one-stop shopping for information. The system is designed to connect the user into public information services, videotex services, full-text services, numerical statistical databases and in-house services. All these services can be tapped with only one sign-on, and then communication with the system can be conducted either at a novice level through menus or at an expert level by means of commands.

One of the fastest growing fields in the communications business is the new mobile radio technology also designated as portable communications. The cellular radio is a computerized radio service which is geographically divided into so-called cells each of them featuring a low-power transmitter effective over an area within 10-12 miles in diameter; as mobile users pass from one cell into another the central system allocates another frequency to them. All cells are connected to this central switching point which also ties into terrestrial communications lines. Cellular radio has found numerous applications already and has the potential to bring information services to people "on the move."

2.2 Analog and Digital Information

2.2.1 General Concepts: Analog Versus Digital

In electronic publishing systems we encounter information in two basic forms: analog and digital.

Analog information, such as humidity, temperature, velocity, etc., was the original form of "signal" encountered by humans; it varies continuously with time and can be conveniently investigated by converting it into voltage, frequency, current, etc., whereby a detector generates analog signals whose magnitude represents the quantity of the investigated phenomenon. Analog signals are difficult to store, and although they are easily transmitted they are liable to degradation by noise and distortion. In our context we are concerned with the video or audio type of analog information.

The digital signal on the other hand is not continuous but rather characterized by discrete values, and is represented by symbols called bits which assume either of two values, 0 or 1, in correspondence to two different voltage levels; these bits form digital words that designate values of continuous phenomena, such as temperature, pressure, humidity, etc., at any given moment. Digital signals express information by the existence of pulses not their absolute values and thus are less liable to degradation during transmission.

This duality (analog/digital) is due to the particular character of information in question and is a severe impediment to an even faster pace of technological advancement. The convergence of the two different technologies—analog and digital—is being feverishly sought and is subject to a great deal of research activity. The differences manifest themselves first at the capture stage when analog data are recorded and digital data are input or scanned in; the differences result also in different storage media. The transmission of analog signals in our context (including video) requires transmission media with 6-MHz bandwidth in fast-scan mode whereas digital data can be sent over the voice-grade lines of only 3 kHz capacity. Incompatibility obtains in displaying video data and digital data and this creates an obstacle in integrating text and graphics as well.

An example of digital data is data output by a computer in the form of a discrete stream of on/off pulses which represent binary ones and zeroes. An analog signal may be seen on an oscilloscope as a con-

TECHNOLOGY: THE BACKGROUND

tinuous line of electric waves; radio, TV and telephone signals may be represented by such waves. In order to be able to receive and process this information a computer must receive it converted to the digital form by an A/D (analog to digital) converter; a D/A converter ordinarily accompanies the A/D converter.

An A/D converter samples the continuous analog input (audio or video, e.g.), breaks up the signal into a number of segments at the rate called sampling rate. The readings are assigned digital codes in the quantization process whereby each sample becomes a pulse codemodulated (PCM) code acceptable to the computer. The device called codec (coder-decoder) is a circuit for conversion of an analog signal into a digital code for transmission and vice versa at the other end.

In electronic publishing, as elsewhere in the information industry, the A/D and D/A conversion are common phenomena. Any remote terminal-computer interaction, e.g., involves digital signals generated by the terminal converted to analog ones in a modem and transmitted, e.g., over voice-grade telephone lines to the computer where a modem (modulator/demodulator) transforms them into the language understandable to digital computers. Modem is the inverse of codec.

Another occurrence of A/D and D/A phenomena in the electronic publishing area is associated with the telefacsimile. If the electric current representing the image is based on a digital method of processing, it must be processed by a modem when a voice-grade telephone line is to be used in that this transmission mode is analog in nature.

Processing halftone images involves digitizing processes and processing color images involves separation scanners based on the digital principle as well.

The problem of D/A and A/D coexistence and conversion has become preeminent with data transmission, as well as with processing, storing and transmission of visual and audio information, using computers.

In data transmission sending digital as opposed to analog information obviates accumulation of undesirable noise in digital repeaters as the signal travels along the transmission line and this constitutes a major advantage; also the channel may be better utilized by time-interleaving of different digitized signals or by time-division multiplexing. Computers can add value to transmission and process digital data in many other ways, e.g., by encryption for better security. Another possibility is bandwidth compression in devices called codecs: interframe compression is based on the fact that subsequent video picture frames frequently vary only to a minor degree, which allows only differences to be transmitted. Intraframe coding avoids duplication by transmitting condensed signals to the receiving computer. Transmission of vast amounts of data will be required of many electronic publishing systems and any means of improving the transmission quality and cost must be exploited. An idea may be formed about the advantage of transmitting data in digital form if we realize, e.g., that one satellite transponder can carry only one analog TV signal but it can accommodate as many as 20 T1 carriers in digital form after compression in a codec: a T1 carrier is a standard offering of the Bell System, SBS and satellite companies, and can combine video, voice and digital signals of, for instance, a videoconference room at the rate of 1.544 Mbits per second (Elton 1982). Work is proceeding on codecs that can squeeze the bandwidth required to carry color video pictures at a ratio up to 1440:1, making a teleconference over 56-Kbit per second digital telephone lines possible.

It is interesting to note that there is no unanimity among the scientists and technologists in the field as to whether the future belongs to the digital or analog form of representation, storage and transmission of information. But one way or the other, electronic publishing will immensely benefit from the continuing and eventually, complete merger of the two technologies. The trend in the telephone industry is clearly towards digital and so is the trend, shown elsewhere, in the evolution of scanners and phototypesetters (third and fourth generation), to name two examples. Digital encoding treated below has become the common language of electronic communication into which signals representing voice, text, data and graphics are converted if they are to be carried on one network.

As analog transmission on international telecommunications networks is gradually waning, analog-to-digital signal conversion on digital circuits is being performed closer and closer to the endpoints of the network, reaching the telephone handset itself (Hall 1986); bearing witness to this development is the fact that modems for digital-to-analog-to-digital modulation and demodulation are being displaced by codecs which in the process of sampling and quantization translate the analog signal into its digital representation.

2.2.2 Digital Representational Form of Information

By "digital" we mean the opposite of "analog." Two possible states to represent values of information (e.g. ones and zeroes, "on" and "off") may be applied in two fundamentally different ways: either by character coding or image coding systems.

Character Coding System. In character coding systems any character of a defined set is represented by a unique definite set (word) of binary digits forming a binary number. There are several coding systems in existence, e.g., ASCII (American Standard Code for Interchange of Infor-

TECHNOLOGY: THE BACKGROUND

mation) and EBCDIC (Extended Binary Coded Decimal Interchange Code). The ASCII character set provides for 128 discrete characters, each composed of 7 bits (without the parity bit). Because each character has a meaning assigned to it, text material may be sorted, retrieved and otherwise operated upon.

The meaning of individual characters or codes may be recognized in scanning text by methods utilizing artificial intelligence. These scanning devices are based on optical character recognition (OCR) and are known as optical character readers and optical code readers, respectively.

The Working Principles. In an OCR device the text to be digitized is presented mechanically or manually to the scanning mechanism. The source document is illuminated either entirely (so-called "aperture" method), or successively spot by spot (so-called "flying spot" method) by a source of light, and the varying intensity of the reflected light (corresponding to the light or dark spots on the document being examined) is converted into electrical signals by one or more photocells to represent the lightness or darkness of each scanned spot. There are several possible ways of capturing the analog values (optical intensity) and transforming them into the discrete digital values for storage and/or manipulation and/or transmission and display. In the spotlight method the scanning beam moving along a line is focused only at a spot at a time and the optical intensity values are read by one or more photodetectors. If the entire document is illuminated, the focused photocell is restricted to read only a spot at a time (aperture method). As a source of light a laser beam is being employed in some scanners. The image may be also, in some devices, projected on a vidicon tube or rather on a group of vidicon tubes. Some scanners are based on the charge-coupled device (CCD) (see Note 1) array and the image of the examined document may be projected line by line on the CCD array, e.g., by a rotating or oscillating mirror. Whatever the method of illumination and conversion applied in a particular scanner, either the paper is mounted in a fixed position and the photocell(s) moves or vice versa, the photocell(s) are stationary and the paper document must be transported as necessary. After the dark and light spots have been captured and their patterns established for individual characters, these patterns have to be recognized by matching them against stored patterns of individual characters "known" to the system. Those patterns which for some reason could not be recognized are singled out for manual recognition by the operator.

Kurzweil Data Entry Machine Optical Character Reader. The older models of OCR device had a limited capability to recognize one or

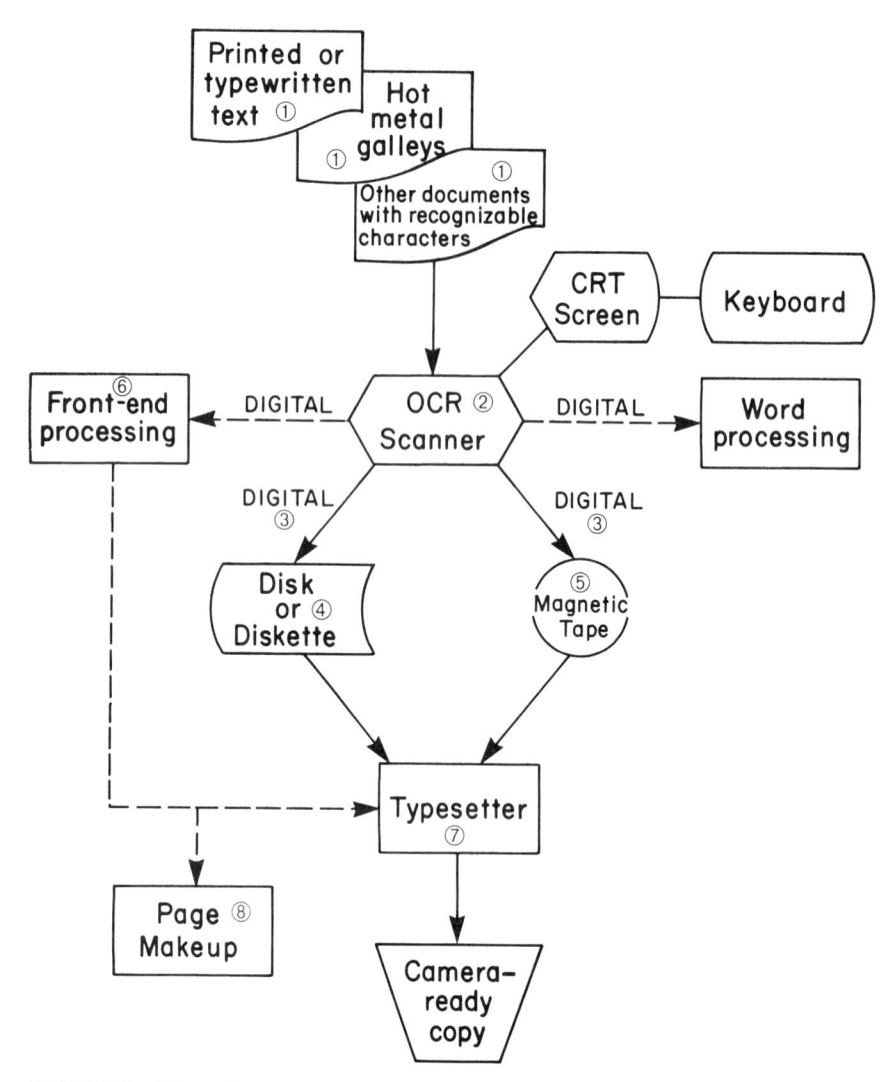

FIGURE 3 OCR—device-facilitated publishing.

several well-defined sets of characters. A diagram of a publishing system utilizing an OCR device is sketched in Figure 3.

Figure 3 depicts a publishing scheme in which documents (1) with recognizable characters enter an OCR scanner (2) and their digital representation (3) is stored (on disk [4] or tape [5]) and/or further processed (6) into whatever form is acceptable to the typesetter (7); page makeup may be interposed (8).

The Kurzweil data entry machine (KDEM) is representative of a much more powerful new OCR generation of devices which have the potential of revolutionizing the input side of many electronic publishing systems: e.g., typescripts may be scanned, digitized and stored for typesetting. Another application is creating databases from documents, articles and other printed materials. By combining a font-versatile OCR scanning device and a suitable phototypesetting system one can, in many instances, obtain formatted typeset copies from typescripts: this has been made possible by taking advantage of the device's ability to recognize not only fonts but also font and format changes and insert typesetting commands automatically.

Hardware of the KDEM is composed of a minicomputer with a CRT screen, keyboard, disk drive and optionally a tape drive, all of which are fed by a scanning camera. The machine displays characters it cannot "understand" on a CRT in the context respective and the operator "trains" the machine how to interpret the character the next time it is encountered; but the system also wields a 40,000-term dictionary, which further alleviates the need for operator's intervention. The device scans 20-50 characters per second (maximum 75 characters per second).

The disadvantage, on the other hand, of the OCR devices is their inability to tackle any graphics whether line art or halftone. Their storage (and transmission) economy, however, may be illustrated on the background of the amount of bits with which they work: a typical typewritten page may contain between 2000 and 4000 characters, which calls for some 15,000-30,000 bits to represent a page. If we used the image facsimile coding technique instead, then it would require at least 10 million bits to represent one 8 1/2 -inch × 11-inch page minus any code compression.

Image (Raster) Coding System. "Image" coding has been used interchangeably with "raster" and "facsimile" coding. Unlike character coding systems, the image coding systems do not interpret the meaning of the scanned image but perceive a page (or any other area, e.g., a character) as a pattern of dots which may be either white or black, on or off, 1 or 0, etc. Image-based systems may be, by their nature, both analog or digital but digital systems are in our focus here because they may be processed by digital computers. The reason for our interest in the digitally encoded image systems is the fact that they have distinct advantages in the display and processing of graphics and offer the key to the solution of the difficult problem of merging text and halftone, among other things. If we want to merge text and art, either we can store text in the character coding form and art in the image coding form or we can store the entire page, text and art, in the image coding form; in the latter instance we forgo the manipulation and searchability inherent in character coding systems; conversions are possible as needed: e.g., raster image processor will convert character coded text into image coding form, an OCR scanner will convert text to the character-coded form, a facsimile scanner will convert a page (either text or art or both) to the image coding form, depending on what the underlying technology postulates. Microform images also may be scanned. In essence, scanning art in an image (or raster or facsimile) scanner is done in a manner similar to that described above for the OCR scanner except that digitizing art does not involve understanding characters. In fact, each reading's analog information in the form of a continuous analog waveform is sampled and quantized, which means that samples are assigned digital values of either black and white or gray values as well, depending on the number of bits available for one scanned picture element (pel or pixel); 1 bit can only express black or white, 4 bits may record 16 shades and 8 bits can represent 256 levels of gray for any pel. These values are stored in a given matrix in the so-called bit-map memory and may be displayed, reproduced or adjusted as needed.

There are essentially three types of image scanners in use today: (1) camera-based, (2) flatbed design and (3) sheet feeding systems.

In an electronic digitizing camera, the image of an object or document is focused by a system of lenses, as is the case in a photocamera; but instead of being exposed on a photosensitive film it is scanned by a CCD array containing from 1728 to 4096 elements. When scanning, e.g., a 8 1/2-inch × 11-inch document, the 4096 element scanner can record approximately 480 dots per inch (4096:8.5) horizontally and make 5280 successive moves in the vertical direction to record 480 dots per inch (5280:11). The quality of the resulting digitized image is defined by the 480 dots per inch (dpi) (also lines per inch—lpi) resolution which depends on the size of the document and the number of elements in the photoreceptor. As the photoreceptor, in our case a CCD array which is most widely used, moves down the page the image is scanned line by line and the analog signal (reflected light) captured by the sensor is converted into digital representation in an analog-to-digital converter. Each element of the photoreceptor captures one picture element which may be represented by one bit as one of two possible states: black or white; shades of gray may be captured. Digital values of these picture elements are fed under computer control into computer memory and stored as a bit map whereupon the image can be displayed or printed. The gray scale information may be redundant or undesirable for some applications (e.g., line graphics): in the process called thresholding all shades of gray above a certain level (threshold) of reflection become white and values below it are interpreted as black:

the continuous tone image turns into a black and white picture where each picture element can be stored and transmitted as one bit only.

In flatbed scanners, much the same as in electronic cameras, the document remains fixed during the scanning process; so is the photoreceptor (unlike electronic cameras) which receives the optical density (the amount of reflected light) information from the moving light source and mirrors.

In a sheet-feeding system the entire optical system is immobile and inserted single sheets of paper are scanned as they move past it. Flatbed scanners and sheet-feeding systems are easily portable and less expensive than electronic cameras.

An important concept in image scanning is that of the "resolution," which practically means the number of spots or points that were scanned per an area unit such as a square inch or centimeter; it is important to realize that the output resolution may be not only equal to but also smaller or larger than the input resolution. Image scanning has found important applications such as imagesetting, both monochrome and color, platemaking with the potential to circumvent typesetting, and telefacsimile in its document delivery function as well as in other transmission roles.

Data Compaction or Compression. In the subsection "Character Coding System," we mentioned that this is a more efficient system of encoding characters than the image (raster or facsimile) coding system. But if the image coding has to be employed because of its other merits, then various expedients may be used to introduce some measure of economy into the endless arrays of ones and zeroes.

One method of data compression is called "run-length" coding and it is claimed that a compaction ratio on the order of 1:10 may be achieved. The basic idea behind this method of coding is that it does not record all bits along the line being scanned but only the binary address of each borderline between black and white and vice versa, which means the relative distance from the preceding run end. "Run-end" coding on the other hand, indicates the distance of the end of each run from the beginning of the line. Other compaction codes have been designed, e.g., Huffman, READ and two-dimensional run-length, which claim even higher rates of compaction.

Vector Notation. Besides the character and the image (raster) coding systems, there is one more kind of information coding namely the vector notation used mainly in computer graphics and also in the videotex image definition. For instance, a line would be sufficiently defined by two points plus a command to draw a line, a circle would be defined by the coordinates of the center and the radius, etc. It may be easily imagined how much more efficient vector coding may be as compared with the necessity to scan the entire page in order to capture a line or a graph. For computer graphics relying on vector notation to be processed, stored and displayed along with other data in character or image (raster) format, it must be first converted for compatibility. This aspect is outlined where applicable in this study. For instance in the Canadian alphageometric videotex system called Telidon, graphics are defined by picture description instructions (PDIs); when these arrive via telephone lines at the user's workstation, they are converted in the modem from the analog form into the character coding form as ASCII characters, and subsequently these are interpreted as PDIs in the Telidon decoder and painted as graphics by the electronic circuitry on a red, green and blue (RGB) monitor; this allows economic coding and provides a display whose resolution is limited only by that of the display device.

The vector image notation has become more of a factor in electronic publishing with the increased prominence of in-house publishing, especially with respect to technical publications and with the integration of CAD/CAM systems into the electronic publishing technology.

Notes

1. *Charge-coupled devices (CCDs).* CCDs are silicon chip-based integrated circuits which, because of their light sensitivity, can be used as image scanners. Each chip may contain typically 1024, 2048 or 4096 light-sensitive elements to pick up the light reflected from an illuminated picture; charge builds up in the elements in direct proportion to the amount of reflected light and the duration of exposure. This picture information (voltage) in analog form is corrected after being taken off the chip, and it is digitized to yield typically 8 bits of data per scanned spot (or light-sensitive element). The device can also serve as an analog or digital storage medium although not as random access storage.

3

Non-Print-based Electronic Publishing

The terms of reference of this chapter embrace the corpus of technologies in which printed output, although it may be available, does not constitute the main mode through which the output may be obtained. The only exception to this rule might be offline (batch) retrieval which used to be presented on cards or utility computer printout; however, from the historical perspective it is expedient if not more appropriate to treat it here as a predecessor to online retrieval. Besides, batch retrieval can be conducted in a video display unit (VDU)-based environment even though video display terminals (VDTs) are now associated with the online interactive mode as a matter of fact. The technologies reported here encompass, in addition to the already mentioned batch and online retrieval, the other VDT- or TV monitor-based modes of electronic publishing: end user-oriented online services to include user-friendly low-cost services with broad content and easy access, videotex to subsume both viewdata and teletext, cable TV in the publishing context, hybrid online/videodisk system, optical digital disk and finally the electronic journal. In the Appendix we address, among other things, problems of casual users in the editorial process, user response and costs as related to electronic publishing as well as issues of human performance and information processing in the context of the electronic journal; these three topics have been dealt with recently in three separate papers as indicated and thematically belong in this chapter.

Also included in Chapter 3 are two sections covering matters related to electronic publishing of the nonprint nature: electronic mail and teleconferencing. Even though electronic message systems have been designed with interpersonal communication in mind, they can potentially handle a variety of tasks germane to our study area, viz., videotex service, transfer of files such as papers, chapters, reports, etc., consulting remote databases, submitting interlibrary loan requests. Teleconferencing is still too young to assess its future contribution to the field.

A paradox of this non-print-based variety of electronic publishing resides in the fact that it all started with the machine-readable magnetic tapes prepared for use in printbased (paper-bound) publishing—namely computer composition. The first stage was the offline computer retrieval which eventually turned into an online mode of operation and use—online retrieval, videotex. What we are witnessing now is, in a sense, a return to the offline mode of usage as videodisks, CD-ROMs and CD-Is are supplementing the traditional product—the printed word—which will coexist with the above offline and online products in their respective areas of excellence. In introducing the information technologies forming the contents of this chapter it is appropriate to put them in a historical context in order to illustrate the acceleration rate of the development of means of communication in general: it took approximately over 5 million years to arrive at writing from spoken word; about 5,000 years from there to printing; 500 years from the ability to print to telephone, film, radio and television media; and a mere 50 years from rudimentary television to the demonstration of videodisks.

3.1 Offline (Batch) Retrieval

In the 1960s typesetting was computerized, and text prepared by the indexing and abstracting services on magnetic tape for this purpose gave birth to a new electronic publishing business—offline computer processing of databases. Information centers sprang up to "spin" the tapes acquired on mainframe computers and began building considerable retrospective files in which current tapes were merged after being used for current information purposes.

Services Offered. Three kinds of services were offered: (1) printed indexes, (2) selective dissemination of information (SDI) or current awareness service and (3) retrospective searching. Among many indexes produced at that time were author and title indexes, KWIC indexes (keywords in context) and KWOC indexes (keywords out of context) pointing to an abstract or full text. Selective dissemination of information is an alerting service in which users' profiles (formalized statements of their information needs) are periodically matched against an update database containing the most recent document surrogates—e.g., titles or abstracts—and the resulting information is delivered on a user's desk. This retrieval product had a form of cards as printed by computers, and usually contained a means for users' feedback; this feedback was an essential part of the service because it allowed for profile evaluation and modification if the results were in some respect unsatisfactory. Retrospective searching usually involved a much bigger database and was conducted as a response to individual requests.

Even though this form of electronic publishing has not survived on any massive scale and never really represented a lucrative enterprise, it did, nevertheless, have a pioneering mission in awakening public awareness to the fact of publishing by electronic means. Computer batch services could not achieve any economy of scales and were often directly or indirectly subsidized. Centers providing this service were not in a position to provide all text information because they often did not own the information store on which retrieval was based. Searching involved some time delays owing to the batch character of processing to perfect the profiles and there was no interaction with the database.

3.2 Online Retrieval

3.2.1 Definition

Online information retrieval is a publishing system in which the end user retrieves, more often than not, with assistance from intermediaries, the information he needs; this is done online (in direct communication/interaction with the computer), which allows for formal query specification and adjustment during the interaction with one or more databases housed in that computer: the interrogator (either intermediary or the end user) interacts with the computer by means of a terminal linked to the computer via communication lines (typically telephone lines but potentially, and to an increasing extent, involving, at least partly, satellites, cables, fiber optics, etc.). Online information retrieval may also be a document delivery system if document surrogates as abstracts, titles, etc. are sought and locally printed; an alternative is to have them sent from an online vendor. Full-text delivery may be arranged in the same terminal session that retrieved the references.

Online information retrieval services were conceived in the 1960s and were commerically introduced in early 1970s when large-capacity storage, high-speed computers, terminals and telecommunications were ready to accept the challenge of processing large databases ap-

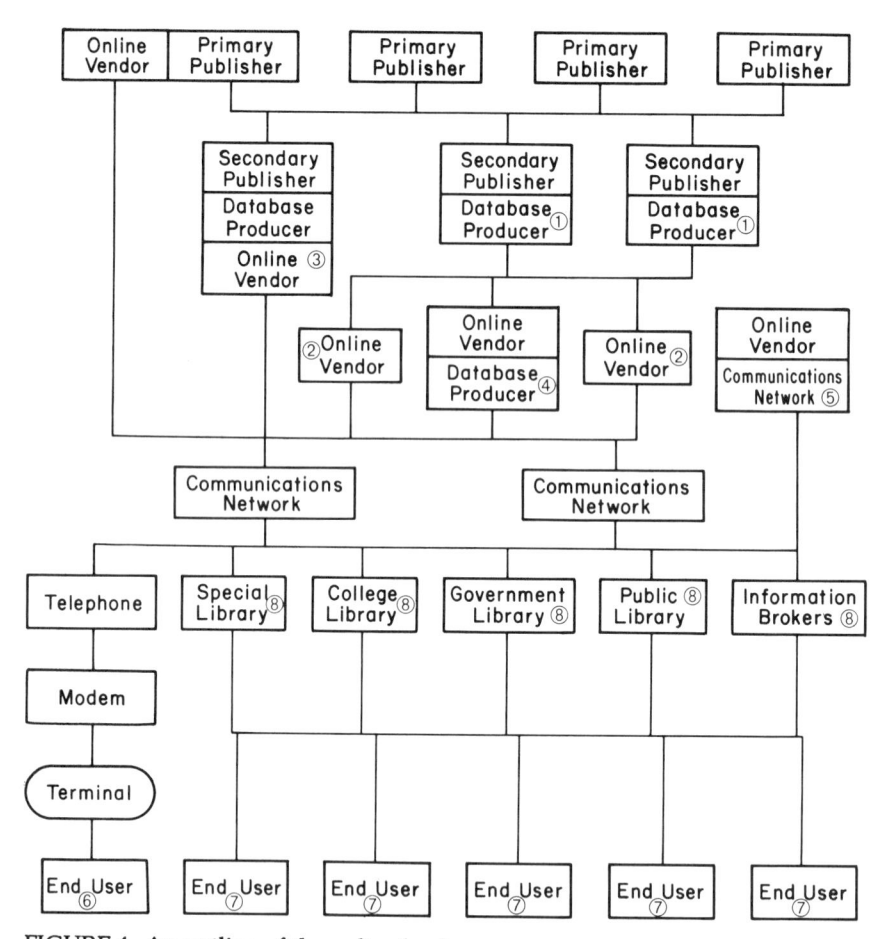

FIGURE 4 An outline of the online business.

pearing on magnetic tapes for computer composition and typesetting. Online services thus evolved as a natural outgrowth of time-sharing made possible by the appearance of multiprocessors and efficient communications interfaces. Value added networks (such as Arpanet, Tymnet, Telenet, Uninet, etc.) based on packet switching techniques, satellites, fiber optics and microwave improved communication between users and remote hosts; the single most important enhancement of the end user's capabilities is the microcomputer.

3.2.2 Online Systems: Market for Suppliers and Consumers

Online information retrieval is a growing business with some very sophisticated relationships (Figure 4). Secondary publishers—abstracting and indexing services—(1) prepare magnetic tapes in the course of their traditional publishing and sell copies of them on an exclusive or nonexclusive basis to (2) online vendors (search services). Secondary publishers (database producers) (1) became in some instances their own (3) online vendors; in doing so the database producer aims at getting a bigger slice of profit, direct communication with database users and regular updating of files, but the ultimate user has yet another online system to learn. On occasion the online vendor is himself involved in creating (4) a database or establishes (5) his own communication network. (6) End users may conduct their own searching but (7) in an overwhelming majority of cases they depend on (8) an intermediary to query the database on their behalf. Intermediaries may typically be specially trained librarians, information specialists in information centers or information brokers.

Searching. To perform an online search, the searcher needs to be trained; online services and some database producers organize training sessions and supply necessary documentation. The searchers formulate the search ahead of the online interrogation based on an interview with the ultimate user and on knowledge of the system by availing themselves of all available tools. Searching can be done on a video display terminal and retrieved items from one or more databases may be printed on an attached printer. The terminal is connected to the communications network through a modem (or accoustic coupler), which translates the digital code generated by the terminal into the analog signal for transmission via telephone lines at rates of 110, 300, 1200, 2400 and more baud. If the output is too bulky to be printed locally, the results are ordered to be printed offline and delivered through mail. Relevant full-text documents may be ordered online for mail delivery.

Microcomputers are becoming increasingly popular also for use as intelligent terminals. On the other side of the communications link, the online vendor maintains a time-sharing host computer with extensive communications capabilities for simultaneous use by many users. Databases are mounted on large-capacity disks and are regularly updated to remain current. Individual databases have different access points that may be used by searchers in retrieving information, and online systems themselves have different sign-on procedures and retrieval protocols, which poses certain problems to searchers if they are to query multiple systems. Users are charged for connect time to a database, for telecommunications and for offline-ordered citations; a searcher's wage is yet another direct cost. Additionally, there is considerable indirect cost including hardware, documentation, supplies, training, promotion and management.

Information Organized in Databases. Databases are collections of information (or data) in machine-readable form stored on storage devices under computer control and may be retrieved by searchers from their terminals. Databases are often machine-readable equivalents of printed indexes and abstract journals. Databases have evolved as a by-product in the genesis of printed journals: text was key-captured onto a magnetic medium (tape), which was used to drive a typesetter, and copies of tapes were sold to be used for offline SDI (selective dissemination of information) or retrospective searching; this service has been nearly exclusively replaced by online retrieval services in the 1970s. Online services fill the role of electronic outlets distributing databases produced by database publishers.

Databases may be divided using a number of criteria. Cuadra (1981, 1985) distinguishes between reference and source databases; reference databases are those that serve as referral pointers to the information sought, whereas source databases do not need any referring because, as their name implies, they are themselves the information source. Reference databases are divided into bibliographic and referral: whereas the former consist of titles or abstracts related to published information, the latter point to nonpublished materials. Source databases are subdivided into numeric, textual-numeric and full-text databases.

Williams (1983) states that the number of databases has risen from 300 in 1975 to over 1000 in 1983 with a corresponding increase in the number of searches from less than one million to eight million; this exponential growth has not been paralleled by a similar increase in the number of records (50 million to about 300 million, respectively) during the same period, tapering off at the latter figure. In a more recent presentation Williams (1984) gives the number of publicly accessible databases as more than 2000 with the yearly growth rate of between 20% and 30%, but 80% of all usage within the library/information center market is accounted for by only 25 databases; the author presents an interesting account of online database usage in 1982 for the above user segment: 1.3 million hours and $127 million total user cost with the average cost per hour equal to $102.59. These figures reflect a respectable growth given the 15 years of online information retrieval's existence, but indicate also tribulations of those producers and online vendors who do not participate in the boom of the main players.

Databases have been traditionally understood to be collections of document surrogates as prepared by secondary (i.e., abstracting and indexing) services, but one current trend in the trade is for more and more documents, newspaper articles, papers, etc., to be published in full text; this may tend to make the distinction between primary and secondary publishing services rather arbitrary. Telecommunications costs, storage costs and general unavailability of suitable software were the main obstacles on the road to full text. Until recently online searchers were limited to retrieving pointers to the full-text documents and had either to scour for documents in a major local library, possibly ordering documents unavailable locally through interlibrary loans; later in the game major online vendors instituted online ordering, which facilitated the process but still involved time delays.

3.2.3 Trends

One clearly perceptible trend points to wider adoption of microcomputers in online information retrieval as reflected in the literature on the topic. Micros provide automatic dial-up and sign-on links to one or more systems, storage of profiles and automatic SDI service (selective dissemination of information on a periodic basis), act as an umbrella system in accessing multiple systems with different protocols, function as an online training device, provide downloading of both data or software ("tele-software"), manipulate output locally for better relevance or fit the output to individual preferences, and package information. Other applications include distribution of results to users and administrative functions such as cost accounting, accounts payable, billing, etc. Whereas downloading of databases was a source of concern for database producers initially, it was not considered a prime issue in 1985 (Neufeld and Cornog 1986).

More and more full-text databases are offered online, a major proportion of those being newspapers. The prudence of this has also been questioned (Monitor 1984b).

Business databases seem to be spawning more interest and attract more customers.

As some online systems simplify their access methods, a growing number of end users are conducting their own searches through bypassing intermediaries. Yet the problem is not so simple as to replace the existing protocols of menus that have proven to be inefficient for the experienced user: at least a dual (novice/expert) system is the answer.

Because it has been discovered, rather predictably, that online users do not enjoy contending with multiple systems, various strategies are being devised to enable users to interrogate several online retrieval systems employing one interface language only. "Transparent information systems" have been often advocated (Williams 1986) as a means of information retrieval designed to free the user from having to deal with the complexity of multiple database searching: front-ends, interfaces, intermediary systems and gateways have been suggested as means to this end.

Whereas more attention was initially paid to bibliographic services, it now appears that nonbibliographic services may play an even more important role in the economics of future libraries and information centres.

Whereas some tendency towards vertical integration in the online information-transfer chain has been reported (Neufeld and Cornog 1983), a contrary trend, and reasons for it, have also been noted (Monitor 1984a). Vertical integration in this context means assuming more than one function in the chain of primary publishers, secondary publishers, online vendors, telecommunications carriers and libraries/information centers. There are intimations that libraries/information centers may forego subscribing to a file that requires learning how to operate yet another online system unless the file is indispensable (Knapp 1983).

Online information retrieval systems are becoming outlets for electronic (and nonelectronic) document delivery. This raises questions about the future role of abstracts and indexes and their relationships with full-text documents.

In the long run artificial intelligence will bring natural languages to bear on retrieval problems associated with an involved index, possibly with the advent of the fifth generation of computers. Speech recognition and speech generation both have the potential to revolutionize the way humans are able to utilize online information services. Videodisks and especially optical digital disk (ODD) hold big promise for local retrieval systems.

Online retrieval has come a long way from searching titles to searching abstracts and eventually to the full text of documents, with information ranging from bibliographic citations to directory-type information, handbook-type factual information, encyclopedias, numeric numeric data and statistical data, to name a few. Though it may sound commonplace, a successful online operation, like any other publishing venture, is one based on a sound analysis of users' needs in relation to a publisher's own circumstances. The debate on whether or not the online business causes cancellations of printed materials has been going on for some time with no clear-cut outcome; but thanks to more realistic pricing algorithms, databases are now a financially self-supporting business (Neufeld and Cornog 1986).

For the future we can foresee other means of database distribution beside online systems: floppy disks, optical storage media and possibly videotex.

3.2.4 Online Versus Videotex

These two forms of electronic publishing were rivals a couple of years ago. Videotex failed to prove the advantages it claimed. One of them was color graphics capability: graphics are now offered at an increasing rate on microcomputers as well and are steadily improving, and there are also numerous computer graphics systems. Besides, the inclusion of graphics in many applications has been found not to be so urgent as it was once assumed. Another claimed advantage, namely use of the standard TV set because of its wide availability, is also questionable because of the home-market penetration by personal computers, which are a much more versatile output (and input) device than TV, especially when it comes to text: TV is capable of displaying only up to around 450 characters owing to its poor screen resolution. Online systems with user-friendly software may be accessed by personal computers which have some user-friendly features as well, and this refutes yet one more "advantage" claimed by videotex systems: the user-friendly menus. As a matter of fact, menus alone, if not accompanied by the advanced-user option, may be more of a bane than a boon in using online systems. The same may be said about the page format in which videotex presents information. Microcomputers possess yet another feature that makes them superior to videotex in accessing large online databases, namely the capability to download large amounts of data (and/or software) in nonprime time and then "massage" and print data as desired.

3.2.5 Online Versus CD-ROM and Other Optical Media

CD-ROM (see Section 3.7) poses a serious challenge to online systems because it relieves end users of the fear of high connect-time charges: more users may be able to do their own searching. CD-ROM is mostly suitable for databases that fill one disk inasmuch as users would not want to search multiple disks; online service may be more complete and more current. What will likely happen is the creation of hybrid systems in which current information would be online, whereas less current information would be on periodically updated disks. Frequently used information may be expected to migrate to locally stored CD-ROMs. Serious hurdles that optical disks face are lack of standards which might force users to acquire multiple hardware, as well as the copyright.

In any case, all industries concerned in this development face a major shakedown before the market regains any degree of stability (if indeed it had ever possessed any at all).

3.3 End User-oriented Online Services

3.3.1 End User Orientation

Under this heading we single out time-sharing microcomputer-based services geared to the general public because of their easy use, typically through a menu interface, and low cost which makes it possible for tens of thousands of customers, often computer hobbyists, to subscribe; the sizable paying clientele distinguishes them from many experimental trials, which have to be heavily subsidized and fail to prove themselves on the market after demonstrating their technological feasibility. They cannot be classified as "pure" online retrieval services because they offer a broad mix of services; neither do they have all the requisite ingredients of videotex (TV set, graphics or special code requiring decoders) to qualify for this label. Thus they are considered both part of the videotex environment (Veith 1982) and dealt with in online literature.

Repackagers of information have found that, in order for electronic publishing to be economically viable, it is necessary to make the scope of the service more diversified to suit the whole spectrum of information needs; a wide variety of databases makes these systems worthwhile for business office, library and consumer alike. But traditional databases alone would not warrant sufficient interest and this is why other services were added such as financial advice, computer-assisted instruction, electronic messaging, sports, news, weather updates, consumer information, astrology readings, home decorating tips, games, general computer capability, programming, banking services, etc.

There are presently over 1.4 million passwords in effect issued to users of online line systems in North America according to the Digital Information Group of Stamford, CT, which includes both the Online retrieval systems described in the previous section and the End user-oriented online services which are the subject of this present chapter: among the leaders are CompuServe with nearly 260,000 passwords followed by Dow Jones (235,000), Mead Data (180,000), Dialog (70,000) and I.P. Sharp (37,000) (Library Systems 1986).

3.3.2 Major Players

Services falling under this category are, for instance, The Source, Dow Jones News/Retrieval, Easy Net and CompuServe. The Source is produced and operated by the Source Telecomputing Corporation. There is an initial fee of $100.00, minimum charge of $10.00 per month and $ .10 per session. Service is available 24 hours a day every day and connect charges are lower in the nonprime time. It is designed to cater to diversified interests: databases stretch over a wide range of subject areas such as health care, real estate, restaurant guides, movie reviews, travel, airline itineraries, entertainment guides, job vacancies, energy conservation or social assistance. Weather, sports and news complement the assortment of information. Educational and shopping services are also accessible as are general computing facilities.

Source Telecomputing Corporation is also marketing a software product designed to facilitate the use of their services with personal computers. The Source Link Disk, as the telecommunication software is called, allows users to dial up and sign on automatically, download data from The Source into the memory or onto disks and control a printer; it also bestows the ability to dial up as many as five other online services and provides editing capabilities. Features such as these are bound to further user acceptance in the competitive world.

A distinctive feature of the "enhanced online services," which distinguishes them from other information utilities (such as offline information retrieval, online information retrieval, videotex/teletex), are the standard services ordinarily provided by computer time-sharing services such as database management utilities, services for computer program development including compilers, text-editing programs, games, electronic mail and various applications programs; The Source makes over 2000 programs and utilities available online.

Easy Net is a menu-oriented online system from Telebase Systems, Inc., which tries to make access to different systems and databases so easy for the users that they may not be aware of the differences. It offers 800 number access and payment by credit cards.

Dow Jones News/Retrieval is another enhanced online service with a mass market and also evidence of the online business gravitating towards microcomputers, business and financial databases, transactional services, easy access and affordable prices. The synergy of the online service/microcomputer association is brought out by their personal computer software Spreadsheet Link, which enables any subscriber/microcomputer owner to download data from the host computer into Visicalc and Multiplan spreadsheet programs for local manipulation.

Dialog's Knowledge Index and BRS After Dark feature simpler interface languages than their full-fledged search services and are used by members of the general public who own personal computers.

The enhanced online customer services bring home the point that new technology in itself is not a panacea, and that customers do not buy technology per se but a product. These services sell and they do so because they are easy to access (albeit at some cost of a slower response) all the time and at an affordable user cost, while the content promises something for nearly everybody. Investment into a microcomputer is more lucrative than buying a videotex decoder because it opens up a whole new world of computing, whereas a decoder leads into videotex whose databases and services have been lacking in depth and variety. In these times of convoluted technologies, the enhanced contents of time-sharing services may make it necessary to redefine electronic publishing once more and answer the following questions: is a lesson in a foreign language an electronic publication by virtue of the media and the manner of acquisition employed or is it just another computerized service (computer-assisted instruction)? Evidently, it may be both.

3.4 Online Public-access Library Catalog

3.4.1 Definition of the Subject and Delineation of Scope

Online catalogs in libraries are an important tool for library users to be able to search bibliographic records representing the holdings of one or more libraries. The objective of such a search may be manifold: it may be a search for an item (book, report, microform, etc.) which is known to be in the collection, or it may be a search for items on a certain subject or items by a certain author, etc., depending on the access points to records available in the specific online system. From the library's point of view, an online catalog is a combination of hardware and software in which the online catalog function is either a part of the total library automation package or is combined with the circulation function.

The interactive capability makes online catalog systems familiar to those patrons who have been previously exposed to online bibliographic services; this interactivity is the distinctive advantage of the online systems when compared with the traditional manual catalog.

This section is directly relevant to those information users who are in the habit of acquiring their information through libraries regardless of whether by electronic or more traditional means; those who do not may be doing so in the future thanks to the new wave of electronic publishing by libraries. If we categorize library users such as professionals, into classes and disregard for a moment those who get away with cursory skimming one or two journals, then we may designate them as one-library, two-library, (and so on) users depending on the size of their information horizon; the net result of public access to electronic publishing in libraries will be a new breed of library (information) user—the multi-library user who will be able to draw on information contents of a number of libraries, large and small, search their store in a more or less sophisticated manner and obtain a full text of relevant documents (or at least inspect them) instantly on a VDT or local printer. The first part of this scenario has become rather common already in the form of public-access catalogs; the second part aiming at full text is in the making to grow out of the first part or rather along with it. One qualification must be made at this point, namely, that libraries may not be the only places to offer this service in the future.

The concern of this section is primarily the online catalog with public access, whereas possible extensions of this concept leading to provision of full-text documents from a full-text electronic data store in the future, such as online full-text retrieval, videotext, videodisk, telefacsimile and other similar concepts are covered in separate chapters; their bearing on the present topic is evident.

3.4.2 Historical Perspective on Online Catalogs

The online public-access catalog has evolved through a number of stages. The old-time book catalogs were in their time replaced by card catalogs which kept growing until their size in large libraries made them unwieldy and difficult to manage. Maintaining card catalogs is a laborious process and card catalogs have suffered from the growing time lag between the time material arrived in the library and the time the card representing the material was inserted in the file for public access. A card catalog offers limited access points to holdings and suffers from frequent changes; remote access is not possible and search methods are primitive. In the meantime libraries have gradually adopted online bibliographic retrieval services, which made it possible for users in a growing number of subject areas to search massive stores of secondary information (information about information) with better precision and recall in a manner convenient to the user, albeit with the assistance of an intermediary. Various databases allowed computerized, efficient searching which often pointed to materials extraneous to the local library, and the contrast with the tedious and inefficient searching of library's own holdings inherent in the manual catalog became all the more obvious. Thus the role of online bibliographic searching may be historically viewed as a precursor of online public-access catalogs and a catalyst influencing the thinking of both librarians and users and paving the road to a wider acceptance of the computerized access to information.

Computerized reference services in many libraries have evolved along with other functions being automated: depending on their specific conditions and needs libraries got involved in the computerization of acquisitions, cataloguing, circulation, serials control, interlibrary loans, binding, accounting and some other areas; in some cases an integrated library system approach was elected. Manual library catalogs benefited not only from the activities in other library areas and from their common database but also from external shared databases whose objective has been to reduce the amount of expensive original cataloging. Participation by librarians in these automation projects changed their perspectives on computer applications in libraries. Library catalogs in many instances were supplied with cards that were printed and sorted by computers which expedited the process somewhat but they still remained card catalogs as seen by the end user. Some libraries adopted computer-output microfiche as a space-saving innovation thus facilitating somewhat the process of searching as well. As another intermediary stage, computer printouts allowed for distributed viewing by library patrons in the earlier automation endeavors.

But it was not until the arrival of the public-access computer-based online catalog that libraries entered the era of electronic publishing as active players in the role of database providers and online operators; let us hasten to say that the computer need not be on the library premises and that the database nearly always is a result of shared cataloging among libraries and library bibliographic networks (bibliographic utilities.) The online catalog is a landmark on the long road of evolution whose importance is often not fully appreciated. First of all, communications are soon established to enable remote usage of the catalog from places of user's choice via telephone lines. Secondly, libraries join their forces and catalogs, and provide the user with a "multilibrary horizon." Thirdly, circulation systems may be integrated into the catalog system and patrons may order hard copies from the comfort of their residences, or laboratories and other places of work. Finally, in addition to providing the information about a known item or result of a subject search, each online catalog allows a certain degree of browsing; all of these lead to requests for full-text documents which libraries procure in the various ways described in other sections of this study. In the times ahead online catalogs and associated services will see a great deal of refinement along the lines sketched above.

3.4.3 Library (Bibliographic) Utilities

Bibliographic utilities are the large bibliographic networks that played a significant role in the evolution of online catalogs in libraries. Their primary purpose is to operate shared cataloging services which enable individual member libraries to access the utility database and to use data records as needed in building the local library's catalog as well as to contribute to the shared database those records that result from local library's original cataloguing. The largest library utility is the Online Computer Library Center, Inc. (OCLC), which presently serves over 3000 member libraries and has special sharing arrangements with another 3000 libraries; the Online Union Catalog contains more than 12 million records supplied by the Library of Congress as well as those contributed by participating libraries. OCLC markets also an automated library system, LS/200, which supports an online public access catalog. Among other major bibliographic utilities are the Washington Library Network (WLN), the Research Libraries Information Network (RLIN) and the University of Toronto Automated Library Systems (UTLAS).

3.4.4 Library Consortia and Libraries

An idea about the size of operation and utility to library user population of online catalogs may be obtained from the public-access services of the Statewide Library Computer System (LCS) maintained by the University of Illinois (Sloan 1984). Resource sharing was the primary reason for expanding LCS beyond the University of Illinois, and any patron may search from an LCS terminal the files of any of the 25 participating libraries using the same commands. Points of access are author, title, author/title and call number. Public access is possible from 222 out of the total of 564 terminals and is not limited to interaction from library premises; this amounted to 1.3 million transactions from the public-access terminals during March 1984. The system may be dialed into directly from a microcomputer, or accessed from terminals placed in public areas of academic departments or through some academic computing networks of participating institutions. The utility of this public-access online system has been enhanced by the bibliographic search capability being complemented with the circulation function; remote borrowing is possible in that every search yields data about which library holds a particular title, if there is a circulating copy and if that copy is available. With this information on hand, the user can initiate the charge-out transaction whereupon the material requested is delivered to the patron's library.

The number of fully operational online catalogs in the United States and Canada was pegged at fewer than 20 by the Council on Library Resources (CLR) in 1980. This number burgeoned to more than 200 by April 1983. Online catalog has had a far more profound impact on library's users than any other technological innovation in the library field in the last several decades (C.L. Jones 1984).

Because user acceptance of online electronic publishing has been a problem in other areas, it is interesting to note the results of a survey undertaken by the CLR based on data from 15 U.S. research libraries with regard to user attitudes toward the online catalog. The study revealed, among other data, that over 80% of users had a favorable attitude toward online catalogs and that over 90% felt that the online catalog was at least as good as the card catalog; nearly 60% of online catalog users use it on almost every visit to the library (C.L. Jones 1984).

3.4.5 The Outlook of the Online Catalog

The online library catalog has not evolved in isolation from other automation efforts in the library and in the surrounding world, and it therefore reflects in its philosophy, hardware and software the contemporary state of the art. As the state of the art advances further, the online catalog will not escape and, in fact, will gladly embrace the improvements introduced in related areas to eliminate some limitations of the present-day technology. Users want to be able to communicate with a multitude of library catalogs while using only one protocol and one set of commands; this demand is being met in online bibliographic retrieval by software interfaces, providing a bridge between different systems so they can be searched using one common command language. Network gateways with multiple services will make it possible for users to avoid multiple logons. Full-text services will, doubtless, find their way into online catalogs either in the on-demand electronic delivery mode or in conjunction with full-text searching. The EIDOS system being designed by OCLC (see Chapter 5) is one modality to increase the efficiency of the catalog by adding more information prior to ordering full text. Because the online catalog is a part of public service, the end user will benefit from any enhancement of terminal ergonomics and from any improvement on the human-machine interface such as pointing devices (mouse, touch panels, joystick, electronic wand, etc.), icons, standardization of procedures and user-friendly access languages or voice input and output capabilities. The online catalog will be able to be tapped from a variety of terminals and microcomputers with improved display capabilities and through a variety of communications options. Good printers, which are already being provided along with VDTs in public areas, will be supplemented by telefacsimile devices and mass storage devices (such as videodisks and optical digital disks) situated close by, so the documents, if required, might be procured with little or no delay. All this is subject to resolving copyright issues and is dependent on economic viability.

It may be safely stated that the future of libraries will be closely tied with and revolving around the online public-access catalog, and that even in this area they may be facing stiff competition from publishers, bibliographic utilities and various information providers. The online catalog is sure to survive even though some other parts of the traditional library, such as acquisitions, may not.

3.5 Videotex: Viewdata and Teletext

3.5.1 Terminology

In the terminology pertaining to this technology there is some chaos causing a degree of confusion in the related literature. In this section we shall use the term "videotex" as a generic term encompassing two somewhat different technologies: viewdata and teletext. Some other authors use the term videotex in place of viewdata to denote its generic character. Some authors view videotex as a technology composed of hardware, software and database, others deal with it as one or more protocols, and yet others see it as predominantly a social issue. In this section we discuss the videotex phenonemon, which, as defined below may be called the "classic" (the concept has been around for almost ten years) videotex definition as apposed to others, e.g., Veith (1983b), who sees Videotex as "any system for bringing computerized information/entertainment systems to the public."

There is a great deal of overlap in the reporting of online systems (bibliographic, numeric, textual, directory-type, etc.), videotex proper, microcomputers, terminals, computer graphics and areas related to mass media as the technologies respective continue to converge.

3.5.2 Definition

Viewdata. Viewdata is an information system offering a wide variety of services (among them electronic publishing functions) whereby databases stored on a host computer are accessed via telecommunications links by subscribers in an interactive mode. Whereas the television set was almost exclusively used in the beginning because of its widespread availability, microcomputers are becoming more and more involved in this area. Users themselves determine which frames (screens, pages) they want to receive at their terminal and specify these frames by means of a hand-held keypad or a keyboard if textual information is to be entered as, e.g., in messaging or in entering keywords (see Figure 5). This figure shows database suppliers (1) (called information providers in the videotex business) delivering information to one or more host computers (2), which store and serve information to users (3). Gateways (4) may be interposed with the advantage of providing information from multiple services while using standard logon/logoff and simplified interactive procedures, thus sparing the user of the imposition otherwise incurred in dealing with a variety of systems. Information frames are selected by answering questions in menus that successively appear on the screen to guide the user through hierarchical

60   THE ELECTRONIC ERA OF PUBLISHING

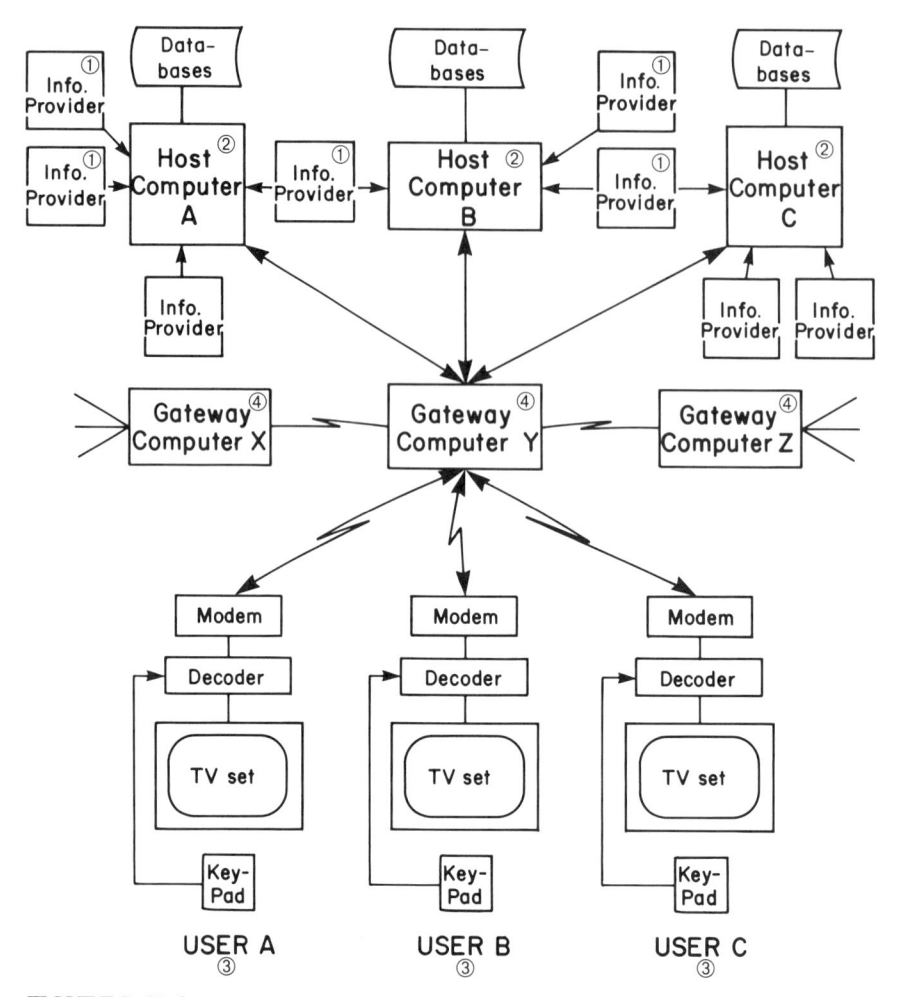

FIGURE 5 Videotex: Viewdata.

"tree-structures" although keywords also have been introduced in some systems to alleviate the retrieval problem.

Even though information pages are received on the TV screen, they are still frames; an important characteristic of viewdata, namely that textual information may be presented along with graphics and photographic pictures, has been successfully demonstrated as well despite the problems ensuing from the large amount of information bits transmitted, resulting in considerable time delays if full-page photographics are displayed. The online interactive character of viewdata enables users to originate transactions if need be in any particular application: in electronic publishing this would mean that subscribers could express their reaction to the material presented to them and even act as authors or publishers themselves. Another important asset of viewdata is its capability to display both monochromatic and color information: the number of colors varies from system to system and is anywhere between eight and several thousands. Nonstandard typefaces are accommodated as well.

The distinguishing feature of viewdata is that, unlike online bibiliographic services, it is not targeted to selected groups of experts but rather to the public. It must be stated, however, that despite all marketing efforts, the main thrust so far has been in business markets rather than in the home market. The reasons are that hardware cost makes the technology unaffordable to individual owners, and private usage during field trials is not followed up by private subscriptions when user charges are instituted. Viewdata provides information directed towards consumers of all kinds which makes it distinct from services catering to science- and technology-oriented markets.

The telephone is most widely used in existing viewdata undertakings but that does not preclude optical fiber, cable television, broadcast radio and satellite from being potential carrier candidates; wideband channels would make additional services on viewdata possible. Besides a telephone set and a modem to connect into the host computer, users need a TV set, decoder and a keypad or keyboard. Information frames have been created by a variety of information providers in special information-provider terminals and stored at service operators' host computers ready to be tapped.

At the present time this medium is established in 26 countries and over 500 systems are installed with over 5000 access ports worldwide; Great Britain alone accounts for over 400 systems (Yeates 1986).

Teletext. Teletext (distinguished from teletex which is something totally different—a combination of telex endowed with word-processing capability) is the other kind of videotex technology that enables television viewers to choose and have immediate access (typically in a few seconds, depending on the size of the database) to individual frames of information such as sports, news, weather, travel, directories, schedules, programs, etc. This kind of videotex has also been referred to as "broadcast," "one-way" or "noninteractive" videotex to differentiate it from viewdata, and to express the fact that the user has the capability to select but not to "talk" back. The database made up of screens (pages, frames) of data is transmitted in an endless loop and is continuously updated as it revolves in repeating cycles. A subscriber equipped with a remote keypad can select a page from a menu (index page), which circulates in shorter intervals; the keyed number designat-

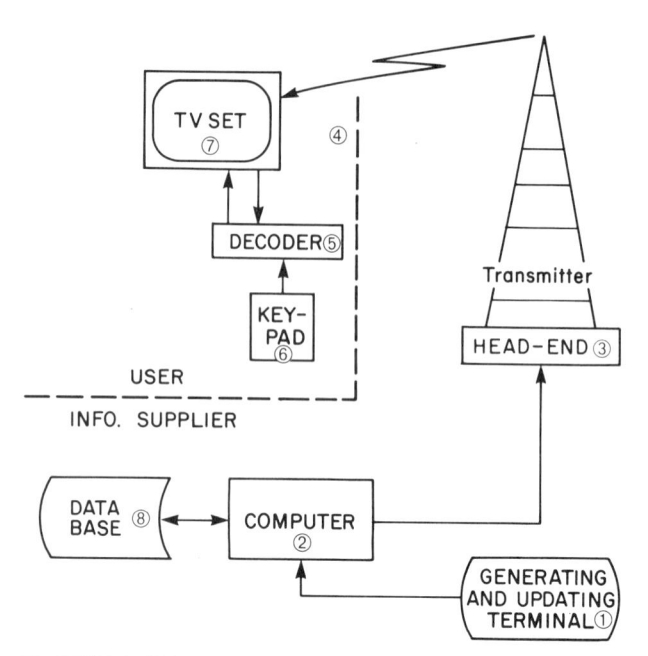

FIGURE 6 Videotex: Teletext.

ing the selected page will cause the page to be grabbed by the receiver's decoder and displayed (see Figure 6).

Figure 6 outlines the terminal (1) linked to a computer (2) where a database (8) is generated or updated, stored and presented to the headend (3) wherefrom it is broadcast to homes (4). The crucial role of the decoder (5) is shown wherein it receives commands from the user operating a keypad (6); this is instrumental in having the desired information displayed on a TV set (7).

Because the teletext technology is based on inserting digital pulses into the analog television signal, more specifically into its unused portion called the vertical blanking interval (VBI), this feature gives a television viewer the option of watching the television program proper telecast on a particular channel, or the channel's VBI carrying the teletext data, or the latter superimposed on the former, as e.g., captions. Alternatively, an entire full channel might be dedicated to teletext, which would dramatically increase the size of the database being retransmitted, i.e., a volume of pages on the order of tens of thousands rather than a few hundred on a VBI basis; such a teletext program could be received with no modification of an existing TV receiver but would preclude captioning on the same channel.

Teletext in the context of electronic publishing holds an appreciable promise. Besides the considerable rate of data transmission (around 7 Mbits per second) it has the unique advantage, namely, that the cost of broadcasting is fixed regardless of how many users (readers) receive the signal, which distinguishes it from viewdata. Veith (1982) suggests that teletext can be utilized as a vehicle for selective distribution of computerized information systems to special groups of customers or to individuals both in the broadcast and cablecast environment. One can easily imagine how conveniently databases and software could be downloaded for local display, processing and repackaging.

3.5.3 Impact of Videotex on Conventional Publishers

Videotex technology is still too young to assess its impact on conventional publishing with any degree of certainty and only some general statements may be made. Viewdata and teletext represent technologies which may be dubbed electronic publishing proper or "nonprint" in that the primary output medium is a display screen and hard copy, albeit possible, is not an important output form of any videotex-related publishing venture. Because current display screens are not suitable for reading any extensive amount of text, videotex is not likely to become a threat to conventional book and magazine publishers. Who then, if anybody is going to be affected by this technology?

In forecasting the speed, direction and force of the impact of Videotex on newspapers, Winsbury (1979) reminds us to consider seven main factors:

1. Legibility
2. Investment (the scale of investment by telecommunication carriers, TV manufactuers, information providers, software and system designers, etc.)
3. Price
4. Terminal
5. Screen display
6. Choice
7. Acceptability

After having considered these factors we may now speculate on whether newspapers might possibly get squeezed by this nonconventional technology. Winsbury (1979) offers the following answer which has been borne out by others:

1. Financial information is well suited for all computerized systems.
2. Classified advertising by its nature is a logical target.

3. Videotex has good chances in areas such as news, sports, weather forecasts, entertainment directories, etc.
4. Display advertisers are also potential patrons of videotex.

We may add that, in the meantime, travel agencies and real estate companies, among others, have availed themselves of videotex services in recent field trials.

How do publishers explain their motivation for going electronic? Zabel (1982) quotes four reasons:

1. To protect their existing revenues and influence
2. To expand their economic base
3. To alleviate the fear of missing out
4. Realization that the industry is facing something of a revolution

Obviously though, whatever the preoccupations of publishers with videotex, there must be some benefits for users to accept this new technology and change their habitual ways of acquiring information. In the area of news, Simeone (1983) summarizes the benefits of videotex as added value to the basic information, e.g., the selection, review and fast distribution; he also suggests that videotex may be a way to minimize the cost.

Reviewing the role viewdata (telephone videotex) might assume in publishing, Martin (1982) concludes that it will not become a substitute for newspapers or magazines but that it will complement the established ones; some old corporations will take on the challenge and exploit their existing information resources, whereas some newcomers will be given an opportunity to enter the arena of electronic publishing.

Viewdata technology, linking television set, telephone and computer, is seen as a suitable medium for ordering merchandise, making reservations and sending simple messages; besides it can be employed in systems displaying video films, teletext services, live TV, display of photographs from optical disks, as well as supplying interacte services such as telebanking, teleshopping and telesoftware (Yeates 1986).

3.5.4 The Present Outlook

On the basis of our experience and a survey of the literature, it would appear that viewdata (and teletex) terminals cannot be cost-justified for casual use of published materials only, especially if one wanted to penetrate the home market to a more appreciable degree than has been possible so far. Videotex services must provide more than that and offer not only entertainment and education but also transaction services, especially telebanking, teleshopping and electronic messaging if any degree of user acceptance is to be achieved. Before that happens, other changes must take place. If the contents are not improved, accessing the databases is not worth the cost. Learning how to access a service of limited scope and value is considered wasted time by most users: one access protocol to many useful services is needed, and this will be made possible by the gateways which are already being put into place in some countries.

Technology forecasts and market analysis conducted by different individuals and agencies differ diametrically, depending on which interests they are supposed to be serving. Their role is made no easier by the competition of personal computers, which are building their user base much faster. The distinction between these two products targeted at the same market will most likely attenuate when a videotex user terminal can perform some computing functions on the host computer or the information provider's terminal (which is microprocessor-based) can be used as a microcomputer as well. The designers of micros, in the meantime, have learned their lesson and are offering such videotex-like features as graphics and colors. Also, any future of videotex cannot be predicted without taking into account the vast capabilities of the videodisk which might make this medium much more attractive for mass distribution. Furthermore, videotex services encounter fierce competition of other TV-based services such as cable TV, pay TV, interactive TV, time-sharing information services (Source, Dow-Jones News Retrieval, Compuserve) and online retrieval services.

The above considerations that augur ill for videotex-type services have been corroborated by Raitt (1985), who concluded that the public is unlikely to consult videotex services for information that is widely available from other less expensive sources such as newspapers, radio or TV. There are now too many competing, well-entrenched sources to which potential users have been already exposed. The major U.S. videotex undertaking, Viewtron, launched in 1983 by Knight-Ridder Newspapers, Inc., has ceased operating after the service has been found unprofitable; in a similar vein the Los Angeles Times Mirror has closed down its Gateway videotex service started in 1984 (Online Newsletter 1986). From among corporate users Digital Equipment Corporation (DEC) has a videotex service based on VAX VTX videotex software for purposes of internal electronic publishing designed for DEC's employees; VAX VTX supports all of the major graphics standards (Carlisle 1986). In Canada, the Grassroots project provides a farm-oriented electronic information service for western Canada; four Winnipeg firms got the Manitoba Telidon Project underway offering information on tourism and highways (Holman 1985). There are other applications but none of them represents a major advance into the forefront of the evolving electronic publishing market.

3.5.5 National Systems

Unlike other developments in electronic publishing that evolved at a corporate level, videotex has emerged as a result of national efforts mainly because of a direct or indirect government support of what was regarded as a major advance into the hi-tech field. The pioneering work has been done in the United Kingdom; their teletext services (Oracle and Ceefax) can be currently viewed on some 800,000 TV sets enhanced with proper decoders. The British viewdata system Prestel with 24,000 subscribers has its clientele mostly in business; it is characterized by building its pictures from small blocks, which give it a "saw-toothed" appearance and hence the designation "alphamosaic." The French system Antiope is also alphamosaic by its nature but it employs parallel coding of attributes (e.g., single or double height, color, flashing or steady) whereas Prestel uses serial coding. What this means is that Antiope is able to store most of the attributes within each character because it typically uses 16 bits for each particular character while only 7 bits are used up to represent the character proper. The Prestel's serial coding implies that character attributes have to be stored as one or more special characters, which appear on the display as blank spaces, because Prestel uses 8 bits per character and that leaves only 1 bit unused. In 1978 Canada unveiled the alphageometric system officially known as Telidon. In this system drawing commands are transmitted as so-called picture description instructions (PDIs) defining basic geometric shapes as line, rectangle, arc and polygon, in addition to a dot, and are interpreted in the decoder as such. The advantage of this approach is that it is independent of terminal hardware implementation and the picture resolution is limited only by the terminal's capabilities. An existing database is unaffected by later changes in hardware. Alphageometric pictures are devoid of the mosaiclike rough outlines of the alphamosaic design. All three systems, named alphamosaic serial, alphamosaic parallel and alphageometric, are capable of applying the alphaphotographic technique in which every dot is stored and transmitted separately to represent any shape in a manner familiar from slow-scan TV and telefacsimile. This method provides continuous tone quality but is demanding in regard to storage and transmission. Another expedient applicable to the above described systems is called dynamically redefinable character set (DRCS) designed to improve the quality of coarse graphics and extend the character set: the shapes of characters (letters and graphics) are not predefined but they are downloaded from the database and subsequently used by the terminal.

3.5.6 Standards

Presently there are three major videotex coding standards:

1. North American Videotex/Teletext Presentation Level Protocol Syntax (NAPLPS). This is a joint ANSI/CSA standard based on the Telidon alphageometric philosophy but enhanced by some additional features. It also accommodates the French and British mosaic code table.
2. The Conference of European Post and Telecommunications Administration (CEPT) Videotex Presentation Layer Data Syntax, is composed of British Prestel, French Antiope, West German Bildschirmtext and Dutch Viditel, and includes alphanumeric text, geometric shapes, DRCS and photographic coding.
3. CAPTAIN is a Japanese standard (Character and Pattern Telephone Access Information Network) easily convertible to the NAPLPS standard. It encompasses the Kanji, Katakana and latin character sets along with geometric and mosaic tables, DRCS, photographic coding and music/sound.

3.6 Cable TV

3.6.1 One-way, Two-way (Interactive)

Cable TV (or CATV for Community Antenna Television) is relevant to electronic publishing in two ways: first it is a communications channel of some awesome capacity and secondly, it is an information content carrier of a great potential. The capacity of a single broadband cable represents up to 300-450 MHz with 34-54 (with dual cables 108) television channels, which may be capable of transmitting signals not only down but also upstream; however, this capability has not been widely exploited and at present only a few cable companies are equipped with this feature. It is not likely that cable TV will develop into a serious competition to telephone companies mainly because it does not have switching capabilities. It does have the potential to play an eminent role in applications such as downloading massive files, in the framework of electronic publishing, to subscribing users such as microcomputer owners, as part of software or database distribution schemes.

The utility of cable television for information services is apparent when one considers its capacity for digital data transmission. Given the bandwidth of one video channel equal to 6 MHz and the bandwidth of 30 kHz required for simultaneous two-way data transmission, it follows that one video channel can provide enough bandwidth for 200 such digital channels.

Two concepts pertaining to cable TV, in general, and to its electronic publishing aspects, in particular, are the notions of interactivity and addressability. Interactivity is a relative term; in a way, a remote channel selector may be viewed as a tool for achieving a certain level of interaction. In contrast, the better selectivity present in teletext systems appears to the user as a higher degree of interaction on a one-way cable system whereby a desired page may be captured from the database and viewed at leisure. This apparent interaction is more limited in comparison with that of the videotext user, who browses through various levels of tree-structures, and even more limited than that of modern retrieval systems with all their bells and whistles. But, for a cable TV service, at least a minimal degree of interaction is essential in order to qualify as a member of the electronic publishing family.

Addressability on cable TV refers to the vital feature of the cable system's computer to communicate effectively with the individual TV sets it serves. In electronic publishing and document delivery, this translates into being able to deliver selected text and graphics to subscribers based on their specific (documents) or standing order (magazines and journals). Addressability can be achieved with addressable converters employing various techniques and their large-scale adoption by cable TV users is likely to precede any extensive use of cable television systems for data communications (Veith 1983a).

Whereas cable TV had originally evolved with the purpose of broadcasting to areas with bad reception, cable TV received an impetus from the satellite communications technology whereby cable TV operators could enrich their programming by carrying quality program from remote sites in addition to local TV stations and local programming.

But the one-way entertainment medium is now slowly changing its image. Rogers Cablesystems, Inc., in their search for useful services, is working in conjunction with C-Cor Electronics, Inc., with an addressable packet-switched modem which will enable various services to professionals to be offered as part of the Cablepac services (Rivenburgh 1984); an agreement with Tymnet, Inc. secured access through a gateway into the Tymnet value-added network and will provide database services and records transfer among other things. This approach opens up a new highway to a variety of services for microcomputer owners as an alternative to using voice-grade networks.

Two-way cable television with a degree of interactivity was introduced under the name QUBE by Warner Amex (Warner Cable Communications, Inc. and the American Express Company) in which users can press buttons on a small keyboard in response to multiple-choice questions appearing on the screen; the answers are processed at the central site and results of the polling are displayed. In 1980 QUBE III with 110 program channels was ushered into service capable of delivering data retrieval in addition to the existing pay-per-view, polling and other services. QUBE has recently been canceled in franchised cities (Rivenburgh 1984). The general principle of polling would appear to be relevant to electronic publishing as one of its added benefits as opposed to conventional publishing which is deprived of an immediate feedback. Information thus garnered could be used for planning and marketing information packages such as an electronic journal, in determining the popularity of authors, systems and topics and in ascertaining when materials are no longer current and are more appropriate for archival storage, to name a few of many possible applications.

A news service on cable has emerged recently (Di Sante 1986) called X*PRESS (by X* Press Information Services, Golden, CO.). News are brought to customers 24 hours a day and 7 days a week as selected from menus listing keywords and phrases. Current reports are from information providers—established news services worldwide—who transmit their reports via satellite and telephone lines to the X*PRESS office; the organized stream is sent back to satellite for distribution to cable companies who deliver it to subscribers equipped with microcomputers. A color or monochrome display adapter, RS 232 communications port and the X*PRESS software are also required.

Another system featuring interactive communication over the cable TV is Index (interactive data exchange) developed by Cox Cable Communications. One part of Index provides for interactive communication at 28 Kbits per second while another part transmits pages in cycles in a manner similar to teletext; among the services available are home shopping and banking, educational programs and access to the Source.

These are only a few concrete examples of data services offered on cable and there are many more being designed, tested, implemented and either operated or abandoned.

3.6.2 Teletext on Cable

Cable TV can deliver teletext services equally well as broadcast TV; cable TV can either rebroadcast the teletext signal received off-the-air or generate its own teletext as a variety of text service. To complicate the matter even more, satellites can also deliver text and graphics in teletext format to the cable TV head ends, which can either pass the teletext information to users equipped with compatible decoders or turn the teletext signal into a billboard channel (see below); besides, cable operators can insert teletext information into any of the television signals received via satellite. This illustrates the difficulty of determining who actually owns the portion of the signal designated as the vertical blanket interval (VBI).

Although teletext is commonly understood to be a computerized information system delivering digital data along with analog signal to

TV sets and monitors capable of receiving them through compatible decoders, the term is sometimes incorrectly used to denote other related services with somewhat similar attributes.

We have dealt with teletext in conjunction with videotext in a separate section and here we only want to elaborate on a few aspects of the cable TV/teletext combination. Although cable TV presently considers its main mission to be the delivery of broadcast signals along with some subscription TV (pay-TV) to our homes, there are other modes of service either being contemplated, researched, tested or offered. Teletext is one of them; it may be supplied either in unused lines of the VBI part of a channel, or a channel may be dedicated to teletext exclusively. Teletext is thus the only visible information on the screen as selected from a keypad, or it appears in a reserved window in parallel to other programming, or it may intermittently fill a certain reserved area or overlay the entire screen. Not all text appearing on the TV screen is teletext. So-called billboard channels are part of many cable TV systems and bring news, sports and weather on a multicolored background with text scrolling or crawling from left to right. Billboard channels are delivered to TV sets as regular television signal although it is originally produced in digital form. The advantage of teletext over billboards is that, by wielding their keypad and knowing a given page number of interest, users can order the page and view it at leisure; in contrast to online retrieval systems, the access time on teletext is not affected by the number of users connected into the service at any particular time. The contents of the database on teletext at any given time can only be limited (unless a full channel is dedicated to it) lest the waiting time for the desired frame to arrive at the decoder might be intolerably long. This determines the nature of the information circulated repeatedly in loops until it is updated by new information: brief items with topical content of general interest as found in newspapers and magazines but much more up-to-date. Many field trials have been conducted proving feasibility of the service and garnering some market research results but the requisite momentum has not yet been reached to make teletext a large-scale service.

3.6.3 Library/Information Center-related Services

While text and graphics-based services of various kinds have been used on cable TV and numerous tests have been conducted and commercial services established, other applications in the context of electronic publishing and document delivery are in the stage of planning, development, implementation or still in the realm of speculation. Bivins Noerr (1983b) foresees a chance for cable TV in libraries and information services in several areas: (1) document transmission in point-to-point or point-to-multipoint dissemination; (2) video loans in which a tape can be ordered to be played to clients; (3) conferencing of users on a cable channel belonging to a library; (4) renting a library's local channel; (5) a local database containing local information; (6) full-text searching with electronic preview of some part of documents including graphics to enable relevant ordering. Concrete examples of cable TV applications in libraries have also been reviewed (Bivins Noerr 1983a) and although limited in size, they demonstrate lucidly the wide gamut of services open to cable TV in the subject area under scrutiny: remote browsing utilizing slow-scan TV, database searching, selective dissemination of information, document delivery, teleconferencing, video encyclopedia, video catalog, automatic circulation control using a remote mainframe, catalog information retrieval possibly with reservations and information sharing over distance, by a library consortium, of data, facsimile, visual and printed information.

The bandwidth below 50 MHz is not used for video and part of it can be utilized for upstream communication. On this fact is based an interesting experience of the Wayne Oakland Library Federation (WOLF): they use four Zeta Z-19RF modems to interface their data terminals and transmit data upstream to the cable company's head end at 29.63 MHz whereupon data transmission is switched to 109.28 MHz in the direction toward the computer center, and vice versa (Whitaker 1985). WOLF's conclusions indicate that digital transmission over cable should be less expensive; what remains to be done is to develop cable/telephone interfaces, to solve problems related to reliability and to investigate the effects of amplifiers on data integrity.

These endeavors will prove that cable TV can mean more to the information industry than merely teletext, and that a valuable contribution of cable will be possible if there is understanding of the problem and willingness to accept the risk associated with an innovation.

3.6.4 From the Present into the Future

Cable TV has a big potential for electronic publishing which has been so far realized only to a small extent (this is relevant to broadcast TV as well). This potential will increase in the future spurred by satellite technology and optical fibers. The success of cable TV in this field (especially in regard to conventional data carriers) will depend on (1) pressure from users and user groups for new services, (2) shifting the focus of cable TV companies in combining other services such as digital with existing ones, (3) widening the field of expertise held by cable TV companies, (4) continuing education of users and (5) a favorable economic climate. Cable TV can prove to be a valuable catalyst in the electronic document delivery systems of the future. User acceptance of information services delivered via TV screen certainly cannot be described as overwhelming but it may change when the TV picture itself, as a frontend facing the user, improves with the advent of high-definition television, (HDT), increasing resolution to 1100 lines from the 525 currently used in North America, which will improve not only the image information but will assist in text acceptance by users. Flat picture tubes should reduce objections as to the lack of portability much the same as has been happening with flat-panel CRTs. This development is paring down the size of the output device, whether it be the TV set or CRT, to look more like the familiar newspaper or a book and is bound to be favorably received by the end user, especially if optionally equipped with a printing (or copying) facility. As so often transpires, this tendency toward compactness is paralleled by an opposite one, namely toward larger screens.

In summary, television, whether cable or broadcast, has been able thus far to enter the domain of electronic publishing mainly as a supplier of news—worldwide, national and local—something akin to an electronic newspaper. A promising direction is access to large databases where cable has the capacity to carry not only video information but also text and sound (even stereo). The spectrum of services that TV is able to offer is necessarily restricted by the low resolution inherent to contemporary TV sets and the limited amount of text that can be accommodated on each page (screenful) of information; this makes today's TV suitable as a medium for short-lived topical information or abstracts rather than a medium for reading the full text of extensive documents. But TV is a powerful means of communications into corporations, institutions and homes, and electronic publishing takes advantage of TV's omnipresence. Electronic publishing alone could not sustain cable TV and cable TV is not able to meet all electronic publishing's aspirations: electronic publishing via the TV screen can conquer user acceptance only in association with entertainment, video conferencing, educational programming, games and transactional services (home shopping, home banking). The point of contention has been only how much of the market will be gained and, consequently, how much of the total bandwidth will be occupied by each of these contenders and this relation will be subject to dynamic change. The cause of electronic publishing will be well served by recent developments in which cable TV channels are exploited as efficient communications means in local area networks; broadband transmission of voice, data, video and facsimile is possible and clusters of up to 32 devices may tap the network resources in the terminal-to-terminal and terminal-to-computer communications modes (Wallace 1984). A significant indirect benefit to electronic publishing will accrue from microcomputers able to share in the cable systems capabilities and to communicate among themselves and with remote computers. The availability of special databases and services will lead to service offerings aimed at select groups of users instead of the general public, thus changing broadcasting into "narrowcasting."

Attempting to make a more accurate assessment of the role cable TV may assume in electronic publishing is not possible in view of such variables as advancing technology, changing attitudes both of producers and users, the economic climate and legal implications. Cable TV may well take on functions traditionally provided by other media such as communications carriers and document delivery, and vie for the aggregate time and money that consumers spend in acquiring information.

3.7 Optical Memory Media

3.7.1 Introduction

In this section we will outline the general aspects of a category of media designated the optical memory media and their implications for publishing. Terminology, working principles and the representation of information will be discussed, and new developments will be broached as relevant to the broad concept of electronic publishing. After that, trends in the evolution of optical media will be traced in examples illustrating some recent applications of 12-inch laser disks, the compact disk read-only memory (CD-ROM), the hybrid "online plus videodisk" system and the optical digital disk (ODD).

Needless to say, the examples introduced here are not claimed to be exhaustive (with new ones being now announced every day) but rather a sample of activities on the background of which the profuse number of new service and product modes and patterns may be better understood.

"Optical" in the sense here means that optical principles rather than magnetic ones (or others for that matter) are employed in recording and reading or replaying of information, the optical agent in our context being the laser.

In treating this subject, we encounter a problem right at the outset: the problem of terminology. There has been some vagueness in reporting on topics such as laser disks, optical disks, videodisks and digital disks. Let us attempt to put the terminology into some degree of perspective before we examine the present and future impact of this relatively recent (some of it very recent) media on electronic publishing. To further simplify matters, let us use consistently the spelling "disk" (with "k" rather than "c") unless otherwise dictated by trade name usage.

Videodisk is a broader term and includes both nonoptical and optical (laser) technology. Videodisks may be theoretically based on a number of recording techniques (e.g., mechanical with a continuous modulated groove, or electromagnetic as has been common in videotapes) but practically, only capacitance and optical laser recording deserve our attention in the context of electronic publishing. The former, the capacitance principle, may be subdivided into grooved and grooveless varieties.

An example of the grooved disk is RCA's capacitance electronic disk (CED) in which a diamond stylus travels in a groove and senses changes in the electrical properties thereof; this disk has found a relatively broad customer acceptance in the home entertainment sector (movies). Disk wear, easy contamination and lack of interactivity put brakes on its application in electronic publishing.

The high video density (HVD) by JVC is a representative of grooveless technology: capacitance variations are detected by a stylus which moves on the surface of the disk and "reads" variable-length depressions on the surface (hereafter called "pits" with "lands" in between); the disk and stylus function as two plates of the capacitor.

Even though "pits" and "lands" are used in videodisks their interpretation is analog (see Section 3.7.3).

3.7.2 Optical Memory Systems

Optical disks, also called laser disks (laser being by far the most widely used light source), deserve more attention from the point of view of publishing (unless we broaden the concept of publishing to encompass home entertainment audio and video). In optical recording and replay, we are dealing with nonmagnetic storage media which have been lately designated as optical memory systems, a buzzword that is here to stay subject to modifications, both in details and in some far-reaching aspects such as, for instance, the emerging disk changer or autochanger (known in popular jargon as jukebox) or the issue of erasability (writable, alterable or erasable disk), etc. Data is both optically recorded in a continuous spiral and scanned as pits and no-pits (lands) by laser. An aluminum shiny layer is provided to increase signal reflection; recording is covered by a protective polyvinyl chloride (PVC) coat which makes the disk very resistant to wear. Information is scanned, as mentioned above, by a low-power laser which follows recorded data along the spiral and sensors—photoelectric cells—detect pits or lands either as changes in the amount of reflected (reflective disk) or transmitted light (transmissive disk). Laservision (by Phillips and Pioneer) is a representative standard and system in the reflective group.

A meaningful criterion along which to subdivide optical reflective disks is as to whether they are constant angular velocity (CAV) or constant linear velocity (CLV) disks.

CLV implies that, because there are more records near the outer edge than near the center, the velocity of rotation diminishes as the head moves toward the rim. The CLV disk has higher video storage capacity (108,000 frames) and is predestined for home entertainment: up to an hour of a movie can fit on one side.

The CAV disk stores one frame (one TV frame consists of two fields with two vertical blanking intervals) per track which produces one video image per revolution. Since there are 54,000 tracks (i.e., 54,000 frames) and 1800 revolutions per minute, the CAV disk contains up to 30 minutes of straight play. The advantage of the CAV disk is that it offers features such as freeze-frame, slow motion, random access to any frame, reverse motion, fast forward. This type of optical disk is of primary interest to the information manager and to electronic publishing: it may figure as a publishing commodity designed for the education/instruction/promotion market, or it may find application anywhere in the communication cycle beginning with the author and ending with the document delivery to the ultimate user.

Although the most common disk diameters are 12 cm and 12 inches, the 14-, 8- and 5 1/4-inch disks are also in use.

Contemporary optical disk systems cooperate with computers in what may be called a synergistic rather than symbiotic manner. Microprocessors are either built into the player or may be attached to it. A video database may be combined with a textual database residing on the optical disk itself or in microcomputer storage. Instructions for the microcomputer may be digitally encoded on a part of the disk. In this manner, text, sound and video (graphics and photographic pictures) may be combined interactively. Expert systems will add yet another dimension (or vice versa) to this multimedia world: the expert answer will be able to be expressed not only by a single piece of data, a sentence, a report (verbal or printed), but also by a whole multimedia presentation which will help in understanding and retention of the expert answer.

3.7.3 Representation of Information

In that audio, video, text and data can all be stored on optical memory media, the question arises as to how the information is encoded on it. In Section 2.2 we explained the analog and digital methods of encoding information. The general answer to the above question is that the medium itself is neither exclusively digital nor analog. Optical disks of any kind contain information encoded in pits; thus the superficial appearance would indicate that optical disks are all digital because the disk player only reads "pit" or "land," or in other words, it has to recognize two discrete states. But in reality the interpretation of the encoded information on output may be either analog, as is common in movies, or digital as is the case with the optical digital disk. Moreover, digital encoding may be embodied either in the raster (facsimile) or character form.

Analog Form of Encoding. This form is suitable for recording and replay of movies and pictures. It is based on the National Television Standard Committee (NTSC) standard which specifies 525-line image consisting of two interlaced fields; 30 frames are read per second (hence 1800 revolutions per minute) to achieve continuous motion or the same frame is read 30 times a second in the freeze-frame mode. In mastering an optical disk the amplitude-modulated (AM) video signal is converted into a frequency-modulated (FM) signal of constant amplitude. Drawing a line through the middle of this wave and clipping off the top and bottom parts of the signal produces a pulse-code modulated (PCM) signal which denotes the area of a pit whenever the wave is above the central line. This signal modulates a laser which writes the pits on the surface of a disk; pits of varying length are detected when the disk is read. The original video signal is reconstructed and displayed on a TV tube or on a monitor. One track on the reflective CAV optical disk contains all picture data to display the 525 lines required to generate one frame on the TV tube.

The analog interpretation of the signal has a serious liability in the TV tube's not being able to reproduce a 8 1/2 × 11-inch page; in fact between 5 and 10 frames are needed. Therefore, whereas a laser disk can store 54,000 frames of video information, it can store only somewhere between 5400 and 10,800 pages of textual information to adequately reproduce fine figures of text. An adequate resolution of the display device is another must.

Digital Form of Encoding. Because of the above storage limitations of the optical disk with regard to textual data and full-page images, digital modes were developed. Digital data can be displayed on high-resolution CRT screens as full pages.

There are two modes of digital recording (and replay). One is the raster (also facsimile or image) digital mode, which is well suited for document processing. Binary bits are represented by pits and lands. Typically a document might be scanned by a CCD scanner and its digital representation transferred to a disk serving as a buffer for data verification and compression. Then the data would modulate a laser burning singular pits onto the disk. The storage capacity of optical disks is around 2×10^{10} bits or 20 Gbits or 20,000 Mbits on both sides. With 300 dots per inch and 1:10 compression, the disk should be able to hold around 22,000 8 1/2 × 11-inch pages; but disks able to store multiples of this amount have been reported depending on the resolution and the compression respective.

Another method of digital encoding is the character digital mode. Sets of individual bits are interpreted as bytes which is the language of computers. This compact method of coding may be illustrated by an example. If a page generated on a microcomputer holds over 2000 characters or approximately 20,000 bits, then the disk with 10^{10} bits capacity can store some 500,000 such pages on one side. Pits may be read not only as singular bits, but also in such a manner that, e.g., a pit of varying size may represent up to four bits so that two pits form a byte. Whereas today one mark represents one bit in most cases, systems are feasible which will have marks storing up to 8-10 bits (Laub 1986).

If digital data are recorded on the disk directly as characters (such as ASCII characters), then we call the disk an optical digital disk.

3.7.4 New Developments in Optical Memory Systems

We have outlined above the concepts of videodisks, optical or laser disks and optical digital disks. All these disks presume data (information) prerecorded on the medium; this is not any handicap in situations where the user only wants to access prerecorded information, such as in information retrieval, and depends on regular updates from the publisher; another such instance is archival information which is not expected to require amendments. Other applications include users who want to be able to "write" their own information either once (write-once optical disks), or who need to be able to alter the information at will just as is the case with magnetic disks; such disks are called erasable (also alterable, writable).

Write-once optical disks are those which are purchased in a condition ready for one-time recording, but once recorded the information cannot be erased. The disks are marketed in the compact size of 5 1/4-inch or 12-inch diameter. Recording is typically digital as is required in large databases for bibliographic and archival purposes. This technology presently allows

for storage exceeding 1 Gbyte per side, permanence of at least 10 years, random access, data transfer rate of 2 Mbits per second. Another term associated with the write-once disk is DRAW—direct read after write; one of the advantages of this recording mode is that errors can be discovered right after they have been made so that data can be reentered at a different disk location while the data in error has the address erased from the index and cannot be accessed.

Write-once disks are a step in the right direction, but eventually merging of magnetic and optical technologies will culminate in the development of magneto-optic (erasable, writable, alterable, erasable DRAW) disks. These disks are being demonstrated as prototypes in the 5 1/4-inch format. When successful, erasable optical disks will position themselves ahead of magnetic media owing to higher storage capacity, lower storage cost per bit. Erasable optical disk is much different from its ROM and write-once relatives because of its potential capability to act in direct competition with magnetic media. They must be seen in the dual role both as replacements for fixed magnetic disks in large mainframes and personal computers alike and as mass storage devices threatening the future of microforms.

The coexistence of the described read-only, write-once and alterable disks stresses the need for multifunctional (read, erase, write), multimedia (read-only, write-once and alterable) or multiformat (5 1/4-inch, 12-inch and possibly others) drives; this awesome task must be addressed lest users be faced with the necessity of acquiring multiple disk drives which would negatively affect the acceptance of the new optical memory systems.

Large databases, as has been shown in this chapter, fit onto one optical disk. If, however, more than one disk is needed, then a device called a disk autochanger (jukebox) may be called for whose primary task is to provide rapid access to any record on any of the stored disks. Jukeboxes housing from 20 to 128 disks have been reported. Each system consists of a high number of stored disks accessible via a much smaller number of disk drives providing access points to the hundreds of megabytes of stored text. Jukeboxes for both write-once and erasable disks have been described.

3.7.5 Hybrid Applications

The term hybrid systems in the optical memory context implies optical disk drives in cooperation with other information technology components in the provision of information/publication services; the number of instances will keep growing as new optical memory systems advance from laboratories and beta test sites into the mainstream of our information society following the already widespread use of consumer disk varieties.

One hybrid system entails searches in a textual database residing on a remote host, and retrieved results supplemented by pictorial information from a local database housed on an optical disk; pictures are displayed on an additional console. Another hybrid system may be cited as an arrangement whereby a search is conducted for more recent data in a local database stored on optical disk(s) using a microcomputer followed by an automatic dial-up into a remote host in order to continue the search for earlier years. The list of hybrid applications will burgeon and will include cooperation (and strong competition) with telecommunications among other things; shipping data recorded on CD-ROMs costs less than two cents per megabyte and compares favorably with telecommunications: cost is one or two orders of magnitude below that of microwave or satellite communication; it is 10,000 times less than connecting into direct dial lines via a modem (Laub 1986).

3.7.6 12-inch Laser Disks

Info Trac has been introduced by Information Access Company as an in-house laser disk system to access IAC's periodical databases. The hardware configuration encompasses an IBM PC microcomputer, a Laser Data controller to look after communications between the computer(s) and disk player(s), a Hewlett-Packard Thinkjet printer and a Pioneer videodisk player. Up to four microcomputers and printers can be connected to a database consisting of one or more laser disks which are supplied to subscribing libraries as monthly cumulated databases. The capacity of the disk may be best imagined as including 2.5 million references which represents 5 years of citations to 1000 publications. The Info Trac disk with its 800 Mbytes of storage has a memory equal to 2000 floppy disks or 80 hard disks at 10 Mbytes each (Carney 1985); up to four laser disk players can team up to an awesome storage of 3.2 Gbytes. For laser disks the maximum data transfer rate of 400 Kbytes per second, corrected error rate of 10^{-12} and typical access time of around 1 second may be expected at this stage of development.

The first systems contain indexes to over 1000 publications as far back as 1982; although the initial selection of periodicals was to reflect collections of major public and academic libraries, it is feasible to custom-tailor databases on disks to suit specific audiences served by specific collections.

Library Systems and Services, Inc. (LSSI, Rockville, MD) is marketing the MINI MARC Laserdisc System which replaces a microfilm reader and 2800 floppy diskettes (8 1/2 inch), thus making it possible for clients in 2700 libraries to access any record randomly (instead of sequentially) (Pezzanite 1985). MINI MARC includes the Library of Congress's LC MARC database containing catalog records of all monographs (both English and foreign) and serials. Customers who need this data for their own cataloguing can now access any record in less than 2 seconds. This large database resides on two laser disks: the first disk holds some 1.5 million records on 52,900 video frames, the other disk 600,000 records as well as indexes on 17,000 frames. Each videodisk frame carries analog video information which has to be converted into digital information in the Laser Data LD110 controller (Laser Data, Cambridge, MA); each frame comprises 15,224 bytes. These type of disks are referred to also as "digital videodisks" or "analog optical data disks" because of the analog/digital conversion and to distinguish them from purely digital and analog disks.

The laser disk can be employed not only for distribution of centrally created databases, but also for databases which are generated as a result of distributed cooperation; a union catalog (a catalog containing records of holdings of multiple cooperating libraries) has been put on laser disk and installed at the headquarters of the Ramapo Catskill Library System (Middletown, NY); any of the 600,000 records can be directly accessed, and as a result the processing of materials has been expedited which will be reflected in cost savings (Freund 1985).

The National Gallery of Art has produced a catalog of 1000 oil paintings from their collection with accompanying information. The other side of the double-sided laser disk 12 inches in diameter houses a complete tour of the museum. This is an example of integrated text and pictorial information brought together in a new product which is highly competitive with the conventional product and is a substitute for really being there.

3.7.7 Compact Disk–Read-only Memory

The Compact disk–read-only memory (see also the more general note in Chapter 2) has grown from a buzzword into one of the most talked-about issues in the publishing and information industries. The number of committed players in the industry assures that we are not witnessing a temporary fad. The CD-ROM is an example of a technology that has found a fitting field of application (there will be a number of areas in that field of publishing) dovetailed to its characteristics.

Data is recorded on the 12-cm diameter disk as "pits and lands" which are interpreted by the reading laser as digital binary codes. Reading is nondestructive because the recording is under a protective layer of transparent plastic. Library Corporation packs over a billion characters of MARC data and indexes into 600 Mbytes (Murphy 1985).

The disk is 1.2 mm thick, the pits are 0.6 µm wide and 0.12 mm deep; with 1.6-µm distance between adjacent turns of the spiral, the track density amounts to 16,000 tracks per inch (floppy disk up to 96 and Winchester disk accommodates on the order of several hundred tracks per inch) which enables nearly 2 billion pits to be recorded on a single CD ROM disk (Laub 1986a).

While CD ROM is an efficient storage medium of respectable capacity (anywhere between 500 and 700 Mbytes depending on how far toward the disk edge the data recording stretches), CD ROM has also some characteristics which may cause some concern in certain applications: the radial access time (the time to complete the radial move of the read head over the specified track) is typically 500 milliseconds (ms) compared with approximately 40 ms for a fixed magnetic disk. The time required for the desired data sector to appear under the read head (the rotational delay or latency) may be up to 150 ms whereas a fixed magnetic disk can accomplish the same in about 8 ms. CD ROM with its 1.23Mbits per second does not measure up to the fixed magnetic disk (5Mbits per second) when it comes to data transfer capability.

The notion of "pits" and "lands" representing bits (ones and zeroes) needs some explanation. User data on magnetic computer tapes, as a result of premastering, are subject to mastering. First, user data undergo error correction encoding to enable data to be recovered in case of defects for whatever reason. Then user data are converted from their 8-bit format into so-called channel code consisting of 14 bits in the process called "8-to-14 modulation." The mystery of CD ROM data coding lies right here in the relationship between the ones and zeroes of the channel code on the one hand and the pits and lands on the other hand: laser in the mastering device is instructed to start burning a pit upon receiving a channel "one" bit and stop burning the pit on reception of another "one" bit. The length of the pits and lands is determined by the number of intervening zero bits of the channel code. Three more bits must be added for technical reasons to the 14 channel bits so that a total of 17 channel bits are needed to represent 8 user bits (1 byte); this indicates the ratio between "productive" and "nonproductive" bits to which we still have to add bits needed for error correction, synchronization and control purposes.

Pits are recorded by laser into the coating of the glass master disk from which negatives are prepared, serving to mold the actual CD ROM disks as we know them, made from transparent plastic and provided with a reflective metal layer as well as with a protective coat. Laser beam is also used to read data from the disk. Photoreceptor receives the reflected light from the disk surface, less from the pits where light is scattered and more from the lands, and transforms the fluctuating light (optical) signal into a corresponding electric signal. From this signal the digital signal, as submitted on the premastered magnetic tape, is recovered by decoding which involves procedures encountered in encoding except in reverse order. The error rate of less than 10^{-16} means that error correction codes built into CD ROMs correct all bits in error except one in ten quadrillion.

Although CD-ROM has a huge potential as a publishing medium a major breakthrough in the number of products and their acceptance by libraries and end users has been so far hindered by the lack of standards; prospective publishers of CD-ROM-based products, vendors of

CD-ROM hardware and media as well as networks, libraries and other users are holding off until such time as when compatibility will remove their respective apprehensions. Before that happens, undoubtedly de facto industry standards will be implemented.

Applications are expected to be in the area of database publications and only later, in corporate management information systems (MIS). Through elimination of online communication charges CD-ROM promises economy achieved by local search on a CD-ROM workstation; once the information is found on the disk, its transfer takes place at the speed of laser disk technology, which will ensure faster display, printing and browsing. Once the database has been acquired, the CD-ROM may be used any number of times; disks carry not only the database but the required software as well. Database producers and online services must consider not only the nature of optical media, but the complex marketing and business issues too; it is unclear whether CD-ROM will attract new customers or whether existing customers will switch over (Summit 1986).

The following examples indicate the expanding role of CD-ROM in publishing.

Disclosure (Disclosure, Bethesda, MD) introduces COMPACT DISCLOSURE on a subscription basis which includes the Disclosure database and the software required to search, display and print the information retrieved from the database; the two-level software allows searching by leading the novice user through menus, yet it offers a command language system for the more advanced user as well.

Psyc INFO (producer of the Psyc INFO and Psyc ALERT Databases, American Psychological Association) is developing Psyc LIT on compact digital disk as a joint venture with Silver Platter Information Inc; Psych LIT provides users with material from Psychological Abstracts published since 1974 to include quarterly updates and the requisite retrieval software at total cost to the user of $5000. The system has been put to test in two libraries to determine user acceptance and the impact on the libraries' operations and staff. End-user searching is supported by tutorials, help screens and the guidance of librarians (Psych INFO News 1986).

The British Library initiated development of the first U.K. compact disk which was mastered in Philips production facilities. The disk holds nearly 600,000 bibliographic records available for search on the British Library's online service BLAISE-LINE. BRS-SEARCH software with Boolean logic and positional searching is installed on an IBM-compatible microcomputer supplemented by the Philips CDR-X1000 disk drive.

A combination of CD-ROM and electronic encyclopedia was reported by Bender (1986). Grolier Electronic Publishing is yet another entrant into the world of CD-ROM publishing with their Academic American Encyclopedia in 20 volumes. The encyclopedia exists both on a laser disk and on CD-ROM with the latter offering enhanced searching capabilities supported by an electronic index of a size nearly equaling that of the encyclopedia proper. The next version is intended to include audio, video, text and software.

Also in the area of full-text publishing, University Microfilms International (UMI) has launched a major prototype system for electronic information delivery which integrates information retrieval, ordering and delivery using a microcomputer. Called IDM (Information Delivery Module) it contains the OCLC M300 workstation or an IBM-compatible PC, a disk player (12 inch and compact disk), a desktop electronic printer, a facsimile interface and database retrieval software for the optical disk. One optical disk holds UMI's Dissertation Abstracts and Comprehensive Dissertation Index.

The wide gamut of contents stored on CD-ROM is further demonstrated by Datatek Corporation which will publish the full text of 10 newspapers, newswire services and databases known online as Data Times; Reference Technology Inc. is engaged in publishing software for the IBM PC on CD-ROM in addition to their main activity geared to producing optical products for clients (Desmarais 1986).

Library Corporation (Washington, DC) is marketing the Library of Congress MARC database on CD-ROM (Murphy 1986): two disks store over 1,400,000 MARC records representing all English language cataloging efforts of the Library of Congress since 1964 plus popular titles dating from 1900. Another Library Corporation product is the ANYBOOK database carrying data on more than one million English language books including also prices and ordering addresses.

Finally, we have to note the dual role to be assumed by Digital Equipment Corporation (DEC) in this new publishing business. DEC will act not only as a service bureau in support of database producers by mastering and replicating disks including also database adaption, consulting, training, etc., but will also function as CD-ROM distributor for some widely used databases.

The above examples are only a few in a rapidly expanding area but they do indicate the present focus: the large database business. Publishers already faced with the online challenge have yet another adjustment to make: to cope with this new medium and to assess what the implications will be to their markets, revenues, personnel and facilities. Online vendors see the potential danger of end users and intermediaries doing their searches locally. Libraries and end users are asking questions about the cost of equipment, availability and compatibility of disks. It appears that where searches are being frequently conducted the cost of replicated disks might be offset by savings on online charges and offprints. New companies are springing up as service bureaus to take care of disk mastering and reproduction as well as related services in preparation of data; an interesting development is CD-Publisher, an IBM based PC-integrated system which allows users to format data files, build database indexes and premaster tapes for CD-ROM replication. Publishers can also test CD-ROM products in the PC-oriented environment in an interactive mode (Electronic Publishing Business 1986).

CD-ROM seems predestined for use with microcomputers controlling the disk player in local applications including distribution over local area networks or local telephone lines. CD-ROM is not intended to replace magnetic disks or large optical digital disks; rather, it will add to the existing variety of media. CD-ROM has thrown a wrench into the present mechanism of database distribution and usage but in the end most parties involved will likely benefit: intermediaries and ultimate users through avoiding online charges and more opportunity to browse, database producers through better control of their wares (although they may choose not to sell directly to clients). Central online database operators need not loose because, as Pemberton (1986) points out, many users appreciate the one-stop shopping on large online databanks, which he likens to the trend in the U.S. toward multibrand car dealerships.

3.7.8 Optical ROM Disks

Distinction is sometimes made between CD-ROM and optical ROM disks (Vacca 1986): both have similar storage capacity but optical ROM is a CAV type of disk which predisposes it for faster access; optical ROM can be two-sided with either a spiral or concentric track whereas CD-ROM arranges and reads information in a spiral track. Both disks find similar applications.

3.7.9 Hybrid "Online Plus Videodisk" System

The hybrid technology brings a powerful extension to the relatively well-established online retrieval, namely, the interactive videodisk enabling the user to obtain pictorial materials along with the text, thereby considerably increasing the utility of this publishing service (see Figure 7). Figure 7 demonstrates the pivotal role of a microcomputer (1) which may be directed by the user to conduct an online search on a remote host (2) and then to display video information stored on a local video disk (3); both textual as well as pictorial information may be either displayed (4) or printed (5).

NON-PRINT-BASED ELECTRONIC PUBLISHING

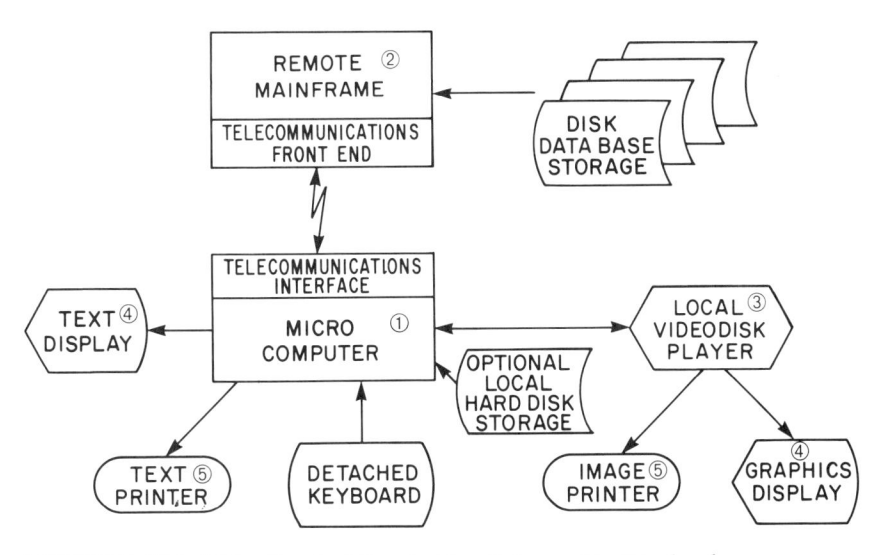

FIGURE 7 Hybrid "online text/local videodisk graphics" technology.

The absence of graphics has been a major drawback of online services, thus limiting their scope to areas where immediate access to illustrations is not a sine qua non condition and the user can wait until a hard copy could be procured, possibly through the same online system. The videodisk player serves the purpose of storing the illustrations locally because the cost of transmitting images in each individual case of need from a remote location might not possibly be cost-justified; also, storing pictorial information on magnetic disks locally would require so much storage space that it also cannot be economically justified and storing it on microforms poses problems with fast retrieval unless expensive, complicated automated systems are introduced.

The following limitations still encumber this hybrid setup:

1. Relatively few reference services are backed up by full text, which would be required in order for this system to be a full-fledged alternative to conventional publications of similar nature.
2. Resolution still leaves much to be desired.
3. Hard copy printout although possible is still lacking in quality.
4. There is an appreciable time delay before pictorial information is gathered and an update disk is mastered, replicated and distributed for local storage.

The advantages of the videodisk technology not only hold promise for the future of publishing but have been perfected to function in some systems of the present; they have to rely on microcomputers to serve as intelligent terminals in relation to remote hosts and to interact with the videodisk player. The role of micros is practically unlimited: they may serve to download software, databases or their segments, function as word processors, etc., in addition to their controlling function.

Video Patsearch. Video Patsearch is a trademark owned by Pergamon International Information Corporation. The database contains U.S. patents issued since 1971 on eight (as of today) videodisks and makes it possible to make subject searches without leaving one's office. The database is housed on Bibliographic Retrieval Services, Inc. (BRS) computer facilities in New York and the Pergamon Info-Line system in London and may be accessed from there by anyone who pays annual subscription fees (which includes installation and maintenance) as well as an online connect charge plus communication charges.

The subscription fee buys:

1. The hardware—a specially designed microcomputer with:
    a customized detached keyboard
    text display screen
    graphics display screen
    interactive laser videodisk player
    text printer
    graphics printer (optional)
    integrated communications interface for
    automatic dialing and logon procedure
2. Software for microcomputer-controlled videodisks
3. Database of video images on a set of videodisks, quarterly updated

First the online search, based on a query, is conducted on the remote patent database by applying any strategy that is deemed productive: using Boolean connectors, proximity indicators, masking, etc. The search words may be from a number of categories such as inventor name, assignee name, patent number, application number, foreign priority and date of issue, in addition to common words found in abstracts and titles, U.S. and international patent classification or references cited. The search may need to be adjusted in response to the result and the scope of the search formulation may be either narrowed or widened depending on whether the number of retrieved items is regarded as excessive or insufficient. The text of selected items can be displayed on the terminal as desired. The database items resulting from the search are then automatically translated into image locations on one of the videodisks and the videodisk is notified accordingly: one can display text of a document on one screen and the first page drawing of the same document on the other screen. One can then move from patent to patent, store relevant documents as a group for later reference and/or make a copy on the text or video printer.

Medical Information Retrieval System. Medical Information Retrieval System (MIRS) is yet another representative of this hybrid technology. This product of the Medical Division of Bibliographic Retrieval Services is predicated on the same philosophy of using a local store of illustrations on videodisks while at the same time accessing text—abstracts, titles, full text, etc.—on a remote mainframe, but the role of the local microcomputer has been expanded to store optionally textual information as well, in addition to its coordinating function. This provides the service supplier with a tool whereby he can distribute data in a manner thought most economical under given circumstances.

3.7.10 Optical Digital Disk

Besides applications in the entertainment area, optical memory media have considerable potential to bring far-reaching changes to education and training, office automation, archives, museums, general information retrieval, document management and last but not least, to electronic publishing. As a matter of fact, the videodisk technology has already made its mark in publishing as described in the previous text. An ODD is an optical disk encoded digitally and produced by the DRAW method with erasability to be added as a desirable feature when available.

This technology offers the following advantages:

1. High storage capacity: typically 1 Gbyte per disk side, 2 Gbytes on a two-sided disk (Rose 1983); 10,000-100,000 pages may be stored on a disk (Hendley 1983). This storage is multiplied by the number of disks in a jukebox.
2. Relatively high access speeds: from a fragment of a second to several seconds to reach any document (slower than magnetic disk); high data transfer rates on the order of megabits per second.
3. In contrast to microforms, there is no delay in accessing documents entered into the system.

4. Recording on disk is more permanent compared with magnetic media.
5. Recording/replay on same unit designed for office environment.
6. Some similarity to magnetic disk: easier to integrate conceptually into electronic systems than microforms.
7. Integration of text, audio and graphics on same disk.
8. Encoding is always digital with possibility of compression; graphics can be handled as black/white as well as color.

On the other hand, there are yet not many systems operational and those in operation have been tested in very specific environments. Cost of larger configurations is still prohibitive. Multiple-disk units are yet not common despite the efforts of at least 20 companies. A comprehensive publishing system based on optical data disk has yet to be set up. A great deal of research and development is still underway to put the above advantages to work, so the optical technology can prove its superiority in relation to microforms and magnetic media and gain acceptance of the end user. The question today is not whether but when the optical digital disk will make major inroads in capturing a portion of the market. The write-once type will assert itself in 1-3 years while erasables will take closer to 10 years.

With the currently available technology, one may already envision an optical disk publishing venture which would be versatile enough to meet a wide range of user expectations.

A publishing system based on ODD (Figure 8) might input a variety of source materials. This could make it a complete publishing system. We can easily envisage a situation where original typed papers (1), after an internal or external review, are scanned in a digital page image scanner (2) in much the same way as camera-ready copies are requested by a publisher to be copied by conventional methods. Other input materials may include out-of-print materials, materials no longer stored on magnetic media online, archival copies, etc. As an alternative, paper may be entered directly into the computer (3), thus circumventing the scanning loop. Scanned materials will have to be verified (4) after the scanning process has been completed. At this stage data is compressed (5) and entered in a computer storage (6) ready to be output on a disk (7). In our example, we outline a publishing system relying on distribution of replicated disks to regional or subject area-specialized centers (8, 9). This is not to discount the alternative method, namely, centralized dissemination of information from an automated computer-controlled multiple-disk storage. Looking at a system like this from the point of view of the end user, there are several options of how to draw on the vast database: for information relevant to a specific need, users would first consult a central (preferably) (10), regional or

NON-PRINT-BASED ELECTRONIC PUBLISHING

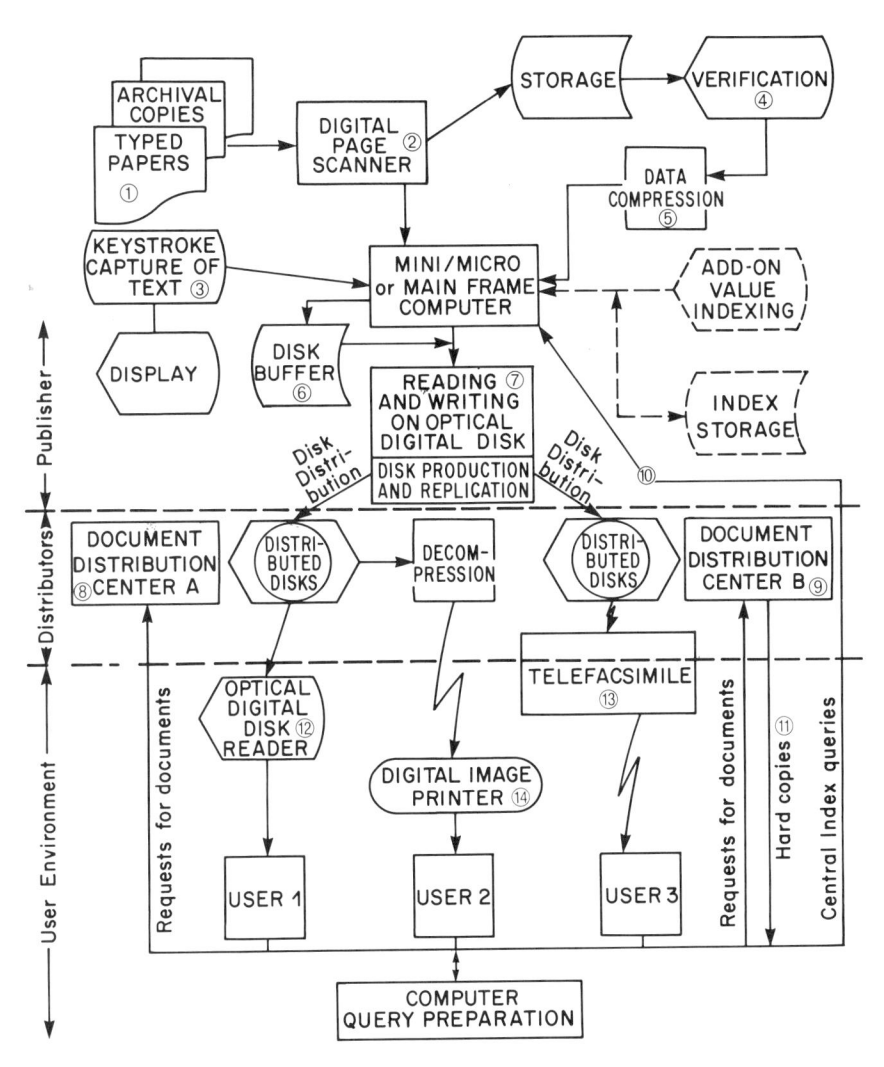

FIGURE 8 Publishing system based on optical digital disk: one of several possible scenarios.

even private database containing database pointers to the physical location. The user would then issue requests for particular documents and receive them, depending on circumstances, either as hard copies (11), on a magnetic or optical storage device (12), if the width of the interest respective warrants it, or via telefacsimile (13). Other alternatives are output from a high-resolution image printer (14) or downloading of digital image information for local recording/replay on disk.

Typographic attributes, if desired and not present already, could be imparted to published materials at the input or output stage; otherwise, the system could function as a mere electronic document delivery facility.

Some systems based on the optical digital disk are outlined in Chapter 5 on electronic document delivery.

3.7.11 Concluding Remarks

Our present knowledge of optical memory systems leaves many questions open, but it already allows us to conclude that much the same as television did not eradicate radio and audiotape did not obliterate the phonograph (even though digital audio may prove to be a tougher customer), the optical disk in all its manifestations as dealt with in this section will suit particular functions because of its inherent (and improving) qualities, and will likely supplement other already entrenched media rather than totally replace them. Thus we can easily envisage a document delivery system involving an array of memory systems in which noncurrent data are stored on microforms, magnetic tapes or in hard copy, whereas more recent data might be on optical disks while magnetic disks might serve the current database for processing or for transmission. The challenge to system designers will be to know the relative merits and liabilities of these media and to employ them accordingly. There has been discussion in this book about convergence of technologies; optical media have characteristics that will make them live and let other media live in a complementary manner.

Optical memory media offer high storage capacity, high durability of the media themselves, longer lifespan of recorded information (probably much more than the suggested minimum of 10 years), lower cost per stored bit owing to the huge amount of accessible bits, less head wear as there is no contact with a disk, less frequent head crashes. The main asset, however, is the ability to store sound, pictures, graphics and text. The speed of access and data transfer rates are also appreciated. Publication-related applications will benefit from a possibility innate to distributed systems, namely to exercise local control over data even though this may entail actual physical manipulation of disks until jukeboxes become commonly available. Also, the portability of small disk drives is certain to add appeal in support of user acceptance. All the above advantages are relevant to different varieties of electronic publishing, both print-bound and nonprint, as well as to electronic document delivery which revolves around huge archival storage and distributed media processing.

Optical disks are in direct competition with paper-based information warehouses and microform repositories including COM (computer output microform). Optical memory systems pose a real challenge to on-line information services because a database may be exploited at fixed cost with virtually no limits imposed: no transmission costs, no online costs, no royalties. Optical memory systems in regard to COM will prove themselves in situations where a large database contains relatively long-lived data that needs updating, wide distribution, frequent access and fast retrieval. COM on the other hand can distribute at reasonable cost large databases that do not require frequent retrieval and can be read at inexpensive stations. Both media have pictorial/graphics capability. Will optical storage replace microforms? This is not likely in the foreseeable future. Paper still towers as an even more awesome adversary (Rothchild 1986): only 2% of business information is stored on magnetic media, 3% on micrographic media, whereas 95% is on paper. A similar situation obtains in publishing when it comes to books and journals which may become a primary target for penetration by optical media in their quest for markets in electronic document delivery. Large databases will be installed in the ROM format and large paper-based stores of information will be digitized onto write-once media with erasable disks (when they finally arrive), occupying those niches where erasability is either required or not undesirable. Erasable disks are not intended to substitute for write-once and ROM, and this should appease all those hesitant to buy for fear of obsolescence. (It is mandatory that industrial standards be in place to eliminate the need for multiple drives.)

Compatibility between the competing media—hardcopy, microforms and optical (as well as magnetic) disk is technologically secured; both OCR (optical character recognition) and raster scanning can provide computer-readable data for further processing and/or transmission, which in their turn can be converted into hardcopy or microform. The only problem remains the cost justification for the expensive facilities.

The high storage capacity makes optical disks eminently suitable for the mode of electronic publishing (explained elsewhere in this volume) known as "on-demand" publishing which envisions only the delivery of articles of interest. As opposed to publishing of mere document surrogates (such as titles only, abstracts only, etc.), optical storage will be a fertile ground for the continuation and escalation of the trend already perceivable towards full-text publishing.

An interesting and typical aspect of the contemporary development in the optical memory systems is the high degree of affinity to microcomputers. This kinship may be observed in micros adding interactivity to disk players, in micros functioning as information retrieval tools from CD-ROMs, etc.

Publishers and in general disk program designers would be mistaken if they conceived of the new optical memory media as a new version of the old, static storage media endowed with enhanced memory. Unlike the old-fashioned book this dynamic medium provides a combination of sound, video and text with random access; various degrees of interactivity enable the users to better exploit the contents to their advantage in pursuit of either education or entertainment. This opens new horizons for publishers; the new wave here does not mean dead hardware with impressive performance parameters but live programming which is heralding the arrival of a totally new product. The applications in the publishing field of laser disk-oriented end products presently include large bibliographic databases, databases to aid in cataloguing, encyclopedias, educational/instructional interactive materials, commercial catalogs, potentially telephone directories, interactive books with multiple plots and endings, art gallery and museum catalogs; but the full potential has not yet been tapped and includes projects like on-demand printing of books in the bookstore as a result of selection from a catalog also stored in the bookstore and supplied by publisher. Conversion of a bookstore into an electronic document delivery site or adding a printshop capability to its long tradition of warehousing has been made possible by the marriage of convenience between the laser disk and the desktop laser printer which forces rethinking of where to store and where to print most economically for all those concerned. A bookstore can thus deliver a work either in machine-readable or human-readable form, whichever is more convenient to the reader; some of these services might be provided on a self-serve basis on coin-operated hardware. Libraries of all kinds will be faced with similar opportunities even though their primary bailiwick will be information provision (both with and without charge) rather than sale of major works; but the distinction becomes rather blurred when we think in terms of full-text delivery to patrons. The specter of copywright lurks behind all these considerations. Another implication of optical memories for libraries is that patrons may be able to do without a librarian as intermediary when the station is inexpensive, the interface language easy and telecommunications costs absent.

A final point for this section is that optical disks will force people to deal with a new order of magnitude—the terabit—after they have moved up the scale from kilobits to megabits, and gradually to gigabits, as milestones in memory development. The main consequence of optical memory, however, will be its far-reaching impact on the respective industry infrastructure accompanied by profound changes in the way people receive and "consume" information: from passive, sequential reading to assimilation controlled partly by program, in part by user and, where applicable, characterized by interaction, participation, multiple choice and decision making.

3.8 Electronic Mail

3.8.1 Definition:

The notion of electronic mail (EM) may mean different things to different people. In the broadest sense electronic mail has been with us for some time and includes diverse means of communication, some of which were in use before the term electronic mail was invented:

1. Public telegraph incorporating services such as Telex and TWX
2. Facsimile-transmitting documents between remote sending and receiving machines on public or private networks
3. Communicating word processors provided with data communications devices
4. Computer conferencing
5. Teleconferencing (audio, video)
6. Voice message systems as a computer technology with a huge future potential. When a signal is received, it is converted from analog to digital form, compressed and temporarily stored until it is retrieved by the addressee, whereupon it is decompressed and delivered in the original analog form. Some systems may be integrated into existing digital switching equipment and may be accessed by callers through rotary dial systems.
7. Computer-based systems which provide computer equipment, specialized software and data communications networks, national and international, for creation, transmission, storing and receiving of messages. Editing facilities, mail-waiting notification capabilities, announcements of messages of general interest in "notice boards," the possibility of sending messages to an unattended terminal and filing of incoming messages are some of the conveniences that make this mode of electronic mail attractive for a number of applications. Connection of this mode of electronic mail to conventional mail services as well as to public telegraph has been established.

Electronic mail in the narrower sense is understood to be a system falling under point 7 above. There has been a proliferation of systems of this class recently introduced by computer manufacturers, common carriers, time-sharing services, online system providers, etc., based on similar principles and capabilities yet using different logon procedures and command languages.

3.8.2 Modes of Communication

There are essentially three possible modes of the sender/recipient communication. (1) In the point-to-point mode, the message cannot reach the recipient unless connection is established between the sending and receiving devices. This obviously creates some inconvenience if the nature of a message cannot tolerate a delay and may require repeated attempts to establish connection. This is applicable to the concept of electronic mail in the broader sense to include telephone, TWX, Telex, communication word processors and telefacsimile. (2) The store-and-forward communication systems have a storage function built into them so the message can be delivered to the recipient whenever the link to the address station can be established or at any desired time such as during off-peak hours. (3) The "mailbox" principle is predicated on the existence of a mailbox for each participant and messages are deposited in and read from these mailboxes by authorized users. Electronic mail systems in the narrow sense are ordinarily mailbox systems which may also be adapted to store and forward messages to unattended terminals termed as automatic delivery.

Electronic mail systems may provide a vehicle for communication between humans and computers in essentially four modes. (A) The human-to-human communication may be exemplified by an editor corresponding with an author and many similar one-to-one or one-to-many situations. (B) The human-to-computer application arises, e.g., in an editing system in which local reporters or editors gather information to be centrally collected before being processed into pages. (C) A computer-to-human message in an electronic publishing environment is, e.g., instructions to authors which may be initiated by a prospective author or may be broadcast from a publisher's computer to a number of pertinent mailboxes. (D) A computer-to-computer message may occur, e.g., in the scheme of selective dissemination of information when information relevant to a stored profile is transmitted automatically to a user terminal or microcomputer.

At another level electronic mail may be either direct or indirect depending on whether or not a delivery system has been interposed between the communicators. If we distinguish between the highly structured (e.g., an ordering form for hard copy) and unstructured information (such as discussion of the editorial board), then electronic mail can do both and anything in-between. Present electronic mail systems are based both on text and voice.

3.8.3 Electronic Mail and Electronic Publishing

Because some members of the broader electronic mail family have been treated elsewhere in this book, we shall focus on the EM systems as defined under point 7 above with a view to applications in electronic publishing.

Electronic mail has been hailed as a new, versatile medium of communication but to put its potential applications in electronic publishing into perspective, one must be aware of its inherent limitations. EM systems do not have, as a rule, sophisticated retrieval facilities as information retrieval systems (IRS), and hence cannot be used as an efficient tool in the user selection part of document delivery. EM systems have sufficient facilities to edit messages but are devoid of formatting and editing capabilities that enable users to enter their papers; the available character set is limited as well. EM systems do not possess means for efficient database generation, updating, sorting or report writing, as is common with generalized database management systems (GDBMS), nor can they effectively manipulate files as file management systems or general computer systems.

However, despite the above shortcomings, EM systems have established themselves on their own merits as proven component parts of major systems. Their impact, unfortunately, may be felt only in relation to the size of their user population. On the document delivery side, EM can be employed with advantage in interlibrary loans in a one-way electronic delivery scheme whereby it cuts down on mailing costs and eliminates the time delay associated with placing an order on materials from lending libraries; forms may be used as well and unattended terminals are an option. Electronic mail requests could well be answered by telefacsimile document delivery, thus making up a two-way electronic delivery system. Online ordering of documents in the framework of online information retrieval has been done for a number of years, and it is essentially an electronic mail system using a simple set of commands with the on-line provider acting as an intermediary between the user and the actual hard copy store.

Communication in the editorial process involving authors, editors and reviewers has been facilitated by EM as far as message exchange is concerned, whereas materials to be published need a different vehicle to be able to move from the author to the editor, from editor to reviewers and vice versa as needed. Such a vehicle, e.g., computer conferencing or general-purpose computer systems, may be employed in which either copies of articles, papers, etc. can be created by each user or else a group of people may share an article, paper, etc. located at a central location in the main memory if proper access has been granted. Electronic mail may be used as a channel between users/readers and publishers as well, thus enhancing the publication cycle by feedback related to the quality of papers, suggestions for improvement and general inquiries; this feedback is to be distinguished from publication schemes whereby readers may append their comments to papers, articles, etc. themselves, which then become retrievable by other users as integral part of the original article. It is also possible to provide communication channels among users/readers, which has been the case with microcomputer owners in some publishing undertakings.

Besides being a helpful tool in diverse publishing functions, EM has come to be one of many services offered to the general public on some computer online utility systems which provide a variety of services, among them online publishing.

3.8.4 Advantages and Hazards

It would be an unwarranted expectation to view EM as a panacea in solving communication problems; EM is not more nor less than a "utility," as this term has been known in the computer world, and any application requires a thorough systems analysis to make sense from the technical, economical and functional point of view.

A properly planned EM system can justify itself by the benefits that can be reaped in reward for a careful analysis. Perhaps the most frequently quoted and readily observed advantage of EM is the absence of any delay in delivering a message; unsuccessful attempts to reach an unavailable person, as is the case with telephone communication, are eliminated; time may be also saved in editing and dispatching a message while received messages may be filed or redirected with little effort to other people potentially interested in a particular subject matter, and an answer to a received message may easily be dispatched in an economic manner. Mailboxes may be "opened" at any time convenient to the recipient, thus avoiding unwelcome interruptions as well as failures to receive messages.

The broadcasting feature of EM makes it easy to dispatch a message to multiple recipients. Any mailbox in the system may be accessed with a compatible terminal by authorized users from anywhere on the communications network. EM systems are usually available 7 days a week and 24 hours a day. In contradistinction to the telephone, a written record of any communication is produced and may be filed electronically or in physical form as hard copy. Messages do not get lost and confidentiality is as safe as a password. Reception of a message can be confirmed with minimum cost and effort. Linkage to other computerized functions in an organization is possible such as data processing, access to external files, document storage and retrieval, file management, etc.

Even though EM may be introduced as a stand-alone function in any organization, it should be always first considered as a component part of an integrated system in resolving a complex problem.

An example of a network with EM which gained prominence in the service of scholarly communication is BITNET, a cooperative undertaking open to all postsecondary institutions in the United States. Established in 1981, it has grown fast to comprise over 500 institutions as of the middle of 1985 through gateways linking it to the EARN

(European Academic Research Network), Mailnet (EDUCOM's network), ARPANET (U.S. Department of Defense Advanced Research Project Agency) and to the NetNorth, a Canadian college network established in 1983 and increasing its membership base. BITNET's activities have been supported by EDUCOM (a professional organization in the area of higher education and computers), which among other coordinating functions, electronically publishes a bulletin board with active user involvement and a user directory. The existence of networks like this, mutually interconnected for easy communication devoid of incompatibility problems, cuts through the jungle of proliferating electronic mail systems with different protocols and can be potentially very useful for further development of computer conferencing and electronic publishing ventures.

Problems associated with electronic mail systems present a list at least as impressive as the benefits. There are too many incompatible systems on the market and similarly to the case of information retrieval systems, users are reluctant to learn a multitude of protocols to talk to a few more correspondents. Electronic mail is often implemented as an isolated measure out of context of broader issues, and it is indiscriminately applied to solve communication problems where a more serious analysis is called for than a mechanistic cure-all of automation. Penetration of files, confusion of authorship, unethical use of privileged information, invasion of privacy and other undesirable phenomena have been reported in conjunction with electronic mail (Carroll 1982).

3.9 Teleconferencing

There are several types of teleconferencing systems:

Audioconferencing

Enhanced audioconferencing (audio with facsimile, slow-scan TV)

Videoconferencing (two-way)

Live television with two-way audio

Written conferences (facsimile, electronic blackboard, teletype)

Teleconferencing has been defined as the use of telecommunication systems by groups of three or more people at two or more locations for the purpose of conferring with one another (Elton 1982).

What exactly is the relationship between teleconferencing and electronic publishing? If we start reasoning from our definition of electronic publishing adopted in the Introduction, we realize that the common denominator of both is the electronic form in which information is captured, processed, transmitted and represented. When we look at the differences it becomes obvious to us that electronic publishing produces a finished product in the form of a book, journal, database, collection of pictures in an art gallery, etc. This holds true even if, because of a built-in feedback mechanism, users can send comments to the publisher or can elaborate on the topic for the benefit of others. If a published piece becomes public property, then what follows is an unstructured, ongoing computer conference. Teleconferencing, on the other hand, does not denote a product but rather a process, interactive in nature, with the degree of interaction varying from an active participation as a speaker to a passive "interaction" as a viewer (or listener), with at least the potential to react in real time, perhaps in questioning the speaker. If on the other hand, a teleconference is recorded and the resulting recorded product is sold on whatever kind of storage medium for user replay, then this product may become part of the electronic document delivery in the realm of electronic publishing. The above dynamics of teleconferencing make it different from electronic mail itself, which spans geographic distances but is not designed to serve synchronous meetings as teleconferencing does. Also, electronic mail is not preorganized as is teleconferencing; neither does it yield a finished product as does electronic publishing. The most difficult to define in our context is computer conferencing, which can handle the message exchange as electronic mail proper and can be utilized to produce an electronic journal but cannot deliver the immediacy of an audio or video conference as part of the teleconferencing scene; for this reason it will be discussed, as a disparate issue from teleconferencing, in the next section.

Before we dispose of the subject of teleconferencing other than computer conferencing, we might say that despite its interactive, real-time synchronous nature, teleconferencing could be useful, at least theoretically, in publishing situations where these qualities are called for. Coauthoring books, for example, could benefit from real-time conferences where the general theme and individual chapter topics could be conveniently discussed and coordinated as the project progresses. Editorial board meetings could be held in this manner as well. Unfortunately, the slow-scan television's resolution does not suffice for a 8 1/2 × 11-inch page to be scanned and displayed in its entirety as typed or printed text; large lettering is required. Other problems are the availability of facilities when they are required, where they are required and whether teleconferencing is economically justified—here distinction must be made between audioconferencing and videoconferencing. Audioconferencing is much less expensive; it is conducted over the public telephone network with channel bandwidth about 3 kHz, whereas videoconferencing only can take place over channels of around 5 MHz, and although telecommunication channels are not the sole cost factor the bandwidth does give some indication of cost relations.

In teleconferencing there is a similar concern as to what we noted in electronic publishing based on its strong reliance on data transmission, namely, the possibility of bandwidth reduction. The present trend is from the analog mode to digital transmission, which will lead to improved signal quality as well as bandwidth compression.

At present audio- and videoconferencing does not potentially reach an audience large enough for us to envisage papers being first presented to a synchronous teleconference with solicited reaction from the audience and subsequently distributed by a variety of means such as audiotape videotape, and others, to emulate proceedings of a live conference; this all could change depending on teleconferencing facilities being both available and economically justifiable in the light of existing options. Certainly users (listeners, watchers) would gain from the added value of the "publication" thrashed out by conference participants, who in their turn would save on travel expenses, whereas "publishers" would recoup some costs associated with organizing the "conference" and its logistics.

3.10 Electronic Journal

3.10.1 Electronic Communication/Publishing via Computer Conferencing

These are computer-based systems for multiple-person communication either synchronous or more typically, asynchronous.

There have been several experiments conducted with computer conferencing systems which were found useful in replacing means of communication that require synchrony in time and place, such as face-to-face meetings, telephone, etc. Computer-directed conferences simply remove the limiting factors of time and place and enable conferees to deposit information into the system and receive exchange information at any convenient time. These systems are distinguished from electronic mail by larger files, which may be destined to an individual (e.g., in a scientific information exchange) or more commonly, to a group of individuals (a "conference") who share some interest. Thus it is important for these systems to be easily accessible to authorized individuals while at the same time ensuring that proprietary rights are not encroached upon. Because of their innate properties, computer conferencing systems have come to be eyed as potential vehicles of electronic publishing.

The computer software available on the host enables participants to enter, edit and format their submissions; the process of journal editing or refereeing can take place on the same computing system. Additional services useful to all those involved in the total communication cycle—writing, editing, refereeing, publishing, distribution and reading—may be tapped, such as simulation, modeling, statistical, mathematical or financial packages, along with graphics capabilities; other useful tools include encyclopedias, dictionaries and a wealth of online database services. Connection to typesetters may be welcomed in many instances. All the above facilities may be resident on the same host as the conferencing software or may be reached through a gateway on the same network; useful facilities however, may be also housed on a local micro. Computer conferencing systems may reside on mainframes or minicomputers; there is also at least one conferencing system called Communitree (see Communitree Group in List of Organizations), which is designed to work on a microcomputer. Although the system is geared to relatively unsophisticated applications, which makes it easy to learn as opposed to some large systems, one can enter messages employing a line editor, read messages in a selected file ("conference"), obtain titles of subconferences if any, branch into other topics of interest and obtain instruction if needed.

Computer conferencing offers electronic publishing a promising technology in which practically all vital functions of an electronic journal can be accommodated. A number of tests and trials have taken place, some of which are sketched below, but the acceptance by prospective authors, editors, reviewers and potential users has fallen short of expectations as regards replacing the conventional journal. Other forms of an electronic journal were more promising (Turoff and Hiltz 1982). Commercial exploitation of computer conferencing systems to create and publish an electronic journal has been scarce although a number of systems have been available for other purposes (Lerch 1983). The reasons why electronic journals on computer conferencing systems have not been embraced by the publishing community are essentially twofold: technology-related and of immaterial nature. In the first category it is the sophisticated procedures for the unsophisticated user, "abstract" nature of the interface, where users get lost in complex branching structures, difficult access to terminals and micros, incompatibility of equipment, VDUs not conforming to ergonomic requirements, the interface not allowing users to do their job as conveniently as in the conventional manner. While the physical shortcomings are being improved upon, the social, more immaterial ones are difficult to overcome: cost advantages offered by an "electronic" journal are not significant enough to entice the user, there is still reluctance in some circles to change the traditional means of communication, there is some apprehension about possible infringement on intellectual property and the electronic journal does not grant the same level of recognition to authors as the conventional journal. The issue of responsibility for archiving is open as are the problems of marketing, pricing and distribution. Because many journal publishers attract authors from a number of countries and most rely on the international market to sell their products, the legal and economic aspects of the transborder flow of information must be also resolved before the electronic journal really takes off on any appreciable scale. Many of these problems are not limited to this kind of journal and the advantages it offers have been proven in numerous tests.

3.10.2 Electronic Information Exchange System

The electronic information exchange system (EIES) is a computer conferencing system, which provides among other things advanced features to facilitate electronic journals as described by Turoff and Hiltz (1982). Designers of EIES have realized that this new facility would not be good at emulating the existing journals and that users must be able to create new forms of publications that meet their particular needs. Four types of electronic publications have been portrayed as being either in existence or under development:

1. A newsletter called Chimo is a two-page weekly journal about members, groups and system news and also an abstract service pointing to items in conferences or public notebooks.
2. "Paper Fair," a totally unrefereed journal, to which members of the community can contribute and deposit their comments on other participants' submissions. The editor's role is limited to user guidance, deletion of papers and provision of table of contents.
3. A classic print-based journal produced electronically was planned to have all the characteristics of the traditional journal. It was to be entered, refereed, edited, copyrighted, subscribed to and electronically distributed. Even though feasible, the original projections did not materialize; the main reason for the failure has been diagnosed as being in the motivational area with political regulatory factors also playing a major role. An electronic journal did not seem to be able to confer enough prestige to authors for them to switch from conventional to electronic means of publishing their findings.
4. Tailored and structured journals. The journal *Legitech* is based on the motivation of contributors to exchange information to a larger extent than in the classic journal. Items published in this successful journal are threefold: inquiries, responses and briefs. Any member of this structured journal can initiate an inquiry and receive responses to it, which are subsequently summarized in a brief of 3-15 pages and published in a public notebook.

A feature of interest to anybody seriously studying the underlying principles of electronic publishing is the capability of the EIES to undergo constant developmental change to accommodate users' needs, wishes and preferences. These changes include human roles as well as software (Turoff and Hiltz 1982). The designers of the EIES recognize that the motivations and habits of users as well as the reward system of their communities are equally important as the technology around which the system is built.

3.10.3 The BLEND Experiment

The Birmingham and Loughborough Electronic Network Development (BLEND) is an experimental program organized jointly by the University of Birmingham, which provides the hardware plus system software facilities, and by Loughborough University of Technology, which contributes the usage research, documentation, training as well as a community of scientists (the Loughborough Information Network Community, known under the acronym LINC) to explore the working of an electronic journal and information network. The aim of the project has been to study system and user performance, costs, usefulness and acceptability (Shackel 1983). Communication between scientists and researchers is studied inasmuch as about 50 specialists in the subject area of computer human factors are connected through the public telephone system to the host computer; a subgroup has been equipped with communicating microcomputers to explore the use of color, sound and running of programs as constituents of papers while raw data are supplied online. In the course of the project, experimental journals have been developed such as a journal of refereed papers, a poster papers journal and a journal with bibliographic references and abstracts supplemented with reader annotation.

3.10.4 Commercial Application

The first commercial application of a computer conferencing system to newsletter publishing has been described by Bechhoefer (1983). The newsletter called IIF (Independent Investors Forum) is produced using a system known as Confer II available on the Michigan Merit network and may be accessed through GTE's Telenet network or leased lines. The Confer II has some capabilities, like other systems, that are helpful in this kind of electronic publishing: the agenda for a newsletter can be readily established; it enables the reader to read selected items in full or in abridged form, react to them, comment and forward information to others. Responses may be addressed to some or all participants who are encouraged by the system software to take active part in the formation of the electronic newsletter. This particular electronic publication is designed to respond to the needs of stock market investors and is predicated on the belief that readers should have a chance to communicate with the editorial staff both by asking additional questions and by letting views be known, and that the readership ought to have the opportunity to contact other subscribers as to their views. IIF's experience shows that subscribers are willing to spend up to 15-20 minutes per session. Microcomputers can be used with advantage to interface with the conferencing system, if provided with a modem and suitable telecommunications software; this involves both downloading information during off-peak periods as well as to uploading messages to the publishers. User support includes a monthly printed user's guide, on-line tutorial, technical advice over the telephone or online and a conference facilitator.

The marriage of a computer conferencing system and a microcomputer seems to be able to prove itself in the rigors of real-life competition.

3.10.5 The Electronic Publishing Project at the University of Calgary

This project has been made possible through a grant from the Social Sciences and Humanities Research Council of Canada, and support from the University Libraries and University Press. The objective of the project was to investigate the editorial process of scholarly publishing with creation of 10 papers in the area of Social Sciences and Humanities with all functions being performed electronically. This having been completed (1) the human-machine interface was explored, (2) the system and user performance was investigated as related to the project and electronic publishing in general, (3) activities taking place on the interface were scrutinized from the perspective of human information processing, (4) reader response to the outputs of the trial was studied and costs of the alternative forms of output were compared.

Additional particulars of the Project and its findings are given in the Appendix enclosing the three following papers: (1) "Casual Users and the Editorial Process," (2) "User Response and Costs," and (3) "Human Performance and Information Processing in the Context of the Electronic Journal." Each of the three papers retains its own numbering of references.

4

Print-based Electronic Publishing

Print-based electronic publishing has evolved historically from traditional publishing. Most of the time its products cannot be distinguished from those prepared by the traditional methods and therefore it is the production technology that makes the difference.

As we have already noted in Chapter 3 with regard to non-print mode, one of the characteristic features of technology development is its rate of acceleration. The same can be demonstrated for the historical evolution of print-based publishing: roughly speaking, cave art (pictorial information) discoveries date as far back as 15,000 BC; Sumerian phonetic writing is 12,000 years younger (2900 BC); another 4000 years later Chinese art was printed (around 800 AD); 650 years later we note another landmark—the Gutenberg press (1450 AD); it took 430 years for typecasting machines to arrive on the scene and mechanize the handling of type (1880) which coincides with the introduction of photoengraving in the preparation of letterpress printing plates. From those milestones the invention of photocomposition was only 60 years away (1940s) and computer composition followed after 20 plus years (early 1960s); early attempts at full page make-up appeared 10 plus years later (1970s) with the desktop phenomenon surfacing in the early 1980s.

Print-based (paper-based) electronic publishing has been also occasionally referred to as computer-aided publishing (CAP) and computer-aided reproduction (CAR) to stress the vital role that computers assumed in its genesis. When addressing any of the processes of prepress, we have to bear in mind that some of the elements and methods discussed are limited to one section (segment or sector) of the industry, whereas some are applicable to more than one or all of the following: (1) book, (2) magazine, (3) newspaper, (4) technical (in-house, in-plant), (5) commercial (graphics and printing) and (6) automated office publishing. The difficulty of choice of the right hardware and software in each particular case is compounded by the diversity of underlying procedures in each segment and by the overlap of conventional, not-so-new and up-to-date equipment on each site.

From print-based electronic publishing, we will isolate the processes of prepress as focus of our discussion while fully realizing that modern electronic printers make the definition a not completely clear-cut matter in that they may produce all of final copy, a proof or a typeset page depending on circumstances. The author's and editors' sphere has been included as well because their tools and concerns relate directly to the modern prepress whose task it is to produce resulting pages as image carriers printable in the print shop (see Note 1).

If we attempted to simplify the prepress technology despite its diversity, convergence and overlap, we could come up with several schemes on which to illustrate some recent developments in a rough outline. The starting sequence of the processes might be characterized as follows:

1. Text (typed)
   Set (galleys)
   Proof
   Art (manually)
   Page (manually)
   Proof
   Film
   Plate
   Print

The wave of electronic technologies has led to several alternative sequences which are suited to and have been adopted by different publishing sectors to a varying degree.

2. Text (keyed or OCR-scanned)
   Art (scanned)
   Page (electronic)
   Proof (soft or plain paper)
   Set (entire page)
   Film
   Plate
   Print (offset or gravure)

3. Text
   Art
   Page
   Proof
   Film
   Plate
   Print
4. Text
   Art
   Page
   Proof
   Plate
   Print
5. Text
   Art
   Page
   Proof
   Print
6. Microcomputer plus scanner
   printer (electronic printer)

These six sets of simplified production sequences do not to tell the whole, complex story of the evolution of the prepress industry, but they do attest to the trend toward streamlining the entire process in both its editorial and production aspects.

Today (sequence #2), more and more text, whether it be a scholarly paper, newspaper editor's copy, technical publication writer's report etc., is key-captured and optical character recognition is increasingly applied where applicable; many workstations are capable of creating line art and halftone illustrations (see Note 2) can be raster-scanned and manipulated in a special workstation (such as a color graphics workstation) or, to some extent, in a page makeup station. Proofs are either "soft" on the screen or on plain paper. The setting of type and also of graphics occurs on "image setters," which can paint the entire page without even understanding what matter is being set. An alternative (sequence #3) exposes film from which the plate is prepared while another alternative (sequence #4) outputs directly on the plate. Electronic printers are available today, which can produce technical publications in-house (alternative sequence #5), and their resolution has steadily improved to the point that their typographic quality is acceptable for an ever-expanding range of products. Finally, another alternative (sequence #6) symbolizes a configuration comprising a microcomputer as the sole workstation, which when equipped with the proper peripherals and software, can handle text entry, line art creation, halftone scanning, composition and page makeup, whereupon the pages may be output to an electronic printer or if desired, to a compatible desktop typesetter.

The method of division of prepress technology along these lines is far from perfect, but it may serve as a basic frame of reference to keep things in perspective in a situation where a similar piece of hardware with different attributes may perform various functions (display screen serving as data entry terminal and/or page makeup terminal or display-ad terminal or system monitor or soft-proof terminal or color graphics workstation) and some function may be performed on different hardware (word processing, setting of type, etc.).

Whenever, in the following chapter, we describe the achievements of modern technologies streaming on the market from the world of computers, care must be taken to avoid the impression that the large, complex problems of prepress have been all solved, and that we are headed into times of relative stability. Far from it: no one single vendor has it all. Mergers, joint ventures and original equipment manufacturer (OEM) arrangements (the OEM is a vendor who purchases equipment and sells it, under his name, with added value as a complete configuration for a given purpose) are ways out of this dilemma. The cost of complex, color-electronic systems is still prohibitive for smaller operations inasmuch as it can run easily from hundreds of thousands into millions: what is basically happening on the cost-side when one acquires a system of this complexity and cost, is a trade-off between a labor-intensive process and a capital-intensive one; this becomes a must when color effects have to be achieved on pages in minutes that might take hours or days on conventional equipment.

Data entry and the editorial office are the focus of the first section in which different possible arrangements of the changing author-editor communication are examined in the light of the new technology. The computer-assisted editorial office, formatting and typographic codes are dealt with next. Word-processing equipment is then described as an impetus for the ongoing revolution in this area of publishing.

Typesetters and their front-ends logically follow; after a brief historical outline, the relationship between typesetters and front-ends is reviewed in terms of intelligence distribution between them, and examples of both are given. Modern digital hardware, both of the CRT and laser-scan variety, are characterized in some detail.

The automation of the prepress technology makes it possible to design complete or "total" systems which encompass all steps necessary to arrive at the final paper copy or to produce film, plate or gravure cylinder, all in one more or less continuous, coherent process. This is the subject of the next section. Color graphics stations, which are essential parts of the "originator to film or plate or gravure cylinder" systems, are described with special regard to their capabilities in handling color pictures; color graphics workstations may be thus seen as subsystems whose services may be needed in any total system that needs refined color graphics for a magazine, report, book, etc., whether it be an illustration, advertising, or actual pages.

Technical documentation systems are being developed at an increasing rate by a growing number of manufacturers. Both new impetus and a challenge to the field are represented by systems with the CAD (computer-aided design) capabilities which require conversion of vector to raster and raster to vector. The latter is required for raster-scanned graphics to be processed as vectors whereas the former can interface a raster output device to a CAD system.

A brief review of typical developments in the print-based variety of electronic publishing would not be complete without highlighting the emergence of the microcomputer-based publishing systems which are attracting more and more attention on the part of hardware manufacturers, software developers and users. As computers have shrunk to a fraction of their former size, so the coming generation of electronic publishing systems will fill not more than large, desktop dimensions with increasingly more sophisticated products rendering requirements of demanding typographic quality.

The last section of the present chapter focuses on selected prepress subsystems apt to fit into a variety of possible configurations depending on their nature; this contrasts with the previous section which examined electronic prepress more from the point of view of system completeness.

Scanners certainly deserve our attention in view of the increasing number of makes appearing on the market in different categories; new applications open up in all sectors of prepress on the input as well as output side of systems.

The new electronic technology introduces some measure of vagueness as to which processing functions will be performed on what hardware and software. This applies specifically to the topic of "page makeup stations," which has moved to the screen from the old ways of manual pasteup. The wide variety of possible setups is outlined as page makeup is moving closer to the "originator" in the changing relationship of word processing, typesetting (text processing) and pagination.

Integration of text with graphics may be accomplished in yet another subsystem which is called the "graphics pasteup to plate" subsystem; it illustrates the method of producing printing plates from different ingredients: text from a text entry terminal and graphics pasted on a carrier sheet. It is necessary to include the raster image processor-facilitated subsystem as a separate subject to stress once more the versatility of this new type of indispensable device even though it will have been mentioned before on a number of occasions.

An interactive picture editing and management system is described as a special case of a digital graphics system which is able to act as a production control tool as well; although designed for the newspaper wireservice market, it has all the capabilities required to handle graphics in general.

Two other subsystems are also reported: the plain-paper proofing subsystem and a digitizing subsystem for types and logos.

Chapter 4 attempts to distill in a few sections a picture of a subject area which is in a state of turmoil with new companies entering the field while others are dropping out of competition or merging. In the short space reserved for this section, an idea may be obtained about the impact of digital computers, the growing significance of microcomputers, the amount of attention that the merging of text with graphics is receiving as well as the amazing power of machines to manipulate pictures. The boundaries between traditional processes of text entry, typesetting and pagination are no longer sacred. Digital typography will have changed much more in two decades the way the progress of civilization is recorded than has happened in the past several thousand years.

Yet it would be a serious mistake to conceive of electronic publishing, print or nonprint, as merely replacing an old piece of equipment with a new, electronic one. Such attempts have already been doomed to failure and, on occasions, ended up in electronic graveyards. New attitudes are needed: parochial, departmental views must be superseded by a total, company-wide systems approach. Some "dirty, old words" are being brushed up again in discussions of people responsible for decisions, such as productivity, profitability, return on capital investment and efficiency. Some conventional values are being painfully rediscovered in attempts to harness the unconventional technology, for instance, the need for user analysis or for proper planning, close cooperation, etc. Even the need for doing one's own homework has been reinstated as a virtue in eliminating blind reliance on "false electronic prophets" in the ongoing discourse among users, vendors, systems integrators and others. Another issue, which is hardly ever mentioned and yet is vital for survival of any industry, is the question of attracting young people to the trade: present curricula do not safeguard that we will raise professionals able to cope with problems that we ourselves have a hard time in sorting out; this, of course, is not a dilemma unique to publishing.

Print-based electronic publishing is an important segment of the industry. The total potential market for computer-aided publishing systems from 1984 to 1988 has been estimated at roughly $41 billion, according to industry analysts at Inter-Consult of Cambridge, Mass. This opportunity exists within the printing industry, with $200 billion of yearly sales worldwide, and $82 billion in the United States alone (Efi Arazi of Scitex at the Seybold Seminars, March 1984, Santa Monica, CA). The importance of effective and efficient prepress operations by far exceeds the size of their share in the above totals. Whereas some sectors of electronic publishing, such as videotex and teletext, are busying themselves with plans on how to encroach on the more traditional publishing media, the publishers of newspapers and magazines are not standing idle and are applying electronic means of design and production to make their operations more effective and efficient. Book publishers are similarly engaged. Thus the dynamics of the electronic onslaught may be perceived in two directions simultaneously: both in replacing the "traditional" publishing techniques as well as struggling with other competing "electronic" technologies to capture a major slice of the business and home market; the battle is on in the home market for the finite commodity: the patron's leisure time.

On the general plane it is easy to observe that computerization of print-based electronic technology is the single predominant factor in shaping its present and the foreseeable future; it is more difficult to attempt to forecast what the consequences of this will be. One of the trends observable on the prepress scene at this junction is a move away from the traditional proprietary technology to technology in the public domain where proper software plays an increasingly important role. As noted elsewhere in this study, the mushrooming software technology poses both great challenges as it frustrates investors searching for suitable, portable packages. Before any futuristic assessment of the trend can be made, it must be qualified as to the function of time that necessitates short-term, intermediate and longer-term evaluation. The short-term effects are making themselves felt already and involve perfection of functions of considerable complexity but still of relatively "limited" scope, such as computerized page makeup, picture manipulation, composition, image setting, etc. In the later 1980s these functions, which are already solidifying, will be perfected, integrated with each other and with other functions in a particular environment. Medium-term development in the early 1990s should see a fruitful symbiosis of various computerized systems on local area and wide area (long-haul) networks, the trend sporadically begun in the 1980s, but this time it will be strongly reinforced by a wide adoption of artificial intelligence and, especially, expert systems which will be applied to single tasks. At this stage networked computers will still be supporting print-based (paper-based) operations in which screen-based, totally electronic publishing systems will be taking hold, gradually spurred mainly by affordable, powerful personal computers endowed with an interface to which humans will easily relate. In the long term to commence around the middle 1990s, paper-based publishing will probably be giving ground to what may be called "integrated electronic communications" to a larger extent than before mainly because of low-cost, high-resolution, flat-panel displays, natural language processing and expert systems, which by then will be able to answer questions and question answers as well as make decisions, solve problems and cooperate in running entire businesses and complex tasks.

Print-based publishing will not cease to exist but it will coalesce with nonprint-based publishing with mutual redistribution of markets, or rather with a new division of labor between the two and electronic document delivery. Publishers by then will have placed their stakes on screen-based technologies, the underlying expert systems and on-demand distribution of knowledge in addition to dispensing information. At any rate, solving the problems of transition to computer-integrated publishing requires top management commitment and long-range planning that accommodates the overall corporate goals; if this is not provided, then the new technology will not deliver increased efficiency—the piecemeal solution will result in a patchwork of automated islands which will defy the very purpose of integration.

4.1 Data Entry Plus the Editorial Process

Each mode of publishing has peculiar problems to tackle in entering data into the system. Videotex information providers' concerns, for instance, are different from those of online information providers and of a still different kind from those in optical digital disk-based systems. In paper-based electronic publishing systems we observe both similarities and distinctions in how information is entered and editorially processed; from newspapers to magazines, journals, books, technical reports, the variations may range from subtle to very substantive.

In this section we touch upon some methods of data entry with implications for editorial processing, highlight the issues encountered by authors capturing keystrokes electronically and then look at the problem posed by formatting and typographic codes. We conclude this section by dealing briefly with the dedicated word processors (WP), electronic typewriters and WP software-equipped microcomputers as vehicles for data entry into publishing systems.

Data entry/editing is interdependent with editorial processing and the convergence of technology brings it closer to typesetting; or perhaps vice versa, typesetting is being brought closer to the originators, even literally to their desk top. Typesetting and its alliance with front-ends is subject to some closer scrutiny in the subsequent section. A study of these closely related areas becomes even more intriguing when we consider the manifold roles that some of these devices may assume: a microcomputer may serve as a keystroke-capturing device which may transmit information to the front-end that drives the typesetter; but microcomputers are provided with software these days empowering them to drive typesetters themselves. Another confusing factor is the increasingly blurred distinction between some devices, e.g., the difference between electronic typewriters and full-fledged word processors as well as between the latter and microcomputers provided with WP software. Even the roles of front-ends vis-à-vis typesetters have to be defined each time we discuss their cooperation, owing to the intelligence distribution between them made possible by the variety of emerging software. Certainly modern technology has made many things easier but reporting on it is not one of them.

4.1.1 Methods

System A: Traditional.

1. The author types a paper or has it typed.
2. Internal editing and review take place with requisite retyping; paper is submitted to a journal publisher.
3. Editor begins the editorial review. Depending on publisher's established procedures, the paper may be forwarded to one or more reviewers.
4. The reviewers referee the paper and return it to editor.
5. Editor negotiates with the author on the final text. Steps 4 and 5 may be repeated if need be. Several rewrites and multiple proofing may be involved as copyediting progresses.
6. Final text is passed to typesetters.
7. Typeset galley is sent to editor.
8. Proofing by editor and author follows.
9. After pagination has been done, another round of proofing takes place.
10. Platemaking and printing ensue.

The proliferation and ready acceptance of word processing has left its mark on authoring and subsequent operations of the editorial process with repercussions all the way down to typesetters. Even though there are many possible variations of applicable procedures, the impact of this new technology on traditional publishing methods is far-reaching. Instead of a typescript, the author wields a "manuscript" on a floppy disk ("compuscript"), which may not be compatible with publisher's and editor's devices as well as those of the typesetter. Problems arising from this jumble of formats may be eliminated totally or in part by (1) standardization of equipment and protocols, (2) adhering to specifications of publishing institutions, (3) using one online system for all participants, (4) transmitting information over telecommunications lines and (5) designing multiple format-to-format conversion systems.

Implementation of these measures either will take time or is difficult to enforce or is applicable only to some situations. An expedient, with some inconvenience, used in many publishing houses, is to deal with "compuscripts" as if they were the traditional typescripts. A setup of this kind may look like this:

System B: Compuscripts.

1. Authors prepare their papers (or whatever) on a word processor. They keep the diskette(s) and mail the printed compuscript to publishers.
2. Editor initiates the editorial process and may communicate with reviewer(s). The annotated original compuscript is returned by mail to the author.
3. Author revises the original compuscript on the word processor and mails the revised version of the printed compuscript to the editor; if this is the negotiated final text the respective diskette with final draft is enclosed.
4. Editor checks that revisions have been implemented as settled and passes the diskette with the pertinent marked-up printed version to copy editors and then to typesetters.

This setup presumes compatibility between author's disks and the typesetter's devices or the existence of a conversion system. It is also based on an agreement as to who inserts the typographic codes driving the typesetter. The process of proofing must be established as called for by the changed technology and procedures. If compatibility between author's and typesetter's diskettes has not been secured, rekeyboarding may be required which entails additional proofing.

System C: Originators to Commercial Typesetters. Transmission over telephone lines can be implemented without waiting for any standardization to be completed and has proved to be an efficient means in resolving the problem of compatibility between the word processor and computer only if the parties involved have the requisite standard communications equipment which has come to be quite common (Buckland 1984). If the word-processing machine does not have error checking built into its telecommunications capability, then parity checking is the only protection against transmission errors. Figure 9 outlines the traffic between originators of information and a commercial typesetter

PRINT-BASED ELECTRONIC PUBLISHING

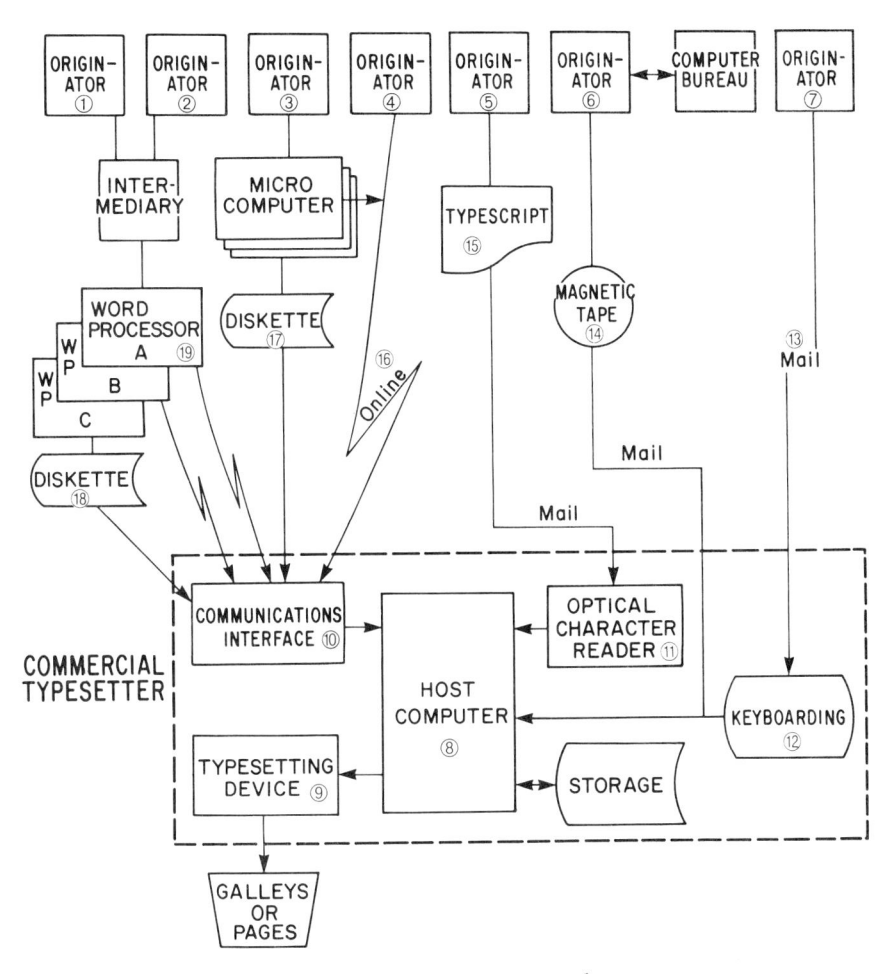

FIGURE 9 Information traffic between originator and typesetter.

as explained in methods C1-C6; originators may be authors publishing on their own or in cooperation, an office where original or nice-looking typeset copies are needed, small publishers, or publishers of technical reports. Editorial processing is done in-house. The typesetting device in instances C1-C6 is located on a commercial typesetter's premises but may be situated in campus printing services, print shops, etc. Figure 9 illustrates the information transfer between the originators (1-7) and the commercial typesetter's computer (8) which drives the typesetter (9); the computer receives data via a communications interface (10), optical character reader (11) or keyboard (12). Originators (1-7) submit copies through mail (13), magnetic tape (14), typescript to be scanned

(15); some are connected online (16) but many more transmit text on diskettes generated on micros (17) or word processors (18) or use communicating word processors (19).

C1. Originators enter their text themselves or through an intermediary using dedicated word processors or software-equipped microcomputers and the information is transmitted to the commercial typesetter's front-end computer over the phone lines. This system offers the originator all advantages of word processing (unlike system A) and saves time involved in sending compuscripts through mail as under system B. If any major revisions should be necessary after the originator reviews the typeset text, these must be made on the originator's word-processing device and retransmitted.

C2. Originators may enter their text from remote terminals online into the typesetter's front-end computer. The advantages are the speed of entry and direct editing but communications and online connect charges may be prohibitive.

C3. Excessive transmission costs may be avoided if originators prepare their text using their organization's computer resources and send the text in an agreed-upon format on a magnetic tape to be entered into the typesetter's front-end machine.

C4. Originators may send in their typescripts to be digitized in an optical character recognition scanner on the typesetter's premises. The economy of this method is determined by amount of human intervention required.

C5. The application of paper tape in submitting text to typesetting has become a rare occurrence.

C6. Most typesetters provide rekeyboarding of text into their front-end.

System D: Data Entry/Edit Plus the Entire Editorial Process in a Total Electronic Environment.

D1. Authoring papers, copy editing and the entire editorial process can be conducted in one and the same system which connects authors, reviewers and editors in one or more institutions (campuses, corporations, etc.) or cross-country and internationally. A system serving this purpose may comprise one or more computers communicating with each other; users are connected with the computer via their data entry devices while applying a computer conferencing system (see also Section 3.10.1 on computer conferencing) to enter and edit their papers, and transmit them to the editor; alternatively, the papers may be retrieved by the editor from their files upon proper authorization. The editor sends papers to referees with a single command and conducts all correspondence electronically with them and authors. Authors make corrections and revisions to their papers without any need to rekeyboard the originally entered paper.

This technique can be achieved if a customized computer conferencing system is employed. It is able to provide an easy access for all authorized users as well as transfer of files from user to user, privacy of privileged files, security against abuse and unauthorized use. Reviewers and editors must be allowed to avail themselves of split screens with the possibility of simultaneous scrolling in all directions so they can reference back and forth, compare text and make annotations and comments. The system must be able to be used by a casual user.

Computer conferencing systems can, in some special applications, act as total publishing systems (see Section 3.10.1 on computer conferencing); the finalized papers can be made accessible to subscribers as electronic journals or may be either printed on an "on-demand" basis and delivered as hard copy or handled electronically.

In a paper-based publishing environment, a system like this comprises a text editor, formatter and an electronic mail system; it transmits processed papers to the typesetting establishment, if a typesetter is not available in-house.

D2. A modification of the above system is practicable with general computerized conferencing systems which do not have facilities customized to the editorial process. Formatting and typographic commands require specially trained personnel. Reviewers and editors cannot annotate text on the screen efficiently and prefer working with a printed copy; results of their refereeing and editing effort must then be keyboarded and forwarded by electronic mail or appended to the electronic paper. This procedure still avoids rekeyboarding the paper but does involve additional printing and paper manipulation. The time delays inherent in regular mail are saved. Authors revise their papers online and present the revised copy to the editors in the same manner as they submitted the original paper. Proofing may be limited to checking the differences between the original and amended versions.

In both systems D1 and D2 the author's creation never leaves the system and never changes its format.

System E: Newspapers' Data Input. Newspaper publishers are in a better position to control their information input than book and journal publishers who deal with geographically remote authors in diverse subject areas and using a variety of data entry modes. Newspaper publishers provide their staff writers with standard entry equipment which eliminates the format incompatibility problem. Staffers' original keystrokes are captured at copyediting terminals (and at display ads terminals) either to fit the assigned article size as predetermined by the editor or to prepare articles and leave it up to the editor how the final page will accommodate the diverse items.

Newspaper publishers have been front-runners in implementing computerized data entry systems in paper-based publishing but some of them were also quick to realize the potential of having their printed matter available in the electronic form in parallel. This enabled them to enter the online information business and some have been showing keen interest in the videotex/teletext developments in which, of course, data entry is subject to different principles.

System F: Editorial Processing in Book Publishing. Book publishing has not been computerized to the degree utilized by newspapers. Systems have been designed that are production oriented but there is little to assist editors and authors. In addition to such factors as long standing tradition, the multiplicity of authors and editors, both internal and external, with diverse systems, there is the sheer size of "file" to contend with on the road to automation.

An editorial system for the book publishing industry must enable the author, reviewer and editorial staff to access any part of the text efficiently in pursuit of their specific tasks. The above participants should be able to exchange messages and files and also share tools such as calendars, spreadsheets, schedules, etc. Workstations ought to be provided with modems so that assistance from remote encyclopedias and databases can be obtained without too much inconvenience. Dictionaries and thesauri should be available online.

The editorial system of a book publisher could have yet another important spin-off benefit, albeit in an area different from editorial: an online file of their book information. This file could prove useful in increasing a book publisher's productivity and might be tapped by internal as well as external seekers of information for reference, ordering and other purposes. A system currently in use called Titlebank (see in Inforonics, Inc. in List of Organizations) serves as a complete book catalog/marketing support system to typeset yearly catalogs, indexes, price lists, new book announcements, etc., directly from one's working environment. An ideal system would have a program for checking errors in spelling, and even some help in choosing the right word. Some kind of assistance as specified below in this chapter in Section 4.1.6 "Word Processor Plus" would be most welcome considering the file size common in book publishing.

For editors and reviewers, it is essential to make edits and comments and still be able to determine who made the changes. Changes are best implemented if split screen is available with annotations being made alongside the original text; this calls for fast access to any element of the text and scrolling at optional speed, optimally simultaneously in both windows; if these expedients are not provided, editors will be always tempted to revert to printed versions which afford easy referencing. Editors must be allowed to keep track of all book components and people involved in order to be able to expedite the editorial and production processes. The specifications of an ideal editorial system in book publishing are more exacting than in other publishing sectors.

4.1.2 Computer-assisted Editorial Office

In much the same way that book publishers struggle with the size of their "files" and require systems to help them inventory book elements and the people involved in processing and producing them, journal publishers could considerably benefit from a system which would manage the file of received manuscripts and eligible referees. The concept of the editorial processing center (EPC) has been reviewed by Hills (1983) and Lerner, Metaxas, Scott, Adams and Judd (1983). The editorial computer system described by Rhodes and Bamford (1976) contains a referee file with information on referees so they may be selected as suitable for a particular manuscript, while at the same time allowing for equitable workload distribution among referees and automatic dispensing of reminder letters. The manuscript file contains all necessary data on all manuscripts including present status with automatic generation of forms and letters.

Systems of the EPC type, while themselves computerized, can make a considerable contribution to electronic publishing because they improve its economy by increasing the productivity and throughput of the editorial office.

4.1.3 Authors to Originate Machine-readable Text

Although the pace of development varies from country to country and fluctuates within a wide range among various segments of the publishing community, it may be safely stated that there has been a general shift in the author-publisher-typesetter relationship toward authors preparing their manuscripts, fittingly called also "compuscripts," either themselves or with their secretary or other persons acting as intermediary, in electronic machine-readable form. The acceptance of electronic data entry and editing has been overwhelming in large newspapers and large-circulation magazines where economics of scale and tough deadlines warrant equipping the editorial staff with electronic data-entry machines, thereby streamlining the entire production line or portions of it. Smaller publishing operations competing for independent authors face serious problems in the transition from a conventional to an electronic flow of materials. The current practice, as already briefly outlined above, of many publishers is characterized by the scenario in which some authors prepare their manuscript on word processors, but editors treat manuscripts prepared in this way as they did typescripts; typescripts are eventually rekeyboarded on the typesetter's front-end before they are typeset. In this case the potential advantages of electronic data entry by the author have been wasted. Webb (1984) lists the problems encountered by publishers who work with independent authors and want to utilize author-keyboarded disks, as some amount of general inertia, resistance on the part of typesetters, difficulty in inserting codes, incompatibility from machine to machine and reluctance of editors to surrender their "control" of manuscripts.

The advantages of electronic keystroke capture accrue to all participants and ideally papers should be keyboarded by authors for editorial processing. The author benefits from working on a word processor; author, editor and typesetter save considerable delays if papers are transmitted over communications lines and they all stand to gain by eliminating, or at least reducing, the time spent otherwise in multiple proofreading.

4.1.4 Formatting and Typographic Codes

Because the trend points to an increasing number of authors entering their papers in a variety of modes—online, via word processors, microcomputers, etc.—havoc both in publishing houses and in typesetting shops is a distinct possibility. Aside from the problem of compatibility in general, there is the issue of inserting codes into the stream of text to control the typesetting machines in performing both formatting and typographic functions.

The practical question arises who would embed the codes into the text. Theoretically it might be the originator—the author—but to ask authors to do that would not be fair because they have already taken the first step on the way to prepare an electronic copy from which all subsequent players stand to benefit. Also, most formatting languages are not designed with the casual user in mind. Publishers, on the other hand, deal with many authors, hence many different formats, and often a multitude of typesetters on their output side. In many cases typesetting firms are best equipped to do this.

There are means of avoiding the coding dilemma. Generic coding can help smooth the author-publisher-typesetter cooperation or the text processing of an in-house operation, however organized. Generic (generalized) coding (tagging or markup) does not insert codes denoting formats or typographic attributes; what the author, or any other text originator does is to mark up the paper, abstract, report or other document with tags defining the individual elements of that document such as title, author, subtitle, paragraph, chapter, etc. The "real" codes governing the typesetter are inserted later by a person who has a better understanding of the document format and typography. That allows authors to work with a limited, one-page list of generic codes and frees them for their specific tasks.

The work on industry standards and author guidelines to aid in keyboarding manuscripts electronically is being pursued vigorously.

The Association of American Publishers (AAP) has announced the release of the provisional Standard for Electronic Manuscript Preparation and Markup, which is the first industry-wide application of the Standard Generalized Markup Language (SGML) (a draft International Standards Organization standard). Manuscripts can be stored as searchable databases and processed on anyone's computer system.

The advantages of generic coding include smooth substitution of "real" codes by very simple and fast programs which look up a generic tag and replace it with a complex real code fitted to the particular publication; moreover, each application may have its specific style sheet stored in the computer, which allows for customized publications to be produced from generalized tags. Generic coding removes dependence of source files on a particular text formatter and a particular output device, improves usability (e.g., including page numbers in cross-references), and results in better consistency of formatting, standardization within one campus or corporation, more efficient writing, reduced lead time and reduced editorial support (Donovan 1983). The benefits accrued from generic coding reach into the area of bibliographic control; codes for automated indexing and cataloging can be provided in the original electronic file.

It should be noted in this context that it is possible to do away with codes completely if the video display workstation can serve to develop the final format and fonts on the screen, as is possible with advanced workstations suitable to certain publishing environments.

4.1.5 Dedicated Word Processors

Word processors are preprogrammed, microcomputer-based systems designed for automated input, processing and output of words to create documents. They are designed to display the text on a screen as an exact image of the document page and allow for editing before the text is printed. Because keystrokes are captured on magnetic media, text may be manipulated which obviates the tedious and labor-intensive retyping: this also points to applications where word processors prove to be most cost-effective. Word processors owe their wide availability to office automation and their wide acceptance to similarity with typewriters. Because of this they have become an important factor in electronic data entry into publishing systems.

A typical configuration includes a microprocessor logic unit, a (preferably detached) keyboard, a video monitor, a floppy disk drive, possibly a hard disk drive, and one or two printers (impact or nonimpact; dot matrix for common printing, or daisy wheel for letter-quality printing). The individual elements may be either of a floor-standing or desktop design, physically integrated or built as modular units.

Word processors may be either (1) stand-alone machines or (2) clustered where several, typically two to four users with their terminals and a diskette, are controlled by a common central processing unit (CPU) with WP software. In larger systems storage is shared as well.

Stations that share common logic are designated as a "shared logic" system. Local area networks are designed to integrate a larger number of units to share communication facilities, textfiles, printers and other devices connected in the network.

Typical Capabilities. Word processors are judged by their respective features. Text editing includes text entry with insertion and deletion of characters, words, lines and sentences, cut and paste, text merging, replacing of text strings with limited or global searching, entering a prestored phrase at any place in text. Scrolling back and forward and efficient cursor control are necessary features of any WP system.

Formatting of text is possible by defining line spacing, line length, the number of lines per page, margins, headings and footings, footnotes, tabs, page numbering, subscripts and superscript, and text may be centered, left or right adjusted, or left and right adjusted. Margin justification may be accomplished by interword spacing, interletter spacing or proportional spacing with letters of different width.

Special Capabilities. Special capabilities encompass a report generator which enables the user to specify the overall layout of a document to be created. Mathematical and statistical capabilities are also available to varying degree. A desirable feature for text entry is a program which verifies correct spelling based on an extensive dictionary; this spelling program may check correct spelling in foreign languages and help in generating one's own customized dictionary. Word processors are as a rule endowed with archival storage to store documents no longer needed on a day-to-day basis. Record management in WP systems is concerned with facilities for creating, adding, sorting, merging, deleting and modifying records.

Unlike early word processors, the newer devices can communicate with other devices of the same or different model and make. Asynchronous and binary synchronous transmission protocols are widely employed. Some typesetting establishments accept WP data via telecommunication to avoid problems associated with diskette incompatibility.

Dedicated word processors may have their capabilities residing in the ROM memory as firmware or as software which may be easily upgraded. Some word processors may even be transformed into a business microcomputer by fitting them with an operating system which can accommodate a number of application programs. All this development makes the distinction between word processors and microcomputers vague indeed: for microcomputers can be provided with WP programs and as such compete with their dedicated counterparts.

4.1.6 Word Processor Plus

It has been generally recognized that word processors, both dedicated and microcomputer plus WP software, can be of considerable assistance to authors, but word processing helps the authors only after they have overcome the infinitely more stressful conceptual part of their task, one that also takes up much more of their time than processing words after the intellectual groundwork has been laid. As a case in point, it would be useful to this author to be able to recall on the screen the structural elements of what he has done so far, possibly in alphabetic order, in causal relationships, in a hierarchical order, and also search term A in connection with term B or term C but not term D, etc. Given the logical capabilities of computers this is possible, and it is only a matter of time when either existing WP programs will be refitted with these features or new programs will be written while still retaining the "conventional" WP power. Ideally, electronic publishing should not be yet another outlet for available technology becoming cheap, but should relieve at least some of the tribulations experienced by humans in the information cycle. One of the problems authors have to grapple with is that they have read, heard about, seen, experimented with or written about some concepts, facts, events, etc., and they need to refresh their memory with regard to them: this may help both to organize a work in progress as well as to gain additional insight into a problem or obtain inspiration. As an author's product grows it becomes increasingly unwieldy and it is difficult for the author to keep track of what has been treated already and what has not: the problem is compounded by vague terminology. Perhaps all authors have arrived at a point in the creative stage of their writing where they felt that it would be great if it were possible to quickly overview where they stand to determine what is to be done next. Has the terminology been used consistently throughout the work? Is the level of detail as intended, are subheadings informative and do they fit into the hierarchy? Have all the conceptual elements been dealt with in proper logical sequence and level of hierarchy? Have acronyms been explained as they first occurred? Is the work going to remain logically structured if a given rearrangement takes place as regards sections, chapters or paragraphs? Have I explained simple concepts first and continued proceeding toward more involved ones? At which points have I referred to certain authors, journals, methods, systems, places? Associated with these issues are problems of easy indexing, table of contents, list of tables, references, illustrations, etc. Authors expect answers to all these and more with the progress in the area of hardware, but even more so in the new microcomputer software.

"Idea Processor," the Light at the End of the Tunnel. Fortunately, there are some programs appearing on the market which may be described as thought organizers; both Thinktank (from Living Videotex, Palo Alto, Calif.) and Zyindex (from Zylab Corporation, Chicago, Ill.) go beyond word processing in assisting authors.

Thinktank (Hershey 1984) displays an outline of a complex text at different levels of detail and allows an author to visualize how logically coherent the text is. It has sorting capabilities to alphabetize subheadings. One can move down the tree structure or stay with the broad headings and one can move items (sections, chapters and paragraphs) up or down in similar manner. Lemmons (1984) likens Thinktank to a spreadsheet where the former manipulates text and the latter handles numbers. Zyindex treats text in a similar manner, that is to say, as a database ("textbase"), which may be searched for occurrence of individual words or their combination using Boolean connectors. Printed passages relevant to the request may then serve to analyze the "textbase" in any way the author may find useful in organizing his ideas.

4.1.7 Electronic Typewriters

The electronic typewriter is a potential candidate for text entry into publishing systems. Whereas a microcomputer plus WP software is a more versatile tool than a dedicated word processor and has become its equal partner with a brighter prospect for the future, the electronic typewriter stands on the lower side of the spectrum between the ordinary typewriter and a word processor. Electronic typewriters resemble typewriters but strive to perform some tasks inherent in word processors, thanks to the intelligence residing in their microprocessors and their captive internal memory. The WP capabilities feature easy correction of the text stored in the internal memory, merging it with additional keyboarded information, automatic underlining, automatic boldface printing, automatic double-spacing, storing text for later recall, printing with right-justified margins, hot zone and other features that facilitate commonly encountered typing tasks. Some electronic typewriters exist in several levels of sophistication which eventually can store tens of thousands of characters on a captive mini-diskette. Higher levels offer single or dual removable-diskette drives and enhanced editing capabilities. Some may be fitted with a limited-size light-emitting diode (LED) display and communication capabilities. As more options are added with corresponding increase in cost, the borderline between electronic typewriters and dedicated word processors becomes blurred.

4.1.8 Microcomputers Plus WP Software

As noted in Section 4.1.5 on dedicated word processors, the borderline between them and microcomputers equipped with WP software is becoming elusive and will vanish eventually. We may view it in more general terms as the coalescence of two formerly distinctive areas: word processing and data processing; although this sounds theoretical it has very concrete implications for authors. The ubiquitous microcomputer is suitable both for word processing and data processing and becoming more widely available—as business computer and home computer—to authors (and others involved in the publishing cycle including readers) not only because of the versatility of micros but also because of their lower price as compared with dedicated word processors. Micros per se do not remove the problems of diskette incompatibility.

There is a variety of WP software on the market to satisfy a user's need at all degrees of sophistication and cost. There are around 20 WP packages available for some microcomputers and it has been claimed that dedicated word processors and microcomputer WP programs are comparable in their abilities (Lanham 1983; Naiman 1983) even though it must be cautioned that software for these machines may not solve all the aspects of a publisher's input problem.

Microcomputers in a publishing environment have the advantage of being able not only to provide the vehicle for data entry, editing, formatting (and printing) but, as the latest development, software is appearing on the market to turn a micro into the front-end for a typesetter. The case for micros in publishing will be strengthened on account of their additional abilities: electronic mail, accounting or statistics. Microcomputers in wide-area networks and in local area networks (LANs) will continue enhancing their applicability.

4.2 Typesetters and Their Front-ends

4.2.1 The Long Road to Digital Typography

The art of typesetting has come a long way and combines an age-old trade with the latest hi-tech advances of the space age. The original setting of type by hand was largely replaced by Mergenthaler's linecasters in the 1890s and was to remain unchallenged practically until the middle of this century. After World War II hot metal was gradually superseded by phototypesetters which were better suited to the age of planography and increased productivity. The first generation of these machines were characterized by emulation of the hot metal process with types being photographed instead of cast from hot molten metal. The second-generation devices stored fonts on strips, disks, drums and grids of film as font masters and a negative image of exposed characters was obtained on film or photosensitive paper. The third-generation devices store digitized type (even though the first machines stored a photographic master) which is imaged on CRT and transferred to film or photographic paper. Characters may be digitized by creating them on a digitizing tablet or simply by scanning tailor-made characters, thereby saving time and cost. The fourth generation employs laser in a raster scan mode as the imaging element rather than an electron beam; a number of other principles is contending for acceptance. The third generation, which is CRT-based and uses digitized fonts, is meeting the quality standards of the industry and its use is widespread. Digitized fonts require huge storage. Not many manufacturers can afford to design and digitize all fonts available today (more than 1200) in several sizes at fine resolution, and for that reason fonts are acquired in machine-readable form from specialized suppliers. A comprehensive study of digital typesetting with associated writing and editorial tasks has been published recently by John W. Seybold (1984).

Typesetting belongs somewhere between text editing and pagination and is moving closer to the originator. The convergence of technologies is putting it on top of a desk. The general trend is to aggregate all of the above three operations (text editing, typesetting and pagination), at least in some applications, and to merge text with graphics with the prospect of adding color somewhere along the line.

It is useful to mention in this context that a digital laser platemaker is an analogy of a digital third-generation phototypesetter in which we replace the electron beam by a laser beam and substitute plate for film as a substrate.

1985-1986 is the period during which the last vestige of photo optical typesetters, known as "second generation," ceased to be manufactured even though, of course, thousands of them remain in operation (Romano 1986).

The arrival of digital typography represents a landmark in human written communication, and as such it has a profound impact on the human civilization. Often as readers we do not realize that traditional printed characters are analog by their nature, and conversely, we are often not aware of some newly printed matter as being based on digital typography; nevertheless, the difference makes for a far-reaching change. Letters can be expressed by configurations of bits called bit maps, and may be displayed, altered, modified, manipulated in different ways, transmitted efficiently, printed, read not only by humans but also by machines and the semantic content understood and changed; or letters can be represented in memory by their outlines or combination of both. Digital typography can utilize the CRT to generate letter forms as a result of an electron beam moving on the screen horizontally and vertically and illuminating picture elements called pixels or pels, successively in each respective horizontal line; alternatively, a laser beam can expose photographic material on a similar principle.

4.2.2 From Typesetters to Image Setters

Any discussion of typesetting and typesetters meets with similar difficulties as other topics and subtopics in electronic publishing: the subject area is one of the fastest advancing because of the present deep penetration by high technology. It also matters whether one reports on what constitutes the current production base or on what is perceived as the leading edge in the trade or perhaps what is on the drawing board. The streamlining of operations, which has always been present in applied technology in general, begins manifesting itself in the prepress technology as well. It is impossible to evaluate the present trends in typesetting without taking at least a cursory glimpse at the preceding text preparation and then to pagination as the logical follow-up of conventional typesetting; an up-to-date, serious study of setting type cannot ignore developments in other associated areas such as capture and integration of illustrations with text, raster image processing, computerized typefont creation and storage, new proof printers, etc., all of which demonstrate how the prepress technology becomes both convergent and diversified.

In dealing with the area in which type is set, we must state first of all that the preeminent trend indicates a fundamental change in the trade. Whereas once we considered the function of a typesetter as providing a galley of text, machines of today and tomorrow have more to offer: they can handle entire pages including graphics, both line art and prescreened halftone, and rotated type or rotated pages in varying degree increments, reverses, tint areas, rules and borders. This is not to say that all typesetters/image setters on the market have all of these features, but they enable users to make their choice depending on their present and future needs and based on their financial circumstances. The current state of flux in the whole trade makes a reasonable choice all the more difficult, and it appears that the more sophisticated the equipment, the more difficult the choice. Prospective buyers have to adjust their purchase of the "back-end" output device (output "engine") to their existing front-end or vice versa, or they can start from scratch and buy a complete set from one vendor, or a system integrator assembles a complete set from different makes. Front-ends maybe defined in our discourse as text-editing and composition devices working either as dedicated systems with a specific make of typesetter or as self-contained devices capable of driving a variety of output devices: "front-end" in simple terms denotes any equipment that prepares data for the output device ("drives" the output device or "marking engine").

With regard to handling text and graphics, we can descry three typical situations:

1. Front-end produces text in generic font; generic font is converted into true font in the digital typesetter using digitized fonts stored on disk. Graphics are added in the pagination process after typesetting in one of several possible ways highlighted elsewhere in this report.
2. Front-end produces text in true font; text in digital form (mostly raster form) is merged with graphics in same form to make up a complete page which may be output by different means from the same source. The prevailing trend points in this direction; this would involve a raster image processor.
3. There are typesetters which set type in the "traditional" manner (i.e., text only) but may be fitted with optional devices enabling them to process graphics.

Any of the above may be minicomputer-oriented or microcomputer-oriented, which is increasingly the case; this distinction will be less and less significant as borderlines between low-end minis and high-end micros will become more and more blurred.

4.2.3 Front-end Versus Typesetter

Modern typesetters cannot be discussed in isolation from front-end processors and their mutual symbiosis in any particular installation is determined by the distribution of intelligence between these two cooperating classes of devices. Compounding this complex relationship is the fact that some types of typesetters may be able to split the intelligence with the front-end and the operator in more than one way and act as a slave typesetter accepting fully composed text while being alternatively able to work as a direct-entry (direct-input) typesetter if provided with a suitable entry device. When we talk about front-end this may mean a computer controller with multiple data entry/edit terminals attached to it as was common already in the 1970s; in this manner the high capacity of an expensive typesetter may be better utilized. Direct-entry typesetters on the other hand are inexpensive, but with new facilities added to them they are losing their identity. Division of intelligence between front-end and typesetter implies that both partners have some computing power built into them and the term "intelligence" means, in more concrete terms, software capability resident in both devices or in either of them. Thus the typesetter, on one side of the spectrum, performs all the composition functions on text received from the front-end whereas, on the other side of the spectrum, a slave typesetter obtains all major composition decisions from its driver front-end, or more precisely, from its composition software. The function that entitles a typesetter to be called intelligent is hyphenation because it involves sophisticated processing often in multiple languages, embracing extensive dictionaries and complex hyphenation algorithms. Typesetters with intermediate intelligence are not able to hyphenate, but are endowed with some intermediate composition capability within a line of text including justification. In direct-entry typesetters it may be left up to the operator to hyphenate even if other functions have been computerized; second-generation typesetters, in the majority of instances, were in fact direct-entry devices fitted with some data entry facility. Digital typesetters are slave devices typically driven by one of the above front-ends.

A special case of front-end/output device symbiosis arises if the front-end is supplemented with a raster image processor which translates the output into the raster format. Then we have a typesetter, or more appropriately an image setter, which images characters (and even graphics) line by line in a vertical pattern as is the case with laser scan typesetters. The same source "database" may also be used to paint a page on a VDT or print a proof on plain paper before "setting."

Typesetters/image setters may be divided into distinctive groups with respect to some of their features.

If we conceive of a typesetter as being an output device then this device either depends on a peculiar front-end device or it accepts output from a wide variety of them, hence division into (1) front-end-dependent and (2) front-end-independent typesetters; this dichotomy presupposes the existence of two separate units working in a compatible manner. Looking at the output device alone, the most important distinction between them is their capability, or lack of it, to output graphics but often "image setters" are also called "typesetters" by inertia. The difficulty in classifying typesetters should by now have become evident and although we are able to lay down some theoretical lines of division, typesetters and associated equipment sometimes elude the straight-jacket of exact classification. We can tell a second-generation typesetter from a third-generation one but it may not be easy to pinpoint a direct-entry device from the rest of the bunch; fourth-generation typesetters involve different technologies and the term has therefore, a somewhat dubious value for a rigorous review. To add to the confusion, laser printers are now often being classified as typesetting devices.

Another criterion by which to divide typesetters is as to whether only a part of the film material may be exposed from a limited area on the CRT tube called the exposure aperture or whether the entire page ("full face") may be exposed without film transport. If typesetting from an exposure aperture, the film material must be transported accordingly to allow for the entire film area (all columns) to be exposed successively; this is called reverse leading. The trend points towards full-face or "full-page" typesetting.

4.2.4 Front-end Plus Typesetter

The working relationship between a front-end and a typesetter may be manifold with some brands, as is illustrated in Figure 10. This figure illustrates how a typesetter (1) is fed via telecommunications interface (2) from various sources: paper tape (3), microcomputer (4), remote terminal (5), word processor (6), optical character reader (7) and magnetic tape (8); a cluster controller (9) can enter text keyed locally at workstations (10) or from the above sources. The typesetter may be driven by a front-end but it may optionally receive typesetting information from other devices such as microcomputers, word processors, etc. The front-end for its part can generate typesetting information in its workstation(s) but it may be connected to other sources of typesetting data and communicate with them in either direction. If a microcomputer is considered as an input to the typesetter, it is as a rule easier to link it with a front-end, but, needless to say, the front-end would not be an

PRINT-BASED ELECTRONIC PUBLISHING

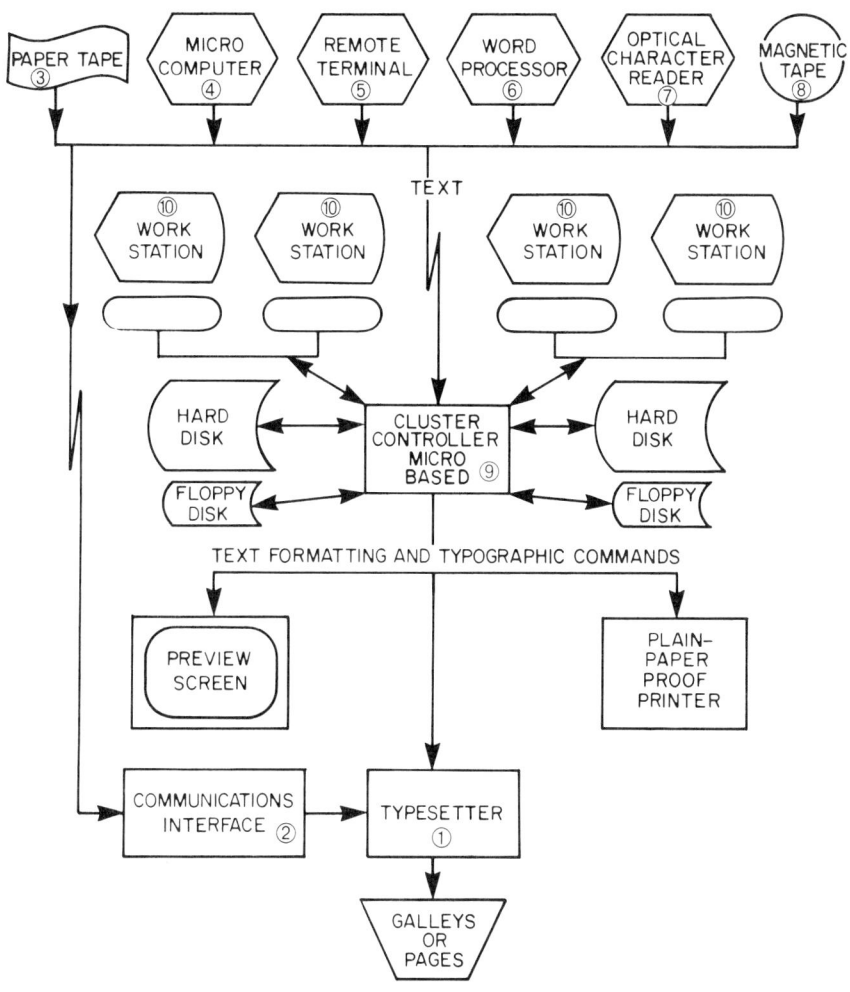

FIGURE 10 Front-end-to-typesetter subsystem: a possible setup.

economical interface to purchase in order to accomplish this link. Microcomputers in 1980s began seriously challenging the established minicomputer-based front-ends of the 1970s (roughly) as their software grew more sophisticated and prices were affordable.

Compugraphic Corporation's modular composition system (MCS), among many others with multiterminal capabilities in the low-end market may serve as an illustration of a combination of devices.

4.2.5 Front-end

The MCS42 front-end system consists of two display screens, two keyboards, one controller and one disk drive. At the heart of the system is a microcomputer-based controller. Two controllers may be coupled to accommodate eight terminals and to drive a single typesetter. System memory is 512 kbytes, the floppy disk accommodates 160 kbytes. As an option, one or two hard disks (10 Mbytes) may be added to store the entire type library. There is an indicator which keeps the operator posted on how many picas and points are left on the line. Hyphenation may be automatic, manual or by use of programmed logic rules. Lines may be ended automatically, semi-automatically or by operator. Screen capacity is 13 copy lines, one message line and one parameter line. A maximum of four floppy disk drives may be connected and hard disk is an optional addition with 5- or 10-Mbyte capacity. A preview screen may be added to enable the full soft copy to appear before it is typeset. A proof printer can be used to obtain plain paper proofs before typesetting, either without typesetting codes or inclusive codes. There are communications interfaces available for the MCS42 to be able to receive typesetting information from word processors and computers and to send information to other MCS systems, word processors and computers which are equipped with the receiving interface; both the receiving and sending interface are RS-232 compatible. Optionally, MCS can be provided with automatic kerning, multiple column processing with automatic or manual column breaks and windows for illustrations, vertical justification, foreign language hyphenation and justification, etc. The MCS42 can be turned into a microcomputer by providing it with a CP/M86 operating system; it can then run various application programs such as the WordStar word-processing system or Spell Star which checks documents created on WordStar for spelling errors. CBASIC-86 is a compiler that enables MCS front-end systems to run user-made programs.

4.2.6 Typesetter

Any of the MCS front-end systems may be used to drive one of the MCS typesetters; the typesetters store fonts either on a flexible film disk or they store digitized fonts on an 8-inch floppy disk (MCS 8400) or a rigid fixed disk (MCS 8600). The MCS 8600 has a maximum speed 860 lines per minute. This typesetter has 100 typefaces accessible to the operator online, each font encompassing 118 characters; the number of typefaces online may be increased to 254. The regular resolution of 1300 scan lines per inch can be increased, as an option, to 5200. Although normally the typesetter is driven by front-end systems, it may

PRINT-BASED ELECTRONIC PUBLISHING

be provided by an optional programmable communications interface which makes it possible for the MCS 8600 to receive typesetting information from computers or word processors directly through data communications, either through direct cable connection or over the dial-up telephone link.

The MCS 8400 has a CRT optical system (3-inch moving CRT with reducing lens); the MCS 8600 is equipped with a fiber optic system.

4.2.7 Typesetters: The CRT and Laser-scan Variety

Modern digital typesetters/image setters are mainly of two kinds when it comes to their optical system:

1. The CRT typesetter has an electron beam to reconstruct each letter as a series of closely spaced vertical lines. These machines utilize different means of projecting the images, as they appear on CRT across the measure (line length), onto the output media (i.e., photosensitive film or paper): movable mirror, traveling small tube plus lens, stationary tube and traveling lens, etc.
2. The technology of the laser-scan typesetter employs a laser beam in place of the electronic beam to scan the full width of the photosensitive material directly; alternatively, it may scan a drum and generate a pattern of charged dots to which toner adheres to be thermally fused onto paper (Bigelow and Day 1983). The laser beam "paints" a page while scanning across the whole width of the page line by line, each time adding a few more details to each character on the sweep. It is claimed by promoters of the laser-beam typesetter that characters are sharper than in CRT systems owing to the coherent character of light that allows for precise focusing to a very fine writing spot; the laser beam is also more power efficient. The size of the "writing" spot in digital typesetters is around 1 mil (0.001 inch) with a few tenths of a mil above and below in different makes.

The top speed of contemporary digital typesetters is given as up to 4000 lines per minute or 24 inches per minute (see Monotype Corporation, Ltd. in References) or up to 15,000 characters per second (Bigelow and Day 1983). The speed of laser-beam typesetters is independent of column or page width because it is scanned in one stroke all across the measure. Today's devices handle line widths up to 108 picas.

If we look closer at a laser-scan typesetter we may identify several stages in the production cycle.

1. Input to the typesetter may be online from a front-end system, or offline from magnetic tape, a floppy disk or a paper tape. Input includes text in galley form plus formatting commands defining the page format.
2. Typesetting commands received are used to compose a page, which involves preparing a list of positions and characters which are subsequently sorted, thereby generating a page on a disk.
3. Digitized font information is obtained from the font disk—either a floppy or rigid disk of varying capacity—on the basis of the sorted composed text.
4. Modulation signals to drive the laser are generated as determined in the previous steps.
5. The laser beam writes on the photographic material as directed.

At the heart of digital typesetting is the power of a computer, without which some capabilities would not be feasible at all (such as graphics, full-page composition, etc.) and the speed of modern digital typesetters would not be possible to attain. Computers employed are mini- and microcomputers even though text editing may be supplied from a mainframe as well. Computers perform the overall control, support text editing in the front-end and tend the composition programs; special software makes input from remote front-ends possible. Hyphenation and justification may be performed in the typesetter if it has not already been done. Text-editing and composition software may be incorporated in the typesetter as well, thus making it a direct-input typesetter. Computers must accommodate software to handle fonts on disks in either bit-map format or in outline (or both of them combined), provide for conversion between formats if necessary and fetch characters as needed with possible "look-ahead" through text or under operator's control. Graphics require special software in addition to enhanced processing capability and extensive storage. An important computer-control function in a laser typesetter is modulation of the laser beam as it sweeps across the entire width of the photosensitive material. The functions outlined above are an indication of the multitude of different tasks computers may be asked to perform in typesetting and these will vary with different makes and models. Micros and minis serving in these applications are mostly 16-bit machines (rarely 8 bit) with from 32-kbyte up to 1-Mbyte main memory often available as options in increments, sometimes with addition of an array of dedicated processors as in handling graphics. The size of random access memory (RAM) required for handling a job of this variety and magnitude maybe up to 2.5 Mbytes.

Modern digital typesetters receive output material in rolls up to 400 feet long supplied in cassettes and deliver output pages onto take-up cassettes of the same or smaller capacity. Output material may be typically panchromatic lithographic film, stabilization paper, rapid access film and resin coated paper, with positive or negative image and reverse or right reading.

Typesetting devices can handle a wide variety of point sizes from 4 to 256 (even over 400), which in some devices have to be stored in more than one master size to cover the point-size range of a given model. Output resolution may be the same in both directions or higher vertically and lower in the horizontal direction: resolution of 1000 line per inch is considered good, but may reach over 3000 or even exceed 5000 if required. Type may be sized up or down in fine increments of 1/30 point to 1 point and may be expanded or condensed in either percentage (e.g., 25%-250%) or in increments expressed in point fractions. Fonts are delivered on floppy disks and may be stored on floppy disks or, preferably, on fixed or removable rigid disks of 10-300-Mbyte capacity capable of storing hundreds, even several thousand fonts. Typically, there would be 128 characters per face; before some or all characters in typefonts required by a job are available, they must be loaded into the RAM memory either by operator intervention from a keyboard or by commands imbedded in the text.

Some typesetters of this category can rotate characters, lines or entire pages and set reverse type.

4.2.8 Typesetting and Printing: Where Do They Belong?

Lately, this question has been posed in the business areas concerned, the reason being the emerging new technologies and the consequent shifts in the economies. The questions raised may be: "Does typesetting better fit in the editor's realm (that is, the publisher's) or is it better placed in the printer's shop?" (Soon typesetting could be moving into the realm of authors.) To better understand the issue, it is necessary to view it in the historical perspective because typesetting, unlike other functions in publishing (e.g., photocopying) or in the office (e.g., communications), has a long-standing tradition. In a medieval monastery the typesetting and printing functions were, of course, performed under one roof and they were united with the publishing authority of the monastery; because a great deal of authoring also took place within the same walls, these institutions exercised an important influence on contemporary publishing activities.

Later the typesetting and printing functions divorced themselves from publishers. Undoubtedly, both sides were content with things as they were and publishers were not equipped to deal with the involved technology of typesetting as it then stood. The division of labor left the white collar functions with the publisher, whereas the printer took care of typesetting and printing as a subcontractor; there were only a few exceptions to this rule, one of them being newspaper publishing where delays inherent in the editing/typesetting dichotomy were plainly intolerable.

To be sure, the delays involved in the communication of author-editor-typesetter-and-back were always felt to be cumbersome, but they have been coming under scrutiny only with the appearance of the VDT screen-based technology, which holds a potential for the user/author to be able to supply a machinable copy to the editor who, in his turn, possibly through a technical editor or an editorial assistant, could provide a printable matrix. The net result of this development would be reduced production time and some cost saving. Placing the typesetting function at the finger tips of the editorial staff and thereby under the publisher's control poses yet another question, namely, the fate of the print shop. It appears that printers can survive all this if they can do what is expected from them, on a cost-competitive basis: as a result of the shake-up in the prepress area, they will be required to deal with a variety of typeset outputs coming from a wide spectrum of hardware and to produce a wide variety of print matter on an assortment of paper in a cost-efficient manner. It would appear that the print shop will survive in performing major print runs, which would be uneconomical to print in an office or on a small publisher's premises, but that the new technology will create conditions where it will be increasingly difficult to compete. How far towards the user typesetting will move depends on the user friendliness of the procedures involved.

The possibility of providing on our campuses editorial services as well as typesetting and printing, along with authors working within the same community, creates in a way a semblance of the medieval monasteries.

The copious abundance of all kinds of both prepress hardware and printing/duplicating technology presents the challenge of multiple options where only an adequate systems analysis can make the difference between a sensible use or abuse of the new opportunities.

In Figure 11 a denotes the integration of all essential functions under one roof; b depicts the separation of typesetting/printing from the publisher; c reflects the present perceptible trend to move composition closer to intellectual creation; d represents one option made possible, especially for short-run publications, by some less expensive copiers, laser printers, and ink-jet printers; e shows universities as organizational units comprising in some instances all essential elements of publishing.

Typesetting as an Office Procedure. Until recently, typesetting was considered irrelevant to the office environment. This can be explained by the high cost of equipment as well as the high level of skill required to

PRINT-BASED ELECTRONIC PUBLISHING 137

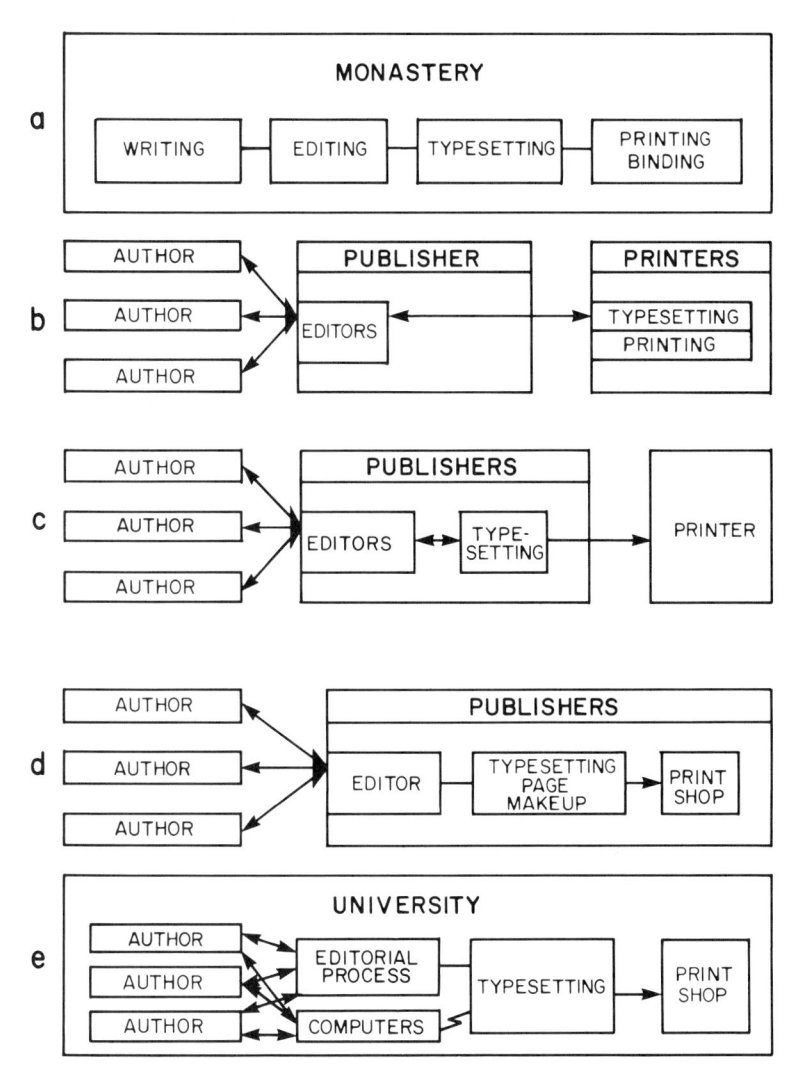

FIGURE 11 Authors, publishers, editors, typesetters, and printers.

become a productive operator of such an equipment. Lately, the cost of hardware has dropped within the reach of larger corporations where usage warrants the cost and the amount of training needed to acquire basic skills to operate a front-end unit has decreased to around 4 hours. In addition to these main factors, there are other incentives which can increase the motivation of an office manager to start looking at typesetting and its benefits: recently introduced phototypesetting processors which are easy to maintain and operate and a wide range of supplies such as paper, films and chemicals.

Typesetting, as applied to documents in an office environment, confers the advantages of a better general appearance, when required by the character of a document, and an improved readability because of the availability of different typefaces. Also, characters can be set in different sizes; often highlighting is possible through the use of boldface types, italics, bold italics, underscore, serif and sans serif. Characters may be set at different angles both ways. Proportional spacing, ligatures and kerning cut down on the volume of text; in our project at the University of Calgary, we achieved one-third saving by having our journal typeset but savings of up to one half of print volume are possible.

The relevance of typesetting in the office environment has been on the increase with the spread of microcomputers and with the progressing convergence of the automated office and electronic publishing; wide implementation of local area networks and the desktop electronic printer/typesetter working in tandem with a microcomputer will accelerate this trend.

4.3 Complete Prepress Systems

In Section 3 we use an approach different from that taken in Sections 1 and 2. Here we single out five types of more or less complete systems by which present trends in prepress may be illustrated: the pervasive role of computers leading to the automation of many functions previously performed by humans, the change in skills humans must possess to operate this new technology, the streamlining of individual functions with simultaneous miniaturization of space requirements for some functions, integration of text and graphics, and further opportunities for process color in the new enhanced systems. Other trends involve automated page makeup, increased acceptance of "soft" proof, plain-paper proofs of both black and white and color for fast and lower-cost approval. In-plant technical documentation systems are included to stress their importance as the primary catalysts of progress in this area by virtue of the bourgeoning activity in response to the need for more effective ways of providing new products and services of growing sophistication with up-to-date high-quality documentation. The role of microcomputers in this fast-developing field has also been recognized by treating them under a separate heading.

4.3.1 Originator to Paper

The title of this publishing mode implies inclusion of the production steps required to arrive from the incipient stage of text entry to a final copy on paper. This state of the art has been reached with certain qualifications: (1) the print copies are monochrome (even though quality color illustrations are presently in an advanced stage of development), (2) the quality of graphics merged with text is not yet fully satisfactory, (3) cost efficiency must be carefully considered. The output from this system is directly on paper with no intermediate steps with possible savings on labor and material. The typographic quality does not suit all publications, especially as regards resolution.

In this category, we may identify at least two groups of systems, both of which are computer-driven.

1. Smaller in-house or office systems, possibly desktop size, where the final paper output can serve as the final print in limited-size runs, a master for photocopying or a paper master for preparation of plates.
2. A total system of a higher performance capable eventually of combining text and halftone graphics in color; this setup would be very suitable for on-demand publishing by providing short-run presses even in distributed units. They will be able to deliver the final product to the ultimate users, tailored to their specifications, and will possibly revolve around some nonimpact print technology such as electrostatic, electrophotographic or ink-jet, etc.

Group 1. As a prototype of the group 1 systems, we may examine in some detail Xerox's 8010 Information System as a pioneer system in this category. The Xerox 8010 Information System is essentially a desktop workstation combining a word processor with a phototypesetter complemented with central storage; a laser printer serves as the master-maker or to meet the need for small print runs. For more on microcomputer-based systems enabling the originator to render a final product, see Section 4.3.5.

Among the areas of general application are office automation, especially on a local area network, along with other devices, and electronic publishing. Word processing is too narrow a concept to accommodate this setup.

The existing display systems are based on the character-coded principle whereby characters are keyed as ASCII codes and are converted on the screen into a matrix of dots (the number of dots per character varies from system to system and determines the resolution of the resulting character), which comprises typically 40, 80 or 132 characters in up to 24 rows; this conversion is performed during the refresh cycle without any need for programming and any CPU involvement. The bit-map technology referred to at different locations in this volume, on the contrary, is based on the storage of an exact character image in the memory and its movement to any desired location on the display screen. Therefore, with "soft" keys available, we can store an amount of characters which is limited only by the storage capacity; in some systems one can even create one's own characters. In order to be able to move any image from the storage to any place on the screen, each pixel on the screen must be represented in the memory at least by 1 bit (for black and white) or more (for halftones and colors). Obviously, the advantage of an image representation as compared with character coding is more typefaces even of a complex nature and better resolution limited only by the resolution of the screen, i.e., number of pixels. The Xerox 8010's display is image-based.

The display of the Xerox 8010 is nearly the true likeness of what will appear at the output end; in fact, it is 95% of the output size. Displays presenting true characters are called WYSIWYG in short for "What you see is what you get." This is desirable at least in some applications even though it demands more resources.

Learning how to use the system and the ease of retention are helped by the mouse, menus, consistency of commands, built-in online training module, icons, familiar office desktop environment and multiple display windows with both horizontal and vertical scroll.

The Xerox 8010 can emulate, given the optional hardware and software, some terminals and talk to some non-Xerox workstations and mainframes, in addition to the Ethernet-based equipment.

Electronic publishing applications include production of technical papers and journals, training manuals, reports of all kinds; also preparation of presentations, business proposals, technical drawings, forms, as well as graphic layouts, charts and graphs, contracts, specifications, etc.

Similar principles underlie the microcomputer systems described also in this section. A general configuration of devices grouped on a local area network is shown in Figure 12, where the central processing unit (1), the file server (2), the laser printer (3) and the communications server (interface) (4) are all linked into the local area network bus (5); a letter-quality printer is also provided (6). Information is input on the workstation (7) and the output master (8) is either duplicated (9) or an offset plate is prepared (10).

Group 2. As we mentioned above, the systems in group 2 also involve some nonimpact printer technology; they do not produce either the speed or the quality of a print shop, but their throughput is nevertheless impressive. Chapter 8 on electronic printers is a logical continuation of this topic for it outlines the potential and promise these devices hold, as such and in conjunction with complementary gadgets,

PRINT-BASED ELECTRONIC PUBLISHING 141

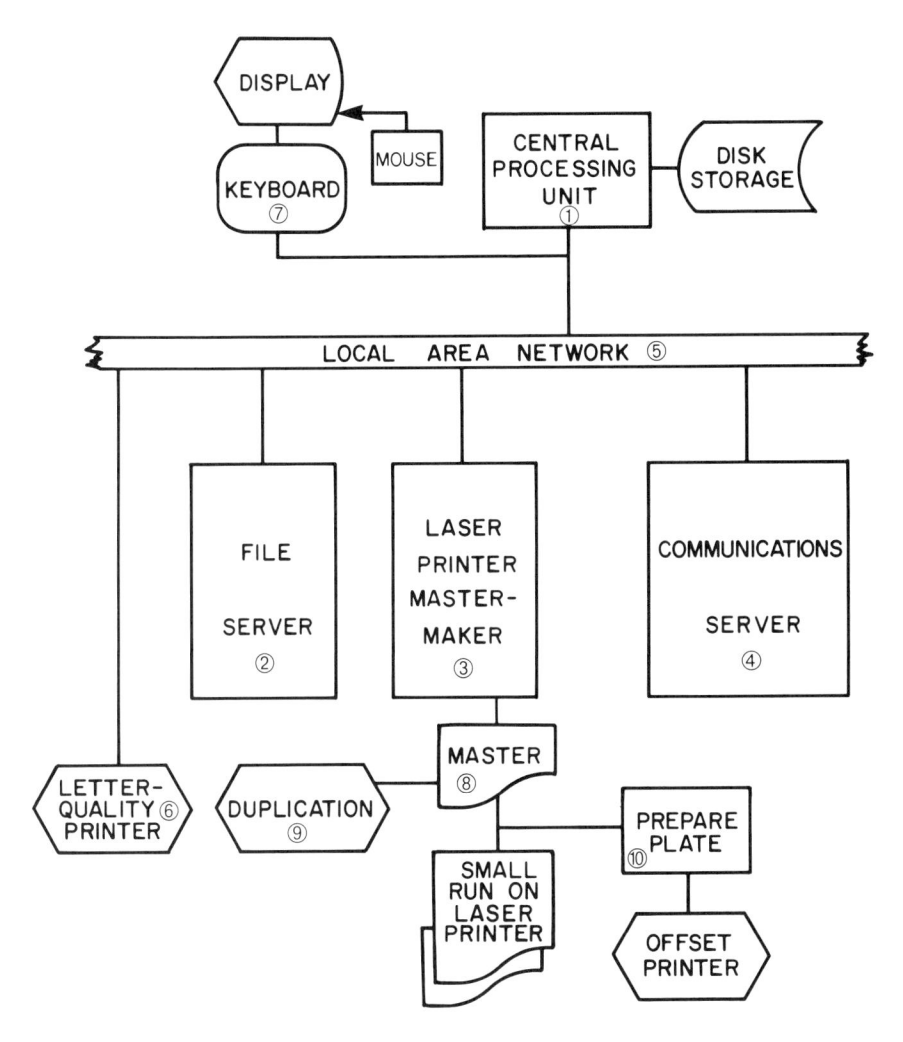

FIGURE 12 Originator-to-paper system.

to make up major subsystems and even complete publishing systems suitable for an ever-growing range of applications.

4.3.2 Originator to Film

Originator to Film (Monochrome). An example of the originator to film (monochrome) is the prepress system of Information International Inc., called NPS (for Newspaper Publishing system or TPS for technical publishing system). This is a working system capable of producing fully madeup pages composed of text, line art and halftones.

The input may occur on video terminals of the text editing and composition system (TECS) where text is entered, edited and illustrations positioned from the keyboard with an automatic text runaround. The user specifies font, point size, lead, line measure and justification mode and the system algorithms take care of the rest. A stored page guide program creates pages as the text is being captured; typographic commands appear as single symbols within the text and are displayed in a reserved area on the screen. Hyphenation is done by a large dictionary and the preferred (widely used) form of hyphenation may be ordered by the operator, thus eliminating those less appealing ones. Footnotes and tables may be defined. A special terminal may be added at this stage to display the true typeset page.

A less expensive system of text/edit terminals (Text/Net 3400) may be employed which are not equipped with the composition function. One cluster controller can support up to 16 terminals.

Another means of input is for the artwork, both line art and continuous tone, performed by the Illustration Scanner 3600; it can do sizing, cropping, screening at different grid density (65-135 lines per inch) and it can modify contrast (soft to hard, hard to soft). The original artwork is scanned and the degree of gray for each halftone dot is converted to a number corresponding to that degree of gray. The values of gray established by this digitizing process are then stored in a computer database and may be recalled from it to reproduce the original picture at a given resolution. This scanner is suitable for magazine size applications. The new 3700 Illustration Scanner is a flatbed design adapted for scanning large newspaper-size originals, equipped with a Motorola 68000 microprocessor.

Once both the text and artwork are captured in machinable form, the process of pagination can start at a Page Makeup Station (PMS) model 2025. This station encompasses a display tube, a graphics tablet with a grid, a puck which can manipulate items around the screen while being moved along the tablet; also, a proof printer has been provided at this stage. Although many pages can be made up interactively at the TECS editing system described above, the 2025 PMS station can handle even those most complex ones. Thus, the 2025 takes over many labor-intensive and highly skilled functions performed manually to date. Both text and halftone may be called up from storage, positioned, sized, electronically cut and pasted, and finalized for typesetting. One cannot manipulate pictures in prescreened format to the degree one can do continuous tone pictures in raster format. An important adjunct to the 2025 PMS station is the 2083 proof printer which produces an electrostatic printout of the page as composed on the screen, either 11 or 22 inches wide. The proof print takes 2 minutes to complete.

On the output side of the NPS system is the 570 VideoComp Typesetter, in which finished pages are automatically set, both text and graphics. Characters are set at 1000 characters per second or more, depending on the quality expected, on a continuous sheet of film, 300 or 310 mm wide, and 400 feet long. VideoComp is a CRT full-face typesetter working continuously in the page-by-page mode. Halftone exposure, contrast between tones and dot range can be specified on the typesetter which is also capable of automatically balancing the intensity of both the graphics and the text. NPS is suited both for centralized and distributed operation.

A block diagram charting a general viable layout of an originator-to-film system is depicted in Figure 13 in its monochrome variety. Figure 13 illustrates four text entry and edit workstations (1-4) all arranged on the local area network (5) and working under a cluster controller (6). A central processing unit (7) oversees a graphics input scanner (8) and passes text and graphics on to a page makeup station (9) provided with a graphics tablet (10) and mouse (11). Pages may be proofed (12), transmitted for remote output (13) or image-set locally (14) on film (15) or microform (16).

Originator to Film (Color). A general diagram of one of a number of possible arrangements is shown in Figure 14 presenting a general outline of a system in which the original (1) is color-separated electronically (2) or by conventional means (camera) (3); in this system the four separations (4) are digitized and screened (5) and sent to the page makeup station (6); text (7) in character code is converted into raster code (8) and united with images in (6). Complete pages are produced in an image setter (9) and output on film (10) ready for platemaking.

INFOCOLOR I. The production cycle from the originator to film has been a reality not only in monochrome but in color as well. As an example, the InfoColor system (Information International Inc.) used in conjunction with the NPS system may be cited. The original color picture in the form of a color film transparency is converted into four color separations in the conventional manner or by means of a color-separation scanner at a resolution range of 500-1000 dots per inch. These separations in the form of reflective prints are scanned by a readscan unit. At this point we end up with four pages as compared with one page in the black and white process and these are stored in the common database.

InfoColor I along with InfoColor II and InfoColor III has been described by Pasricha (1984).

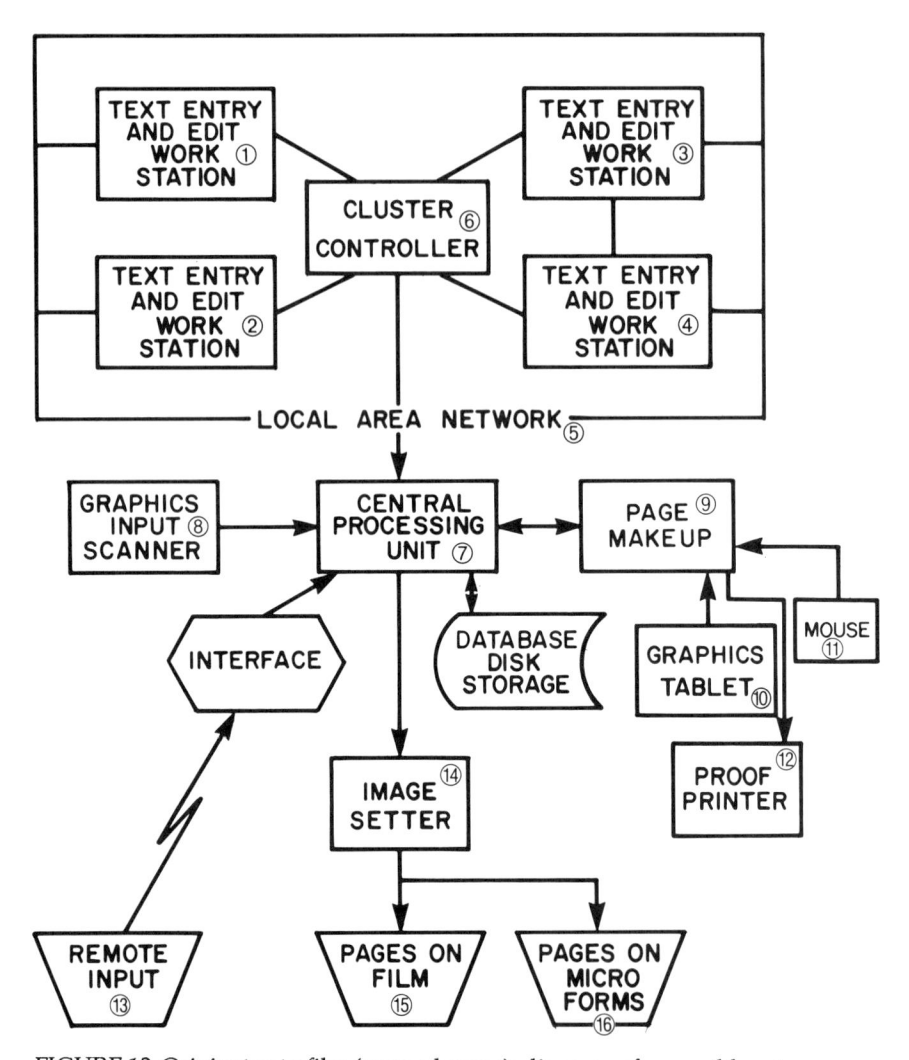

FIGURE 13 Originator to film (monochrome): diagram of a possible setup.

INFOCOLOR II. This is the higher developmental stage of InfoColor I. InfoColor II can accept input from a number of color-processing prepress systems as Hell (Chromacom), Scitex (Response 350) and Crosfield (Studio 860) or directly from a color-separation scanner. At this stage the digitized contone (digitized separations) are fed into the InfoColor Conversion Unit (ICU). It is this piece of equipment that makes InfoColor II unique: other manufacturers convert text into the raster format, merge it with continuous tone pictures in raster format and then transmit and/or manipulate both as such; they may screen

PRINT-BASED ELECTRONIC PUBLISHING 145

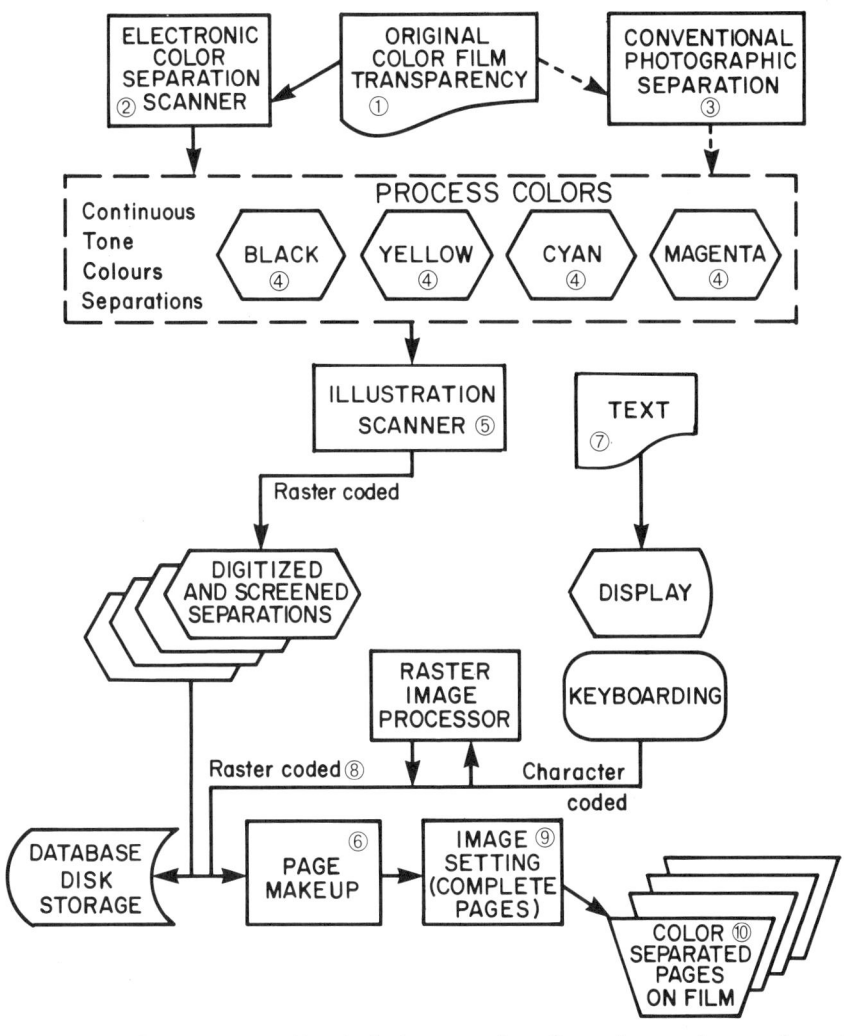

FIGURE 14 Originator to film (color): general outline of one of a number of possible arrangements.

pictures at the output stage. In contrast, ICU accepts illustrations in raster format, screens them and outputs them in a character-coded format in which one halftone cell is coded as 1 byte; each byte represents the size and shape of a halftone dot which will be recognized as such and output by the typesetter in due course. Four-color pictures require 4 bytes per halftone cell.

The point here is that both text and illustrations are stored and transmitted (if necessary) as text (character coded), where bytes represent

ASCII codes (for text) or halftone cells (their size and shape) as far as illustrations are concerned.

InfoColor II is 1984 technology. It does away with separations and the need for reflective positives. Storing and transmitting text in character coded format is more economical, but storing and transmitting illustrations as characters does not allow quite the compression one can achieve when compacting rasterized data (around 10:1); one obtains a 4:1 compression due to the fact that illustrations are stored and transmitted in the prescreened halftone format rather than rasterized contone.

INFOCOLOR III. Information International Inc. is working on a new version—InfoColor III. This new model will not store and transmit screened picture data as the previous two models did, but screening will be done only prior to typesetting on the VideoComp Pagesetter; screening will be performed in a special raster image processor (RIP). This will allow for a better data compression ratio (7:1) than with the existing models since continuous-tone data will be involved. Text will continue to be typeset as it has been, but picture data will be set in raster form which will speed up the setting process.

4.3.3 Originator to Film/Plate/Gravure Cylinder: The Complete Digital Color Systems

Systems of this class are computerized publishing systems that provide a continuous electronic path from text editing and graphics scanning to the page makeup module with text/picture merging and from there to a laser write-unit, which exposes plates, film or gravure cylinders ready for replication.

The interest in these systems has not been overwhelming but there are several successful installations: systems producing black and white pages as well as digital color graphics systems processing full color pages. A market has opened up in the newspaper field and that does not come as a surprise when one considers the mammoth scale of the newspaper business which can cost-justify acquisitions requiring capital investment of this magnitude; some innovative ideas originating in the newspaper area can benefit others in the prepress and printing industry. Color systems are also being adopted by magazines, for production of promotional literature, maps and catalogs and for packaging purposes.

The raison d'etre for these systems is higher productivity and reduced material cost which means lower production costs accompanied by higher throughput as the production cycle is shortened. It is easier to meet deadlines and management likes the greater control of the process and of the product afforded by this new equipment. Multiple proofing may be obviated. Standard quality results from computerization of the variable human skill used formerly. Timeliness of publications is improved. Better planning of resources is also possible owing to estimates being made easier; also, several alternatives can be prepared and assessed. Labor-intensive procedures are substituted by capital-intensive ones. Multi-edition publications can use the same page layout. Any application requires a thorough preliminary study into economic viability.

This technology is new but well established with several major prepress equipment suppliers (among them Scitex, Crosfield, Autologic, Hell and Information International Inc.) on the market.

Although not yet perfect the digital color graphics systems are one of the most impressive developments in the entire prepress area. They have similar capabilities but they do differ in several aspects. One of them is how they approach the problem of text entry. Text may be scanned into the system or, preferably, it may be supplied from a text processing front-end. Another line of division is the data format (i.e., text and graphics, jointly or separately) employed in processing:

1. Text may be rasterized and processed along with graphics.
2. Graphics may be converted into what amounts to be character-coded data (representing halftone dots expressed as ASCII characters) to be processed as such along with the text.
3. Text and graphics may be processed in different formats.

Other distinguishing characteristics are the point at which picture data is screened (at input or output stage); how it is compressed, stored, transmitted and manipulated; the human-machine interface, as in all computerized systems, bears on users' satisfaction and product acceptance and receives an ever-increasing attention. Digital color graphics systems may be programmed for different combinations of press, paper and ink and results of changes may be checked immediately on a display which is very time- and cost-effective. If we divide the functions of a digital color prepress system into input, processing and output, multiple overlapping operation may be accomplished on the more sophisticated systems where high productivity is essential. Considerable economy arises from the fact that pictures may be reused any number of times. Transmission of full-color pictures is viable via satellite links, but with a high degree of data compression, it is even possible to send data over voice-grade lines which will make it a matter of minutes rather than seconds. Transmission of color pictures is required from a place of data capture (e.g., scanning a slide) to the editorial office or full pages may be sent to remote printing sites.

"Direct to plate" means a competitive edge translating in many production situations not only into savings on labor by elimination of pasteup, stripping, camera, etc. (by use of expensive equipment which will entail high purchase cost, high depreciation rate, high maintenance cost, high cost of training, high hourly rate where applicable, etc.), but also into extended deadlines important particularly in newspapers and newsmagazines as well as the possibility of meeting deadlines and specifications in rush jobs that it would otherwise be impossible to accept. Nevertheless, the alternative of going to plate through the film stage still offers, and likely will continue to offer for some time to come, a few advantages. These advantages will be eliminated only with further advancements in technology: less expensive and more compact magnetic or optical storage which will meet the taxing demands of electronic color processing, improved platemaking procedures to shorten the time required to burn a plate or unification of the platemaking job with the printing function under one roof are some of them in addition to lower cost. Gaffin (1985) uses the example of the color scanner in his argument that electronics provide the most valuable services if they combine the advantages of computerization with film's storage capabilities: in support of his argument he goes on to state that a single set of separations, while costing less than $100, would occupy a major portion of a multi-megabyte disk pack worth $1000; also (1) data needs to be online each time additional plate is burned; (2) when multiple plates are required for long print runs, each plate will take the same amount of time to make; (3) complications might arise in case extra plates are needed in the print shop if the printer does not have control over the platemaking process including separations.

New relationships arise between computers, platemakers and printers when newspapers (and possibly other publishing ventures) use satellite transmission of their newspapers from computer to film or computer to plate. *The Wall Street Journal* has been using the computer-to-film mode for 9 years and now 7 of its 17 plants go directly from computer to plate making use of satellite communications; the *New York Times* has ordered 22 Datrax 765 laser platemaking and facsimile transmission systems for the same purpose (Bruno 1985). The new factor in this scenario is efficient communications of transmitted information: the totally digital character of these systems presents a strong impetus to go electronic all the way.

A large, hypothetical, digital color prepress system (see Figure 15) might work as outlined below. Obviously this large configuration could exist at several progressively smaller sizes to suit different budgets and to meet particular needs. Also, identical objectives may be accomplished by various means; the underlying philosophies keep

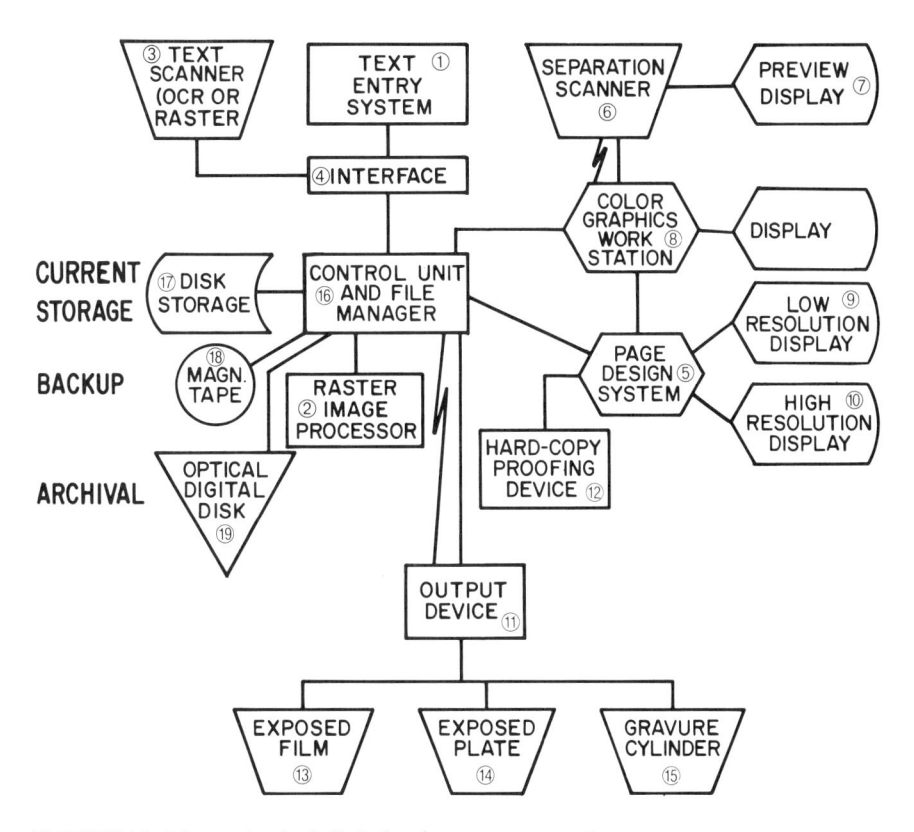

FIGURE 15 A hypothetical digital color prepress system.

changing as this relatively new technology matures and clients' needs become more articulated, while they in turn, get a better grasp of the new opportunities. Understandably, each vendor defends its own approach and because the technology is too complex for the uninitiated to debate it on a theoretical ground, the best strategy for a prospective user is to adopt the "show me" stance. Although the technology is still in the process of early solidification, viable products are successfully working in full production.

Text may be fed into the system from a text entry device (1) such as a front-end, dedicated word processor or microcomputer, either locally or from a remote location through a suitable interface (4); text received in character-coded format is translated into raster format in a raster image processor resident inside the system (2). But text might be also scanned in and chunks of it may be treated as images (3). Alternatively, text may be generated on the system's workstation (such as captions) and handled in raster format, or ideally, it may be fully composed in the character format on the system itself. This would be simpler than to shuffle it back and forth between the text system and the page-planning (5) workstation if this is at all possible.

Color illustrations may be acquired into the system through a color-separation scanner (6) producing four process-color pictures (cyan, yellow, magenta and black); the configuration might be furnished with a preview screen (7), some storage, and manipulation capability (8) and transmission ports.

Both text and color pictures may be input remotely and transmitted over a distance using modern communications technology and advanced methods of data compression allowing compaction on the order of 1:10 all the way to around 1:80; this reduction of the transmitted volume of data makes it possible to use even dial-up voice-grade lines if necessary and if the time delay and cost are tolerable. The amount of storage required in handling color is one of the restrictions imposed on use of micros in this area at present. The amount of bits and bytes needed to represent a picture depends on its size, on the resolution, on whether black and white or color, and if color, how many component colors. With a resolution of 300 dots per inch 90,000 pixels (pels) are generated per one square inch and approximately 9 Mbits per one A4 page (8.5 × 11 inches) in black and white; if 256 variations of color or as many levels of gray are desired per 1 pixel then we have to multiply by 8 (1 byte per picture element), which leaves us with 72 Mbits per page or 9 Mbytes. In fact, on a screen 1 pixel may be represented by a triplet configured of 3 pixels: 1 pel each of red, green and blue; if each of them has 8 bits this amounts to 24 bits or over 16 million different colors per triplet. This is more than human eye could ever be able to descry. Digitized color pages with four process-colors take four to eight times more storage space than black and white pages, in other words 36 Mbytes and up. Taking the systems information into account, a 300-Mbyte disk could accommodate anywhere between three and eight color pictures, or more if pages contain also text and data compression is applied. Of course this calculation may serve only as an example, and it is liable to collapse as would a house of cards when we change the parameters: if we for instance increase the resolution from the low definition of 300 line per inch to a typographic quality resolution of 900 lines per inch, the storage requirement will rise by a factor of nine; if on the other hand, we compress data at a 1:10 ratio, we put it back close to the original value and similar fluctuations will be obtained by changing other parameters. In transmitting pages we depend heavily on yet another variable, namely, the transmission rate: considering the above-defined example of a color page of 36

Mbytes, compressing it to 3.6 Mbytes (28.8 Mbits) and transmitting it at 1.544 Mbits per second, which requires the capacity of a T1 carrier (a standard offering of the Bell System and satellite companies), we find that we need around 19 seconds to send a page under these simplified conditions. The economy of transmitting character-coded data in lieu of raster data has been mentioned earlier in Chapter 2.

The input image may be further enhanced in a color graphics workstation (8)(see next paragraph), whereupon it can be stored for further disposition by the page-planning (design) station (5). The page-design station may serve as a complete page makeup station arranging type and illustrations in an electronic manner with elimination of any manual pasteup; the page-design station may work with true fonts and true colors or it may only lay out the page possibly in black and white and pass it to the color graphics workstation (8) for final processing before the page is output (11). The page-design station ought to be equipped with a high- and/or low-resolution (9, 10) display, either black and white or color, to furnish a soft proof; similarly, hard-copy proofs (12) should be available in color if possible to assist in the final approval before a page is sent to one of output devices. In the case of a remote input or output, data compression and decompression units are fitted into the system as appropriate. Depending on how the text aspect is handled, the page-design station may be assisted by a raster image processor and fitted with a considerable amount of storage to hold page components, output-ready pages and pages to be kept ready for reuse. Assembled pages may be output to a laser-imaging film exposure unit (13) to produce electronically screened halftone films as required for offset plates or continuous tone films as suitable for gravure purposes. Plates may be also directly exposed (14). Gravure cylinders (15) may be prepared by direct electronic engraving methods but may also be obtained by chemical etching with help of contone films. The control unit and file manager (16), assisted by varied storage devices as appropriate (17-19), provide the focal point of the entire configuration.

Color Graphics Workstations. These stations are essential parts of digital color prepress systems and are the consoles at which most of the human-machine interaction in the design of color pictures takes place; the way they are designed, therefore, will determine the relative degree of ease or difficulty experienced by operators using them and also the amount of training needed to master these devices. The length of time and cost of training may have been underestimated in some cases. To traditional graphic artists, the tools were transparent while the artists worked to realize their vision; the computer graphic artists have an enormous amount of machinery interposed between their vision and the creation. If this complex tool is not made similarly transparent, then many achievements in graphic arts accumulated through hundreds of years might be jeopardized for the sake of illusory expediency.

Being subsystems in larger configurations implies compatibility with input devices, such as scanners, and possibly with front-end systems if text processing is envisaged on the system, and with the rest of the system. The design phase is followed up by the production stage and graphics data created totally or partly on this console are then output on film or plate or may drive engraving devices to produce gravure cylinders. Workstations work either in batch mode or preferably in interactive mode, and display may be monochrome, or mostly and preferably, in color, either in low or high resolution.

Capabilities. Color-imaging stations employ color monitors which display the images as they are called in from computer storage, typically from a 300- to 480-MByte disk drive. The operators then use various tools at their disposal to manipulate the picture or multiple pictures to achieve their goal. They call up pictures by assigned names or numbers or pictures may be presented as miniatures for easy reference. Typical manipulations include sizing, moving and duplicating pictures, framing (creating borders), rotation, cropping, creating geometric shapes and freehand drawing. Color may be adjusted over the entire area or locally and airbrushing may be applied even at the pixel level. Retouching is possible and some details may be moved in or left out. Overlays and underlays are usually feasible when handling multiple pictures. Operators can at will keep the original picture, duplicate it or decide on replacing it if the assembled page meets with their approval. Geometric shapes may be generated in a manner similar to alphageometric videotex systems; e.g., a line is defined by two points, rectangular shapes are formed by specifying two extreme points of the diagonal, a circle is made up by inputting its radius coordinates or an ellipse is created when both of its axes are defined. Lately, while text-processing systems struggle to acquire at least some graphics-processing capabilities, the suppliers of image workstations suppliers are increasingly interested in adding composition features to their products.

Tools. The operator of a color-imaging station, in order to realize the above capabilities, has at his disposal the following standard tools: a color monitor, a monochrome monitor with a keyboard, a digitizing tablet with an electronic stylus and a cross-line cursor, a keypad with function keys, a trackball to position pictures and a mouse, paddles, joystick, etc., to control the screen cursor.

In the IMAGER console by Scitex for instance, there are seven high-speed microcomputers dedicated to image data processing. Multilayered memory allows for simultaneous display and independent processing of several pictures at once. At any time this color monitor can display any ink layer of the entire palette of colors of printing ink: each ink individually, any combination of them or the complete four-color ink picture, at a resolution of 512 × 512 pels in interlaced raster mode. The console displays either process color for contone pictures or line art with up to 256 adjustable sets of color values as tints. At their discretion operators may create, store and use grids, which do not show in print.

The monochrome monitor indicates which key labels are currently in effect and brings up system messages and function status. The keyboard enters alphanumeric data and can serve to communicate with a front-end text system and make up text/graphics pages using the Texta typesetter. The digitizing tablet can be applied to drawing and airbrushing as the operator moves the stylus (or cursor) across the tablet. The trackball helps the operator to position a picture and a dial controls the image's angle and may be used to zoom anywhere on the page. The keypad has 13 keys representing various operational functions. The operator can assign different functions to these keys and read their new meaning on the monochrome monitor.

Vista Plus Response-300 Electronic Page Design and Page Makeup. The Vista system (by Scitex) is an example of a digital color system which is being successfully integrated with a number of different makes of front-end text-processing systems. This makes Vista an electronic page design and page makeup system; graphics, either photos or line art, may be input through a scanner either in low resolution for page layout or at high resolution for color manipulation. Both black and white and color graphics can be handled. As far as text is concerned, Vista interfaces with several front-end makes and stores text and graphics separately while being able to display them alongside each other; Vista can communicate with front-ends, e.g., it sends along a layout specification and then displays the text received from the front-end.

The page designer works on the Vista's console and can perform basically all functions that were accomplished manually on conventional systems. Pictures are stored on the system and may be used any number of times without the operator having to create them each time they are needed. Graphics may be generated on the screen. Picture windows of all geometric shapes may be prepared and, under the operator's control, pictures may be magnified, positioned, rotated and rough-cropped. Text is displayed in the typeface, point size and color in which it will be finally output. Text and graphics are copyfitted in an interactive manner as required. The approval process is expedited by the possibility of obtaining proofs anytime during the design stage.

The Production Stage. The Scitex Response-300 system is the production system that takes over where the page design and page makeup of the Vista system have been left off. There, the rough mask provided on Vista is replaced with fine cropping and electronic airbrushing and color balancing is done. The output from a Response-300 system may be:

1. Film to be further processed for offset or gravure printing
2. Lithographic plates, or commands to drive an engraving machine to produce a gravure cylinder

The color-imaging station IMAGER is described above under the subsection "Color Graphics Workstations."

Business Graphics Systems. Also falling under the category of computer-manipulated graphics are images generated with the objective of enhancing communication in the business world; despite this orientation, which does not have the word "publishing" in it, it is self-evident in the context of the present volume that business graphics bear heavily on a number of systems described in it, especially in conjunction with microcomputer- and minicomputer-based workstations.

Computer graphics systems may offer other end products (Fiteni 1986) as well: (1) video output is possible whereby artists' creations are transferred to videotape in a studio using videotape sychronization devices, and merged with voice, data, photographs, slides, graphics and film clips into a complex, new kind of an information/publishing product; (2) a graphics output film recorder can be employed to convert computer-generated images of a 512 × 512 resolution into photographic quality slides with 2000 or 4000 lines per inch; (3) a color plotter can produce a color image of lower resolution and with a limited range of colors.

4.3.4 In-plant Technical Documentation Systems

The Case of Technical Publishing. The volume of technical documentation has been growing steadily in the past decades commensurate with the expansion of technological innovation. Technical publications have lately become a major driving force behind the progress in prepress technology much the same as newspapers and color magazines were in the 1960s and 1970s. The amount of human effort expended in this endeavor can easily be estimated from the volume of publishing and cost per page in this area alone: Krummel (1984) puts the production volume at 500,000 pages per minute and the typical cost per page of a document at $400, not including original writing and final printing.

There have been systems in existence for some time that handle text satisfactorily and other systems that handle continuous tone and halftone, while computer aided design (CAD) has evolved in parallel in recent years to serve the needs of architects, cartographers, mechanical and electronics engineers, plant designers and others. Lately, however, hardware manufacturers have emerged with the necessary software to automate the preparation of technical documentation such as maps, maintenance and repair manuals, user guides, assembly instructions, training manuals, technical reports, etc., bringing together both text and graphics in a streamlined operation.

The benefits of modern electronic in-plant publishing accrue from lower cost per page owing to the reduced labor component and lower skill level required to perform some functions. The competitive position of companies that can offer timely, precise and attractive documentation along with product delivery may improve. Xyvision estimates that its customers decreased production times by as much as 68% and production cost per page by 30%-50% (Davis 1986): but as Higginson, the president of Caddex, points out, systems that concentrate on typographic and production problems of in-house publishing help the efficiency of the entire technical documentation only to a slight degree because production constitutes a mere 10% of the total documentation cost. Obviously a good technical documentation system must address other aspects, such as those of document generation, system management and support (Davis 1986).

Specific Traits of Technical Publications Systems. A modern electronic publishing system to tackle technical documentation is expected to have the facilities to:

Enter and edit text

Prepare line illustrations in vector format on a digitizing tablet or on a screen as part of a workstation

Capture original drawings via a scanner in raster format and transform them to the vector format, if need be, for efficient storage, processing and transmission

Convert vector-coded data to raster format data in a vector-to-raster converter for display or setting if required

Compose a page and merge the text and graphics either generated on the system or read in from an original or received from other CAD systems

Preview pages on screen as "soft-proof" and/or provide a proof from a hardcopy

- Deliver a suitable output to a typesetter, laser printer, pen plotter, electrostatic plotter, dot matrix printer, etc.
- Integrate continuous-tone photography scanned into the system as halftone inasmuch as a good publication must be able to include photographic illustrations along with line art
- Display pages at resolutions up to between 3 and 4 million pels
- Be easy to learn so a number of specialized workers (editors, authors, layout designers, artists, draftsmen, administrators, etc.) all can perform their particular tasks utilizing the common user interface with each drawing on the resources specific to their task and utilizing a subset of the total interface

In this study, we have been discussing prepress systems in which the typesetter/imagesetter is "driven" electronically and more particularly, digitally. In looking at the logic of development in prepress, we may expect that this digital control will extend one stage farther, and that presses of the future will be driven digitally as well. In dealing with special traits of technical publishing systems (in-house, corporate, in-plant), we must stress that it is in the technical publishing field where a start of this trend may be discerned, whereas similar development in commercial publishing is still a matter for electronic prophets to contemplate: for example, the IBM 3800 printer or the Xerox 9700 now take on printing jobs in corporate environments where rigid typographic standards do not apply.

A distinctive feature of all technical publications is the need to update them and any such system must make it easy for the user.

In treating technical publications or, more properly, in-house publishing, a mistake that authors make quite often is to treat the subject as a monolithic topic. At the same time they do not clearly define the differences that separate in-house publishing from the rest of the paper-based (print-based) industry. These distinctions have very practical implications for hardware design, software engineering and system integration because the parameters involved may be quite different.

Sargent (1986) differentiates three categories, the first two of which fall into the in-house classification: (1) word and desktop publishing, (2) office and technical publishing and (3) computer-integrated publishing.

1. Word and desktop publishing deals with short documents (1-10 pages) produced by an individual (inclusive of graphics); revisions are not a major issue, database management is simple. Composition is not demanding. Output is on laserprinter with 300 lines per inch resolution.

2. Office and technical publication produces longer documents mostly with line art; it involves cooperation of more individuals. Revision control is more complex. Output is mostly on laser printers even though typeset output may be required at times when the final appearance really matters.
3. Computer-integrated publishing is a complex production process which embraces a number of publishing professionals delivering documents typically 50-250 pages long of typeset quality with line art and halftone illustrations. Although systems of class 3 produce books, newspapers, magazines and journals, they do share some applications with class 2 in production of directories, catalogs, technical documents, specifications, repair manuals, policy manuals, etc.

Dyson and Seybold (1986) view desktop publishing as preparation of typeset or near typeset documents involving desktop computers; output devices are electronic printers as well as highest-quality output devices; multiple computers and multiple users may be part of such publishing systems.

The above division of systems serves to bring forward the vagueness of terms, such as desktop, office, in-house, in-plant and technical publishing, and demonstrates the need for a definition; in-plant (technical) publishing discussed in this chapter includes a variety of products with characteristics ranging on a wide scale.

Some Features of Technical Publishing Systems. Practical implementations of electronic technical publication systems, as might be expected, manifest some divergent views.

One of the differences resides in the presence or absence of user interaction: whereas on some systems operators can make changes to pages in real time by direct interaction, on some systems they have to avail themselves of batch processes which require them to go through the whole procedure sequence again (and again) until the result meets their specifications. Batch processing may be done "in the background" which allows the user to proceed with other functions simultaneously "in the foreground."

Another difference relates to whether or not the display shows the page as it will be eventually output or only a mere approximation of the output. There are conflicting views on this subject and it all boils down to the conflict between the convenience of having it and the cost of implementing it: to store or not to store all fonts and their point sizes ready for display, for example. Screen resolution may be typically 72-100 dots per inch with some high-end products offering much higher resolutions.

Essentially, graphics may be imparted in desktop publishing by (1) paint programs that provide the operator with an electronic painting tool which creates geometric shapes and free-hand drawings on a pixel-by-pixel basis or (2) drawing programs in which objects are presented as mathematical expressions and can be output on a screen or paper in a resolution-independent manner; finally (3) graphics such as bar charts, pie charts and line graphs can be generated by computer data directly, as a graphic representation of output from business programs, such as a spreadsheet.

Another line of division between technical publishing systems is the way the user works with graphics on the system. One user may be working at a digitizing tablet or another on the screen to generate the vector data.

Another important feature that characterizes the human-machine interaction is determined by the manner in which text composition is handled. One can either embed formatting and typesetting commands or preferably generic codes in the text or one can manage them in real time on the display using more advanced features as icons, mouse, pop-up menus, etc.

Because in most organizations technical publications will be the result of cooperation between departments and a multitude of individuals possessing a variety of skills and located throughout the organization, it is imperative that the entire team be able to participate in the creative, editorial or production aspect of publishing at all stages of the document production. Some systems allow for clusters of workstations to work within a cluster controller's sphere; other systems have workstations linked into local area networks and can avail themselves of services provided by all peripherals on that network.

Some technical publishing system vendors sell their own proprietary hardware with software whereas others design software products to be run on other manufacturers' hardware.

Generic coding is common in technical publication systems. Formatting and typographic commands may be also entered from the keyboard by means of dedicated keys.

There are technical publishing systems that stake out the area of technical documentation and forms whereas other claim to be more versatile so as to be relevant to book publishing and the commercial environment as well.

With regard to input and output, some technical publishing systems accept input from front-ends, word processors, or microcomputer, mainframe and minicomputer text editors and serve in the composition and page makeup capacity, whereas other systems perform text entry and editing as well. On some systems one can do minor corrections in the text on a universal terminal, other systems require that any editing be performed on the workstation of original entry—systems of this nature must ensure that text be capable of moving both back and forward as needed. This passing of files is made possible by maintaining three separate databases (text file, graphics file and format file), as is transparent to the user on sophisticated systems.

Graphics may be created on the workstation itself by tracing or original creation or may be acquired from a personal computer which has the requisite capability; CAD/CAM systems are another possibility of how to enter line graphics. Pictures may be scanned into the system electronically and may be screened either as they enter or they may be screened on their output from the system. Once in the system they may be manipulated in their full resolution or in their low-resolution version to save processing and storage capacity. In high-end systems 32-bit microprocessors are required to handle the complex software.

Another kind of input into electronic print-based publishing systems is image input via still-video camera. Conceptually, this is not dissimilar to a photographic camera, the difference being that the image of the object captured is encoded digitally and the medium holding the image is a mini-diskette or optical disk. Video images have been recently designated as another source for news photographs as well as color prepress systems such as Crosfield, Hell and Scitex, among others (Dyson, Edwards, Seybold and Solimeno 1986). But still-camera input should especially well suit desktop publishers who base their output on electronic printers featuring 300 line per inch resolution: the still-video camera in question is Canon RC-701 using charge-coupled devices (CCD) to capture the image at 780 × 488 line per inch resolution on a 2-inch floppy disk (The Seybold Report on Publishing Systems 1986).

On the output side technical publishing systems can drive typically a laser printer to furnish a hardcopy proof or the final camera-ready master if resolution does not meet with objections as to typographic quality. Both CRT and laser typesetters are supported for the most demanding jobs. Inasmuch as the resolution of laser printers continues to improve, one may expect that they will satisfy even more rigid standards imposed on some publications and will increase their share of the market. Laser printers are furnished with powerful raster image processors and can print complete pages encompassing text, line art and halftones. In addition to laser printers, the electrostatic principle, LED-based technology and ion deposition are well entrenched in the electronic printer trade.

Technical publishing systems communicate with similar systems and peripherals online, offline (magnetic tapes of various density, length, width) or via telecommunications. With view to the growing volume and number of titles, serious consideration must be given to separation of current documents from archival materials. Archiving is usually provided on magnetic tapes, but if long-term storage is envisaged, then storing on microforms and on optical digital disk offers longer durability. Because of high published volumes, data compression is an important issue in data storage and transmission even with the appearance on the market of optical storage media and wideband communications technology.

Technical publishing systems offer features which can spare the originator, paginator and compositor alike a great deal of worry and repetitive chores: tables of contents and lists of illustrations are automatically set up and updated, footnotes are placed where they belong, all components of a publication (sections, chapters, paragraphs) including tables and figures may be automatically renumbered to correspond with changes made. Pages are automatically numbered and provided with running heads and feet. Multicolumn pages are possible, pages are automatically balanced and vertically justified, widows and orphans are eliminated during pagination. Tables in text may be composed as a result of interaction or they may be designed automatically. Hyphenation may be done at the user's discretion manually or automatically with help of a dictionary. More than one dictionary may be available for different languages and purposes; hyphenation dictionaries may be accompanied with computer logic for end-of-line decisions. Systems differ in how they tackle the ripple effect throughout the document during repagination.

Automatic kerning and ligatures are supported; intercharacter as well as interword spacing is controlled under user specification. Technical publishing systems vary in their abilities to handle foreign alphabets, mathematical and chemical symbols and pi characters.

User interface is an important feature in technical publishing systems because short training time and increased productivity are considerations influencing the purchase of a system. Software design attempts to achieve this plus a fast response time despite the huge amount of the programming code necessary to support the sophisticated text entry, composition and page makeup features. Although hardware is often the main preoccupation of corporations considering in-house publishing, this area will progressively develop in the manner of word processing and become an arena for a contest of diverse software packages. Anybody heavily investing in-house publishing can ill afford "savings" in software that may cost him heavily in increased labor cost.

Raster to Vector and Vector to Raster. Most of what has been said in this context pertains equally to other processes in the prepress phase of publishing, but coexistence of CAD with text (and continuous-tone images or contone) poses some special problems in technical publication systems. In the "ordinary" electronic publishing systems, we have to contend with the character-coded format for text, which may have to be converted to the raster format if it is to be merged and imaged along with graphics. In electronic technical documentation publishing systems however, we encounter one additional format, and as CAD-CAM people will argue, the more important and advantageous data format, namely, the vector data. The complexity of technical issues associated with this compels various competitors in the area to join their forces in tackling the problem. Instructions based on vectors are used widely to represent type fonts, bar charts, pie charts, line charts and other low- and medium-resolution business graphics.

To be sure one does not need necessarily CAD to publish technical documentation: line art could be scanned in, but inclusion of CAD allows publishers to cash in on the obvious advantages of the otherwise costly CAD systems, namely those associated with the vector data format.

In many systems pictorial information (including line art) is scanned to yield rasterized format; CAD systems, in contrast, generate vectorized data while drawing is being done on a digitizing tablet or on the screen, using keys, mouse, puck, joystick, etc. The advantages of having line art in vector form are

Efficient storage (and transmission) allowing existing archives to be vectorized for computer storage and future processing. Krummel (1983) documents the savings in storage depending on the code: an average engineering drawing requires 90 Mbits in the raster mode, 2.5 Mbits in vector code and 0.5 Mbits in element code used for further compression of the already economical vector code. Pictures in vector format can be moved, duplicated on the screen and reused any number of times as such or their parts.

Easier editing than in raster format

The disadvantage of the vector form of picture representation becomes apparent when involved graphics requiring stacks of vector instructions take away the storage advantage that simple graphics enjoy; also, in applications where the frequent recreation of graphs is called for, a raster-based system pours bits from RAM's bit-map memory into pixels on the screen under the guidance of a modestly sized program whereas graphics in vector form have to be redrawn each time using the same voluminous program.

Because one has to accommodate both formats—vector and raster—on the same system, "bridges" must be established to convert from one to the other as needed. Vector-to-raster transformation is needed whenever data in vector format (after being stored and manipulated) is directed to be displayed or set; in addition to the picture data in vector and/or raster format there may also be text in either format, or in the character-coded format, and such a situation must be handled according to what is acceptable to the output device.

As already mentioned, the raster-to-vector converter may be called for in the input stage when scanned data must be made conformable to the vector-oriented CAD portion of the system.

4.3.5 Microcomputers in Paper-based Electronic Publishing

After their entrenchment in data entry and editing, microcomputers are making their mark in other areas of paper-based electronic publishing: here we will briefly examine their place in composition, as image processors and in total publishing systems; a host of other applications will be mentioned where appropriate.

Microcomputers have matured to the point where their main memory and processing power enable them to tackle jobs previously thought unrealistic for this class of hardware, and are already perceived as a very real threat to the existing, mostly minicomputer-based prepress equipment. It is not going to be the lower cost of micros in itself but a better cost-performance showing that will influence potential buyers in their purchasing decisions. Before any real breakthrough on the markets can take place, micros must both accommodate the steady, professional user and avoid the tribulations of the occasional user as outlined elsewhere in this book (see Appendix). In this respect micros face a dilemma: either to maintain an extensive and costly distribution mechanism and after-the-sale-service or build a forgiving interface right into the system and sell it "off-the-shelf." In fact, this dilemma leaves only the second option open which would shift the cost in the triad, hardware-software + interface-customer service, from both ends to the center. This would finally remove the equally interesting and agonizing contradiction surrounding the computer business, namely, the obsession with physical parameters and by and large blatant disregard of the end user thinly veiled by piles of documentation written in arcane language, extensive training sessions and an army of consultants. Whereas this was possible with mainframes operating in corporate environments, it will not work with micros which are promoted as tools for the ultimate user and are professed to be easy to learn and operate. This need has been perceived and the ideal of a forgiving micro is being vigorously pursued.

Micros may be purchased off-the-shelf or they may be included in turnkey systems. They offer the possibility of lower cost, decentralization of computing power, multiple choice of software for the same or similar purposes and applicability for a multitude of tasks. Micros generally fit into the scheme of a multiuser environment and networks of micros are becoming common even though their functionality leaves a great deal of room for improvement. Micros presently have the potential to handle virtually all tasks in the electronic prepress with the exception of those involving the processing of sophisticated color pictures, which optimally require disk storage on the order of gigabytes rather than megabytes, processing time per instruction measured in nanoseconds rather than microseconds, main memory in megabytes instead of kilobytes and high-resolution display devices. The problems now experienced by electronic journals on mainframes with regard to management of large files would be aggravated on networked micros at the present state of the art.

Microcomputers will find their place in publishing first in organizations not now owning any "conventional" hardware and software for the purpose and will slowly blend into the mini-dominated environment; this migration will likely be slowed down by the inertia of the already installed systems and by the existing organizational infrastructure of the industry in general.

Composition. Microcomputers today offer a lucrative option in the area of composition which used to be an exclusive domain of mainframes and minicomputers. The list of features that micros can take over has been growing constantly and it is now easier to enumerate those functions they cannot perform but soon will rather than vice versa. Microcomputers have simply moved in to challenge the supremacy of the "conventional" front-ends. The problem with front-ends is that because of their high cost they are not affordable to the mass market, and because they cannot be produced on a massive scale they cannot be less expensive. Microcomputers, with their already impressive base of installations, threaten to cut into the front-ends' potential markets because the micros are presently establishing themselves in direct-input and minicomputer-based systems. Microcomputers are already becoming users' preferred data entry devices and that will be a contributive factor to making the entry device serve as a composition tool as well. In the same train of thought, microcomputers are fitting more and more into the role of an image workstation and page makeup station. The result of all this is that microcomputers, which already proved themselves useful in so many diverse everyday-life tasks, are now in the process of enhancing their versatility across the field of electronic publishing and, more particularly, the electronic prepress stage. The appeal of micros is thus increased by the possibility of using, if not physically the same device, then the same generic type of device for multiple logically related tasks, as their hardware attributes are being improved and new resourceful software continues to be engineered.

In reviewing microcomputers' composition capabilities, one cannot help but be impressed with the progress made within merely two years. Formerly, micros were thought of as the easier-to-learn and inexpensive alternative to more sophisticated and more expensive systems but this is not true any more. Micros of today represent a new breed of composition device enabling the movement of control in the composition and page makeup areas closer to the creative originator— the author, editor, artist, etc. Microcomputers in more than one application are instrumental in closing the gap between the office of the future and technical publishing. Output from micros is possible through serial and parallel ports in the direct typesetting mode online or offline from a disk; a telecommunication link to the typesetter is possible. Most software packages can drive a variety of typesetters, and output to laser printers and dot-matrix printers is quite common these days. Microcomposition software is available which converts images of text in raster format, as captured by scanning, into a text file consisting of ASCII characters so that it may be "understood" as text by any word-processing system while at the same time allowing also considerable compaction of the file (character code versus raster code). Resulting pages are output on a dot-matrix printer or on an electronic printer.

The possible applications in electronic publishing of these microcomputer-based systems may include technical reports, technical manuals and instruction and maintenance manuals all produced in-house. An important asset of this kind of relatively inexpensive equipment is its ability to store and transmit any type of text as a digitized image (any language, any script) and to process even microforms. There are clear implications for distribution of documents both within an organization and remotely, e.g., in an on-demand environment and, more specifically, in response to a literature search (also online, catalogue, etc.) or in a selective dissemination of information scheme as a result of automatically processing a submitted user's profile. There are ramifications of this technology for distant education and videoconferencing which are marginally relevant to electronic publishing. Yet another application is as high-resolution facsimile. An ideal implementation would be as one of a multitude of various subsystems tied into a local area network.

Systems of this nature may be able to perform functions that presently can be done only by much larger and more expensive hardware.

Total Publishing Systems. Microcomputers have the capabilities around which to build entire publishing systems. Gradually they moved into data entry/editing, became basis of raster image processors and laser printers and took a firm foothold in composition and

PRINT-BASED ELECTRONIC PUBLISHING 165

image manipulation. They are amenable to networking and have the potential to take on controlling functions. They have already proved themselves as being efficient in numerous administrative support roles. It comes therefore as no surprise that some vendors are working on ways how to harness all these ingredients together in complete publishing systems. This is to be viewed as a positive development from which, in the long run, everyone stands to benefit. The user will end up with a broad selection of systems, off-the-shelf hardware and software, local maintenance and lower price owing to the huge installed base and stiff competition. Small and medium software houses may flourish and so should system integrators, consultants and format conversion people. Big prepress vendors will have to reassess their respective positions; there have been indications of that already. All this may be the impetus needed to reach the critical mass capable of moving the evolution of electronic publishing several steps forward on a large scale and wide front.

MACINTOSH XL. In 1985 Apple Computer announced a publishing system whose cornerstone is the desktop microcomputer Macintosh XL with 512-kbyte main memory expandable to 1-Mbyte RAM, 10-Mbyte built-in hard disk storage, 400-kbyte floppy disk storage and 12-inch display unit; mouse, icons and pull-down menus were designed for easier use. Up to 32 Macintosh line products within 1000 feet of each other can be connected through the Apple Talk Personal Network to share resources, and work is underway to develop gateways linking Apple Talk networks among themselves as well as with Ethernet and other local area networks, mainframes, minicomputers and commercial databases. File servers can be integrated into the network to relieve computers from storage chores and to schedule jobs for the printers among other things. Another component of the system is Apple's Laser Writer, a true typesetter or rather image setter, which was designed around a powerful 12-MHz 32-bit MC68000 microprocessor with 1/2 Mbyte of ROM and 1 1/2 Mbytes of RAM. The machine has an RS-232 port so it can be driven via telephone lines by other computers to output both text and graphics on the same page at a resolution of 300 dots per inch (120 per centimeter). It does not require any special paper or chemicals and it prints also on transparencies, labels and envelopes; the replaceable toner cartridge prints up to 3000 pages. For those applications requiring graphic arts resolution, Allied Linotype has put on the market modified versions of their typesetters (Linotronic 100 and Linotronic 300) which fit into the Apple Talk network inasmuch as both Apple and Linotype have based their typesetting philosophies on the PostScript page-descriptor language, containing a comprehensive array of commands to handle line art and halftone graphics. Graphics may be created on micros themselves or they may be scanned in by means of inexpensive scanners. Configurations of devices as described above will attract a host of composition programs from a variety of sources. The above mentioned PostScript language by Adobe Systems, Inc., Palo Alto, Calif., is a high-level language which operates on a model of each page and can perform all image transformations on a wide range of output devices using the same page description. This implies that it is device independent and resolution independent so it cannot easily obsolesce owing to the progress of display and printing technology. If a front-end device produces output as PostScript page description, then a typesetter needs a corresponding PostScript interpreter which would understand description commands coming from the front-end and translate them into concrete raster data controlling the laser that "writes" pages of text and/or graphics. An interesting feature of PostScript is that, unlike some image-setting systems storing characters as bit maps and requiring a bit map for each size and style of every font, PostScript works only with character outlines which are compact descriptions of how to paint characters; Postscript is one of a number of languages operating on the same principle and vying to become recognized as standards.

Currently, the Macintosh-based publishing system is superior to other makes for several reasons: (1) graphics capabilities; (2) user-friendly interface; (3) PostScript language-oriented output to both the Laser Writer and Linotronic 100/Linotronic 300 typesetters, thus satisfying a wide range of user needs; (4) the Apple Talk network for multiple workstations, featuring simple installation and low cost.

MACINTOSH PLUS. The Macintosh Plus, released in January of 1986, has twice the memory—1 Mbyte—of its precursor Macintosh XL (512 kbytes), twice the internal floppy disk capacity (800 kbytes rather than 400) with less noisy operation and twice the speed; the ROM capacity has been doubled to 128 kbytes featuring a new file management system, (hierarchical file system HFS) and a substantially faster screen display routine (a new version of the Quick Draw); the small computer systems interface (SCSI) boosts the input and output data transfer rate to 320 kbits per second; the new keyboard contains cursor keys and an adding machine keypad.

All Apple enhancements can be incorporated in the older products. When 1-Mbit chips become a commercial reality, the Macintosh Plus will be upgraded to 4 Mbytes by inserting the chip strips on the new board.

Equally important for the publishing trade is the new Laser Writer Plus: the ROM storage has been enhanced to 1 1/2 Mbytes (the RAM storage remains at 1 1/2 Mbytes) to increase the original number of fonts (nine) by an additional 16 type fonts or to supplement the original 13 styles by additional 22.

It is still to early to speculate what Macintosh Plus will contribute to electronic publishing; this new hardware frontier will be followed by a new wave of developments in the software area made possible by these advancements. Ironically, what will eventually happen will not entirely depend on Apple.

The respectable memory will be able to be divided into even more sizable partitions. A switcher can create up to four partitions from which to run different application programs by switching among them; this is important for Macintosh because its operating system can handle one task at a time (no multitasking). Larger memory will make it possible to execute large programs faster with fewer overlays. Super-programs will undoubtedly spring up with multiple functions such as editing/composition, composition/formatting, composition/pagination, etc. The RAM cache memory will speed up input/output-oriented tasks because there will be fewer disk accesses; an ideal use for cache memory in publishing will be to set aside a portion of memory, e.g., for screen fonts. But the large memory itself will make it possible to hold more data for programs such as spreadsheets and larger hyphenation and spelling dictionaries in order that major portions of extensive text may be reformatted and rehyphenated; this will make for better line-ending decisions.

The HFS built into the 128-kbyte ROM is one of the main features of Macintosh Plus: it allows a user to build files, group them into hierarchical levels, create any number of levels and easily move between levels, partitions and even disks. The utility for a publisher of this file management system is evident in view of the multiplicity of authors, editors, reviewers, works being planned, processed and distributed, etc.

Foremost among the criteria by which to judge suitability of less expensive microcomputer publishing systems for full-fledged applications in publishing ranks the quality of text composition and page makeup software; the other valuable ingredients of a superior publishing system are present already: merging text and graphics, availability of high-quality fonts, ability to output both to technical-publication quality laser printers as well as to top-quality image setters, a WYSIWYG interactive display workstation, an efficient page-description language, local area network to accommodate the need for multiple devices, creation of line graphics and scanning of contone or halftone graphics.

Text composition programs are being developed for both Apple and IBM microcomputers. "MacWrite" is standard on the Macintosh but it is only a word-processing program that justifies but does not know how to hyphenate. "Microsoft Word" is another such program that can produce two columns of text with footnotes, up to four documents on the screen available for "cut and paste" and also with no hyphenation available at present.

Graphics generated by "MacDraw" are resolution independent and are easily handled by the PostScript language. "MacPaint", in contrast, creates graphics in bit-map form but is accommodated as well. "Page Maker" (from Aldus Corporation) is an electronic page makeup system that can build pages from text prepared by MacWrite or Microsoft Word and graphics generated by either MacDraw or MacPaint. A page is selected and individual components of the page are positioned with a mouse whereby text flows into designed columns or Page Maker will make the line decisions. Graphics may be superimposed on text or vice versa if desired. "MacPublisher" (by Micro Cosmos) is less expensive and is not designed to meet high expectations for graphic arts. It allows both editing and page makeup, and it enables copy to be fitted within a layout. "Typographer" is yet another potential competitor to the Page Maker. It supports PostScript while composing interactively. "Ready Set Go" is still another composition software to vie for Macintosh applications.

There is absolutely no doubt that the above word processing/composition/graphics/layout/pagination programs will mature and new ones will be added, one hopes, in a modular way and mutually compatible not only within one manufacturer's hardware but across the entire micro world.

One does not even have to own a micro-based publishing system in order to exploit the advantages of such devices. One can either rent a set or one can avail oneself of self-service units on the "pay-as-you-go" principle: an Apple Macintosh computer combined with a coin- or bill-collecting mechanism is marketed as Coin Mac by Golden Rule Inc., Chicago; this system is powered all day so the input is not lost when the user's paid-for time runs out and, unlike some coin operated systems of the past, it features concise, user-friendly instructions (American Printer 1986).

LASER WRITER PLUS. The Laser Writer Plus has 1 1/2 Mbyte ROM and 1 1/2 Mbyte RAM memory. The Laser Writer was equipped with nine type font masters: Times Roman, italic, bold, bold italic; Helvetica, Helvetica bold, Courier, Courier bold and symbol font. With italic versions (obliqued) of Helvetica and Courier, this makes 13 type styles. The Laser Writer Plus contains 16 more fonts in addition to the above: International Typeface Corporation (ITC) Avant Garde Book, ITC Avant Garde Book Demi, ITC Bookman light, light italic, Demi and

Demi italic, New Century Schoolbook, italic, bold and bold italic, Palatino, italic, bold and bold italic, ITC Zapf Chancery medium italic and ITC Zapf Dingbats. These additional 16 type font masters can generate 22 type styles including oblique versions of Avant Garde and narrow versions of Helvetica, Helvetica bold and Helvetica obliques. All these type fonts are on ROM but a full set of screen fonts is supplied as well on a screen font disk.

But it would be wrong to assume that one is limited to the above fonts burned into ROM because the Laser Writer software can download any font sold by Adobe Systems; one does not even have to buy the upgrade kit (from Laser Writer to Laser Writer Plus) comprising the fonts. As many as three to six fonts can be downloaded into RAM. Once fonts have been installed in a printer, all users of that printer can copy screen fonts from the printer but these are coded and function only with the printer of origin. The limited available RAM memory for downloadable fonts is not a serious constraint in most publishing applications that do not mix many fonts on a page; for a typical office application, the number of fonts is an already overkill. Another constraint might be the number of screen fonts on the disk of the Macintosh system, but this would pose no problem if the system disk was a Winchester disk.

The Laser Writer owes its popularity to a large degree to the PostScript page-description language which allows for fonts to be stored in one master size (rather than storing all font and size combinations as bit-maps as most other laser printers do); these can be electronically scaled whenever a need arises for any particular size within a font.

In conclusion, the Laser Writer Plus represents a considerable improvement over its predecessor with respect to both speed and size of the font library. The speed comes from faster execution of the PostScript code by the interpreter software in the RIP, which can read in data input from the Macintosh while at the same time printing the preceding page; time per page varies over a wide range contingent on page complexity: 30 seconds per page appears to be an average but speeds of up to three, four, six and even eight pages per minute have been mentioned. In any case 3000 pages per month seems to be the desirable ceiling: this is about the capacity of a replaceable cartridge containing photoconductor and toner.

The impact of the Macintosh (Plus)/Laser Writer (Plus) family of products has been significant: in offices many documents are now typeset that formerly were not, such as proposals, newsletters, brochures, presentations, offers, etc. Applications include the in-house technical documentation market, small newspapers substituting Laser

Writer for typesetting and large newspapers producing editorial graphics on it, books, scholarly journals and magazines. All this applies to the Macintosh and Laser Writer but more can be achieved by combining this configuration with the Linotronic 100 by Linotype.

In section 4.3.5 we have highlighted microcomputers as being a new factor in paper-based electronic publishing, one which has opened the somewhat staid atmosphere of conventional publishing to a flurry of renewed activity: this development will be revisited in Chapter 7. Yet the bridge between microcomputers and long-established conventional publishing based on print is still tenuous; to be sure, text can be efficiently output from microsystems not only on in-house page printers but also on typographic quality typesetters. When it comes to transferring images from computer color-graphic systems to printed publications though, the road becomes rather circuitous (Shafer 1986): digital computer graphics have to be cast on transparency, converted to an analog film transparency whereupon the transparency is subjected to the color separation process to be able to be imaged in the course of the offset printing operation; this cumbersome technology, where all imperfections of the film are scanned into the digital representation, can be circumvented by video-to-print techniques such as the method introduced by ImageSet Corp. (a color separator in San Francisco, Calif.). ImageSet markets proprietary software which enables computer-generated images to be received by the color separator on diskettes, converted from RGB (red, green, blue) color values of a microcomputer system to CYMK (cyan, yellow, magenta, black) values as is necessary for offset printing: the resulting CYMK data is transferred onto a 9-track magnetic tape, digitally imaged and output on film; this totally digital process is microcomputer based.

LINOTRONIC 100. Linotronic 100 (Linotype) offers some unique features with the Apple Macintosh, and in this connection it requires the PostScript interpreter, which translates page-description codes into raster format ready to be painted by laser across the whole page. The Macintosh can accept continuous-tone graphics (or any page image) via a scanner (e.g., Microtek at $3500 or some even less expensive variety such as Magic and Thunderscan) and can create text and line graphics, merge text and graphics on any page, provide a soft proof and output to the LaserWriter for an inexpensive plain-paper proof or onto a Linotronic 100 for a typographic-quality page ready for camera to plate. Macintosh workstations can be grouped together in a network called Apple Talk, and finished pages (or their components) may be stored in a mass storage device. This network can receive files from remote devices as well. The Linotronic 100 can output pages originating from varied sources. The advantage of microcomputer workstations configured in a distributed processing system over a system with multiple workstations outputting through a single device (mainframe or minicomputer) is less downtime, because if any component in the system fails, the rest remain unaffected.

The Microtek scanner is a CCD-based device whose resolution can be selected through software as either 200 × 200 or 300 × 300 lines per inch. Storage and communication cost is saved by the compression of picture data at a ratio of 1:10. Scaling, brightness and contrast are also set by means of software. While in text mode one can digitize text, graphics and drawings; in halftone mode continuous tone pictures can be scanned; in mixed mode both the text and halftone mode may be made to work in up to four rectangular windows. At the resolution of 300 lines per inch an 8.5 × 11-inch size is processed in 26 seconds.

Linotype is also fostering its IBM connection reflected in the so-called "Series 200" products which it fully supports. The series is composed of an IBM PC (featuring 256 kbytes, MS-DOS, two floppy disk drives and a Hercules graphics card) rigged with a synchronous adapter, an 80-column monitor and provided with the Microsoft Word word-processing software supplemented by the Page Planner composition package; this is required to drive the model 100 or 202 typesetter via Cora.

4.4 Assorted Prepress Subsystems

As a follow-up to the previous section highlighting some typical complete (more or less) prepress systems, this section concludes this chapter on print-based electronic publishing with an account of a few subsystems, which do not as such possess the ability to fulfill independently the total design and production function from the outset to the press-ready product (offset plate or gravure cylinder), let alone final printed copy. Nevertheless, they do represent important elements of complete systems: the first three have been already mentioned in this chapter in the context of complete systems and hence their role may be better appreciated: (1) the scanners finding their way into new systems and sites, (2) the difficult-to-define, but practically omnipresent, raster image processors and (3) the much-talked-about page makeup stations as the hub of many new prepress configurations. The remaining four subsystems are less glamorous but represent either a technically interesting variant among other alternatives, (4) the graphics pasteup-to-plate subsystem and (5) interactive picture editing for newspapers, or have an all-round utility, (6) plain-paper proofing subsystems, or are of a specialized nature, (7) digitizing subsystems.

4.4.1 Scanner—A Versatile Component of Prepress Systems

The principles of scanning have been outlined in Section 2.2.2, "Digital Representational Form of Information." On a general level, scanners may be analog, or digital if the analog signal is transformed into discrete digital values. Devices embodying these principles may find application in several areas of prepress. It may serve in lieu of a camera when film is prepared locally from the original by use of screening and perhaps picture enhancement; a scanner maybe used to digitize an image and store it for processing outside the scanner; images may be digitized, transmitted and recorded at a remote location in the telefacsimile mode; scanned and transmitted information may be used at a remote site to expose film or "burn" a plate; or a scanner may be used as a page makeup tool to bring together the diverse components of a page. These examples indicate how versatile an element a scanner can be in several prepress configurations: it can figure as an input or output device, or both; it can be used locally or remotely; it can function in batch or online mode; or it can output on paper or film with no need of chemical supplies and a dark room. Quality may be enhanced with the inclusion of a display screen to preview the result. Advanced capabilities and fast throughput are made possible under the microprocessor control. Although data captured in a scanner may be processed in an attached microcomputer, the trend has been to build at least some processing capability ("intelligence") right in the scanner itself.

Scanning generally may be done in one of three ways:

1. Continuous-tone pictures may be scanned in and output as contone; in this instance, manipulation can be done in subsequent stages and screening may take place on the output from the system.
2. Continuous-tone pictures may be scanned in and screening may be done at the same time, perhaps with some picture manipulation and possibly with compression of data. Screening is performed at densities of between 30 and 140 lines per inch and can be done at different angles and with different shape of halftone cell to suit a particular application.
3. Some high-resolution scanners also scan halftone pictures.

Scanning resolutions of 200, 300 and 400 lines per inch are achieved in inexpensive desktop scanners which typically use charge-coupled devices (CCDs) with a constant number of scanned spots (also called dots, lines, scans, observations or samples) across the width. Many scanners offer a choice of several resolutions. Medium-resolution (450-700 lines per inch) and high-resolution (1000-2000 lines per inch and above) machines use laser beams sweeping across the line, allowing variable resolution to be achieved as needed. Manipulation of the picture may be performed in batch mode on the scanner itself or outside the scanner either in full resolution, or in low resolution for economy reasons, with the file of commands transmitted later to the full-resolution device for execution. Some manufacturers market roller-fed scanners, others turn more toward flatbed types and yet other vendors offer a choice of both.

The Autokon 1000 Laser Graphics System (by ECRM, Bedford, Mass.), for instance, is a menu-driven device which prompts the operator to take action as appropriate; there are also trouble-shooting menus for maintenance purposes and instant calibration. This black and white flatbed scanner offers selection of resolution in the range from 200 to 2000 lines per inch when used as an input digitizer. Halftone screens may be selected from between 65 and 100 lines per inch as well as 120, 133 and 144 lines per inch in the high-resolution mode. Up to 12 setups may be stored on the system to speed up production, and a job may be run while another is in the process of being set up. Type and line art may be enlarged, reduced, stretched, squeezed, reversed and flopped. A threshold for dropouts may be set and the sharpness of the picture may be redefined; highlight masking, posterization and other effects can be accomplished in picture manipulation.

Color-separation scanners are a special kind of scanner (see also Note 3) whose objective typically is to prepare four-color separations (even though fewer or more than four may also be required) from an original color picture such as a color film transparency (35-mm roll of exposed film or single slides): black, yellow, cyan and magenta. Color-separation scanners are the new alternative to the conventional photographic color separation process based on a camera provided with filters. These four-color separations may actually have to be produced as laser-exposed films or as reflective positives to be further scanned and processed in a digital color prepress system; alternatively, they may be fed into the digital color system directly and then viewed and enhanced by the console operator in full color or as single separations. Scitex Corporation Ltd. has recently introduced a transportable color-separation scanner named Satlight (Scitex Publication No. 172F401) which can scan film or single slides prepared and selected by a photographer. Digitized pictures can be enlarged and cropped, with their density and contrast adjusted, and the resulting data optionally can be compressed before it is transmitted to a remote editorial office equipped with the Scitex Response 300 system for further image enhancement, whereupon complete color-separation films are produced locally or remotely. The Satlight scanner is furnished with a 5.25-inch Winchester disk with a capacity of 46 Mbytes sufficient to store up to 15 compressed images. A full-color picture can be scanned into the system typically within 90 seconds and transmitted at 9.6 Kbaud, 56 Kbits per second, 1.544 Mbits per second or 2.08 Mbits per second; the transmission time at a transmission speed of 1.544 Mbytes per second and compression ratio of 8:1, is given as 7.5 seconds per picture. With higher compression ratios of around 85:1 which are presently feasible, it becomes entirely practicable to transmit pictures even via phone lines.

Modern color-separation scanners are a good example of how identical functions may be accomplished at different stages of the process. Cropping and sizing, for instance, may be done right in the separation scanner perhaps utilizing its high-accuracy true-color screen displaying the press/paper/ink combination of choice if such a facility is available; but one can size and crop on a color graphics workstation or on a page-planning (design) station.

It is no mystery to anyone privy to the underlying principles that scanners, facsimile machines and OCR devices share a common technology basis. At a recent Comdex show most of the exhibiting scanner vendors either had, or were contemplating to add, character recognition software to their gadgets (Seybold 1985), and in similar vein, some scanners are being suggested as being suitable for scanning documents in capacity of facsimile machines even though, in an inverse development, Xerox is marketing fax machines that can function as 200 line per inch input scanners and output printers. Densitometers are useful electronic devices which support scanning and plate production (see Note 4).

4.4.2 Raster Image Processor Facilitated Subsystem

The raster image processor (RIP), also called raster imager, raster image controller, raster image device, etc., is becoming an increasingly useful component in a number of prepress system configurations. The RIP, essentially a special-purpose computer, comes into the picture as a requisite intermediate, e.g., between a front-end where a page is finalized as far as text is concerned, on the one hand, and the laser-writing device, on the other hand. In other words, it converts the text data originally in character coded format into the raster format as demanded by the output device and it does so at a remarkable speed of 5-10 Mbits per second. Because it outputs in the raster format, it can be guided to drive a film, paper or plate-imaging device, an electronic printer, output on a video display or a telefacsimile receiver.

RIP may be used, e.g., in connection with a high-resolution typesetter. In fact, a RIP is physically a relatively small device and may be integrated into the typesetter proper or exist as a self-supporting unit to assist a variety of devices. The RIP can accept fonts of a typesetter, translate them into raster image form and store them on disk in this form. Disks are an indispensable companion of any RIP owing to the huge amount of bits they store and process. Because a RIP may share the fonts with the typesetter, it may not only output on laser recorder, but it may add versatility and flexibility to the system; one might, e.g., feed page-bits to a proof printer from the RIP and, after the proof has been found correct, send the same data to be typeset on the "host" typesetter which shares the fonts with the RIP. This substitutes plain paper proof for the more expensive typesetter paper.

Technically, there is no obstacle for the RIP also to handle halftone, which fit well into the above-mentioned applications of RIP. But a RIP must be considered as a rather general output device, which is potentially capable of handling any imaging equipment based on the raster form of output.

Figure 16 displays in a simplified manner how a raster image processor (1) may be harnessed to perform a wide variety of functions. In this system the input, both text (2) and graphics (3), possibly fully paginated (4) may be previewed either as "soft copy" (5) or as hard copy (6) and transmitted to a remote fax receiver (7) with the assistance of the RIP (1); text may be typeset (8) using shared fonts (9) or entire pages can be recorded on film (10), plate (11) or paper (12) by a laser-imaging device (13).

This general concept of a RIP implies that it may be a versatile device which is difficult to define. There are RIPs that possess an all-around compatibility with other devices and there are those that are tied into specific configurations and makes. This poses a serious problem for prospective buyers and reinforces the case for system integrators. Raster image processors have thus become one of the most discussed single items in the preprint technology, and the list of raster output devices that may be fed by RIPs continues to grow. So does the list of capabilities expected from this device (Seybold and Stivison 1984): sizing type characters, slanting, drawing horizontal and vertical lines, outputting line graphics and halftones, and also rotating type, generating screen tints, patterns and reverses, drawing and plotting capabilities and resolution-independent output of line art and halftones.

Raster image processors can be manufactured and sold as part of proprietary hardware or other equipment manufacturers (OEMs) may fit them into their systems in applications such as combining RIPs with various display units and marking engines to match their resolution, speed and other attributes. As to the applicable fonts, a raster imager can support both bit maps created by experienced typographers as well

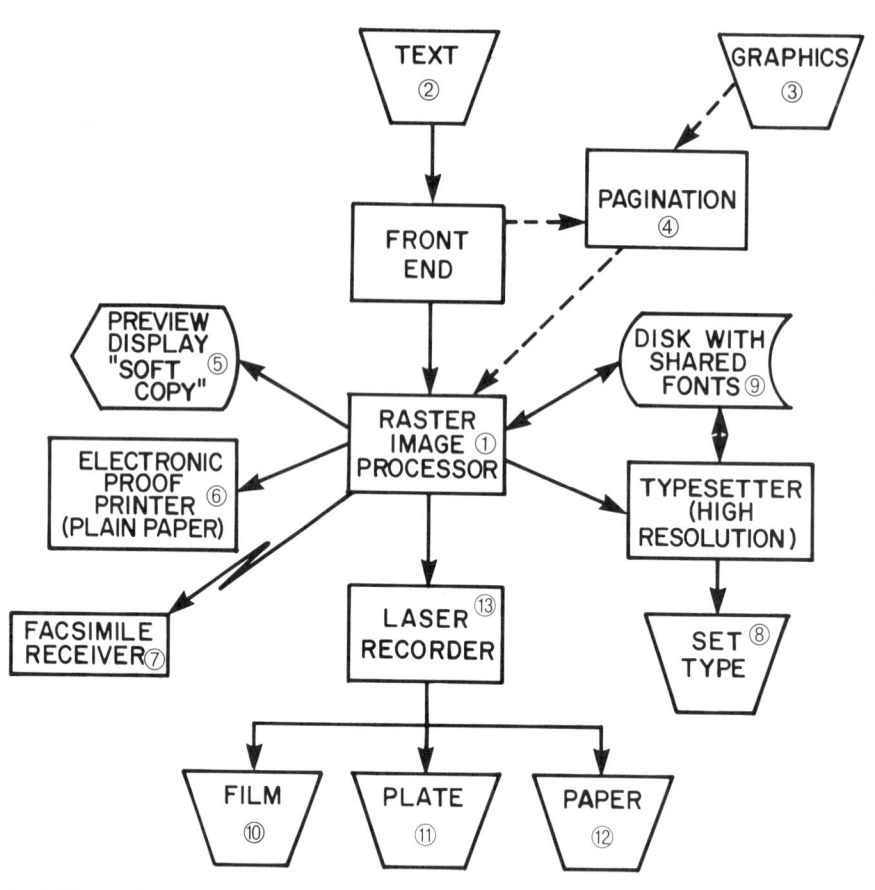

FIGURE 16 Raster image processor subsystem (simplified chart of a possible arrangement).

as outline fonts which are much more storage economical in that they describe characters as spline curves rather than store all the bits necessary to paint shapes of all font characters in all styles and sizes. A mix of bit maps and outlines can be also handled, thus increasing the range of options to meet whatever typographic quality may be required. A raster imager may process locally presented data but these may be also remotely supplied. It should be noted, however, that simple painting of pages would not entirely satisfy the definition of a raster processor, as it is presently understood: to interpret incoming data to include both text and graphics (line art as well as halftones) and translate the input format into an output consisting of pages of bit patterns upon which the particular imaging engine can operate. There is no standard format presently in existence which would allow at least some degree of device independence, and some firms of note are promoting their own formats with hope that they might be accepted as industry standards before national or international standards are established.

Raster imagers are an important phenomenon in the prepress industry as demonstrated by the interest displayed on the part of many vendors. For the user they open up new ways for text and graphics integration, higher speeds of imaging (depending on resolutions and graphic complexity) and a wide range of resolutions from low (around 200 lines per inch) to high (around 1500 lines per inch); they practically remove restrictions on fonts, styles and sizes and offer an array of graphic capabilities surpassing those of conventional technologies.

4.4.3 Page Makeup Stations

Page makeup is the stage of prepress technology after text entry/edit and capture of illustrations, whereby all components of a page are gathered and made ready for local or remote output. It has also been referred to as pagination, pasteup, composition, page layout, etc., although these terms have other meanings as well, because of vague terminology. Sophisticated systems of today have been made possible by the concomitant developments in scanning devices, raster image processors, image manipulation, data compression, bit-map memory and high-resolution terminals, all of them computer-controlled.

In the era of flourishing hot metal systems, pages were assembled from metal columns and lines after the galleys had undergone proofing. Setting the columns of lines was clearly typesetting and what followed was page makeup when columns of text as blocks of metal were fitted together into pages. Phototypesetting still maintained this dichotomy undisturbed inasmuch as pages were made up from paper or film galleys but the development did not stop there.

New Era in Page Makeup. In today's convoluted systems the borderline between text editing, typesetting and page makeup becomes less and less distinct. Page makeup moved from manual pasteup to the screen, and the screen has improved its resolution over the years along with the size. Initially, only columns could be manipulated, later, blocks of text and art could be composed on the screen, finally, the whole page is formed, edited and with individual items placed where desired. Whereas the earlier computerized composition systems were batch oriented, the more recent ones are often interactive, allowing for modifications to be incorporated on displayed pages in real time, whereby changes are done either immediately across the entire page or in several affected lines only, with the entire page being reconstructed later; this can result in considerably better response times.

Pagination systems may be facing, on the input side, individual terminals or microprocessor-controlled clusters, or they may be connected to a local area network, possibly with text-editing terminals, word processors, etc., while typesetting devices are situated on the output side. In some page makeup systems, one can delineate the size of articles and then later on, fill in the text. This allows for better editorial planning. Digitized typefonts stored on disks make it possible to display pages in their real final form including font, character size, leading, etc., thus providing for a true "soft proof" copy, even though some argue that true fonts on screen do not justify the increased cost. Thanks to digitized imaging, text and tone can be integrated, and with some qualifications, color can be harnessed as well where necessary. The cost of hardware and software is contingent upon the degree of sophistication.

Integration of Text and Graphics. One of the topical issues in page makeup is integration of text and graphics and the possibility of achieving such integration is in fact the one most desirable feature of these modern computer-controlled systems.

There are several problems in arriving at integrated pages and they are of an economic, technical or "systems" nature.

Probably the severest one is of a totally nontechnical character: there is the general lack of a "total" approach. Problems have not been analyzed locally and solutions are being sought without clearly stated objectives. It may happen that the solution is not congruous with existing procedures. As a result the prospective pagination system may not connect with the front-end system or is not compatible with the intended output devices. Neither of the alternative solutions is very attractive: either discard the existing equipment and try to purchase a complete compatible set or wait until there is one available, or buy different makes and find ways to make them work together. Although expert advice may be obtained from system integrators, the more knowledgeable the end user is the better.

The economic problem will be similar to that of new acquisitions in other areas and boils down to the questions of cost justification. The merits of electronic pagination may vary depending on local circumstances, but will include some or all of those claimed lately by Solimeno (1984): savings in materials and labor, extended deadlines, better quality both as far as physical appearance and editorial content are concerned, and, perhaps most importantly, a better management of work flow including page layout, makeup, copyfitting and eventually release of pages to production. Advantages are, hence, both quantifiable and difficult to price.

One of the fundamental technical imperatives in page makeup systems is to determine the technical functions required in a given environment (newspaper, magazine, in-plant, commercial printer) and then select (or design) the hardware and software to perform them. Whereas in the conventional pasteup process, integration of text and graphics is achieved manually from approved galleys and illustrations, in the emerging technology some or all integrative functions may be implemented in a page makeup workstation or on the same station as text processing (e.g., artholes or hyphenation) or in an output laser-writing unit. Specifically, graphics may be handled in different ways; they may be manipulated (at least partly) in a pagination workstation (e.g., rotation, scaling, cropping, etc.) or they may be handled in a picture-editing workstation for newspapers (e.g., wire photos) or in a color graphics workstation, both of which have been described in this chapter. What is striking here is the multitude of potentially possible solutions to the same problem in different environments in place of the old, conventional pasteup process. The best solution in any particular instance is the answer to a very straightforward question: It looks all right but how does it suit my work flow?

We cannot, therefore, discuss the page makeup station in isolation from the broader environment and must examine it in a system-wide context.

Page Makeup in Broader Context. Traditional and electronic page makeup are juxtaposed in Figure 17. The conventional (A) setup is self-explanatory. In the electronic computerized version (B), text (1) is entered and/or composed in one of the available front-end systems. We have already stated, and it may be useful to reiterate, that the new electronic technology introduces some degree of vagueness as to which processing functions will be performed on which hardware and software. Thus some front-ends may be entrusted with some page makeup duties as well, such as columns, art windows and text runaround; creation of line art may be possible, too. Conversely, the page makeup workstation (2) itself may be able to look after some text-editing functions such as corrections and also provide some graphics editing such as sizing and cropping. Local graphics (3) are scanned in and digitized (4), and then manipulated in a graphics manipulation workstation (5) described elsewhere. Some text processing may be done there such as captions. News photos received from news wire services (6) may be processed in the same workstation and used, stored or retransmitted as described elsewhere; captions may be inserted at this stage.

A. CONVENTIONAL

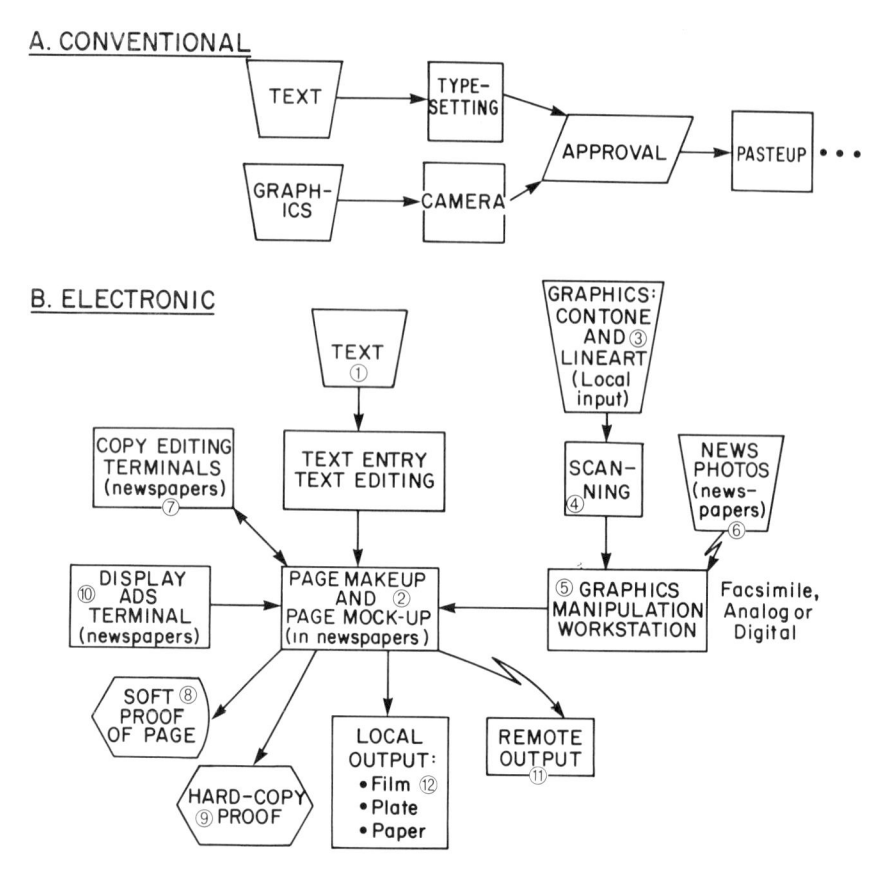

[Flow diagram: TEXT → TYPESETTING; GRAPHICS → CAMERA; both → APPROVAL → PASTEUP ...]

B. ELECTRONIC

[Flow diagram with numbered components: TEXT ①; GRAPHICS: CONTONE AND LINEART (Local input) ③; COPY EDITING TERMINALS (newspapers) ⑦; TEXT ENTRY TEXT EDITING; SCANNING ④; NEWS PHOTOS (newspapers) ⑥; DISPLAY ADS TERMINAL (newspapers) ⑩; PAGE MAKEUP AND PAGE MOCK-UP (in newspapers) ②; GRAPHICS MANIPULATION WORKSTATION ⑤; Facsimile, Analog or Digital; SOFT PROOF OF PAGE ⑧; HARD-COPY PROOF ⑨; LOCAL OUTPUT: • Film ⑫ • Plate • Paper; REMOTE OUTPUT ⑪]

FIGURE 17 Page makeup in broader context (one of many possible arrangements).

In a newspaper operation the page makeup station (2) may serve ideally for preparation of a page mock-up, which is then passed to copy editors (7) to fit their copies where appropriate or else it may serve to lay out the page using copies received from editors. Classified ads will require special software that includes billing, accounting, editing, layout and associated functions. Both soft proof (8) and hard-copy proof (9) should be obtainable before the final page is cleared for remote (11) or local (12) output.

Display ad makeup (10) is a case of an area makeup which thematically relates to the subject of page makeup. Dedicated display ad makeup stations (DAMS) (10) fit into a broader context comprising page makeup station, typesetter, copy-editing terminals, hard-copy proofers, etc., and their final product is a complete display ad including text and graphics to be integrated into complete pages where a window for them has been set aside typically beforehand. Because DAMS have extensive text and graphics design and production capabilities, they are built around powerful graphics processors with a good display monitor; they store all already existing components of ads, call them up and generate new elements sometime through a great deal of manipulation. To avoid an excessive amount of training and to increase productivity of operators, DAMS are based on menus and avail themselves of other user-friendly features such as mouse and icons. They are capable of creating all textual and graphic components within a given shape, provide various masking and handle the background; components may be enclosed within borders and a variety of rules may be generated for an increased appeal. Individual elements of an ad may be reversed, scaled, zoomed or rotated, and selected areas may be filled with patterns or provided with tints to enhance the artistic effect. Needless to say, continuity of the production process must be safeguarded by a compatible environment, especially direct flow into the page makeup.

Integration of text and graphics has been bandied around for long time yet the final solution is still some way in the future. There has been a mismatch between user expectation and vendor performance. Integration is largely a software problem; it takes longer than generally anticipated, and when it is completed, no one is ready to foot the bill (Givens 1986).

4.4.4 Graphics Pasteup-to-Plate Subsystem

We have already described the originator-to-film/plate/gravure cylinder systems; there is yet another way to arrive directly at a plate.

This category of systems may be called graphics pasteup to plate, which might be conceived of as the back-end system to one of the existing front-end systems. These systems eliminate the film as an intermediate step, hence, the name "filmless" systems (see Figure 18).

Although the idea of saving the film material and increasing productivity seems enticing, these systems have not seen any widespread use—at least not yet. Interestingly enough, there was more read-send-write activity (telefacsimile) than reading pasted-up pages and writing them locally on plates, undoubtedly because of the inherent economics. Distributed remote printing holds some promise.

An example of the graphics pasteup to plate subsystem is one implemented recently in real life. It combines equipment of two manufacturers in the field, namely that of Eocom and Hastech. In this setup one proceeds page by page: text (1) is finalized in the front-end part of the system (2)—the Hastech's Page Pro and the Magician editing ter-

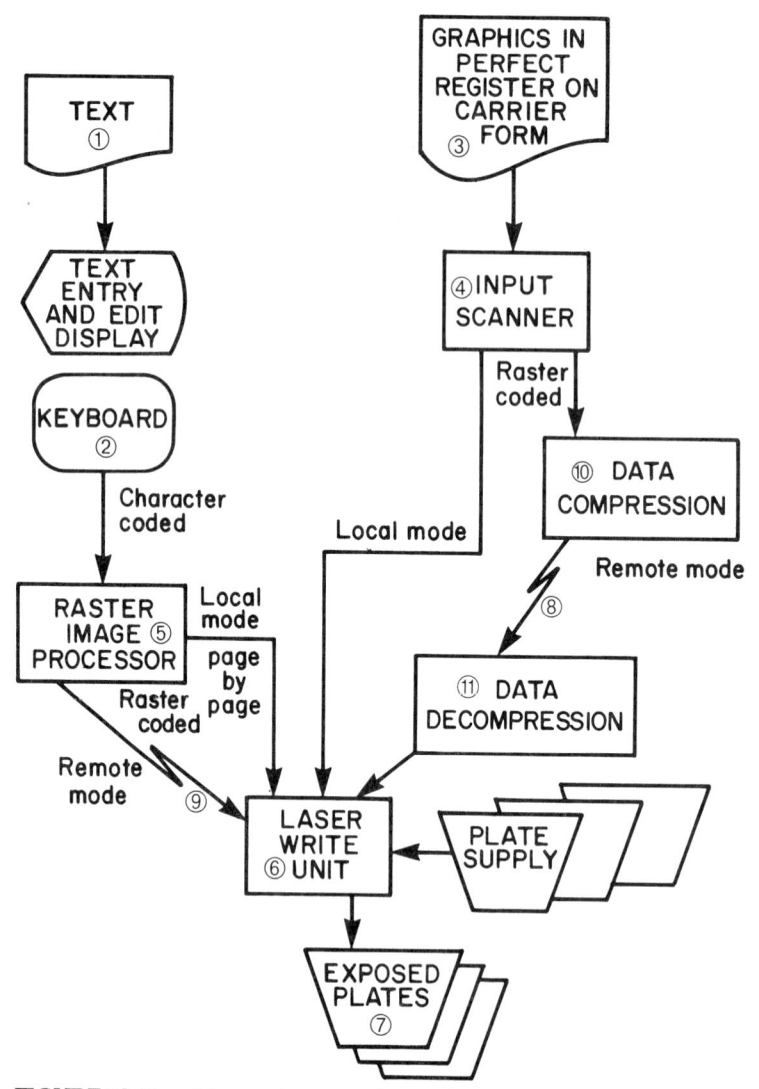

FIGURE 18 Graphics pasteup-to-plate subsystem (black and white).

minals based on the Motorola 68000 microprocessor. Concurrently, the graphics pertaining to the same page are mounted precisely on a page form (3), which is subsequently placed in the scanning drawer of the Laserite laser-read scanner (4). This method necessitates only one page of graphics to be stored in the device rather than having to store the entire job. It must be emphasized that it is imperative to position the graphics exactly where they belong so the following operation places the text accordingly. The text (1) has to be subjected to conversion in the EPC raster image processor (5), and it is then combined with the graphics in the Laserite writing (record) unit (6) to be exposed as a press-ready plate (7). There is no proofing facility. The production on this kind of equipment is between 20 and 30 plates per hour: productivity is increased and the intermediate film is eliminated. Another advantage of this kind of setup is the possibility of remote printing where the transmission line might be interposed either between the Scan laser unit and the Write laser unit (8), or text only could be transmitted (9) to the rest of the system. We have mentioned plate as the final output but photographic paper and film can be equally well exposed on the equipment described above. There are manufacturers active in the area and their products differ, among other things, in using different laser technology and plate-writing techniques. The amount of transmitted data in the remote mode of processing may be reduced by exploitation of data compression (10) and decompression techniques (11).

Basically, the introduction of a graphics pasteup-to-plate system means a trade-off resulting in a higher capital investment cost and lower labor, space and materials costs. Need for a varied output and necessity to provide for remote printing may make the implementation worth contemplating.

4.4.5 Interactive Picture Editing and Management System for Newspapers

Electronic Picture Desk (Muirhead). This is a system designed for the interactive editing of pictures input from a local scanner or received on-line from wire picture services in the newspaper industry. It may also act as a production control tool. In the hub of the system is the traffic management module, which contains the software necessary to achieve the general objective of the electronic picture desk: to receive, store and process graphics of all kinds so they may be integrated into full pages locally or sent on. The system is designed for the wire service market, but is suited to work as a digital graphics system as well. Its salient feature is that it is the first digital wire photo system to supplement the current systems which are analog. This offers the advantages of digital systems, but may also cause problems if compatibility with existing equipment cannot be secured.

Peripheral Devices. Incoming pictures are stored in magnetic disk storage sufficient for 60, 120 or 300 photos. The operator VDU allows the operators to work in any of several basic modes: they can obtain guidance, define operating parameters and default values, generate message files, edit stored images on the editing monitor, display the status of the system and stored images, manage and route these images. These functions are listed on a menu which appears on power-up.

Any stored picture can be displayed in continuous tone on the TV monitor within 3 seconds in 64 levels of gray and at a 512 × 512-pixel resolution. Pictures may be edited—sized, cropped, rotated, tonal range enhanced as needed—and captions can be included at this stage. These functions are effected interactively on the screen while the original picture remains untouched for possible future use. Other peripherals include continuous tone writers, electronic screening cameras, archival subsystem, remote wire photo services and eventually a pagination system. The local scanner may be transformed into a wire photo transmitter by means of an interface card; it scans a 35-mm negative in 30 seconds.

4.4.6 Plain-paper Proofing Subsystems

The issue of plain-paper proofing could be subsumed under the Section 4.4.2 on raster image processor-facilitated subsystems because, after all, proofing is only one of the things at which RIPs are supposed to be indispensable. Proofing subsystems could be discussed under the more general topic of typesetters or image setters as well; they deserve to be at least briefly treated because practically any prepress system can benefit from some sort of inexpensive proofing until such time as we all agree that "soft" proofing is sufficient to obtain an approval.

Essential Attributes. The rationale behind a proof printer is that it saves money by printing on plain paper instead of using expensive photographic film or paper. A proof printer should be able to produce more copies, if needed, promptly and efficiently; a good proofer may be used for short print runs on the "on-demand" basis or when originals are preferred to copies. It should be able to work both locally and at a remote site or sites. It is highly desirable that both graphics and text appear on the proof exactly as they would when set: same font, size and composition format. Preferably, the RIP feeding the proof printer pours the same data into the typesetter (image setter) on approval; the "soft" proofing capability on a display unit comes to be considered a standard feature.

Examples. Camex has the Super Setter which will output complete pages including text and graphics. Their Bit Caster does all the rasterizing at a rate of 6 Mbits per second and pours raster data in the same format into either the Bit Printer for proofing or the Bit Setter for final setting. The Bit Caster rasterizes for any output imaging device at any resolution and any character or image size.

Autologic has the APS-55 Bit Blaster which can work in the dependent mode, whereby data from a front-end streams into the Bit Blaster and after being converted into its raster format, is directed into the laser printer to produce a proof. It may be also displayed on the graphics display terminal (GDT). In the dependent mode, the laser proof printer shares the typesetter's electronics and font disk. The Bit Blaster may also act in the independent mode as a stand-alone unit with its own electronics and a font disk in a disk drive; it outputs alternatively to a display unit, laser proof printer and eventually to the typesetter. Remote mode is also possible.

4.4.7 Digitizing Subsystem (Types, Logos)

In this category we include an array of modular devices that enable a prepress establishment to digitize type fonts, special characters, alphabets, and logos either produced in-house or acquired from a font vendor. Contingent upon the respective configuration, these may be stored in a RIP or typesetter or in a self-contained storage, displayed and edited online or offline, thus creating one's own font library.

The Autologic APS-44 may serve as an example of a digitizing subsystem. In the simplest arrangement the matter to be input is scanned by a scanner at 1000-line per inch resolution in 6 seconds; it is a CCD array consisting of 1024 elements. Attached to it is a control terminal which affords the user the discretion to make minor changes such as to delete characters and obtain some statistics on stored characters. A graphics display monitor (512 × 512 pixels) may be added as well as the graphics edit package, allowing for graphics to be edited or new fonts to be designed and stored on a floppy disk or directly in the typesetter.

Notes

1. Although this section is about prepress, it is by no means contradictory if we look briefly at what is transpiring in the print shop. In general terms, letterpress use continues to decline and its share is being captured by offset and gravure; offset remains in the lead as the most cost-effective technology, which is well in tune with the electronic developments in the prepress area providing print-ready plates. Gravure will likely receive some additional appeal from halftone gravure and wraparound gravure plates as well, but it will continue to compete with offset most successfully only in large runs at least until such time as more

economical ways of cylinder engraving are found. Laser technology is well established in preparation of gravure cylinders as well. Electromechanical engravers may be driven directly by a digital color prepress system without the need for any film; continuous-tone films prepared by color prepress serve for chemical etching of print cylinders. Electronic printers, initially used for proofing and matrix preparation, are moving in not only as typesetters but also as full-fledged printers where printing speed and run size warrant it.

2. *Screening and Halftones.* In reproducing continuous-tone pictures we often employ the concept of halftone inasmuch as contone cannot be reproduced as such by offset printing. The original contone picture is photographed through a screen (even though scanning has become widely used lately), which results in the original image being broken down into a pattern of tiny dots that may be distinguishable under a magnifying glass; in shooting the picture the halftone screen is interposed on the optical axis between the picture and the film. The main characteristic of the screen is its resolution, which is the number of lines per unit of length ranging from 55 to 300 lines per inch. Newspaper illustrations tolerate a maximum of 65-85 lines per inch, books up to around 120, and coated paper can handle around 150; letterpress could cope with a maximum of 110 lines per inch, whereas offset lithography achieves better contrast by accepting a density of 130-150. Halftone screens are made of glass orplastic with crisscrossed lines engraved into the surface and formed by black pigment. The quality of a halftone illustration is directly proportionate to the screen density. Owing to optical laws, the effect of photographing the contone picture through the screen mesh will result in a halftone picture characterized by dots, which are smaller and farther apart in the light areas of the picture and are larger and closer together in the dark areas. Screens may also serve to achieve various special effects such as linen, mesh, burlaplike reproductions, etc. So-called tints are special effects in printing, which are accomplished by making a halftone picture of a solid black resulting in dots that are evenly spaced for a given "mixture" of black and white. Tints are usually available for various proportions of black and white, from 10% of white to 90% as the size of dots decreases.

As one might expect in the electronic age and in light of the ever-expanding range of laser applications, the current glass-etched screens have found a serious competitor in screens produced on specially designed laser scanners, which direct a laser beam to burn dots into polyester film (*American Printer* 1986); such screens are manufactured by Swisscreen and distributed by Graphex Ltd. The main advantages of this new kind of screen are claimed to be consistent quality, elimination of "fog" at the outer edges of the light source beyond the center area of the screen, and higher scratch resistance resulting from a special hardening procedure. Parameters of individual screens are computer-stored and, therefore, may be reproduced precisely, making it unnecessary to reproduce the whole set for other colors.

3. *Color Separation.* All color prints are formed by little halftone dots deposited from four plates corresponding to the three process colors, magenta, yellow and cyan, plus the fourth black printer plate serving to enhance contrasts and shading as well as accentuating outlines and possibly to print the text matter. Process color separation is a production process requiring knowledge of color theory and extensive experience in the field of process camera, platemaking and printing. Process color separation works from the original color illustration or a high-quality color transparency and separates "composite" colors into their four "process" component colors from which four corresponding plates are produced, which through their combination when printed, produce the original color illustration or as close a similitude as possible. As a matter of interest, color separation could be done manually by the artist himself, but we are concerned with industrial applications. Initially color separation was done by means of color filters (green, orange and violet) employed in a process camera with simultaneous or subsequent screening at different angles for each process color. Today color separation is performed electronically including all color correction and picture manipulation, using electronic scanners and color graphics workstations. Although separation into four process colors is common, more or less than four colors can also be used to achieve the likeness of the original color picture. An electronic scanner can scan and output directly acting as a camera, or it can also store the digital data for further processing. Screening could be done in the scanner or in the output device from the color system.

If the original picture is to be transmitted, then a photograph is prepared of each color component by the color separation process; these pictures are transmitted and screened at the receiving site to yield halftone offset plates.

Color separation is based on eye illusion. Each plate is printed with the appropriate ink being deposited on paper as tiny dots of varying sizes and different colors; these dots alongside each other are then perceived by the human eye not as individual color spots but they mix into color combinations approaching that of the original picture.

4. *Densitometers.* Densitometers are devices that are gradually replacing human judgment based on eyesight and gray-scale reference strips. A densitometer is an electronic device measuring the amount of light reflected back from an object (reflection densitometer) or transmitted through an object (transmission densitometer) and relating these quantities respective to the amount of the initiated light. In the prepress, reflection densitometers are practical in measuring the optical density of art in the form of print on paper or photographic prints; the transmission densitometers are useful in consistently determining the density of transparencies, i.e., art on negative or positive film. Densitometric readings are given on the logarithmic scale: a black area with nearly all of the incident light being absorbed, would be indicated by a density reading of 2 which means close to 100% of light absorption.

Densitometers in the prepress serve the purpose of measuring densities of reflective or transmissive originals as well as densities of developed films for dot area percentages (Boyum 1986); the objective is to ensure that the output from the scanner or camera will yield plates that in press will reproduce the original as closely as possible. The main applications of densitometers in prepress are threefold: (1) scanner or camera calibration, (2) precise and reproducible measurement of dot percentages in the negative and (3) better control of film processing. The densitometer can prove to be an efficient tool both in black and white (monochrome) halftone as well as color separation applications with savings netted at the proofing and platemaking stages.

5

Electronic Document Delivery

5.1 Delineation of the Concept

Electronic document delivery (EDD) is a term rightly meriting definition and explanation in the context of electronic publishing. EDD may be conceived of as a service that provides the electronic communication channel through which a client may obtain the desired document(s). The client may be the ultimate user (reader) or an intermediary (e.g., a librarian) who procures the document and hands it over to the end user. The EDD service might be an electronic publisher, a consortium of publishers or booksellers, an independent commercial service center, a library, or other warehouse of information, or a consortium of these, a government agency, a learned association or society, or conceivably, a cooperative of users. The service may be financially self-supporting or may be to some degree subsidized to help it get started. The electronic communication channel is what makes EDD distinct from the conventional document delivery systems, and it may take a different shape contingent upon the technology adopted in a particular implementation. The delivery of the document(s) takes place in machine-readable form and the material is presented to the user in an intelligible form either readable or audible. The aptness of the term "document" may be challenged in the light of the diversity of formats and their manipulability.

5.2 The Rationale Behind Electronic Document Delivery Efforts

The motives for the development of EDD projects are both the availability of technological means and the situation inherent in the existing document delivery systems.

There is a growing discrepancy between the speed with which references to documents can be obtained by online information retrieval and the speed of the subsequent, comparatively sluggish process by which the documents themselves can be procured. Although it is possible to order documents online, the user is still often obliged to wait for delivery by conventional means. The continuing growth of the number of databases and online searches generates more demand and is bound to press for speedier delivery of documents.

The existing infrastructure does not hold promise for improvement in the future. Libraries' collections cannot keep growing commensurate with the increase in the number of published titles while library budgets shrink and cost of published materials keeps soaring. Also, the space needed to store printed materials is becoming scarce and too costly. The number of book and journal titles shows a steady growth but print runs are on the decline; this also calls for rethinking of the extant ways of "document" delivery.

Telefacsimile helps to alleviate the problem of document transmission, but unless put into the framework of a comprehensive system, is no more than a stopgap measure with telecopiers available only at a limited number of delivery points and encumbered by compatibility problems. Interlibrary loan services in our libraries may avail themselves of one-way electronic communication for ordering but they have to rely, in most cases, on mail delivery. Computerized cataloguing and circulation systems allow users to determine what material is available both locally and otherwise to meet user needs, and may be accessed from remote terminals in some cases, but they do not resolve the problem of EDD. In addition, they often do not reflect the complete collections of one institution, let alone comprehensive coverage of a field of study. Some book publishers and book jobbers do have computerized systems whereby books (and other materials) may be ordered but delivery still takes the usual time.

The present systems of document delivery leave users frustrated and publishers, jobbers and libraries groping for solutions. Publishers face rising costs of material, labor and distribution, and they are not content with readers making photocopies while the numbers of subscribers keep declining. It appears that the publishing unit such as a book or a scholarly journal is no longer desirable and may soon not be economically viable and will be, at least in some fields, replaced by smaller units such as chapters or individual papers better suited to meet the needs of the more and more diversified readership; these packages will be more often than not custom-tailored to individual users or to suit specific tasks and will likely be authored by users/readers themselves in most instances.

5.3 Background

There are several factors that help pave the road toward electronic document delivery. New telecommunications technology links together computers, which have successfully invaded the publishing industry in areas other than EDD, namely, text generation and editing as well as production of publications, the result being that EDD can benefit from the availability of hardware and know-how at both the publisher's and user's sites. Perhaps even more important is the increasing familiarity of readers with electronic devices which, in the long run, will overcome the resistance towards new electronic forms of delivery and will cut down on time and cost required for training. A great deal of experience has been acquired by both publishers and online operators in creation, storage, maintenance and distribution of large databases in the area of secondary publications which will be invaluable in dealing with databases of primary materials. Online bibliographic databases generate more demand for provision of full-text documents and EDD should be striving to capture this vast market. When they arrived, online information retrieval systems created something that their predecessor—batch computer retrieval—could not accomplish: they became a marketplace where consumers and producers meet. It is very possible that the same thing will recur once again when full-text documents become available online on a large scale.

The position of publishers in any prospective scheme of EDD appears to be strong owing to the accumulated store of information in their typesetting tapes; even though they require some processing to clean them from typesetting codes, any form of machine-readable data presents a competitive edge at the start.

The fast progress of EDD has been impeded by several factors. There is a considerable risk in venturing an enterprise of this magnitude and it is nearly impossible for one publisher to undertake it. All bits and pieces of technology exist and they offer a wide gamut of options, but they still have to prove their viability in the face of competition on the part of traditional publishing media—readers themselves are not clamoring for change. A single publisher not only does not possess the financial means required, but does not wield a publishing base wide enough to proffer a service of sufficient comprehensiveness; users would be extremely reluctant to subscribe to a multitude of different services to cover a single subject area. No system of full-text delivery can avoid to be costly at the central site in view of the amount of storage to guarantee both comprehensive coverage and retrospective depth, as well as all the administrative, communications, data retrieval and database management functions. However, it must be affordable at the user's end. Only economy of scales can help and a mass market is needed. Users want to be able not only to retrieve relevant items, but also to obtain prices or intelligible order instructions and to check on the status of the order they placed.

Some system components are only at an advanced stage of development, e.g., the digital optical disk in the "jukebox" arrangement. Video display units have not yet reached the state of perfection to become a favorite reading medium, yet the "VDU/print" dilemma has some very concrete ramifications in the planning for EDD systems. Whereas some believe in paperless information systems of the future (Lancaster 1978), a word of caution has also been voiced (Strassmann 1984); VDU is not to be considered as an "enemy" of paper that will replace it but rather as a complement that will dominate the logic of information search.

The situation in EDD is very likely to develop into a parallel of on-line bibliographic retrieval systems in which the user is confronted with too many hosts and too many databases, which makes choice difficult, and when the choice has been made, the search results may be compromised by superficial knowledge of the system and/or database(s). In EDD it will be necessary, in view of the lack of standards, to provide users with a "database of databases" indicating all electronic suppliers, their range of services, prices and subject areas covered. Simple operation is a must; even so it appears that an intermediary will interface with the ultimate user if emphasis is placed on a high degree of completeness of documents required in a "multiple supplier" environment. This will result in increased costs. Ideally, the information retrieval operation should coincide with the "document" delivery operation.

The development of EDD is a viable proposition only if sufficient demand can be engendered for this service. It is by no means clear how many users will be willing to pay for the undisputed advantages of electronic delivery. Speed alone would hardly be enough to generate the critical mass of demand necessary for setting up an infrastructure of this magnitude. Other features of a progressive EDD must be present such as comprehensive coverage, user-friendly interface, reasonable cost, inexpensive hardware if required, and clear and simple instructions. A lucid and convenient method of billing may offset, in many cases, reservations held with regard to cost.

An account of not-so-encouraging factors would not be complete without mentioning the hard-to-crack copyright problem. Legal, economic and organizational obstacles have proved to be the most serious impediments on the way to EDD. None of the many possible solutions should unduly inconvenience the intermediary—whether librarian or broker—and the ultimate user if the encumbrances of the traditional information-gathering habits are to be abandoned and EDD accepted on a large scale.

5.4 Modes of Operation

Electronic document delivery may be a part of an electronic publishing system, as is the case of videotex and teletext services or full-text online retrieval systems, but EDD may be provided by an agency separate from the original publishing system(s) either electronic or conventional. An EDD system may start from a print-based storage such as archived hard copies and microforms or from a multitude of machine-readable storage media such as floppies, typesetting tapes, hard magnetic disks, high-density tapes, videodisks, digital optical disks, etc.; print-based input would require digitization and OCR devices, or facsimile technology could be applied for scanning pages followed by transmission and reception at the user's site. Conversely, machine-readable input would have to be converted into the format of central storage wherefrom it could be retrieved as needed and transmitted to the user.

Systems of EDD may be divided into those that are electronic in one direction only and those that are electronic in both directions, i.e., upstream as well as downstream. As an example of the former, we might cite an EDD system in which the request for a document is submitted at a terminal as a result of an online bibliographic search with the document being sent by a courier; an example of the latter would be videotex systems which are bidirectional electronic systems albeit capable of limited "document" size.

Information subject to dissemination through EDD channels may be supplied to the user either from a central store or from one of several decentralized stores of machine-readable information. In a decentralized store the documents may be either both produced and stored or distributed from a central service bureau to decentralized centers on physical storage devices (tapes, disks, digital optical disks, etc.), or by transmission.

The requested documents may reach the user/reader via communications lines or they may be delivered on storage media for local replay and/or reproduction. A hybrid system is also possible whereby text may be transmitted online and graphics are displayed and printed from a locally stored media such as a videodisk. If documents are sent over communications lines, then two arrangements are possible: either documents are delivered online immediately or they may be received in nonprime time (overnight) by a nonattended terminal to save costs if delay can be tolerated. Documents may be supplied to a user terminal in final form or it may be possible to manipulate them if the receiving device (e.g., microcomputer) has the requisite capability. Generally speaking, documents are received either in the true format of the original as in the case in telecopying (facsimile) or they are reformatted by the receiving device if it is unable to reproduce them exactly.

The central EDD service most likely will not store documents in one type of media but will dynamically evolve in time and will take advantage of technological advancements when they become feasible and economically viable. It may start from predominantly hard-copy files and microforms and build machine-readable files from current materials. Eventually, as backfiles have been progressively computerized, the center may develop an electronic storage encompassing both archival and current materials with the latter being maintained online. Basically, there are two approaches to produce computer-readable files: documents may be digitized as required in the course of on-demand delivery in response to each individual request, or the whole store may be systematically digitized as constraints of the system permit. Depending on the subject area, user demands and technology available, EDD systems may be capable of supplying text only, text and line graphics, or even halftone illustrations. As far as text is concerned, electronic systems outside the EDD concept can deliver abstracts only, as described elsewhere in this book, or the documents may be presented to the reader as synopses of the original articles, or finally, as full-text documents which has lately become a definite trend.

Electronic document delivery can take place as a result of users' being able to retrieve the articles of interest by searching indexes prepared for this purpose that point to the location of full-text documents. Searching may be conducted in one or more searchable record fields or in the full text of documents if searchable. Alternatively, the user states his request for documents in standard format and the delivery service bureau takes care of the rest. Electronic delivery systems, which are paralleled by conventional publishing, leave the users an option as to what form they prefer, whereas systems based exclusively on electronic publishing will demand that users have compatible hardware, software and training to be able to receive the information.

Generally speaking, access to EDD systems may be granted to the public at large or may be limited to closed user groups.

Delivery from the central facility or distributed centers to users can take place:

1. On a regular basis in which a document is supplied to subscribers either as an issue of a journal or some other publishing form, or may be also provided within the framework of an SDI service (selective dissemination of information, also known as current awareness or alerting service), which packages information to suit a particular user profile, rather than as a synchronous conglomerate of diverse information issued within a journal's topical mandate.
2. On an individual basis to meet a particular ad hoc need. On-demand electronic delivery may be requested by anybody possessing an authorized password, which is issued upon conclusion of a formal contract spelling out the terms and conditions of delivery transactions. Access on a credit card has been also made possible.

5.5 Users: Problems and Help

Tribulations of end users confronted with user-unfriendly electronic gadgetry have been dealt with in this book where appropriate, and they are no less felt in the area of EDD systems. Because the same cooperators, human and machine, are facing each other, the nature of problems encountered at the interface remains the same. The benefit a user can derive from interacting with a retrieval and/or delivery system is directly proportional to the amount of training which is expensive and time-consuming. Operating online systems without proper training is cost inefficient. In fact, many prospective users are turned off by these prospects and the situation is frequently aggravated by inadequate documentation. Some systems have adopted simplified interfaces but expert users tend to become frustrated if novice/expert option is not featured.

The task before users who need some information may be best illustrated by the existence of many options available to them: they may visit some local libraries to consult some traditional sources but there are electronic options as well and their number keeps growing. One of them is online databases. At the time of writing, there are 3000 online databases in the public domain, which has already necessitated creation of a "database of databases" cutting across the borders of individual database producers and on-line operators; this service by Knowledge Industry Publications, Inc., called Database User Service (see References and List of Organizations), may be consulted online although a printed directory, information updates in a monthly newsletter, and a toll-free hotline are also at the subscriber's disposal.

Yet finding pertinent references is but the beginning, albeit important, of a sometimes protracted game of document delivery. Wood (1982) distinguishes eight stages in document delivery:
1. Gaining awareness that a document exists
2. Identifying where it may be found
3. Verifying and generating a request
4. Transmitting the request
5. Processing the request
6. Transmitting the loan or copy
7. Paying the fees
8. Returning the originals

The potential bliss of electronic document delivery on the background of these eight steps may be fully appreciated: the entire transaction may take place, ideally and possibly, between a user terminal (microcomputer) and one or two host computers in an interactive mode.

If we focus for a moment on the mainframe computer/personal computer symbiosis, we can detect a trend which runs against, or along, the tendency to establish user-friendly service by way of simplifying the interaction with mainframe's software: it is the new category of PC software which empowers PCs to become a negotiator between the mainframe, on the one hand (its software and databases), and the searcher sitting at a PC on the other hand; Markoff (1984) describes the relationship of a tightly coupled mainframe database system and PC software as approximating the current relationship between operating systems and application programs. This concept is highly relevant both to online searching and to EDD systems in view of the fact that fulltext databases are being included in online providers' repertoires: for example, Dialog, a subsidiary of the Lockheed Corporation, implemented Information Access Company's two databases, Magazine ASAP and Trade and Industry ASAP, which cover 120 popular magazines and publications.

A typical software package between a searcher (plus his PC) and mainframe of potential significance for EDD is the Sci Mate from the Institute for Scientific Information (see References and List of Organizations). The software works on a number of microcomputers. Two separate software packages constitute Sci Mate: Universal On-line Searcher and Personal Data Manager. Whereas the former allows a user to query multiple on-line hosts with an automatic logon and one language only, the latter enables a user to create his own records either directly from the keyboard, from another Sci Mate file, from a word processor or from downloaded information. In terms of EDD, this program allows manipulation of textual data, generation of customized reports and merging of downloaded information with one's own notes or documents. An important feature of this system is that, once a record has been entered, it is searchable with no additional effort on the part of the user. This brings a new element into EDD systems in that the information received may be instantly organized for efficient use and manipulated in a variety of ways.

Software packages such as the above spell the end of the monopoly that mainframes once held with regard to "intelligence" in dealing with possibly hundreds of "dumb" terminals. This is of appreciable assistance to the end user, and other developments along this line are underway such as data compression on large documents transmitted from central storage to local microcomputer users in the scheme of EDD.

5.6 Examples of Electronic Document Delivery Systems

In this section we briefly characterize some different EDD systems in North America and in Europe. This is not intended to be, and in the light of the current flurry of activities in the field, cannot be a comprehensive list of EDD projects but rather a representative sample of activities in the field demonstrating the current trends, the philosophy behind the EDD concept, the underlying mechanisms and technology of various approaches and some concomitant problems encountered in the implementation.

Some projects never left the drawing board, some were run as field tests (AIP) and some were implemented on a sizable scale (ACS). Some of these undertakings have been designed on utilization of their own databases (e.g., ACS and AIP), and others relied on a multiplicity of information providers (ADONIS and Comtex). The projects envisage telefacsimile receivers, ASCII terminals alone and in combination with facsimile, optical disk readers, microcomputers (single or multiple), dot-matrix printers, electronic printers (laser and ink-jet printers) and even phototypesetters on the user side of the system. The storage of documents has been considered and/or implemented both on magnetic disks and on digital optical disks. Both terrestrial and satellite facilities have been used as telecommunications links in the projects. Documents in some of the projects may contain text, line graphics, mathematical notations and chemical structures. The SDDS project has a composition facility as well; this demonstrates the necessity of differentiating between EDD systems proper and EDD systems in the broader sense that function as the "back-end" part of a comprehensive electronic publishing system in meeting the demand of users for full-text documents or synopses. In such systems the editorial part is transparent to the reader in much the same way as the EDD component is transparent to authors, editors and reviewers. Electronic encyclopedias present special opportunities and challenges in view of their classification schemes which make it possible for various spin-off products to be prepared by the ultimate users themselves or by an intermediary to serve specific purposes.

"Electronic libraries," in the context of newspaper publishing, are establishing themselves as commercially viable propositions. Major libraries are busy trying to carve their niche in the electronic delivery infrastructure before it crystalizes. As opposed to publishers, libraries have a long-standing tradition of catering directly to the ultimate user and some of them have sizable collections of considerable completeness, spanning a wide range of subject fields, but like publishers, they lack the expertise in the requisite complex technology. Additionally, the funds required are beyond the means of any single library with the exception of the largest ones.

As is evident from the EDD projects that we list below, and also that we don't include, most systems are a product of the coalescence of elements of several disciplines such as computer technology, communications, information retrieval, record management, artificial intelligence, librarianship, publishing, reproduction, videotechnology, media, etc. Microprocessors have found applications in all of the above areas. One important area with regard to EDD systems is the scanning technology. Those EDD projects that cannot take advantage of the availability of typesetting tapes, or some other machine-readable medium, must depend on digitizing the printed material, thus making it processable in the electronic components of the system. Both raster scanning and OCR are employed in the current projects with the latter applicable to text only, and the former applicable to either text or graphics, or both. One of the advantages of OCR is that it produces an output which can be readily "understood" by computers; raster scanning turns out an output which can be "painted" on a VDU or electronic printer. Raster scanning is relevant to graphics, and if used to digitize text, it takes many more bits to represent a page than with OCR; this is partly offset by compressing techniques which reduce the number of bits required to represent a given area.

5.6.1 The American Chemical Society

The American Chemical Society (ACS) has long been a large publisher of chemical and other scientific literature and was a pioneer in the field of electronic publishing. Known through its successful efforts in the area of abstract publishing by its Chemical Abstract Service, the ACS is also a prominent journal publisher. In our context of EDD, the ACS launched a major project on June 1, 1983 by making the full text of their 18 journals available online; this was preceded by a 3-year study designed to determine the user-related aspects of such an undertaking (Morton 1984). The advantages of electronic delivery were found to be currency owing to biweekly updating, immediate access to the full article and the full-text search ability; the disadvantages encountered were lack of graphics and the limitation of the file to ACS journals (see the report by Terrant 1983). As a natural follow-up to the full-text online venture, the ACS is exploring the use of high-density magnetic tape as a means of delivering scientific journals in computer-readable form. Terrant concludes that, although online access to full text may be a solution to convenient document delivery, the telecommunication cost is too high at present. He envisages a greater role of customized packaging in dissemination of information in the future.

5.6.2 American Institute of Physics

The American Institute of Physics (AIP) conducted a test of publishing and distributing research information by electronic means (Lerner, Mick and Callahan 1980). Several laboratories associated with NASA participated in the experiment whereby librarians, scientists and engineers searched the SPIN database (abstracts of physics and astronomy articles) mounted on DIALOG (Lockheed's online information system). Retrieved references served as a basis for ordering those full-text articles deemed relevant which were delivered with an excellent response time by use of a facsimile transmitter. Two-way communication—both reference searches and document delivery—took place via the experimental Communications Technology Satellite (CTS). The technologies applied in the experiment proved to be up to the task, but the utilization and acceptance by patrons were found to be dependent on the manner in which the service was presented to them at each respective site. The report recommended, among other things, that videodisk technology for image storage and facsimile transmission should be studied.

5.6.3 Academic American Encyclopedia

Grolier (Grolier Electronic Publishing Inc.) has an electronic version of the Academic American Encyclopedia (AAE) consisting of approximately 30,000 articles and 9 million words, which is currently accessible to over 250,000 online and videotex subscribers (Cook 1984). The AAE is available on (1) a videotex system, (2) ASCII nongraphic services (user-oriented enhanced online services sometimes included in the videotex family of services), (3) regular online bibliographic services and (4) videodisk. The videotex system is Viewtron from Viewdata Corp. of America (a Knight-Ridder subsidiary), a system based on selection of desired options from menus. Users dial into the Viewtron host in Miami and, upon selecting AAE from among the menu items, are connected through a communications gateway to the AAE database in Philadelphia. The search of the database can start. It is the first commercial service based on North American Videotex/Teletext Presentation Level Protocol Syntax (NAPLPS) color graphics. Information delivered to the Viewtron user is composed of the frame in the videotex format but the text itself as placed in an active window is supplied in the ASCII code.

User-oriented, enhanced online services—Dow Jones News/Retrieval and Compuserve—also distribute AAE in much the same way as the online retrieval services DIALOG and BRS; the differences between these two categories were outlined in the respective chapters. Grolier has implemented yet another medium as an outlet for the AAE, namely the laser disk and CD-ROM disk.

Encyclopedias in general are versatile products in the context of EDD because of their internal organization by subject-related classification criteria. This enables, e.g., the Arete Publishing Company, a subsidiary of the Dutch publishers VNU, to generate a variety of products such as a book on a specific subject with little additional editorial effort or to transmit the spin-off publications in electronic form to remote locations to be printed, etc. (Maslin 1982).

5.6.4 The Library of Congress

The Library of Congress has launched the Optical Disk Pilot Program (Criswell 1983) which is designed to apply optical digital disks for essentially two separate purposes: (1) for a 3-year "prospective preservation" pilot program and (2) for retrieval of printed documents. High-use serials have been selected as the test material in this project which will eventually produce 100 disks with over a million images. After scanning, the digitized documents are stored on optical digital disks and individual pages or entire documents viewed by patrons on high-resolution VDTs or printed locally or remotely. Optical disk is being evaluated as a means for preservation, access and use of image materials such as architectural drawings, photographs, cartoons, sound recordings, motion pictures and TV programs.

A similar project has been undertaken by the British Library in an effort to cope with the growing demand for documents.

5.6.5 Commonwealth Scientific and Industrial Research Organization

The Commonwealth Scientific and Industrial Research Organization (CSIRO) in Australia has been investigating the Toshiba Tosfile system (Judge 1984) based on a 30-cm digital optical disk designed to store and retrieve 20,000 A4 pages. One A4 page takes 3 seconds to be scanned and output by laser, while concurrently, a file is created for retrieval on a floppy disk; up to six keywords per document may be used for retrieval in a maximum of 10 seconds. Six A4 pages are printed in a minute. Judge (1984) comments that such a device is cost-effective only if the market can generate a sufficient demand (over 500 pages a day).

5.6.6 Electronic Libraries in the Newspaper Domain

Newspaper databases have been installed on online retrieval systems for quite some time, such as Infoglobe in Canada offering the *Globe and Mail* from November 14, 1977 up to the present and *The New York Times* Information Bank in the United States. Lately, the interest of newspaper publishers in "electronic libraries" has soared and many newspapers are available in dual form, in both hard copy and electronic form. It would appear that at present the electronic paper does not pose any threat to hard copy sales mainly owing to the innate portability and readability of the printed version in contrast to its electronic counterpart, which has been used mainly for research purposes capitalizing on the sophisticated retrieval capabilities and fast delivery of the online full text, possibly supplemented by local manipulation on a micro. The benefits accrued to newspapers from electronic libraries are: (1) additional revenue can be earned from the electronic copy which has already been key captured in the process of editing, (2) the electronic library may be a replacement, in total or in part, for the traditional morgue maintained in microform, (3) older material may be called back into the editorial system if needed and if this is technically possible, (4) information may be passed efficiently to branch offices, and (5) feedback from users via electronic mail may be possible. An electronic newspaper library may be operated by a publisher itself or by a third party for a number of publishers and a multitude of users/readers.

Two companies are implementing their ideas of "regional data centers" (Alexander, Edwards, Stivison and Swain 1984), which are conceived as computerized repositories of data on a specific region or state embracing the full text of several newspaper databases and other databases of local interest. One of them, Datatek, operates the BASIS system from the Battelle Memorial Institute and markets the Data Times database containing a number of newspaper databases, a microfilm library index, an annual report and listing of companies traded and residing in Oklahoma, Legis Trak (Oklahoma Legislature information), Sports Trak and electronic mail. Datatek provides documentation, training, marketing and support. The BASIS system may be installed in-house or used online from the central facility.

Another electronic newspaper library has been offered by Vu/Text for subscribers in the United States and Canada and specializes in newspaper and business databases. Associated Press uses Vu/Text as its electronic library for the Washington and New York offices; as a result of cooperation with the AP, AP dishes can be used to upload a newspaper text to the Vu/Text computer in Philadelphia and download data for local decentralized use (Alexander, Edwards, Stivison and Swain 1984).

Electronic newspaper libraries are an application of information retrieval systems in a field with specific characteristics and are proving to be commercially viable. They are EDD systems but they could turn into complete electronic publishing systems if editorial capabilities were incorporated into the software.

5.6.7 Comtex

Comtex is a company engaged in electronic publishing of progress reports on ongoing research (Broad 1982). Submissions to the Comtex journals are refereed by a well-qualified editorial board with experts in every subject area covered, but there is no peer review process. This speeds up the editorial process and reduces the submission-publication time lag to a mere 6-8 weeks. Papers are either accepted or rejected with no author-reviewer-editor negotiation. Reports are then stored in the central computer and made available online to microcomputer and terminal owners who pay an hourly connect fee for the full text of selected individual reports. It remains to be seen whether traditional journal publishers will accept for publication articles which are based on research reports published in electronic journals.

5.6.8 ADONIS

ADONIS (Article Delivery Over Network Information Service) is a document delivery project based on a study completed in 1982 and funded by a consortium of publishers (Elsevier Science Publishers, Pergamon Press, Springer Verlag, Blackwells Scientific, John Wiley & Sons and Academic Press). The project was aimed at counteracting the situation whereby readers obtain copies of articles in libraries, either from the local store or procured for them through interlibrary loans, thus bypassing publishers who are unable to recover their costs incurred in the publishing process. Under the ADONIS scheme the lending center (publisher's store) would charge the requestor's library which, in its turn, would recoup its cost from the user. Scientific, technical and medical journal articles were to be entered into the ADONIS store and delivered to requestors within 24 hours of receipt of the order. The project envisioned participation of any and all interested publishers concerned with the increasing demand for single articles in the above subject areas in the light of the diminishing library budgets translating into a reduced ability to respond to this demand.

According to the projections, a database creation center was to be set up with the objective of converting journal article pages into digitized images in compressed form by means of a high-resolution scanner and storing them in a high-capacity digital store, the Philips Magnadoc, a digital optical disk system. Simultaneously, an index to all stored documents would be established pointing to their address on the disk(s). In response to user requests, the retrieved documents could be either printed on a high-resolution electronic printer or displayed on a CRT terminal, locally or at a remote location, from a single, or multiple optical disk reader or from a "jukebox" device which could retrieve, load and display the requested document automatically.

5.6.9 ARTEMIS

The ARTEMIS (Automatic Retrieval of Text from Europe's Multinational Information Service) is another example of an EDD service.

The ARTEMIS document delivery center would receive requests from patrons in a variety of ways such as mail or telephone or from user terminals just like a centralized library loan system with decentralized storage. References in standard format would be matched by ARTEMIS with corresponding documents stored online or offline and transmitted to users overnight. Information would be delivered in full text either character-coded for text- only transmission through teletex (an improved telex service, not to be confused with teletext) or facsimile-coded (image or raster format) to the user's telefacsimile receiver in the form truly representing the original page and including graphics; both character-coded and facsimile-coded information could be downloaded to user's computer for later printing.

The information for ARTEMIS would be captured from paper or microfilm either by optical character recognition devices or from a machine-readable medium prepared during text processing (typesetting); alternatively, pages would be digitized by facsimile scanners if graphics were involved. Digitized text would be put on information providers' own computer or supplied from an online operators' computer through a telecommunications network (i.e., Euronet) into which user terminals are connected. ARTEMIS was designed to route user requests to the appropriate host computer and look after accounting of each transaction.

5.6.10 Scientific Document Delivery System

The proposal of the Scientific Document Delivery System (SDDS) accepted by the Commission of the European Communities (Canzii, Degli Antoni, Lucarella and Pilenga 1984) is aimed at minimizing the publishing costs of low-circulation scientific books and resolving the copyright and security problems. Accepted documents' surrogates are also published in a printed catalogue. Users can search the database on-line and retrieve prices and relevant documents, preview the documents and order those deemed relevant. Documents may consist of text, line graphics, mathematical notations and chemical structures. The central computer facility files accepted documents, enables document retrieval and text composition using the TEX system and performs the ordering, billing and accounting functions; it interfaces with the network and distributes copies of the stored documents as requested by customer, on hard copy or magnetic media or directly to user's terminal for display or printing on dot-matrix printer or a small laser printer. Because text can be composed by the host, the output may be directed to a phototypesetter or a high-speed laser printer. TEX is a powerful typesetting language invented by Donald Knuth at Stanford University; it has a versatile math-setting capability.

Among the interfaces, ASCII terminals are used to enter text and the TEX composition language is employed producing a file with all typesetting information on the text formatted into pages; this file is still in the character-coded mode and is transmitted in this format across the network or transferred on magnetic media. Another program converts the text into the raster format for final representation of characters. Personal computers serve as workstations with a user-friendly editing program named EASY TEX, which allows for entry of even complex mathematical formulas. Integration of illustrations with text is achieved by means of a digital image scanner. The variety of output devices includes dot-matrix printers, laser printers, phototypesetters and graphic displays.

5.6.11 Project UNIVERSE

The Universities Extended Ring and Satellite Experiment (UNIVERSE) under the sponsorship of the British government, industry and universities explores effective communication over a complex of terrestrial and satellite networks. The satellite contributes to the experiment the high-bandwidth communication at the rate of 1 Mbits per second. These data rates make the UNIVERSE network, supplemented with high-speed terrestrial links and connections to X25 networks, well suited for intermittent transmission of documents (Winfield 1984): four pages of facsimile or 40 pages of text per second. The UNIVERSE experiment has as one of its aims the development of a multi-media workstation based on an affordable microcomputer. This has been accomplished and a mix of text, low-resolution and high-resolution graphics has been created and can be accessed using a workstation composed of three BBC microcomputers. Text is displayed on one screen, the graphics on the second screen, and the third micro functions as a printer server to provide a hard copy on a color ink-jet printer. Simple menus allow users to select and read multimedia documents stored at multiple remote sites across the network.

5.6.12 Electronic Information Delivery Online System

The Online Computer Library Center (OCLC) has been developing a document delivery system called the Electronic Information Delivery Online System (EIDOS) designed to bring the full text of documents to users' microcomputers located in libraries or on user's premises. The database for this project would be prepared from typesetting tapes made available by publishers; the typesetting codes would be stripped out and the database would be formatted to contain title pages, tables of contents and indexes. Subscribing libraries would install this database for public access by their clients, presumably free of charge. This first phase of the process would be expected to positively identify items of interest; the second phase would be initiated from the same microcomputer and its objective would be to bring the full text of selected documents down to user screens from the full-text database initially housed on the OCLC computers or from a publisher. Copyright problems have yet to be resolved.

5.6.13 Other Projects

Apollo. The Apollo system (article procurement with online local ordering) is a European information delivery project undertaken jointly by the Commission of the European Communities, European Space Agency and Eutelsat (a consortium of European Telecommunication Administrations). The unique feature of this document delivery trial is the combination of terrestrial and satellite links in facilitating the processes of retrieval, ordering and delivery. The advantages expected of this system over the status quo are quick delivery and user convenience at a cost per page which, it is hoped, will not preclude use at least for some document categories. Users in a typical Apollo scenario use a packet-switched network to query online databases prepared by database producers and stored on an online supplier's host computer. Ordering data are automatically prepared from relevant documents selected for ordering and transmitted to the repository where these data are verified. The customer confirms the order whereupon the full-text documents are sent to a shared satellite uplink, transmitted via satellite to a downlink on the user's premises (receive-only station), which passes this digital information to the user's terminal, workstation, microcomputer or fax machine.

Transdoc. Project Transdoc is interesting on several grounds: (1) it has been planned to offer a bridge between a major bibliographic database and document storage; (1) it constitutes an instrument for royalty accounting; and (3) it operates in a dual mode delivering documents both from the Thomson digital optical disk system and from an automated microfiche cabinet which may provide valuable insight into how these two different technologies compare in real life. The project involves some 2000 users in France, Belgium and the Netherlands.

Eurodocdel. This European project is on a smaller scale but aims at using optical disks, image scanning systems and satellite delivery; a videotex terminal has been envisaged as the terminal for ordering documents.

5.7 Innovative Distribution Formats

The bestsellers distributed through bookstores by book publishers will not necessarily need to be books. The definition of EDD is broad enough to include both electronic documents (products) and electronic delivery of interactive as well as noninteractive services; by "electronic products" we mean video cassettes, audio cassettes, videodisks and computer software on a variety of storage media. A "new" product such as software may be electronically distributed to a retail outlet to be received by the store clerk or, indeed, the ultimate user. The following outline of some existing schemes for electronic product distribution indicates how sophisticated the document delivery market has come to be.

The first time a videodisk paid royalties to a book publisher (Ditlea 1984) was the case of the videodisk version of *The National Gallery of Art, Washington* published by Harry N. Abrams, Inc. and distributed through traditional outlets. This product is aimed at laser disk players in the United States with the break-even point being estimated at 7000 copies. The 12-inch diameter laser disk can be played on Pioneer, Magnavox and Sylvania devices. Any one of 1645 images can be selected by keying four digits; the contents of the disk are supplemented by a pair of 20-minute documentary style programs on the masterpieces. This documentary part stresses the new capabilities of the electronic interactive medium which still lags behind the print version in color fidelity.

Bookstores have become the distribution channel for yet another unorthodox medium, namely, books on cassettes. Although these audio cassettes do not pose any threat to the sales of the well-liked and entrenched conventional books displayed on adjacent racks, this new medium has proved itself through the trial stages as a new, viable alternative, thus bearing out the prevailing view that electronic delivery systems, in the context of electronic publishing, are not about to take over the monopoly that "classic" print publishing once held, but rather enrich the spectrum of choices. Categories treated on cassettes encompass entire books or title abridgements, dramatizations or adaptations and book-related material by authors of successful titles; subjects include such areas as old-time radio shows, children's books, foreign languages, classic literature, business, biographies, self-improvement and history (Blaiwas 1984). The popularity of books on audio cassettes is due to the omnipresent audio cassette player as opposed to the more expensive devices required by end users of electronic information delivery systems.

It remains to be seen whether videotape will capture as much of the customer favor in publishing as audiotape has. Videotape not only adds picture to the sound, but also includes additional cost, lack of portable replay and the liability that it cannot be enjoyed in all situations of daily life because it demands all the attention span of the viewer.

Boundaries between print publishing and computer disk publishing are also vanishing as print publishers and software developers (and software freelance writers) join forces in marketing their wares. Software distributed through existing retail outlets or textbook channels includes home entertainment, home productivity, etc., but education is an area on which much effort has been concentrating.

An innovative way of electronic software distribution has been initiated by Telesun Corporation (J.C. 1984, see References), which has created a software users' network whereby participating microcomputer owners can use software titles from a rental library and communicate with other users. Documentation on software is either included in the software or is forwarded to subscribers by mail. Users have to connect to the network and pay royalties each time a piece of software is used; illegal duplication is prevented by a special patented protection procedure. Available software is claimed to be compatible with 75%-85% of all computers now on the market.

Software may be also distributed electronically while still remaining in the publisher/bookstore domain. After all, bookstores have a well-established clientele which might welcome an introduction to this new sort of commodity. However, bookstores still often lack the requisite technical knowledge and marketing experience to provide access to the right kind of software for their prospective customers and to safeguard an adequate after-the-sale service.

Three systems for electronic distribution of software were introduced (Hurwood 1984): Xante, a system aimed at the mass market outlets, handling both cartridges and disks; ROMOX, in which customers serve themselves in an interactive mode to obtain cartridges; and CUMMA, in which customers insert money in order to receive the desired software from the machine.

5.8 Electronic Document Management Systems and Electronic Publishing

Modern electronic document management systems (EDMSs) hold some potential for electronic publishing as document delivery subsystems. They are based on economical storage as provided by microforms but unlike the old systems relying on manual cataloguing and in contrast to the initial computer-assisted systems in which a complete microform file is required for every stand-alone microprocessor-based retrieval unit, EDMSs are characterized by computerized indexing and retrieval of relevant documents inclusive of their location information, automatic fetching of selected frames, their scanning, display and a variety of outputs. Even though the EDMS have been designed primarily for document management purposes in a corporate environment and targeted at the office of the future, they contain some features pertinent to our context. As a document delivery system in electronic publishing, these systems offer the microform alternative to the magnetic storage with its inherent advantage in cost and durability. This is practical especially in the on-demand mode of document delivery. It must be noted at this point that there is a noticeable trend to replace microforms with optical digital disks.

The central document store might receive documents as hard copies (1) or in computer-readable form (2) (Figure 19); either of these must be converted into microforms (3) (film, filmstrip, fiche or aperture card). Paper documents (1) are scanned by a raster scanner (4) and a COM is prepared in a raster COM recorder (5); alternatively, a microform camera may be employed (6). Machine-readable input goes

ELECTRONIC DOCUMENT DELIVERY

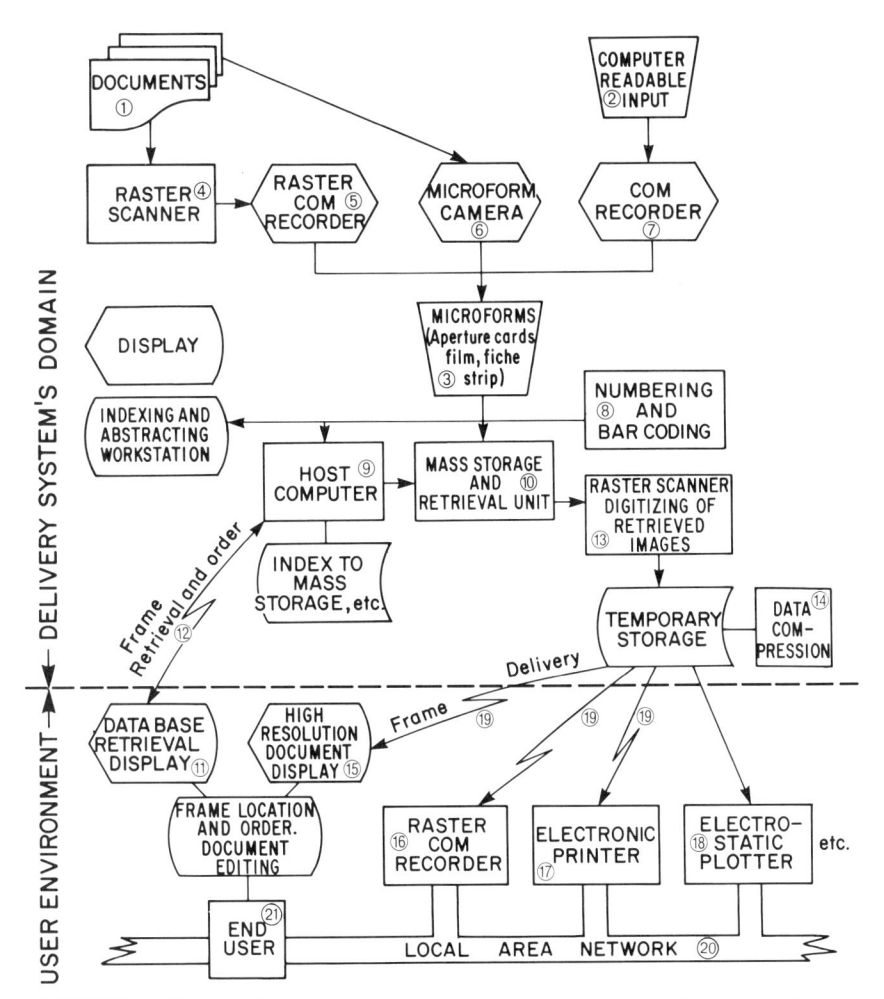

FIGURE 19 Electronic document management systems in the electronic delivery role.

straight into a COM recorder (7). After the microforms have been numbered and provided with machinable codes (8) (e.g., zebra codes) a textual database is generated centrally on a computer (9) either on a publisher's premises or by his distributor. When this has been completed, microforms are placed in an optical mass storage and automatic retrieval unit (10). Local or remote users (21) have at their disposal display terminals (11) and enter their search formulas (12) to query the central database online (9). The optical mass storage device (10) automatically retrieves the frames requested and has them digitized by an associated raster scanner (13). After data compression (14), these digitized images are sent to the user's high-resolution display terminal (15) which may be integrated with the retrieval terminal (11) in one unit. The displayed document may be further enhanced by editing software allowing for page modification before the final page is transmitted to one of a variety of output devices: raster COM recorder (16), electronic (laser) printer (17), electrostatic plotter (18), etc. In view of the vast amount of transmitted bits, the EDMSs can avail themselves of broadband channels (19) (e.g., satellites) tied into local area networks (20) for a reasonable response time.

A vital part of any EDMS-based distribution scheme is the film raster scanner. For example, the Graphix 1 scanner of the Information International Inc. (Painter 1983) can address one billion points in a 35-mm film image at speeds reaching up to two million points per second. Of crucial significance in making decisions as to the suitability of EDMS systems for any document storage and distribution system is the size of the automatic computer-controlled microform storage facility. For example, the system Access 2010 can store upwards to 125 million images if five units are integrated; the same system's scanner can digitize a microform frame in 1-3 seconds at a resolution of 200 lines per inch and display images at resolution of 1728 × 2,200 lines.

A microform-based system might, at least temporarily, alleviate the problem of archival storage. Older materials would be distributed from a paper-based store possibly using facsimile; current materials could be supplied from magnetic disks either online or offline. Microform archives could be built via COM recorders from the magnetic media, thus replacing gradually the paper-based store with the space-saving microform media which also afford more durable recording than magnetic media.

A system combining the microform and the optical digital disk (ODD) is Canon's "Integrated Electronic Filing System." In our present examination of electronic publishing systems, it is relevant in one or two ways: first of all, this configuration may serve as a subsystem in a total system, e.g., it might be enhanced by telefacsimile to deliver information on demand; secondly, components of this configuration might be employed in some other publishing system, specifically:

1. Optical digital disk drive with the DRAW capability, which can accommodate plastic disks of either 8- or 12-inch diameter (20 or 30 cm) with respective storage capacity of 7.4 or 20.8 Gbits. The error rate of 10^{-12} claimed for this device is outstanding.
2. Electrophotographic display, which does not require any refreshing because it is a black-on-white picture drawn by laser on a con-

tinuous photosensitive belt with subsequent toner application; the toner is removed when the image rolls away from the viewing position. Pages up to A3 in size can be displayed.
3. Digital microfilm scanner which automatically retrieves the searched frames utilizing the CCD (couple-charged device) technology and scans them at a resolution of 400 lines per inch (16 lines per millimeter).

Other parts of the system are a document reader, a laser beam electrophotographic printer and a system controller. The system has a RS-232C communications port enabling it to talk to remote systems, and it ties into the Canonet LAN. The "Integrated Electronic Filing System" is a prototype of a universal system which will find application both in the automated office of the future and in an in-house small-run publishing system also fulfilling the on-demand delivery function. It can duplicate the digital optical disk to be sent to a regional or local service center for distribution; and it can write documents from microfilm to disk, in other words from "archival" to the "live" storage. In addition to being a microfilm reader/printer (digital) and (digital) copier, it provides for reading of stored documents without glare. Communications make it much more versatile yet.

5.9 Concluding Remarks on Electronic Document Delivery

It is obvious that the evolution of EDD systems is influenced by political, economic, psychological, legal and social considerations, and is not merely a matter of technology. It has been recognized that an essential role of publishers is that of selectivity, i.e., to decide in a responsible manner what is to be let into the system and what is to be filtered out. With the setting up of EDD systems, there may be an additional "filter" imposed on the information flow toward the end user; this may happen regardless of whether a publisher, a library or anybody else operates the EDD. The motivation to imposing a "filter" might be on economic grounds in anticipation of heavier demand for given matter, which in EDD systems replaces the journal, etc., as the negotiable commodity; this would be highly undesirable because sometimes a published article may be of interest only to a few people but it may cause a major breakthrough in a scholarly discipline. Clearly, a paper (or any other unit of scholarly publishing) may be viewed as having two different value "tags": one reflecting its economic value (with respect to the cost of scanning, storage, transmission, number of "sales" anticipated, etc.) and the other bearing on its scholarly merits. In the traditional scholarly journal, papers of wide interest helped carry along those which were equally valuable but directed to a limited circle of scholars and this vital function must be incorporated into any prospective EDD system.

There is another issue looming above the EDD systems, also related to the processing and storage cost, namely: who will perform the archiving function. On the one hand, this matter is of paramount interest to the scholarly community and to the society at large providing for the continuity of human knowledge preserved in published materials as they pass through the stage of "out-of-print" and beyond, to the point where they possess merely historical value; on the other hand, there will be economic pressures towards jettisoning materials which are perceived as no longer profitable. Initially at least, these materials will be in print form, but later on, when more and more paper-based information is transformed into machine-readable form, the issue will revolve around the storage capacity, costs involved, the storage-medium durability as suited for archival purposes and cost redistribution.

What will be the next likely course of events in document delivery? If we start with users, they will continue to require "documents" which are readable, portable, easy to browse through and, if applicable, well indexed. They will prefer no or little cost, and, if there is a cost, a simple pricing structure. No or little training is a condition of acceptance; service must be available most of the time and must be prompt even though it entails higher costs (in most cases this is negotiable). Online selection and preview have gained popularity already. Users cannot be expected to buy expensive terminals or micros unless they are supposed to serve multiple purposes. Materials distributed electronically already include newspapers, patents, software and encyclopedias and will affect journals sooner than books; journals in the areas of science, technology and medicine are likely to be prime candidates for electronic distribution in their category, followed by business and financial items. On-demand publishing seems to be agreeable to user, libraries and publishers. For a long time to come, dual (parallel) publication is likely to prevail—both conventional and electronic. Journals also may be electronically distributed in dual format: as loosely associated papers in a journal and as closely related papers in electronic packages. Repackaging of information will become common both for redistribution and private purposes.

Electronic publishing will come gradually because publishers are mostly conservative and users/readers are resistant to change unless substantially motivated; libraries as go-betweens do not have funds to initiate any major change. Certainly the situation in the document supply has not reached any aspect of a crisis, but it may soon become confusing to some users who will become increasingly bewildered by the plethora of potential sources; because users cannot hope for any one-stop shopping, intermediaries will prevail in EDD as they have in on-line information retrieval. Various document supply sources will, unfortunately for the user, require a variety of output devices which is yet another justification for interposing an intermediary between the source and the ultimate user; the only exception is an EDD system where hard copy is prepared at a central or regional facility and mailed to the user.

5.10 Telefacsimile

Telefacsimile (also called facsimile or fax) is a technology that makes it possible to reproduce an exact copy of a source document at another location, local or remote. Any facsimile facility encompasses a transmitter and/or receiver or preferably a combination of both, known as a transceiver. Telegraph, telephone, and radio have traditionally served as transmission media, but optical fibers and satellites are likely to be used in the near future. Each scanned picture element may be represented in either analog form as an analog signal or in the digital form as 1 bit if black and white decisions are made or as a series of bits if levels of grey are to be distinguished as well.

Technology. The facsimile technology involves scanning the original document whereby the visual pattern of information is encoded in the transmitter (also called scanner) as an electrical signal corresponding to the visual pattern scanned; these electrical signals, either analog or digital, are transmitted and converted back into the original visual pattern at the receiving site.

Scanner. Principles of scanning have been described in Section 2.2 "Analog and Digital Form of Information" with regard to both character and image coding systems. Scanning finds applications in many areas of electronic publishing and has been referred to on many occasions throughout this volume. If the sending unit feeds only one page at a time then each page of a bound volume must be photocopied first; searching and photocopying of material to be transmitted takes by far more time than transmission itself.

Receiver. The function of a receiver is to convert the incoming electrical signal into permanent representation of the original document as scanned at the transmitting site. Essentially the same scanning techniques are utilized at both the transmitter and receiver whose primary function is to drive a printer. Several reproduction principles have been applied in facsimile printers, among them the following techniques:

Photographic
Thermal
Electrostatic
Electroresistive
Direct-image electrostatic
Ink-jet printing

Resolution. An important parameter in facsimile is resolution which means the number of scan lines per inch; this number may be, even though not necessarily so, equal in both the horizontal and vertical directions. More scan lines are synonymous with higher resolution and translate into better picture quality; scan lines are those spots that are scanned and their number is limited by considerations such as the bandwidth necessary to transmit them. The time involved in scanning, transmission and printing directly affects costs. Resolution in facsimile systems is a compromise between what is desirable in terms of picture quality and what is feasible in terms of the equipment used as it relates to economic viability. Resolutions range from about 100 lines per inch up to (not typically) around 2000 lines per inch encountered in microtelefacsimile. The proper resolution is automatically set depending on the density of transmitted documents but may be also selected manually for better clarity if needed.

Standards. A major obstacle to communication via telefacsimile would be that different makes and models of equipment could not talk to each other. To ward off this real threat, several standards have been implemented by the Consultative Committee on International Telephony and Telegraphy, (CCITT) in ascending order of their performance characteristics:

Group I encompasses analog devices with a speed of 4-6 minutes per page, and transmission rate of 2400-4800 baud per second.

Group II contains analog devices with a speed of 2-3 minutes per page and a minimum resolution of 96 × 96 lines per inch; transmission rate in this category is 4800-7200 baud per second.

Group III includes digital devices outputting a page in 1 minute or less, at a minimum resolution of 204 × 98 λινεσ περ ινχη; τρανσμισσιον σπεεδ ισ 7200–9600 βαυδ περ σεχονδ.

Group IV is designed for high-speed digital facsimile of high resolution with enhanced communications capabilities.

Fax and Electronic Publishing. Telefacsimile is relevant to electronic publishing as much as it is to the business office by virtue of its capability to transmit information, both textual and pictorial. An application of fax technology is the wirephoto services dating back to the 1920s. The use of facsimile has been investigated by individual libraries and library networks since the 1960s. A new dimension has been added to facsimile in that it is possible to scan and transmit microforms and either display them or write them on paper, microfilm or microfiche, which may be referred to as microfacsimile. All these applications fall under the rubric of document delivery (distribution and dissemination) and more specifically, on-demand EDD. But the applicability of telefacsimile ranges over a vast area of electronic publishing systems in which, e.g., pages are transmitted to a remote point to be printed for local distribution after film or plate has been prepared; this in fact is being done to avoid the costs of transporting the printed matter in bulk, or to take advantage of lower printing costs at a particular location. Pictures only can be transmitted to the composition room for pagination as well, if suitable interface is provided between the pagination system and the originating source which might be one's own scanner, picture store, raster image processor or an outside supplier such as a wirephoto service. The above examples involving graphics pose problems with the vast amount of data to be stored, processed and sent and these are aggravated still if color pictures are involved. Color pictures are transmitted as monochrome color separations: either the separation process is combined with scanning and this is repeated with all three filters, or colors are separated in the conventional manner using a camera at the sending site and monochrome separation prints are transmitted.

Technical Development and the Future. The trends in facsimile point in several directions and are aimed at a better and less expensive reproduction. Gates et al. (1982b) summarize the technical development as including automatic paperfeed, color facsimile, high-speed facsimile, high-quality definition of the image, the use of satellites, improved data compression techniques, the use of lasers and CCDs for imaging, a receiver scanning white areas at high speed and dark areas at low speed, a memory unit added to a scanner allowing for automatic transmission to take place during off-peak hours and finally a combination of a character-coded system for text with an image (raster or facsimile) system for graphics. Techniques of telefacsimile are also being applied to microform so that pages can be displayed or output on paper or on microform (McQueen and Boss 1983).

No doubt the above outlined technological features will make facsimile more attractive to those involved in future document delivery systems, especially to organizations providing information on the on-demand basis from a hard copy or print-based store. Yet we must not forget that more and more documents will be stored electronically in the coming years, and then document delivery will be from whatever storage media holds the documents in a particular instance: magnetic tapes, magnetic disks, videodisks, digital optical disks and other mass storage media. In that case no telefacsimile digitization will be required, although conversions between character- and image (raster)-coded and vector-coded data will still be needed. One trend that tries to cope with the present and future competitors of fax is to integrate it in a versatile environment of local area networks and to combine it with a variety of other equipment such as intelligent terminals, telephones, copiers, storage devices, etc.

6

Artificial Intelligence

6.1 General Observations

Artificial intelligence (AI) is an interdisciplinary field spanning a number of diverse subject areas such as psychology, cognitive science, computer science, electronics and linguistics. Even though AI is a rather elusive concept when it comes to definition, it is understood to concern itself with computer emulation of human perception and cognition processes represented as information-processing functions. Artificial intelligence encompasses varied disciplines whose enumeration may serve to give an outline of the field: search, knowledge representation, understanding natural language text and speech, automatic programming, models of cognition, automatic deduction, vision, robotics, learning and inductive inference, planning and problem solving (Barr and Feigenbaum 1982), theorem proving and logic programming, game playing, pattern recognition, AI "tool" building, expert systems and adaptive systems (Cercone and McCalla 1984). All these functions may be conceived of as computer models emulating specific aspects of the human mind with a varying degree of success.

Because electronic publishing is about computer-assisted modes of communication as defined elsewhere in this book, and because the ultimate objective of AI is to develop intelligent systems which would simulate and match the human mind and thus bridge the gap between machines and humans, it follows that both disciplines have common areas of concern. More specifically, electronic publishing stands to benefit from any advancement in AI that would facilitate use by humans of the new automated computer-based publishing systems in knowledge acquisition, processing and final distribution. This may result in improving present technology as well as in introducing altogether new modes of publishing, such as the use of some "publications" in a language of choice, automated consultants and multifaceted interfaces (text plus graphics plus voice). The field of AI is a difficult subject in which research results are not always amenable to immediate practical exploitation and many promising efforts have fallen short of expectation in the past. New optimism flared up in conjunction with the announcement of the fifth generation of computers boasting knowledge-based symbolic computation. The main difficulty in designing AI systems lies, in our opinion, in the ironic fact that the inner workings of the human brain are not yet fully understood so we are emulating something that itself is in the process of being explored.

Artifical intelligence has the ability to manipulate symbols as one of its most distinguishing characteristics and strengths, and this aspect has led to the synonymous designation of it as symbolic processing; herein lies another hindrance to its rapid development in that computer personnel will have to get used to what amounts to a new way of thinking manifesting itself in new programming approaches and languages (such as LISP and PROLOG).

Let us briefly examine expert systems, which have advanced into the limelight lately, and mention some other areas of interest in the present discourse.

6.2 Expert Systems

Expert systems (ES), also known as knowledge-based systems (KBS), serve the purpose of overcoming some inherent inadequacies of the human cognitive system such as absorption and assimilation of information in real time (see Figure 25). Expert systems serve as consultants to humans who present data (queries) to them and receive answers from them as a result of deductions emulating human reasoning.

Figure 20 illustrates experts (1-3) depositing their knowledge into an expert system with the assistance of a knowledge engineer (4) even though it is entirely possible to do so without an intermediary given a suitable interface. Users (5-7) query the system (8) in natural language (9). The expert system "reasons" through the inference engine (10) poring over the knowledge base (11); the global database (12) contains the input data, intermediate results between the "reasoning" steps and system status and history. A good expert system should be able to explain its judgment (13); an editor (14) may facilitate operation.

Users communicate with the ES as they would with a human expert by both answering the system's questions and interogating the system.

ARTIFICIAL INTELLIGENCE

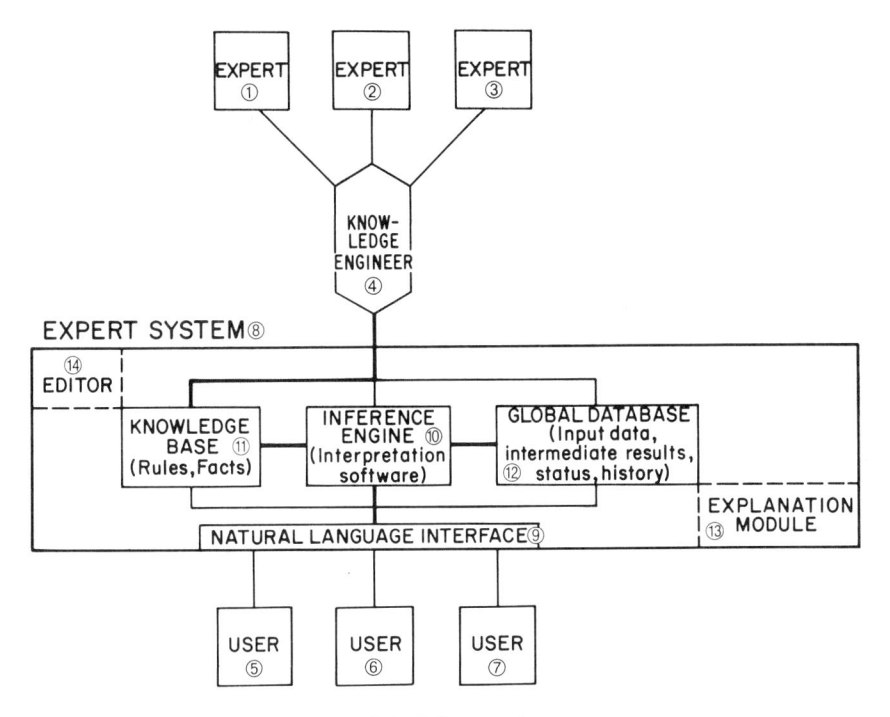

FIGURE 20 Expert system (simplified diagram).

Expert systems contain both the reasoning mechanism plus integrated empirical knowledge of a certain discipline. One of the advantages of an ES is that once the system has been established, unlimited expert advice may continue to be obtained within the system's scope at a cost of maintenance plus operation. Although ES are mostly based on variations of production system techniques (Newell 1973), it is entirely possible that database management systems concepts may be employed as well (Bonczek, Holsapple and Whinston 1984).

The difference between general problem-solving programs and ES resides in the former integrating knowledge into coding and the latter keeping knowledge and code "at arm's length" in discrete modules. Another difference rests in the fact that conventional computer programs concern themselves with numbers and words whereas expert systems operate on a knowledge base, heuristics and intuition. Also, traditional programming is done in such a manner that complete specification of the program precedes coding and testing, whereas knowledge engineering postulates an iterative approach owing to our lack of understanding of the reasoning involved in solving complex problems (Haley and Williams 1986).

Expert systems are able to account for their reasoning in a language understandable directly to users and this feature is bound to be stressed even more in the future.

Typically an ES has two main components: a control mechanism often called the "inference engine" (also control structure, control strategy or rule interpreter), which is the software operating on the knowledge base and data and represents the intelligent, "thinking" part of the whole. The other component is the so-called knowledge base (rule base), which may be looked upon as the expert's knowledge formalized, e.g., in "production rules"; these rules express knowledge of a specific area in terms of premises and actions (IF...THEN statements or "rules"), where the IF portion figures as the basis of questions placed by the system before the user; if the user's answer matches an IF statement (premise), then the THEN portion (action or answer) is true and will be employed in ensuing deductions. The consequence of ES being modular is that a given "inference engine" can be used with a variety of knowledge bases; in terms of electronic publishing, this means that, e.g., a specific inference engine might operate on different sets of productions rules (i.e., discrete knowledge bases), each of them formalizing the expertise required to communicate with an information retrieval host. Vice versa, it is equally possible for a knowledge base to be controlled by a variety of "rule interpreters" (inference engines) as a particular situation may warrant. This portability allows for modifications to be imparted to one component of the system without affecting other component parts of the system. In this manner, the knowledge base can be kept up-to-date or modified in that some production rules may be deleted while new ones are added to bring it up to the present state of the art in the subject area. In this context, a new career in the information/publishing field emerges, namely that of the knowledge engineer whose job it is to extract the subject area expert's knowledge and translate it into formal rules of a particular software package. But "knowledge engineers" may lose their jobs even before their job classification has been firmly established because there are already systems in existence and on drawing boards which are designed to make life easier on the input side of knowledge bases, initially for knowledge engineers but perhaps, before long, experts themselves to make knowledge engineers superfluous.

By database standards, ES are minor databases incorporating around 2000 rules and aiming at the figure of around 20,000. By 1990, however, knowledge acquisition systems are predicted to be in existence that will guide humans in knowledge base generation and expand into areas where there were no human experts before; around 2000, semi-autonomous systems are heralded capable of forming knowledge bases from text (Yaghmai and Maxin 1984).

Whatever the pace, it appears that expert systems will possess the qualities enabling them to outwit their human progenitors, and having no functional limitations imposed on them, they will be certain to make their mark on the knowledge industry of the future, especially in the light of the fifth generation computers and their touted supercapabilities. One of the obstacles to widespread use of expert systems was that the majority of expert systems were not yet available on the most popular microcomputers. But that has been changing too and expert systems may be able to prove themselves in the real commercial world. The programs written for microcomputers are not designed for a specific purpose but rather as expert system "shells" in the sense that users can build their own systems for any particular application.

Expert Systems—Automatic Consultants and Publishers. Computers should never be utilized merely to computerize the existing procedures, and in doing so, to freeze the present status quo albeit employing a new, trendy technology. At the very most, what can be achieved is conserving and perpetuating the old deficiencies and shortcomings by repeating them faster than before. Computers enable us to look at old problems in an innovative, fresh manner and sometimes even leapfrog the former state of affairs with a qualitative change. A fundamental change of the very concept of publishing can occur if, or rather when, the potential of some developments in artificial intelligence will be brought to fruition. The notion of expert systems appears very promising. Expert systems have the intrinsic property with regard to publishing that they can both be sold as "published" works and produce expert judgments (possibly with help of report writer programs), which themselves may be considered published works each and every time one is produced. The merit of "on-demand" publishing rests in its ability to spare the users/readers from subscribing to a collection of articles, some of which are partly or totally uninteresting to them, but they still have to pore over those deemed relevant and evaluate them. By contrast, expert systems will enable the ultimate users/readers/problem solvers to request answers to their questions; in other words, some publishing products and services may evolve from reading media into computerized consulting services. Where expert systems will be feasible, viable and affordable, this would represent one more option for the users to choose if they so wished and avoid the hassle of online bibliographic retrieval, hard copy full-text provision and extensive study of acquired materials. Jones (1984) suggests that a report-writing module would be an expansion of this (ES) technique into the sphere of simple stylized literary effort; the same author quotes timetables as works that may be suitable for replacement by ES whereas encyclopedias and handbooks are brought forward as prime examples of works suitable for front-ending by ES.

One can easily draw an analogy with online systems and imagine electronic journals interfaced with ES to allow users selection of the relevant journal and a paper within that journal. The complexity of the evolving situation and the myriad of potentially possible information and publishing systems may be demonstrated again on this new medium—the electronic journal—which might be either front-ended by an expert system—a relatively newer medium—or even replaced by such a knowledge-based medium altogether if the knowledge inherent to the electronic journal were transplanted into the knowledge-based system. But as Politt (1984) reminds us, expert systems can be expected to be a more refined and dynamic means of knowledge capture than periodicals.

There will be many implications of this information revolution which will, among other things, bring about shortcuts in the entire communication cycle with the resulting acceleration of information transfer. Figure 21 demonstrates development of information technology in evolutionary steps with special regard to the user. In the traditional system (1), the user searched the card catalog and obtained full text from shelves; offline (2) systems alleviated the search effort; online retrieval (3) from exterior databases and later from online public access catalogs (4) further simplified the search effort and improved completeness as well as timeliness; later online searching was complemented by online document ordering and, in full-text databases, resulted in the user acquiring the complete document (5). Electronic journals (6) provide full text. Expert systems (7) supply users with hard facts rather than pointers to sources or documents. Knowledge engineers mediate between experts and the system initially (8) but eventually experts communicate with the system directly (9); expert systems are envisioned that will be capable of extracting and organizing knowledge from human-readable and machine-readable sources autonomously and deposit it into expert systems for direct exploitation by users in varied forms (10), such as answers, reports, text plus image, sound, voice and multimedia presentation. But perhaps the most significant and probably the crucial implication, will be the continuous displacement of the information work force; this on the one hand will eliminate some professionals presently active as go-betweens in the above mentioned areas of online retrieval, hard copy procurement and information analysis, but on the other hand will create employment opportunities in preparation and maintenance of knowledge bases, designing human-machine interfaces, and designing and operating referral services, which will keep track of all the options open to the user with regard to his specific need, to name a few. The problem that can be already identified at

ARTIFICIAL INTELLIGENCE

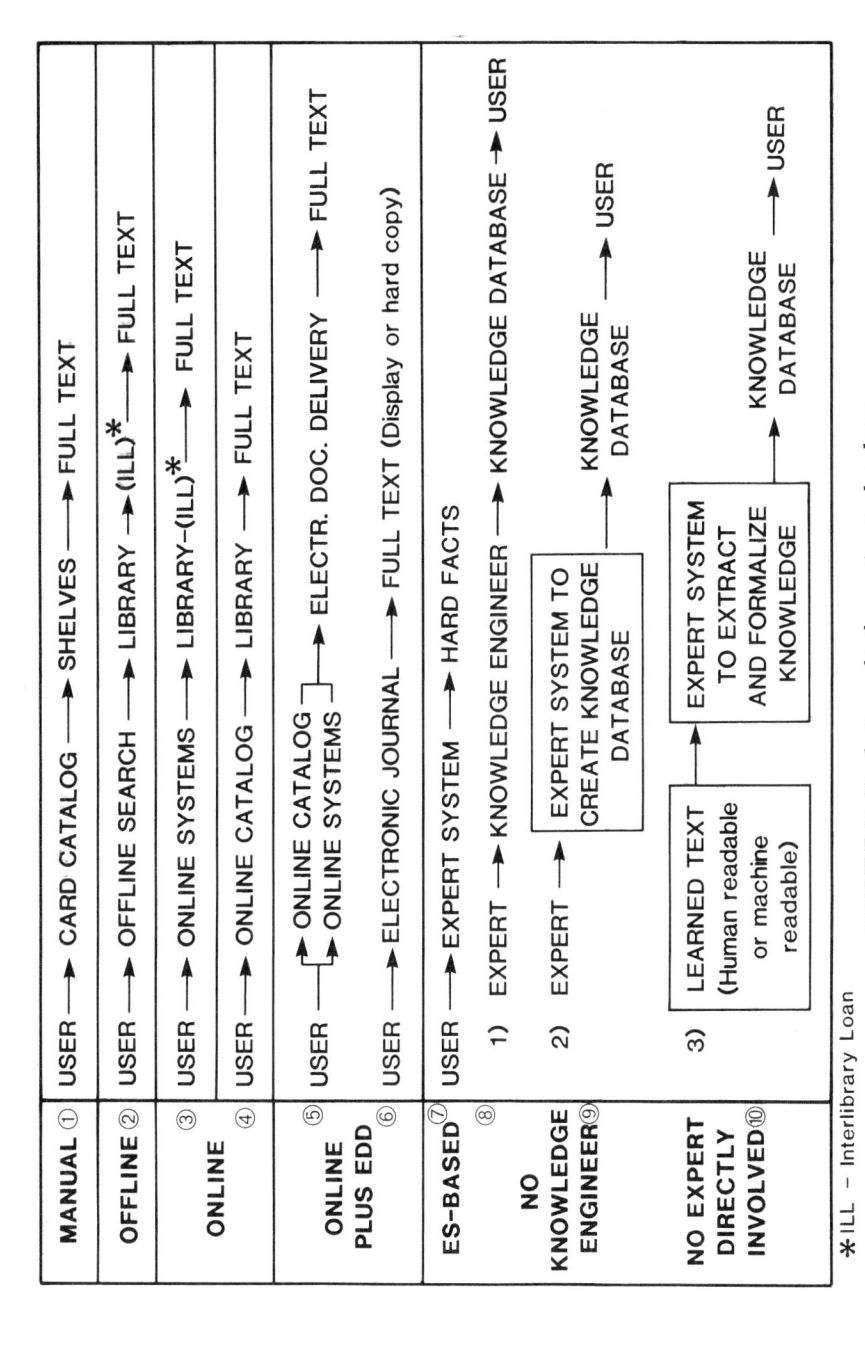

MANUAL ①	USER →	CARD CATALOG →	SHELVES →	FULL TEXT		
OFFLINE ②	USER →	OFFLINE SEARCH →	LIBRARY →	(ILL)* →	FULL TEXT	
ONLINE ③	USER →	ONLINE SYSTEMS →	LIBRARY–(ILL)* →	FULL TEXT		
ONLINE ④	USER →	ONLINE CATALOG →	LIBRARY →	FULL TEXT		
ONLINE PLUS EDD ⑤	USER →	ONLINE CATALOG / ONLINE SYSTEMS →	ELECTR. DOC. DELIVERY →	FULL TEXT		
⑥	USER →	ELECTRONIC JOURNAL →	FULL TEXT (Display or hard copy)			
ES-BASED ⑦	USER →	EXPERT SYSTEM →	HARD FACTS			
⑧ 1)		EXPERT →	KNOWLEDGE ENGINEER →	KNOWLEDGE DATABASE →	USER	
NO KNOWLEDGE ENGINEER ⑨ 2)		EXPERT →	EXPERT SYSTEM TO CREATE KNOWLEDGE DATABASE →	KNOWLEDGE DATABASE →	USER	
NO EXPERT DIRECTLY INVOLVED ⑩ 3)		LEARNED TEXT (Human readable or machine readable) →	EXPERT SYSTEM TO EXTRACT AND FORMALIZE KNOWLEDGE →	KNOWLEDGE DATABASE →	USER	

*ILL – Interlibrary Loan

FIGURE 21 Evolution of information technology.

present, is that we cannot train and retrain people fast enough to keep pace with the opportunities as they present themselves: the reason for this is threefold: (1) people are conservative and resistant to change, (2) training is lacking because of obsolete methods and shortage of teachers knowledgeable in the desirable subject areas, (3) we are uncertain in which direction to move. This discrepancy between the speed of the onslaught of technology and the rate of human awareness and reaction results in the latter becoming the bottleneck of the former as has been the case in so many areas. Expert systems in any application introduce a qualitatively new degree of user-friendliness.

Expert Systems and Online Information Retrieval. Expert systems are one of the methods able to eliminate problems encountered by ultimate users, intermediaries and their respective organizations in the retrieval from databases (there are already programs working in the same general area that are not of the expert system nature; see Section 3.2 on online retrieval systems). These problems originate in the basic fact that users' information needs are complex enough to involve interactions of manifold rules reflecting multiple networks, hosts, databases, formal access languages and specific vocabularies. To cope with this complexity, human operators have to be trained, retrained and even so can only handle a few host-database combinations efficiently. Because the rules can readily be imparted to the knowledge base of expert systems, these are likely to take over a great deal of the labor in database searching. The impact on online information retrieval may therefore, be envisioned on two tracks: expert systems add natural language capability and can revolutionize the database interface, plus eventually they wield the potential of extirpating them, in some areas, gradually as a class while they can offer factual answers to specific queries rather than masses of relevant (and irrelevant) references.

Online information retrieval, much like information retrieval in general, relies heavily on the quality of the index area where matching with the formalized or informal query occurs; at the same time building and maintenance of a thesaurus or other classification system is a time-consuming job requiring consistency and a great deal of expertise in the field. Because this expertise lends itself to translation into rules, it becomes yet another candidate for incorporation into ES.

Expert Systems and Publishing System Selection and Design. One of the problems facing decision makers in electronic publishing is the number of alternatives that all can be applied to a publisher's specific situation: is a videotex system more suitable in a given set of conditions than an ordinary online system to achieve the best market exposure for a certain database? Does a videodisk have a chance in a given publishing situation, all circumstances considered? Which system and make (originator to plate, to film or to paper, etc.) would solve a particular problem (labor cost, shortage of space, low productivity, low quality, need for better control, etc.) of a prepress operation in a given category (technical publications, magazines, etc.) and the size of a run? These are all questions that could one day be answered by expert systems, based as they are, on rules. The above questions demonstrate not only the level of knowledge which an expert must possess when communicating with a knowledge engineer (or with the expert system itself if a sophisticated interface allows for the knowledge to be acquired directly from a human expert), but also the life expectancy of the inserted information, which may have, depending on its nature, a short life span and require frequent updating. Expert systems may be valuable as much for the design of publishing systems as they are for their selection if the expertise can be expressed by rules forming what Newell designated as production systems (Newell 1973). Also, ES can be used to diagnose failures in working systems; of course, system selection, design and failure diagnosis are universally applicable to any subject area for which rules can be established. Expert systems for systems experts are recommended, for instance, by Martin (1985) in working with elaborate configurations such as distributed computing, distributed data, complex networks, small and large computers, with the need for high reliability and availability.

Additional Potential of Expert Systems. Let us briefly mention another capability of ES which could transform publishing into a much more useful service: they might provide the tool for translation into one or more other languages as yet another valuable feature of electronic publishing. Abstracting and indexing too, have been on the agenda of artificial intelligence for decades and now have more chance for success with the more powerful computers on the horizon.

Because of the vast amount of highly qualified work that goes into building the knowledge base with knowledge engineers acting as intermediaries between experts and knowledge bases, a flurry of activity can be observed in machine learning systems. Forsyth (1984) characterized machine learning systems as any automatic improvement in the performance of a computer over time, as a result of experience, with the aim of (1) covering a wider range of problems, (2) delivering more accurate solutions, (3) obtaining answers more cheaply and (4) simplifying codified knowledge. Machine learning systems work on knowledge bases that are erasable and programmable rather than the read-only type prevailing in ordinary expert systems. Forsyth (1984) works on a more user-friendly version of the BEAGLE, which is a computer package for producing decision rules by induction from a database: the rules are Boolean expressions represented by tree structures. Gevarter (1985) foresees systems able to semi-autonomously develop knowledge bases from text around the year 2000.

6.3 Other Artifical Intelligence Concepts Relevant to Electronic Publishing

In electronic publishing as in all other computer application areas, AI could make its mark by humanizing the human-machine interface. This could increase user productivity and enjoyment of work, reduce training costs and thus affect the acceptance of new technology. Of obvious significance in this context is natural language understanding which has already been embraced as a panacea in dealing with problems of accessing large databases if applicable to reasonably large vocabulary. Related to the problem of natural language understanding is speech understanding. Progress in this area to date indicates that full natural language understanding is still far away. Besides, there is the nagging question of what is the effect on the user of a dialog that is similar to his natural language but contains invisible restrictions in syntax, semantics, or vocabulary (Ramsey and Grimes 1983)? Nevertheless, natural language processing (NLP) seems to be advancing from laboratories into the stormy commercial world. The applications span areas relevant to electronic publishing and include several major topics (Johnson 1986): (1) interfacing by means of a "talkwriter" amounts to conversion of spoken word into typewritten word; (2) NLP interfaces to the major database management systems; (3) machine translation (MT) is claimed to double the productivity of human translators by preparing a workable first draft to be polished by human cognition; (4) Dialogue interfaces which go one step beyond simply passing a command and executing it—they maintain a two-way conversation as they build an internal model of the dialoguer's frame of mind during the discussion; and (5) text editing is next on the list of NLP applications, as the logical step after the word processing spelling correctors—its purpose will be improving on grammar and style of written language. With respect to voice input and voice output, it may be of interest to note here that Massachusetts Institute of Technology has been conducting research on their combined application with pointing devices (spatial input) and graphics (spatial output) (Jones 1984) which seem to indicate that joint use of graphics and voice augments their respective individual contributions to a more effective human-machine interaction.

Besides improving the human-machine interface, information retrieval and database management, AI may indirectly contribute to electronic publishing by offering new approaches to the broad area of programming languages.

Applied robotics have also found their first niche in the EDD (see "Enter the robot librarian." *New Scientist* 1984) part of electronic publishing. Sony is conducting a test of robots called "intelibots" in the library of the Kanazawa Industrial University: 60 booths have been installed, each of them containing video and audio cassette players; 34 intelibots designed by Sony page and load cassettes into the cassette players to serve 4500 students involved in the Sony test. Intelibots are controlled by a central computer in performing their functions. A large repository of diverse forms of electronic "publications" appears to be a fertile ground for deployment of various kinds of robots to pick out and "hand"-deliver required materials to certain locations (carrels, booths), machines or end users. Requests for services of this kind would be entered into the guiding computer by keying, pointing on the screen or by voice. Artificial intelligence can thus take on jobs in electronic publishing and document delivery which are both highly intellectual and purely mechanic in nature.

One thing that boggles the mind is the number of possible hybrid systems that will employ multiple components coming from technologies described so far in this book. This convergence of diverse media, gadgets and software has been made possible by the growing computational resources and will be multiplied by the evolving artificial intelligence. How shall we call and classify an information/communication/publishing system in the not-so-distant future, which will unify an expert system and multiple online systems using optical memory media; a system with an NLP capability and which accepts written work or spoken word as input; a system which will scan any graphics and manipulate them in any way with ease equal to that with which it processes text; a system which outputs text alongside graphics and also voice, data, etc., with simultaneous translation; or a system with output both nonprint-oriented and paper-based including videotex format. Obviously, new criteria will apply to the integrated communications media of the future replacing old criteria of the isolated, limited publication means of the present and past.

7
Microcomputers in Electronic Publishing

With the developments in the VLSI technology that brought about the microrevolution being manifest with more and more powerful microprocessors and microcomputers, with ever-expanding numbers of off-the-shelf software packages embracing a growing gamut of applications and with larger, faster and less expensive storage, it was only a matter of time before microcomputers would find their way into the electronic publishing scene. To be sure, there was some use of microcomputers in electronic publishing in the recent past, but it was mostly in areas where the full potential of micros was not realized such as an author's terminal (or reviewer's or editor's). Although this application constituted an improvement as compared with dumb terminals and noncommunicating word processors, the microcomputer was for some time relegated to second-rate functions, such as text entry and editing, and to applications not representing a major slice of the present market. What is now changing is the availability of more sophisticated software packages which will enhance micros' position in publication roles held traditionally by mainframes, and more lately, by minicomputers. This development will make the distinction between minis and micros increasingly blurred. As may be seen below, this process has already started and is certain to gain momentum as computing power is moving to our desktops. Whereas microcomputers started off as isolated stand-alone devices, their utility has been increasing dramatically with communications capabilities being constantly improved.

7.1 Applications

The following summary gives examples of current applications cited in this volume; the list intimates the wide range of roles that microcomputers can assume wherever the information publishing cycle is conceived (authors' sphere plus editorial process) or completed (reader's or user's domain) and anywhere in between (control functions, composition, graphics manipulation, etc.) as well as assisting in administrative tasks such as accounting, billing, fulfillment, editorial processing center, etc.:

> As we briefly mentioned in Section 3.5 "Videotex: Viewdata and Teletext," the videotex information provider's terminal may be used as a microcomputer if equipped with appropriate software; this might involve functions related to videotex and otherwise. But, in a reverse development, microcomputer manufacturers have provided their products with such videotex-like features as graphics and color, which both increases competition between these two technologies and attenuates their differences. Microcomputers may be equipped with special software, digitizing tablets, boards and decoders, which enable users to create pages in videotex format and display, manipulate, store and transmit them, thus converting users into information providers. Somewhat ironically, microcomputers have turned out to be the hottest topic in the rather stale area of videotex. The Apple Macintosh has been recently equipped with a software package called MacNAPLPS, which adds the videotex decoder capability to the microcomputer; the package has been developed by Electrohome of Kitchener, Ontario.

> In Subsection 4.3.5, "Microcomputers in Paper-based Electronic Publishing," we reported on the possibility of a personal computer acting as a focal point in a system at which any type of text may be scanned into the system as a digitized image in raster format with subsequent scanning of illustrations and their sizing within picture boundaries. Text may be generated on the same microcomputer and data may be transmitted. This makes it an intelligent facsimile device among other things, but there are indications that similar systems might be used if properly configured in applications that were once dominated by prohibitively expensive mainframes and minis; microforms may be handled as well. In-house publishing and electronic document delivery, in general, can benefit from microcomputers introduced recently in this area.

> Another exemplary bailiwick for microcomputers is the area of information and document retrieval. We have noted the dual role of

microcomputers working both as intelligent terminals in retrieval from remote mainframes and retrieval from local image store (see Figure 7 "The hybrid online text/local videodisk graphics technology"); the role of the microcomputer may be modified to store databases locally, either original or downloaded. Software for specialized processing may be downloaded from a remote host; when searching database stored on a disk, the software may be located on the same disk as data (CD-ROM or videodisk).

Microcomputers can be utilized with advantage across the spectrum of electronic publishing systems whenever query preparation and negotiation is involved. Local query preparation saves connect and communication cost and also storage cost, especially if a number of user profiles are stored to provide information to subscribing users on an ongoing basis which entails frequent changes to user profiles.

The possibility of text entry and editing has been well established with micros including networks and clusters of micros. Microcomputers were also adapted to typesetting installations via front-ends but this is essentially a misapplication because the personal computers of today themselves have all prerequisites to drive typesetters. Increased attention has been paid recently by software producers to the area of composition to bring micros on a par with minicomputers and to enable them to drive typesetters; programs have been written that can prepare only galleys and others that produce a page without illustrations. Some programs can drive a specific typesetter whereas some can handle an array of devices. Some of the programs work in batch mode and others offer a varying degree of interactivity. Today microcomputers can compose complete pages and integrate text with graphics whether it be line art or continuous tone. Complete pages can be "imaged" on a typesetter or electronic printer. The trend clearly points to micros being able to take over the job of existing front-ends, including hyphenation and justification and display of true type size and position, in interactive mode of composition. This will move composition into the realm of the automated office with complete page makeup capabilities for certain applications and will make microcomputers the most visible factor in effectively removing the last vestige of difference between the automated office and electronic publishing.

It may well be that the upshot of the present trends will be users creating their own "books" and "journals" and personalized files meeting their short-term or longer-term information needs.

Microcomputers provide a tool for repackaging of packages and offer to put all the ingredients of an end user's workstation together.

Libraries appreciate the help of microcomputers in many areas. Stand-alone applications already include departmental files, information retrieval, electronic messaging, statistics, accounting, inventory, personnel files, modeling and similar roles. Microcomputers, however, can prove invaluable to libraries if and when they decide to pursue active electronic publishing beyond the on-line public access catalogue which, by the way, may also be supported by micros in much the same way as other aspects of library automation. A new role for micros in libraries has been as a controller in CD-ROM installations dealt with above.

Microcomputers add "intelligence" to even complex electronic publishing systems and as such control the flow of information (data, text, illustrations) in whatever format (character-, raster- or vector-encoded) from one component to the other throughout the system. For instance, text may be marshaled from the text-entry device along with illustrations introduced through the scanning device to the page makeup device and from there finally to any of the output devices. Besides this organizing function, microcomputers are at the heart of many individual devices as outlined where appropriate in this study. A raster image processor (raster imager, raster image controller, etc.), for instance, may be thought of as a special purpose, dedicated microcomputer based on a powerful microprocessor; such microprocessors may be found in other equipment as well, such as electronic printers, performing variety of functions.

For a more detailed treatment of microcomputers in the print-based (paper-oriented) category of electronic publishing, please refer also to Chapter 4 "Print-based Electronic Publishing" (Section 4.3.5).

7.2 Microcomputers and Current Trends

Microcomputers are being utilized to serve in applications formerly reserved to much larger conventional hardware based on mainframes and minicomputers; this phenomenon has had a profound impact not only on the technological aspect of publishing, but is sending waves across the industry's infrastructure with far-reaching implications particularly in marketing.

A. Microcomputers are instrumental in the trend which endeavors to shift the center of gravity in the publishing process closer to the author or at least to the editor. There is even no technological restriction why authors could not be publishers themselves; new equipment makes it possible to produce camera-ready pages on publishers' premises immediately after the editorial process. This may even include small print runs on an electronic page printer if the resolution suffices for a given purpose. All this may lead to a better control over the process and product and may result in extension of deadlines, better quality, shorter production cycle and possibly in lower cost if the application had been designed in a cost-effective manner.

B. Another observable trend in publishing today is vanishing borderlines between prepress areas once recognized as disparate. On modern micros the distinction between text entry, graphics generation, editing, composition and pagination boils down to the necessity to call up new software whereas typesetting (or better, image setting) will still be initiated from the same workstation to be performed on an adjacent piece of hardware. All the above functions are united in space and partly in time in one workstation or streamlined in a continuous chain of processes. A corollary effect of this is shortening of the technological process: micro-based systems can, as some of their mini-oriented predecessors did, eliminate some proofreading by outputting the same data to the display, electronic proof printer and typesetter; some camera work is saved and pasteup and stripping are done electronically. There are tendencies pointing to complete pages being output directly to plate. In-house publishing may output directly on paper if the resolution of electronic printers is acceptable, which is the case in technical documentation at present.

C. The talk in the trade about integration of text and graphics has been going on since the 1970s; the advent of microcomputers makes this technology affordable even to smaller publishers. Text and graphics may be united on the same workstation where both of them have been generated, but in some situations these processes are separated for reasons of better productivity based on the division of labor. Microcomputer-oriented page layout and page makeup stations may operate on a microcomputer network along with other microcomputer workstations specialized in text entry and graphics generation. Along with line graphics, more continuous-tone illustrations are being incorporated as halftones into publications as a result of microcomputers capable of interfacing with a wide range of scanners on the input side and raster imaging technology on the output side; picture manipulation possible at this stage in some configurations includes cropping, sizing, airbrushing, control of brightness, contrast and multiple resolution.

D. The convergence of electronic publishing and office automation allows for personalized documents to be typeset and various business and technical documents to be published directly from the office; microcomputer-based workstations strung along a local area network and surrounded with an assortment of peripheral devices provide the focal point for this convergence.

E. Whereas in the 1960s and 1970s the newspaper sector was the trailblazer and trendsetter in publishing technology, we can see more attention of system developers being directed toward the growing in-house publishing segment of the industry. Microcomputers have bright prospects in the technical documentation area owing to lower cost, easier training, availability of graphics while the output resolution is acceptable; this is the field where the marriage between the micro and the electronic laser printer has proved to be most fruitful. But microcomputer-based systems have now discovered the newspaper sector as yet another niche to conquer and small newspaper systems are being sold.

F. If some of the trends in "micropublishing" are accompanied by *if*'s and *but*'s, then the number of authors submitting their papers in machine-readable form has been rising constantly. If problems of incompatibility in any particular case are resolved, then all of authors, editors/publishers and typesetters can benefit considerably through elimination of retyping and proofreading.

G. Very far-reaching changes have occurred in electronic publishing, much the same as in other areas, on the human-machine interface. With the advent of micro-based systems, we have been moving away from mnemonic codes to interfaces characterized by pull-down menus, iconic symbols and pointing devices or touch-screens. This development has freed operators from the tedious memorizing of complex codes but changed in its wake the job description and list of qualifications expected from the new breed of an "operator" to include text entry, graphics creation, basics of typography, handling of halftones, esthetics of pagination.

H. The software explosion observed in computing in general makes microcomputers a much more versatile tool while at the same time forcing on users the onus to cope with the flood of information about information tools, thus returning them to the quandary of the precomputer era, which computers were supposed to resolve in the first place. It appears that some degree of an overlap is developing between word processing and composition software. Composition programs on microcomputers are being perfected by inclusion of such advanced features as kerning and automatic hyphenation to a degree of sophistication previously known only on minis; the same is true of software picture manipulation (e.g., scaling, cropping, adjustment of contrast and brightness) and of pagination. Microcomputers in electronic publishing are versatile enough to act in varied design and production roles and at the same time are able to serve in a number of capacities of administrative nature: editors can match authors' data and their creations with attributes of referees and perform various automated functions built around these files. Other specialized software can look after fulfillment, billing, accounting, preparation of brochures, yearbooks, bibliographies, book catalogues. Some single-purpose hardware such as front-ends or disk conversion devices can be provided with an operating system and serve as ordinary microcomputers.

7.3 Roles of Microcomputers in Prepress (1986 and Beyond)

In the "low-end" prepress market, we can find microcomputers performing a number of functions listed below in increasing order of complexity:

1. A microcomputer may play only the role of a low-cost data entry and editing workstation. In this case it depends on a front-end endowed with composition capability; multiple personal computers may be connected into a front-end either locally or remotely, and composed "soft" copy may be previewed on a preview station in generic fonts or even in true fonts before being passed on to the typesetter.
2. Microcomputers can not only serve as inexpensive text entry devices but they can compose as well, thus replacing the much more expensive front-end system. Many software houses, large and small, are busy writing composition programs whose sophistication is already approaching that of the "high-end" front-ends. There is no doubt that off-the-shelf micros will achieve a breakthrough on the market which is already bracing up for possible consequences; besides the lower price there is the added benefit of a much less unfriendly interface.
3. Micros can go beyond editing and composition as vehicles for line graphics creation and pagination. At this level of capacity, they deliver complete pages, which may be previewed on the same workstation, to a laser printer or to a typesetter. The graphics capabilities and composition power of these systems are being constantly enhanced. The trend points to these workstations working in the interactive mode whereby all changes of format, font and style appear immediately on the screen. Often

some task may be performed in the foreground while another job is being run in the background. Some amount of storage and processing time may be saved if composition and pagination operations are conducted on lower resolution copy, which is blown up to full resolution at the time of actual output. Although these systems may be rather slow for a larger publishing operation, the increased processing power and working storage will remove even this obstacle to wider acceptance.

4. Continuous-tone scanning can augment the above functions with illustrations screened and the resulting halftones placed on camera-ready page.

A comprehensive configuration of this type (see Subsection 4.3.5) features a workstation which can accept continuous tone graphics (or any page image) via a scanner, create text and line graphics, merge text and graphics on any page, provide a "soft" proof and output both to a technical publication-quality electronic printer (providing either final print or plain-paper proofs) or to typographic-quality imagesetters. Workstations of this kind may be linked in a local area network sharing a mass storage device; the advantage of this type of distributed processing over a system in which multiple workstations output through a single device (mainframe or minicomputer) is less downtime because, in case of any one component's failure, the rest continue undisturbed. Camera-ready pages go on plate but the trend points to output directly on plate.

Systems of this category are modular with some components easily updated. The number of companies interested in the development works against obsolescence. Orientation on the raster output technology, merging of text and graphics, output in a page description language (it is hoped, standardized), focusing on the microcomputer as the hub of the configuration, easy human-machine interface and mushrooming software packages available are all well in line with observable trends.

A case history dealing with cost benefit of a publishing system built on the above principles may be found in the next section. As a point of interest, we may mention that this category of systems may be used by authors, editors, graphic artists, publishers, the automated office and, in the framework of electronic document delivery, as a facsimile-like service.

5. At a point in the not very distant future, we may expect that both nonprint and print-based publishing will merge. At this stage of development, which we have called integrated electronic communication, all functions of electronic communication will be able

to be performed from a workstation, most likely based on a super-microcomputer: the functions of authors, publisher and readers. It will be possible to participate in database publishing both actively as author and passively as end user, using local storage or remote hosts; it will be possible to participate in electronic journals and videotex-like services. It will be possible from one's desktop both to transmit and receive full-text documents in the framework of electronic document delivery. All publishing functions will be feasible encompassing text, line graphics and continuous/halftone illustrations as described above. Media and format conversion capability will be built into this workstation as well. Advanced software will include products of artificial intelligence such as an assortment of expert systems, translation, abstracting and indexing systems and the plain-language interface.

These systems will be fully integrated into communications networks, both long haul (wide area) and local, which by then will have merged themselves.

7.4 A Note on the Economics

The economy of using a micro-oriented system to publish both technical documentation and typographic-quality materials may be shown on an example of a medium-sized, in-house publishing shop involved in the production of books and journals. Let us assume that typesetting and page makeup have been contracted with a commercial printer; 50% of all author submissions is as typewritten pages and the other half delivered in computer-readable form with charges by the outside service of $50 and $15, respectively, i.e., $32.50 per page on average. The monthly cost payable for 300 pages thus makes $9750.

Typesetting and page makeup may be done today by an in-house publishing system centered around a microcomputer. A system at about $66,000 can be acquired encompassing a microcomputer with a VDT, keyboard, mouse, requisite word-processing, graphics and composition software, scanner, proof printer, laser printer and typesetter. Considering a 5-year depreciation period, the cost per month would be $1100, which amount must be increased by 10% to cover the maintenance contract. Adding $2000 for an operator and estimated $170 for material (photomaterial plus chemicals) makes a subtotal of $3380 per month and the total of $4056 per month including 20% overhead. The investment can be paid off by resulting savings ($5694 a month) in about 12 months. The amount of saving would be still higher because (1) the microcomputer systems of today do not require elaborate coding or complicated key sequences which have to be performed at present; (2) the proposed system is not fully utilized and can take on additional jobs; (3) there is a net saving on line graphics, which can be efficiently generated on the screen instead of being ordered in a graphics art shop; (4) the operator is not fully utilized at the above production rate and may participate in other jobs such as data entry, etc.; (5) there is less proofreading because multi-column pages are produced instead of galleys; (6) continuous tone illustrations are integrated electronically into the page instead of being stripped in.

Another example of the cost-effectiveness of microcomputers in electronic publishing may be cited in the area of peripheral devices. As authors submit their contributions, to an increasing extent, in machine-readable form, mostly as word processor and microcomputer diskettes, publishers and commercial typesetters have been confronted with the problem of compatibility between these media and their own respective processing systems. The only way to transmit text between different computers, word processors on the one hand and typesetters on the other hand, was for some time by telecommunications but this practice often eliminated important codes. Today, there are several media and data conversion systems on the market that are either devices dedicated to this special task or general business microcomputers which may be used for any purpose. These devices allow translations from and to hundreds of different data formats; they operate in a variety of modes—from disk to disk, telecommunications to disk, disk to telecommunications, magnetic tape to disk and vice versa, disk to computer, front-end, typesetter or printer. By acting as a bridge between incompatible systems, the media converters reduce labor and handling, provide in-house control over data and text and increase productivity of prepress while at the same time enhancing the utility of business microcomputers. There is no rekeying and less proofreading. The cost efficiency of acquiring a data converter may be demonstrated on a simplified case history taken from a small press operation. If 10 journals are being published as quarterlies and each of the 40 issues per year contains five papers on separate diskettes, which cannot be handled on editor's equipment, then 200 translations a year may be required. If media/format conversion is done by a service bureau, then a charge between $30 and $70 is incurred per disk; this amounts to an estimated $10,000 a year. Because a data conversion system costs around $20,000 contingent upon sophistication, this investment can pay for itself in approximately 2 years while furnishing all the advantages of machine-readable "compuscripts" over the typewritten copy. The alternative to microcomputer-based format conversion is to deal with both the diskette and hard copy in the author-editor communication and to rekey the copy into the typesetter's front-end if needed; this alternative is inconvenient to all parties involved and is on retreat.

7.5 The Marketing Aspect

Having pleaded that there is a future for microcomputers in electronic publishing technologically and that this future holds some positive potential for the economics of publishing, we now briefly explore how all this may affect the prepress vendor-publisher relationship.

Thus far "traditional" prepress vendors have provided minicomputer-based hardware and software as a package to customers. Vendors have been buying some components of their configurations from other manufacturers in recognition of the fact that research and development are so costly that single vendors cannot undertake it on a broad front on their own. On this research and manufacturing base is built the marketing superstructure with continental, regional and local sales offices staffed with business and technical representatives. This costly arrangement has been often subject to customer criticism with regard to the quality of after-the-sale-service, training, documentation, etc.

The infrastructure of the new micro-based era has only begun to emerge. Microcomputer manufacturers building on a strong research base buy various components, assemble the product and supply microcomputer stores. Software engineering companies, big and small, supply both of the above levels. As micros grow more versatile and software more specialized, it is becoming evident that microcomputer stores will not be in a position to offer adequate advice and service across the entire spectrum of applications. It appears that in electronic publishing as in other areas, there is a place in the marketing infrastructure for new players if standards of customer service are to be maintained, or preferably, improved.

1. Specialized micro stores might be one of the ways how to ensure detailed customer guidance and satisfactory service. Specialized stores would be selling hardware and software of multiple origin, both new and second-hand, to the publisher. The problem of this arrangement is the limited local market. If a multitier marketing organization were to be established, it would easily end up being as unwieldy as the present one.
2. A value-added micro store for publishers would go one step further and provide, in addition to the specialized hardware and software, all the gadgets a publisher might need, for one-stop shopping. This would encompass electronic page printers, scan-

ners, typesetters, etc. This type of store usually supplies a complete line of devices for a given purpose but from a limited number of manufacturers, possibly from only one, for each kind of equipment.

The complexity of the market and the dynamics of the development already seem to be warranting the services of independent consultants divorced from allegiance to any particular vendor(s):

3. System integrators would not maintain any stock but would act as task-oriented problem solvers for customers requiring such a service. It would be part of their expertise to be knowledgeable of hardware and software and to be able to relate it optimally to a specific user situation. This system integration is a step higher from the present state in which integration is done by vendors partial to their wares and would save the customers from having to be their own system's integrators. System integrators can provide feasibility reports as part of the presale service and advise customers as to the after-the-sale service. They sell mostly know-how and act as intermediaries between multiple vendors and multiple users with specialized needs.
4. Finally, the entrenched conventional vendors are all active in the development of integrated systems embracing microcomputers as their pivotal component, in addition to their other products. It remains to be seen whether customers will sufficiently value the service provided by these vendors or buy microcomputers at lower cost off-the-shelf and obtain the requisite service elsewhere.

As far as publishers are concerned, they hope for better quality of service and lower price. For this to happen, it would be necessary to reverse the trend they have been witnessing recently, namely that although the cost of hardware has been falling, the proportion of marketing overhead and acquisition related services has been rising steadily.

7.6 Conclusion

The impact of microcomputers on the contemporary prepress industry has been highlighted by their role in shaping up present trends. Micros are one of those factors shifting the center of gravity of the publishing process closer to the author or at least to the editor/publisher; borderlines between individual areas of prepress are vanishing as data entry, graphics generation, editing, composition and pagination can all be effected on the same micro-based workstation with an image setter standing by. All this means simplification of the technological process resulting in a shorter information/communication cycle.

The integration of text and graphics was not implemented on microcomputer workstations the first time, but it was this development that made the integration affordable to smaller publishers. Line graphics may be created on the workstation itself, whereas continuous-tone illustrations are scanned in through a variety of scanners.

An important trend in which microcomputers have come to assume a pivotal role is the convergence of electronic publishing with the automated office.

Micro-based systems have made a strong impact particularly on technical documentation because of, among other things, the coordination of micros with electronic page printers. Microcomputers are part of the distinct trend toward authors submitting their manuscripts in computer-readable form in which capacity micros are replacing dedicated word processors. Paralleling the spread of microcomputers in publishing is the frantic development in the area of software. Hardly any week passes without new progress being reported in word processing, composition, image manipulation and pagination programs.

The contribution that microcomputers make in various contemporary prepress systems has been shown to be of a varying degree of sophistication. The economics of electronic publishing systems with micros as their underlying components have yet not received enough attention in the literature. Micros do not represent merely a new technological alternative but an efficient problem solution with an interesting level of cost/benefit.

A period of turmoil can be expected with regard to the manner in which new and conventional systems will be marketed and associated customer services offered. It may well be that the upshot of the present trends will be users creating their own books and journals and other personalized information files meeting their short-term or long-term information needs; microcomputers provide a tool for repackaging of packages and for putting all the ingredients of an end user's workstation together.

8

Electronic Printers

8.1 Versatile Output Device

There has been a proliferation of electronic printers in recent years. Even though they do not, by their definition, fit into the scheme of the prepress technology, they are an important member of the family of devices that have helped the electronic publishing revolution to take place and will be treated here. Besides, electronic printers have found applications other than only as high-volume printers: for instance, as proof printers, in preparation of masters for copying as well as masters for platemaking, and finally as single-copy or short-run on-demand printers.

Modern printers may be divided into two general classes: (A) impact printers that imprint by the impact-exerting pressure of type (or extendible needles) against paper with ribbon as an ink carrier situated in-between, and (B) nonimpact printers that produce type and graphics by other than purely mechanical means such as laser, ion-deposition and others.

A. Impact printers include a wide range of devices for office, data-processing centers and in-house publishers: drum printers, cylinder printers, band printers, chain printers, daisy wheel printers and dot-matrix printers.

Dot-matrix printers create type by selectively pushing needles in a printhead against a ribbon facing paper; characters are formed as a pattern of dots within a matrix (typically 9×7). Output is not considered letter-quality but the speed of 50-400 characters per second is the reason of the printer's popularity as are its graphics capabilities.

Daisy wheel printers work with characters placed at extremities of wheel spokes that radiate from a central hub; impact is effected by a hammer which strikes the desired character against a ribbon and paper. Daisy wheel printers have been used widely wherever letter-quality standard is expected at affordable cost, graphics are not a serious concern and higher volume of noise can be tolerated.

B. Nonimpact printers are gaining popularity while both conquering the first-time users' market and encroaching on the traditional markets held thus far by impact printers. This category of devices encompasses the following types as the most discussed printers:
1. Ink-jet
2. Thermal (and thermal transfer)
3. Electrosensitive
4. Laser
5. Light-emitting diode (LED)-array
6. Ion-deposition
7. Magnetographic

Devices 4–7 are also referred to as electronic printers, which is not quite accurate because the other products above also embody electronic components, but the label is nevertheless valid inasmuch as it groups together devices of comparable performance and price, which compete against each other. The same devices are also known as page printers to emphasize the fact that a full-fledged page is generated in the device's raster processor before being presented to the printing (marking) engine which produces the page in human-readable form. Devices under types 4 and 5 are sometimes described as xerographic as opposed to machines under type 6 and 7 which are classified, by contrast, as nonxerographic to characterize the final development process.

We shall now briefly introduce machines in the B (nonimpact) category, which are at present subject to continuous research and development, and when market-ready, will enter the battle raging with the aim of conquering the fast-opening market niches. Without any doubt this is one of few areas in electronic publishing where opportunities are big. Page printers came out from nowhere to become the centerpiece of many electronic publishing configurations.

1. Ink-jet printers are not suitable for text processing; they integrate text and graphics in applications where speed is not of primary importance but instead where color is appreciated in complex,

even three-dimensional drawings. Jets of ink from replaceable cartridges are directed onto plain paper, transparencies or clay-coated paper to produce desired color combinations from the four basic colors.
2. Thermal printers feature a print head fitted with heating elements in the form of pins arranged as a vertical strip which moves along a line; as heated pins selectively hit the paper, characters are generated within matrix patterns on the chemically treated paper.

   Thermal-transfer printers work on a different principle: an ink donor film faces a sheet of paper, which is pressed against it by a pressure roller. The ink film is in contact with the writing head composed of heating elements which impress ink into paper wherever they are heated. Integration of text and graphics on plain paper is possible.
3. Electrosensitive printers use a special aluminum-coated paper which is marked by dark dots where small electrodes contact the paper and change its color through electrical current.
4. Laser printers have occasioned the most remarkable influence on people's view of electronic publishing within practically 1 year's time and are instrumental in placing quite impressive publishing capabilities on the desktop. See also Chapter 4 with regard to their sudden rise to prominence and contemporary applications.

   Laser printers use the highly focused laser beam modulated to "write" the entire page as it has been generated by the raster image processor and stored as a bit-mapped representation of the page. The laser beam is switched on and off as required in "pouring" bits onto a rotating drum (or belt) provided with photosensitive coating. The laser beam scans along the length of the drum and, by changing the electrical charge of the drum's surface, in effect "paints" a latent image of the page; this is transferred to paper which selectively attracts toner to dots carrying the opposite electrical charge. Toner is subsequently fused into paper to conclude the process. The number of dots (also spots, lines) per inch or centimeter determines the resolution of the resulting image: 300 × 300 dots per inch (120 × 120 per centimeter) is commonly achieved and efforts are underway to improve on resolution to push it closer to what is professed to be typographic quality—variably set at over 750 dots per inch or, more often, at 1000 dots per inch. Lasers which used to be the visible-light gas type have been supplemented by infrared solid-state lasers. Production speed is anywhere between 400 and 6000 characters per second or 24,000 and 360,000 characters per minute or 8 and 120 pages per minute.

5. The light emitting diode - array types of page printers work on a principle similar to the above but they simplify the design by adopting LED as the light source.
6. Ion-deposition technology is a newer principle which is intended to compete against laser printers.
7. Magnetographic printers have the unique quality of being able to produce multiple copies without having to re-create the page image each time the page is reproduced (Sommerfeld 1986).

8.2 Technical Features and Performance Indicators of Page Printers

The high-volume printers may print up to 70-120 pages per minute or 18,000-20,000 lines per minute and are intended to compete with line printers. Medium-output machines have a print speed of up to 40 pages per minute and are directed toward the automated office needs to be shared by a number of users in distributed processing. The low-end class of electronic desktop printers has print speed of around 6-12 pages per minute and is aimed at the office of the future as an output device for single workstations.

Even more important than the absolute production speed in characters per second or pages per minute is the average monthly page volume (AMPV) also called duty cycle: an eight pages per minute printer has an AMPV equal to 3000; a 10-30 pages per minute printer has an AMPV of approximately 5000-70,000; at the production rate of more than 50 pages per minute, an AMPV of some 250,000 may be expected (Dempsey and Parkinson 1986).

Another distinguishing feature of electronic printers is their resolution. The resolution of 300 lines per inch is common but 400 and even 600 dots per inch have been achieved and provide better quality halftones. (This compares with 1000 lines per inch and more encountered with typesetters.) Higher resolution may be offset by a slower speed of the electronic printer. Most laser printers have a dot size of 4 mils as compared with the dot size of typesetters equal to between 1 and 2 mils.

Electronic printers are either supplied as printing devices only ("imaging engine") or sold complete with a more or less sophisticated raster image processor (RIP), font storage and controller. The RIPs often have their own storage of fonts and print-ready pages. Fonts are stored on floppy disks, hard disks and plug-in ROM cartridges or they may be downloaded from the host computer into the printer when required. Electronic printers may be supplemented with scanners to input manual graphics and some sophisticated printers have available to them software which translates computer-produced vector graphics

ELECTRONIC PRINTERS

into the raster format. Scanned pictures can be cropped, sized, screened, contrasted, etc. More elaborate raster image processors allow stored characters to be emboldened, rotated, reversed, compressed, expanded or anisometrically scaled.

Graphics capabilities are expected from modern electronic printers; line art can be output in satisfactory quality and continuous tone can be scanned in and screened to 85-100 lines contingent upon the required number of levels of gray. The decisive component of the printer when it comes to graphics is the raster image processor.

On the output side, microfiche output (computer-output microfiche) and back-to-back (duplex) printing may be applied and save material cost. Otherwise output is on plain paper or specially treated paper (chemically or photochemically) in the form of sheets, fanfold paper or continuous web.

Another criterion of electronic printer's versatility is the number of fonts it stores and their point-size range as well as how many type fonts may be used on a page or in a job. Characters may be stored as bit maps or as character outlines. In some printers all sizes of a type must be stored if required; in some machines a master may be sized to the desired point size.

Electronic printers may receive their input either offline, e.g., from a magnetic tape or they may function online and receive information directly from a host computer. Electronic printers vary as to their compatibility with various "front-ends" (in typesetter terminology) and some of them cooperate with a number of different hosts. Some accept data via RS232 ports at rates up to 19.2 Kbaud and others may have IEEE 488 and/or Centronix interfaces.

Factors to look for when selecting a page printer, besides price, resolution, speed per second or minute and AMPV, are paper handling capabilities on input and output, the number of fonts, the number of fonts per page, graphics capabilities, noise level and reliability. As with other equipment, compatibility must be given serious consideration for the present and future applications. Because page printers, although based on the same principle, can serve very different, specific purposes for which they are built, proper selection involving the above criteria must be made. Page printers offer such advantages as speed, reliability, quiet operation, good-quality output (especially the laser type), as well as suitability for a wide range of applications, especially in a variety of multiuser situations.

Electronic page printers have the potential to bring about broad changes both in the office of the future and publishing. One perceptible trend is marriage of the electronic nonimpact printer, desktop and otherwise, with the ubiquitous microcomputer: in this configuration the micro is ideally fitted with composition software of varying degree of perfection while the printer is supplemented by a raster image processor, either as an independent unit or incorporated into a micro or physically attached to printer, with a disk to store pages ready to be imaged and the type fonts.

8.3 Page Description Languages

Users are generally not very aware of the page description language (PDL) feature applied in a particular page printer. This feature should be ideally transparent to the user but often is not. Page description language is software that serves to describe all graphics and text on a page in a manner that satisfies typesetting specifications. On a Macintosh, for instance, Quick Draw commands are translated into PostScript by a PostScript driver; a raster image controller then drives the printer or typesetter. It interprets the PostScript language and prepares bit maps depicting the entire page which is output by the printing engine. There are presently several PDLs on the market as implemented and promoted by their originators—either software companies or major vendors.

Various PDLs are filling a role in diverse applications; some more popular PDLs are:

PostScript (Adobe Corporation)

Interpress (Xerox Corporation)

Reprint (Interleaf Corporation)

DDL (Imagen Corporation)

Needless to say, a PDL power is the single most important factor governing the output device's capabilities; the printing "engine" accepts from the controller—RIP—the page image as a continuous stream of bits and places them in any location on a page (all points are addressable) as originally specified in the PDL. A page printer must always have a full page stored in memory before printing starts in that printing takes place at speeds on the order of millions dots per second so it cannot be sustained by usual transmission techniques; bit map information could also be supplied directly from a computer but it is much more rapidly fed into the printing engine from an internal raster image controller. Modern page printers, laser and LED, have a megabyte plus memory for storing a page; the new controller of the Omnilaser 2115 (by Texas Instruments) is designed with 3-Mbyte memory (*The Seybold Report on Publishing Systems,* August 4, 1986).

The distinction between generalized graphics standards and PDLs is the PDL's capability to specify typesetting features.

ELECTRONIC PRINTERS

8.4 A Few Representatives of the Growing Printer Family

IBM 3800, Model 3. IBM 3800, model 3, is a high-speed, nonimpact printer based on the electrophotographic technology and uses a low-power laser. The underlying design philosophy is one of a subsystem nonimpact printer which is an integral part, along with a suitable front-end, of a total computer-driven system.

This device is also a "page" printer to reflect the fact that all picture elements or pels, on a page may be addressed in the memory which means that print matter—text, graphics, overlays—may be placed (printed) anywhere on a page under computer control; in line printers each line is formatted separately. This model has a pel density of 240 × 240 pels per square inch and is equipped with 59 type styles, each of which may include up to 256 characters; characters may be either uniformly spaced (monospaced) or proportionally spaced, with a density of 6, 8, 10 and 12 lines per inch, and character width of 10, 12 and 15 characters per inch. Maximum speed is 20,040 lines per minute. Special graphic characters other than those supplied with the machine may be designed by users. Multipart paper cannot be used and each copy has to be printed in a separate pass.

This electronic (electrophotographic) printer is suitable for in-house publishing purposes and will satisfy most requirements as far as print fonts are concerned. It also contains special symbols (such as mathematical, Greek letters, etc.) and other characters may be added (such as electrical, chemical, etc.). Black and white graphics may be scanned into the memory and then "poured out" into any of the available pixels on the page; this is why this mode of operation is called APA (all point addressable).

Xerox 9700. This printer accepts input from most IBM large computers either directly online or from a magnetic tape offline and stores it on a disk. Form image is created from prestored digital data and merged with the input data by the "character dispatcher." "Image generator" memory stores character fonts and forms as dot patterns and the image generator reproduces them as electronic patterns which control a scanning laser beam sweeping across an electrically charged, light-sensitive belt; whenever the laser light is on, the belt loses its charge and conversely, the charge is preserved whenever the laser light is switched off, thus marking invisible characters on the belt. The latent image attracts the black particles of dry ink developer; the resulting page image—the ink hanging on to charged areas of the belt—is transferred to a sheet of paper and fused. The narrow laser beam enables 300 dots per inch to be marked on the belt in both horizontal and vertical directions while maintaining the printer speed of up to 18,000 lines per minute or two pages per second. Input data may be transmitted to the printer from Xerox word processors via an RS-232C synchronous communications line at 2400 baud. Data is received on disk without any interference with the printing process. Printing may be done back-to-back on both sides of the sheet.

Alternatively, the image generator may be electronically switched to image pages on a CRT with subsequent film processing of the exposed microfiche to produce computer-output microfiche.

In the printed output the type font size ranges from 4 to 24 points, spacing varies between 3 and 18 lines per inch and 4-30 characters will occupy an inch length.

Xerox Electronic Publishing System. In a complete electronic publishing environment, text is entered via Xerox word processors or into a main frame. Simple textual material may go directly from word processor to printer, whereas complex documents may require some more formatting on the computer using the Xerox integrated composition system (XICS), which takes over after the user-edited and updated text as far as content and typos are concerned. The XICS resident in the computer performs all tasks involved in the production of camera-ready artwork for conventional printing, including formatting, typesetting, placement of titles and subtitles, etc., insertion of illustrations, tables, headers and footers; it also provides justification and automatic extraction and setting of multiple indexes, among other associated features. After appropriate generic codes have been inserted, the text is stored on a disk in the printer or computer system.

Computer-generated graphics from a CAD/CAM output are received in the vector format and converted into compressed raster format which can be handled by the printer; this is accomplished by a software package called Electronic Printer Image Construction (EPIC). Manually produced graphics have to be scanned into the system via the Xerox 150 Graphic Input Station, which digitizes line art and continuous tone (photographs) with some picture manipulation such as cropping, sizing, changing contrast and density; also a halftone screen is selected for photographs.

Finally, the separate textual and graphics files are merged in a device called the Graphics Handling Option equipped with the necessary software to prepare pages in the raster format to be output on an electronic printer.

Xerox 2700. This is an output device for minicomputers and clusters of word processors and, with the printing speed of 12 pages per minute, is suitable for printing a variety of reports and brochures besides letters, insurance policies, handouts, forms and similar outputs.

ELECTRONIC PRINTERS   251

This device is a laser printer with up to six fonts on a page, 300-dot per inch resolution, fitted with font storage and a raster image processor; fonts can be downloaded or supplied on a ROM cartridge. On-demand printing and proof printing are possible applications in the context of electronic publishing.

Canon LBP-20. This machine is designed to print 20 pages per minute and up to 50,000 pages per month depending on the speed of the controler driving it. Vertical resolution is factory set to 240, 300, 400 or 480 dots per inch and the horizontal resolution depends on the clock rate of video signals set to drive the printer.

Canon LBP-CX. This machine is destined to be a printer for personal computers and word processors. In much the same way as Xerox 2700 and similar machines, they could play a major role in any on-demand electronic publishing system as local decentralized output devices. The output is around 3000 pages per month and vertical resolution 240 or 300 dots per inch (factory set) with horizontal resolution being determined by the clock rate of the video signal driving the printer.

IBM In-house Publishing System. There are several possible methods of data entry and editing into the IBM electronic publishing system geared specifically to technical documentation and revolving around the IBM 4250 electronic printer: word processors, personal computers or an IBM mainframe editor accessed via terminals. When text has been edited, formatted and coded, it is then processed by the batch composition software called Display Composition Facility (DCF), which performs all usual composition functions on the text according to the generic codes embedded in the text file. The DCF leaves open space for graphics to be part of that particular document and the raster image processor (software package on mainframe) called Composed Document Printing Facility (CDPF) converts character-coded text into the raster format and merges it with graphics that were translated from vector format into the raster format by software called Graphic Display Data Management (GDDM).

Pages in raster format are presented to the IBM 4250 printer. This machine is based on the electroerosion principle and distinguishes itself with a resolution of 600 dots per inch, which will, in some applications, provide a quality of type as satisfactory as that of a typesetter. An average page may take approximately 1.5 minute to print.

9

Some Implications of Electronic Publishing

Introductory Comments. This chapter will examine phenomena that are bound to play a major role in the gradual development of the emerging publishing scene embodying the new structures as created by the new technologies on the remains of the old infrastructure which may give in under the weakness of its now-increasing internal deficiencies accentuated by the persistent impingement of the new technologies. It is generally agreed that the ensuing changes will be gradual, and that they will affect different types of publishers with varying urgency and timing. It is also generally perceived that this transformation cannot be viewed as transition from one state into another but rather as a dynamic chain of events in which the technological elements are mutually combining, supplementing each other but also competing among themselves in achieving given objectives. This technological interaction is compounded by political, social, economic, psychological and legal factors that all result in the process of change being a multidimensional one.

At the very beginning of this volume we defined the concept of "electronic publishing," which lends itself to ambiguous interpretation. The term "publishing" can be understood only in the context used and it may involve any function in the chain of communication, or combination of such activities, between authors and users (readers). In fact, authors and users are the only links in the chain sure to survive and rather paradoxically, in the extreme case, they do not need any go-betweens as some so-called self-publishers have already proven using the conventional technology; this is going to be made much easier with the kind of equipment now reaching our desk tops. In a sense, authors may be their own readers, and the only readers for that matter, if they repackage information for personal perusal using a personal publishing system.

In this chapter we indulge in some speculation on what the forces of change may portend to authors, publishers, libraries and users. As stated above, we do not address political, social and legal aspects of the problem in this study, and economic and psychological ramifications are dealt with only as related to specific issues.

It is recognized that current development is driven by technology. The main characteristic of most achievements in this emerging new world of communication is that we can do many things faster than before (while acknowledging that we are able to perform some entirely new functions). If we sat down and quietly sorted out our priorities, we would find that increased speed would not necessarily be placed on top of the list. The real danger of this is that fast information may do to our mind what fast food has done to our body: at stake is the quality of being informed (the "informedness" to put it clumsily); this is a danger too real to be ignored for anybody who would consume, for an extended period of time, two-line news headlines that turn one's emotions on and off. No one will argue that a person quietly consuming a well-researched and well-analyzed column in an old-fashioned newspaper may be better served. So what is needed is a new type of integration: assimilation of the new, fast technology to the proven ways of communication honed for centuries, a task that nobody seems to be awfully excited about.

9.1 Authors

The technological options open to authors in the morning of the electronic era are sufficiently explored in pertinent parts of this volume, including associated concerns such as the quandaries of occasional users, human information-processing issues, user performance in the author/editor area, hardware issues of electronic typewriters, word processors, microcomputers and so on. Suffice it to say at this point that authors, on their part, have been adapting very well to the impending electronic era in spite of problems of an ergonomic or psychologic nature. Authors have been submitting their papers increasingly in machine-readable form, a practice that has not been without problems arising for publishers and authors alike.

The major observable trend is toward control of the final product being shifted closer to authors and their desk top, including typesetting, composition of text and graphics, and even print, as reported elsewhere in this volume.

9.2 Publishers

The impact of electronic publishing on publishers must be viewed against the background of the stresses that have developed in publishing of the present day. The pressure on publishers is exerted by declining subscriptions mainly because of (1) shrinking library budgets, (2) document delivery services which have burgeoned, especially with the advent of online bibliographic services, (3) interlibrary loans which also have been boosted by online public access union catalogues, some of which allow circulation on a wide geographic basis, and (4) controversial photocopying which affects both authors and publishers. While revenues have been on the decline, the costs are steadily rising in labor, machinery, paper, auxiliary materials and postage.

All this makes publishers think about going electronic. Whatever the speed of development, and there is no doubt that more and more elements of publishing are going to take advantage of computer and communications technology, publishers have a definite edge over new competition on the scene, because of their undisputed mission in maintaining a reputable quality of published materials by keeping up high standards for editorial process and their expertise in packaging, pricing, marketing, promoting and distributing published materials. Inasmuch as publishers hold manuscripts, and later on, edited copies in machine-readable form, it is important for them that they also hold rights to the electronic form of output along with the printed form.

Having listed publishers' advantages let us examine their disadvantages in the contemporary struggle of many contenders, among them outsiders, to assess the situation correctly and enter the business of electronic publishing at the right time, with the right product, the most suitable equipment and the right marketing strategies, on a sound financial basis.

Publishers face serious problems in raising money because the industry is capital intensive, investment is considered risky and each project requires complete rethinking of basic financial and business principles. It is important to determine in the course of planning whether publishing will be parallel or electronic only, which will significantly influence the cash flow. The possibility of joining forces must, and is being seriously considered. Choices include allying oneself horizontally with others in a consortium or in a cooperative enterprise of various types with other publishers; the alternative of vertical cooperation with printers, libraries and companies of diverse orientation cannot be ignored. Publishers will have difficulty in adjusting to the facts that there will be less subscription revenue (except perhaps for a series of videodisks or an electronic journal) and that nearly all revenue will be delayed in coming because most use will be "on demand." The absence of revenue from advertising will seriously affect the cash flow as well and will require a great deal of innovative thinking on either replacing it or incorporating ads into electronic media. Most of the revenue will have to be raised through subscriptions (e.g., electronic journal), fees for hits, connect time and CPU, royalties for viewing and printing pages, charges for downloaded information, leased databases to be locally distributed or media, rental of compatible equipment, etc.

Another problem of some publishers is lack of expertise and experience with electronic publishing which may give competition a welcome head start. The reason for absence of expertise is its high cost; another reason is the conservative attitude of many publishers, some of whom might benefit from electronic publishing most. Recently there has been an upsurge in publishers' interest to modernize, as witnessed by increased sales of new technology products by numerous vendors.

Technology, which is the source of all the scramble for boons both real and imagined, is also a source of trouble for the would-be electronic publisher. First of all, although it is true that bits and pieces of technological marvels do exist and are not only reported on but exhibited and even demonstrated, it is also true that they are either too costly for a single publisher, or they are not compatible with his existing equipment, or there are some shortcomings that hamper user acceptance. Often publishers do not know how to "put it all together"; sometimes departmental, partial solutions prevent a total solution from being implemented with the projected benefits. Economic analysis as part of feasibility studies is difficult to measure because many benefits are of intangible nature, such as improved control, streamlined operations, better quality; some costs are not fully anticipated as is the case with operations and maintenance costs, retraining costs, etc. Often technology is reported by vendors that has not yet left the drawing board, and it becomes sometimes difficult for the potential buyer to tell market-ready products from the fantasyland gimmickry of hyperactive vendors. Sensationalistic reporting also abounds.

Publishers of secondary publications (indexing and abstracting services) have already moved into the stage of parallel, both electronic and traditional, publishing, some of them more than 15 years ago. One issue before them is whether to go full electronic or not and if so, when. The matter is largely a problem of cost recovery and so their decision is mainly dependent on their end user's preferences. If, for instance, end users in libraries shifted their preferences to online searching from printed abstract journals, libraries could then desist from subscribing to printed copies and switch to online services, something that libraries at large are still hesitant to do. Secondary publishers would then have to recover, entirely from sales to online services, the cost of magnetic tapes now obtained as spin-off from their typesetting tapes. Secondary publishers have, theoretically at least, the option to operate an online service and cater to the end user; problems associated with this are dealt with elsewhere in this study. Alternatively, they can sell their databases on some mass storage device such as CD-ROM or videodisk or download them to libraries or other regional or local distributors directly. If local distributors could afford to store databases and operate a local search and document delivery service from a mass storage device such as ODD, that would also create pressure on online services. Another pressure is libraries searching CD-ROMs on microcomputer-controlled facilities. But let us not forget that secondary publishers depend on primary publishers' product and there is a possibility that some publishers of primary publications might undertake to provide abstracting and indexing services themselves. Abstracts and/or indexing could be provided by authors, and when authors supply a machine-readable copy to publishers, which is becoming commonplace with some publishers, then before long software will be available to prepare a database of abstracts as a by-product of primary publishing. All this indicates a trend toward diversification of responsibilities and redistribution of revenues along the vertical chain.

9.3 Libraries

Whereas it is impossible to make forecasts that would fit libraries of all kinds and sizes and whereas it is even riskier to attach any time figure to projected events, several developments are certain to mark the evolution of libraries in the time to come. Very different predictions have been made for the fate of libraries under the siege of technology both from within and outside the profession, ranging from very optimistic to very gloomy, according to the attitude of the author: electronic publishing may be perceived either as a threat or as an opportunity. We must be also careful to distinguish between short-term and long-term forecasts and we must differentiate between the demise of the library as an institution and the librarians/information specialists who work in it. Last, and not least, electronic publishing will affect different kinds of libraries in various ways.

The online public access catalogue has been already elevated to be actually synonymous with the library of the future and likened to the library user's "window on the world" (Gallup Fayen 1983). The online catalogue will develop into the focus of the library, and other activities will group around it related to electronic publishing and document delivery. The online catalogue will not restrict itself to catalogue records but will encompass more detailed information pertinent to catalogued records possibly in a separate file. Information reaching beyond the local collection will be able to be tapped from the same terminal as a matter of fact. Union catalogues pointing to other libraries' holdings will become common. Subject searching will improve.

Full-text documents will be obtained either from a local electronic store, or online from database publishers, information providers, library utilities or online operators. In the case of fully electronic publishing, materials will be either held locally on magnetic storage devices, ODDs or optical videodisks, or displayed and printed online locally, downloaded for further manipulation or received via telefacsimile. On-demand publishing by itself will change the internal makeup of libraries when such publishing really takes off and will have important implications throughout the library. Aveney (1984) goes as far as to predict that (1) selection will be done on-demand and collection development will not have to be systematically pursued, (2) users will need more selection advice, (3) no acquisitions department is envisaged, (4) a need for few cataloguers is anticipated (5) serials items will be paid for on delivery, and (6) no acquiring, storing, retrieving and reshelving of printed materials is expected to be the upshot of the present wave of electronic publishing.

Dowlin (1984) postulates that the electronic library possesses four characteristics: (1) use of computers to manage resources, (2) use of electronic channels to link the information seeker to the information provider, (3) use of trained staff to intervene when asked by the information seeker, and (6) ability to store, organize and transmit information via electronic channels.

Although many seem to be agreed that there is a future not only for the librarian but also for the library as a physical entity albeit modified by the surge of events, Lancaster (1984) visualizes an institution based on technical expertise rather than on physical facilities and claims that the "library without walls" already exists and that the process of disembodiment will certainly continue; the resulting information professionals may be looked upon as "electronic librarians" or librarians without libraries.

The destiny of the library as an institution must be judged on the background of other events in the publishing cycle beginning with authors who, in the extreme case, might communicate directly with users/readers, publishers who may not get involved in electronic publishing and if they do, may or may not sell directly to users, and wholesalers and retailers who may be left out of the game entirely or might assume distribution to users directly. Academic libraries build their strength on strong collections which for long time will have to be maintained especially as far as books are concerned. Academic libraries have their own large supportive constituency which they already serve with some electronic products and they can build on their expertise.

They might extend their services to the community even more than at present and recoup some of their cost. Their potential to become major electronic document distributors, if not outright publishers, is equally great. Special libraries may be hit harder because their services are much easier to be obtained externally from information consultants and brokers. Public libraries may face strong financial difficulties and may be forced to restrict their services, but they have the responsibility of catering to all social strata of society, and if they were to be closed down, some other institution or mechanism would have to be invented to provide electronic information to such a constituency. Additionally, public libraries may take initiative in playing an active role in public continuing education using modern technology.

It would appear that libraries will weather the electronic storm as institutions if, forced by shrinking budgets, they will develop the foresight to recognize the situation and reassess their priorities, which may in some cases mean a sharp departure from the existing status quo, something that libraries historically are not accustomed to do. It appears that books, especially fiction and study materials as commonly found in academic libraries, will long resist going electronic, whereas encyclopedias, dictionaries, directories, catalogues and all kinds of reference books are positioned on the opposite side of the spectrum, along with publications of ephemeral value, and with scientific journals waiting for the opportune time. If the institution of the traditional journal is abolished, then low-circulation articles will become an acute problem for electronic distribution.

Whereas handling of archival copies will have to remain in the public domain and will have to be looked after by national libraries as electronic repositories, the problem of out-of-print materials resting traditionally with major libraries will have to be renegotiated and is an example of how any change in the communication cycle affects its other constituents. If libraries swing from the present modus vivendi to the on-demand mode of operation, then the responsibility for out-of-print matter can only be with the publisher and would have to be absorbed as additional overhead sustained by the currently in-print operation; the practical effect of this would be the shift of cost from the public (i.e., library-subsidized) sphere into the commercial (private) domain.

9.4 Changing Role of the Intermediary

Librarians will be affected both by the cropping up of more professional functions as a result of technological change and by the reduction of clerical jobs resulting from the higher productivity of the new equipment. No doubt, librarians will be required to be more flexible in their outlook on their job and their profession. They will have to develop a positive attitude toward computers even though the old idea of 1960s and early 1970s that every librarian would have to be retrained to become a programmer has already been proven false. Librarians will have to develop more communications skills in keeping with the trend away from technical services to public services. It would be unrealistic to expect that "professionals" or information "haves" who armed themselves with a microcomputer will be their own financial counselors, doctors, lawyers, accountants, information technicians, travel agents, etc., just because software packages are available. Librarians will have their own share of packages in their own field with which to contend. Librarians or information counselors will be called upon for professional advice as to appropriate systems, relevant databases, efficient search strategies, economic packages, cost assessment, copyright expertise and assistance in operating the ever-growing array of gadgetry which will need to be studied, evaluated, operated, maintained and guarded against misuse and abuse. It is easy for professionals to provide some information and they may even do it right but are they really doing the right thing? Are they searching efficiently the database that offers them the best result at the optimum cost? Only a librarian familiar with the content of databases, and their makeup and equipped with general and specific strategies can achieve good relevance and recall in extracting information from a variety of sources. This indicates that there is always going to be a place for a librarian (or information counselor or specialist) in electronic publishing. Librarians will have to develop communication competence, and interpersonal skills to cope with the gradual shift in their responsibilities. Librarians will have to know the basic jargon of computers and telecommunications to maintain a meaningful dialogue with experts in those areas. Systems analysis and design skills will help those involved in these respective activities to prevent the situations in which outsiders force their systems on libraries without librarians (information specialists) having substantial input into the hardware/software acquisition negotiations.

We have stressed so far the need for the librarian to communicate effectively, understand the computerese, acquire systems analysis and design skills, yet there is a number of additional ingredients in this incipient information professional's job. Dowlin comments (1984) that librarians "add value" to the information, data or knowledge by collecting, storing and retrieving it through an established framework which enhances access and tailors the collection to the community needs, and this makes the librarian both guide and gatekeeper. This will of course, require, more than in the past, that librarians become also knowledgeable of the subject field in which they are working. The increasing amount of information that can be acquired by electronic means may, in fact, call for not one but two intermediaries: one as online retrieval specialist, the other one as discriminator who also summarizes and evaluates the result. Lancaster (1984) considers it possible that librarians will be asked to perform an "information analysis": searching, selecting the best of the information retrieved and evaluating the results for the user. The same author also expects more involvement by librarians in user education and training, planning and designing electronic publications, designing and operating electronic networks, in the organization of electronic files, in devising and implementing new types of information services and in maintaining current awareness of clients.

A new career will be of interest to librarians/information specialists which has been promoted in recent years in the United States and Europe, namely that of information manager. This concept has been plagued by some vagueness and is applied to connote management of all information-related functions in an organization. The concept has relevance to our examination of the librarianship under the assault of new information technology and more specifically electronic publishing, as may be seen from a recent description of the three main areas of competence (Vickers 1984): (1) people (basic management techniques, patterns of information use and basics of ergonomics), (2) information (information transfer, information storage, information retrieval, information resources, communications and reprography, including micrographics), and (3) systems (information technology, computer systems, office automation, telecommunications, systems security, research methods and diagnostic techniques). As may be seen, these terms of reference exceed those of the run-off-the-mill librarian, but they beckon to librarians who are intent on upgrading their professional status.

But librarians/information specialists of the coming era of electronic publishing will have to facilitate communication all along the way from the originator to the consumer, and this will necessitate not only education, which provides requisite knowledge and skills, but also certain qualities; these were listed by Simkins (1983) as adaptability, the ability to learn new tricks, logic and accuracy (as required in dealing with computers), intelligence, thoroughness, commonsense, friendliness and ability to communicate.

The ability to communicate may assume new dimensions with access to an ever-increasing number of databases, containing both abstracts and full-text documents, some of which may be in languages other than English; the versatility and indispensability of librarians/information specialists would be raised to a new level if they were able to provide a prompt translation from the original perhaps with the aid of computerized dictionaries, until such time when translation programs will finally take over the job.

The job nature of the librarian/information specialist (information broker, consultant, counselor, manager) will require both general education to understand the meaning of the evolutionary process in its entirety and specialization of knowledge and skills to be able to take on functions hitherto unknown in the profession, functions that themselves are results of integration of technology. What this means is the integration of information specialists into integrating technologies. Both centralization and decentralization will have their place in the impact of electronic publishing on libraries and librarians/information specialists. Central production, storage and dissemination facilities will thrive along with smaller distributed processing and storage centers and with the completely decentralized self-made user (who in the broadest sense will be not only "consumer" but may end up by being an author, critic, editor or even publisher). A "distributed" librarian/information specialist may be one of many possible forms that electronic publishing will force on the information profession: a librarian assigned on a temporary or on a more permanent basis to a task force, department, faculty, etc. to act as a specialized information counselor or consultant.

The position of librarians/information specialists as important links in the information chain is not dissimilar to other professions on the cutting edge of technology. The substance is assured of continuous growth but the speculation on the form it will take can never be definitely resolved as it will be different in various institutions and will dynamically change to keep up with the changing institutions.

Wherever in this chapter the talk has been about librarians, other designations may be more favored in the future. Wherever the discussion is of libraries, this institution may be in the long term replaced either partly or totally by other decentralized local information service bureaux owned publicly or privately. The above discussion, I hope, has made it clear that the institution of electronic information production and distribution will thrive, and while it will diversify, a wide variety of tasks and functions will be discharged by the new information professional. This will require changes in library schools' curricula and in continuing education which is turning into a life-long experience.

9.5 Users

The community of information users contains, with respect to new technology, both the progressive and conservative elements. In the late 1960s it used to be an exhausting job of persuasion to convert users of traditional library services into consumers of the early computerized services such as indexes, SDI and retrospective database searches from magnetic tapes. In the mid-1980s users are much more adapted to computerized services in libraries mainly owing to the positive experience with online bibliographic searching, reinforced by the likewise successful introduction to the online catalogue and other forms of electronic publishing such as videotex/teletext trials. The ubiquitous microcomputer available in many organizations, schools, universities, research labs and even homes, has rid the minds of a lot of people of the initial technofobia experienced when it came to using computers.

Granted the improved attitudes of users toward computerized services and despite some enhanced human-machine interfaces hitting the market, it is still true that more developments in electronic publishing, much the same as in other computer application areas, are technology-driven rather than user-driven; this has a negative impact on users' acceptance of the new technology. Also, the vast amount of information available electronically today has been used only by a small minority of the "information elite." The "information-poor" or "computer-illiterate" must be drawn into the process not only in their own interest but for the good of the entire concept of electronic publishing, which requires a minimum critical mass for sustained operation. The librarians/information specialists have an important role to play as facilitators of access to electronic information for everyone; even if systems do become more "user-forgiving," the increasing number and variety of services and databases will require the presence of intermediaries to intervene when needed.

A matter of vital interest to users is the price to be paid for the increased convenience, completeness, relevance and timeliness of information. Users are not all alike and the advantages of electronic publishing which might entail a fee for the service will be weighed carefully against the free-of-charge library services of the past. On the whole, both libraries and users might benefit, because even if there is a higher cost per service unit (online search or document delivery, for instance), fewer material goods and services may be required to meet specific user needs.

In conclusion, users will benefit from all the services as outlined in this study insofar as they will be able and willing to invest their time in user instruction and spend some money for services they think worthwhile. Information itself has value but one must also know how to put it to use.

10
Conclusions

When drawing conclusions from a subject as extensive as the theme of this book, one is faced with an awesome task. Not only is the subject field vast but also readers in categories as diverse as to range from authors, editors, publishers to librarians, typographers, system designers, computer specialists and others may require specific conclusions relevant to their peculiar needs and situations; the inescapable consequence of this is that general conclusions, however carefully researched and germane to a large cross-section of the potential readership, may not substitute reading of the entire text on which to base and form one's own conclusive opinion on a specific detail.

In concluding, let us briefly review the major perceptible trends in the (1) nonprint-based and the (2) print-based varieties of electronic publishing and touch on those detectable in (3) electronic document delivery and (4) artificial intelligence. Then, we will attempt to speculate on the likely interplay of these trends as determinants in shaping the electronic future of publishing with full recognition of the shaky grounds on which to base any such predictions. The discipline is so young and fluid that in many areas it has not yet taken any definite form; trends are often difficult to descry among temporary fads and are often passed off by those with vested interest in their success.

In using the "print-based" and "non-print-based" dichotomy, a word of caution is in order. One and the same organization can do and does both kinds of publishing; for instance, a journal may publish not only in the traditional manner or electronically in the print-based fashion but also in the non-print-based mode, utilizing, e.g., videotex and online retrieval technologies. Moreover, both varieties of technology may share some equipment: for instance, a microcomputer may be employed in the process of composition and in the creation of frames for videotex services and abstracts for online retrieval services contingent upon the software applied. Microcomputers and more specifically their software, growing ever more versatile and powerful, thus contribute to the convergence of the print-based and non-print-based modes much the same as they have already enabled, on another plane, individuals and organizations to act both as information consumers and information suppliers. Consequently, some conclusions made with relation to one mode apply to the other as well, thus reinforcing further the argument for their eventual merger. The main criterion in system evaluation that will always apply is how well a system is suited to meet the needs and expectations of the patron, the "electronic addict," the "computer-illiterate" and the middle-of-the-road information consumer alike.

10.1 Non-print-based Electronic Publishing

In non-print-based electronic publishing, batch information retrieval has been all but replaced by online information retrieval which widened its scope by adding numeric, statistical, directory-type and other databases to the bibliographic ones. Searching the full text of documents has become common. The full text of documents may be either ordered online or obtained directly at the terminal. Microcomputers thanks to their software will continue to revolutionize the way information can be obtained online. Optical digital disk, videodisk and CD-ROM promise to be the factors that may change the prospects for local distributed retrieval systems. The whole concept of online information retrieval will be radically influenced by the exploits of artificial intelligence, whereby the interface will be initially further "humanized," but later on with wider adoption of expert systems, we should see even more fact retrieval as opposed to reference retrieval. End user-oriented online services, which already have built up a respectable clientele, may be expected to grow and online retrieval services will try to get their slice of this market by cost reductions, broader scope of service content, easier command language and access.

The online public access library catalogue has been taking libraries by storm. Computerized catalogues will enhance library services so that patrons will be able to retrieve more comprehensive information "published" not only by one but by multiple libraries and do so in an interactive manner, even in remote mode. The computerized library catalog will become a nucleus around which to group the related services essential to library survival, yet at the same time it will enable private enterprise to encroach on the traditional library turf.

The future of videotex, which until now has not been able to make any appreciable inroads into the publishing field, must be seen against the backdrop of competition from cable TV, pay TV, interactive TV and videodisk-enhanced, user-friendly online retrieval services; microcomputers offer what was formerly considered to be videotex's strength, namely graphics, color and inexpensive display. It would appear that, for videotex to compete in this electronic world, it would have to be marketed as a part of a much more comprehensive package on a gateway. Videotex is descending from its position as a different communication technology and is turning into just another computer graphics standard.

Even though cable TV cannot meet all of electronic publishing's requirements and electronic publishing alone cannot sustain cable TV, the possibility to transmit voice, data, text, video and facsimile pages makes cable TV suitable for varied communication services, such as database services, file and software downloading, electronic document delivery, polling, narrow-casting to selected audiences and local area networks. This potential is gradually being realized and will be further boosted by the progress in the satellite technology and optical fiber implementation.

The videodisk medium may be utilized with advantage to store published pictorial information locally while a microcomputer can add interactivity. A microcomputer can also serve to access remote textual databases complemented by locally stored pictures, or it can be applied to support retrieval from textual databases stored locally with images on a videodisk. This technology adds pictures, sound and motion to plain, online text retrieval and is struggling for the attention of the more sophisticated user. On the other hand, the optical digital disk may become one of the mainstays of extensive publishing systems in the near future because of its inherent qualities among which its huge storage capacity predestines it for applications heretofore unthinkable. The CD-ROMs are moving databases from publishers to local processing centers and in doing so, challenge other competing media. The struggle for an erasable, writable disk and jukebox is on.

Practically all essential functions of an electronic journal can be performed on a computer conferencing system involving the entire communications cycle. Other useful tools can be built into the system residing on a mainframe, minicomputer or, recently, a microcomputer. The reasons why the electronic journal has not been generally accepted by the communications community are twofold: (1) technology has made it possible but not yet convenient enough; (2) cost advantages are not significant enough to turn the tide and convert the conservative end user. Also, authors like to contribute to journals with some prestige, reviewers want to be able to comment in the text and on the margins and readily compare multiple versions and readers prefer portable printed materials. Technology is making this possible as well. Other problems of immaterial nature are marketing, advertising, pricing, distribution, archival responsibility and transborder information flow. It would appear that the appearance of the electronic journal has initiated an in-depth reexamination of the concept of a scholarly journal, its strengths and weaknesses, and revived pondering of some old problems such as low-circulation papers. It is likely that the electronic journal based on modified computer conferencing systems may thrive in the hybrid print and nonprint mode capitalizing on the exploits of the modern digitized prepress technology with integrated text and images and use of microcomputer composition software and laser printers. Journals going electronic will open up the electronic highway to experiments with less formal information packages.

10.2 Print-based Electronic Publishing

When observing the field of prepress in the broader sense, the immediate impression is one of computers permeating the entire picture. The ironic conclusion may well be that computerization will help prepress in doing some things faster than humans and some things that humans could not do, but eventually it will lead to the demise of print-based publishing in its present predominant form and usher a new era of coalesced print-based plus non-print-based electronic publishing combined with electronic document delivery where the boundaries will be initially difficult, and later on, impossible to draw. This stage might be perhaps most befittingly called "integrated electronic communication" characterized by ease of use, compatibility of component systems and networks, and a variety of peripheral equipment. The road to this landmark will be highlighted in the late 1980s by systems of respectable complexity but still of relatively limited scope (composition, picture manipulation, pagination, etc.) succeeded later (in the early 1990s) by their perfection and integration into local area networks and long-haul networks (by then they will have merged), which will enable artificial intelligence to become one of main forces in further development. Expert systems and natural language processing will have been widely adopted by then in support of advanced electronic publishing. "Integrated electronic communication" will be able later in the 1990s to look after all human information needs in a selective or on-demand mode. The appearance of low-cost, high-resolution, portable flat panels will have encroached on the last vestige of the print-based status quo—the conservative reader of printed information. At this stage it should be possible to utilize screens not only for "intelligent" or "logical" operations such as page layout, page makeup and logical searching in large databases, but also for selective reading. Display devices should be not much larger than books and might be called "automated books" with some processing capability and sizable storage. Once again, the more we change things the more they remain the same. The circle has returned to the book, apparently. Also, the more familiar things look to humans the more readily they are embraced. One "automated book" might be conceived of as a private library of content-related books, in fact, a library with external communications capabilities. After this stage is reached further development will concentrate on enhancing parameters rather than changing the concept. The "book" will have become dynamic as far as contents are concerned, its contents being of "library" size and being able to be changed and modified. In the era of "integrated electronic communication" paper will not disappear but will become only one of an array of possible output forms of which there will be plenty. The new electronic page printers presently suggested mostly for proofing will be affordable and all of them of desktop size. They will offer typographic quality, and this will make division of communication into print-based and nonprint-based categories meaningless. There will be both print and nonprint output but no print-based and nonprint-based industry per se in the long view. Both varieties of electronic publishing, which themselves owe so much for their advancement to the convergence of computers and communications with publishing and other more conventional fields such as library and office technology, will merge into the knowledge-based, integrated electronic communication. Whereas computerization of publishing started in the 1960s and became more prominent in the 1970s, microcomputers in the 1980s have come to be the major force in restructuring the entire information or knowledge industry.

Computerization has been the foundation on which two major trends developed: (1) digital graphics allow for more graphics to be included in publications of all kinds both in "pure" electronic technologies as well as in print. The CAD/CAM technologies initially on the margin of publishing's interest have moved into the mainstream of events, and melding the vector formats with text and raster format presented yet another challenge to system designers. (2) Use of more and better color illustrations is yet another trend made feasible by the increasing power of computers. Transmission of color pictures is possible thanks to the communications "highways" and to data compression; color pictures may be sent not only via satellites and microwaves at speeds on the order of megabits per second but on voice-grade lines as well because of compressions up to 1:60. Electronic publishing does not know any geographic boundaries and defies distances; it has struck the notion of separateness from its dictionary.

Developments in the changing author-editor-reviewer relationship resulting from the growing volume of "compuscripts" submitted by authors embracing the new technology seek to cope with incompatibility of devices and multitudes of data formats. Some technical problems were discussed with respect to this trend, but the essential impact on the further evolution of the print-based industry is the data capture at the site of the originator, which favorably affects the cost and speed of the total communications cycle.

Developments in the modern prepress, which have already started and no doubt will continue in the future, are characterized among other things, by endeavors to shorten the technological process and in doing so, streamline the component procedures, much the same as has been common in other industries. Associated with this has been the diminishing size of hardware contrasting with the burgeoning power of the new software. This tendency may be exemplified by system designs aimed at eliminating galley proofs and going directly to film, or eliminating film entirely and outputting a plate, or avoiding even plate by direct print. Culmination of these efforts may be encountered in recent microcomputer-oriented systems where a microcomputer, optimally integrated into a local area network environment and equipped with requisite peripherals and proper software, can handle text entry, line art creation, graphics scanning and manipulation, composition and page makeup with output directed either to an electronic printer or to a compatible desktop typesetter. Streamlining of the workflow with resulting time and cost savings manifests itself also on the input side of electronic publishing systems in the general tendency towards "humanizing" the human-machine interface in various ways, the proliferation of systems for data format conversion, scanning text by means of optical character readers and scanning of graphics. Voice input and output will further diversify input and output alternatives: the underused telephone may yet become an important terminal.

Text and graphics integration is a goal that has been strived at for a long time but is being refined only now if we disregard some early less significant attempts. This process is computer-controlled both in the print-bound and nonprint-based communication systems and the data can be manipulated in all of the character, vector and raster formats as required by editorial and production considerations. The main motive for this goal seems to be the desire to streamline the editorial aspects and the production line and to gain better control of the process and product. Savings are also claimed but it is by no means a clear-cut issue. A thorough analysis is called for of the entire process as there are ramifications in all directions including capital investment needed, material and labor cost, training, implementation and maintenance. Even though at present the cost of equipment is still a serious consideration, text and graphics integration is a trend to stay with us and it will become more and more widespread as affordability opens the low end of the market. Technically integration of text with graphics can be performed in a variety of ways illustrated in this study: for instance, it may take place in a scanner, in a microcomputer-based system, to a limited extent even in a color graphics station, in a "graphics pasteup-to-plate" subsystem, but most conveniently in a special page makeup station.

One of the results of the present upheaval in prepress technology is that the borderlines between individual conventional operations are becoming somewhat vague. Whereas formerly one could clearly distinguish between the original data entry, typesetting and subsequent pagination with intermittent proofing, camera and final press, the new technology makes these areas less clearly defined. This requires the reader of any write-up on new prepress to pore over the text to see what the author means: typesetting may mean setting type along with graphics, proofing may mean "soft" as well as hard copy proofing in which the same device may set type or provide the final print depending on circumstances. These moving and ill-defined boundaries have an implication for the author-system relationship, namely in that the control over the final form of publication is moving closer to the originator. It is now possible for a publisher to "typeset" and print and authors may in some instances, if they can and so wish, supply the text and even illustrations into the system, make up a page with type set in the final form and illustrations in place, and proceed even with a limited-run print. How much authors themselves, in fact, will want to use this potential will vary from case to case with the process control moving into their realm for some types of publications. In reality, publishing electronic or not will always require varied skills and it appears that there will be only shift from certain skills to others rather than any "de-skilling" taking place. It is unrealistic to expect authors to make typographic decisions when they may write only one or two books in their lifetime; the availability of 1000-plus typefaces in various styles and sizes at the operator's fingertips will make decisions all the more difficult and will call for professional judgment. In the same vein, decisions about application of color will require an expert versed in computerized color systems offering thousands of possible alternatives. It would therefore, appear that many a skilled operation performed formerly by humans will be conducted by humans albeit utilizing electronic devices. There will be other mainly computer-associated skills for which humans will have to be trained and retrained. Yet high technology in general demands more of a good basic general education than of any single skill attainable by vocational training. Fuzzy and vanishing borderlines between sectors of prepress have other implications too: people who are designing the "interdisciplinary" systems overlapping the boundaries between data entry, graphics, typography, page makeup, etc. are expected or are presumed to have sum total of all the expertise required to master the individual jobs plus knowledge of computers and other requisite paraphernalia. This collective wisdom is expensive to acquire and sustain, and this is one of the reasons why many companies are going under. Customers and prospects encounter the same overwhelming task to keep themselves abreast with the mushrooming technology to be able to grasp it or at least to maintain a meaningful dialogue with vendors. The ensuing communication gap leads to customers being unable to formulate their needs in terms of new technology and vendors offering solutions which do not find sufficient buyers to pay for the high cost of research and development.

When assessing the past, present and future contribution of computers to print-based (and where applicable to nonprint-based) formal communication, one must not only appreciate the design and production area but also the less conspicuous and less frequently reported "nonproductive" applications related to business such as statistics, accounting, promotion, fulfillment, mailing, questionnaires, forms, editorial office systems, varied "idea processors" to assist authors, as well as the potential to help libraries and other information warehouses with bibliographic control.

10.3 Electronic Document Delivery

Electronic document delivery differs from conventional document delivery by the electronic communication channel interposed between the ultimate user or an intermediary on the one hand and the supplier on the other hand; EDD systems may be also the "back-end" part of a comprehensive electronic publishing system either in the "pure" electronic form (such as in electronic journals) or in the "dual" or hybrid (both print and nonprint) form. With full-text systems becoming more common on proliferating networks and because of the wide availability of terminals and micros at the user's end, there is no reason why users cannot receive documents electronically from the same databases which are often being shared already between authors, reviewers and editors. This will make the concept of electronic document delivery increasingly difficult to define as a separate entity in many systems; yet this is not to say that EDD is not going to be viable as an independent service for a long time to come to provide added value by offering broad comprehensive coverage, sufficient retrospective depth and related customer services along with the necessary business infrastructure that individual electronic publishers may not be able or willing to offer.

The problems to be resolved are mostly of a nontechnical character such as legal (copyright), economic and organizational; some problems have been inherited from the past such as the issue of responsibility for archiving and the dilemma of low-circulation journals. Diverse technology has been contemplated for EDD: on the user's site, for instance, telefacsimile receivers, ASCII terminals alone or in combination with telefacsimile, terminals with videotex capability, videodisk players, microcomputers, dot-matrix and daisy wheel printers, electronic page printers, ink-jet, electroerosion printers, etc., even typesetters. Storage of documents is of eminent importance and magnetic disks, ODDs and microforms alone and in combination have been suggested. Both terrestrial and satellite facilities have been planned for EDD as telecommunications links. Where typesetting tapes or some other machine readable medium is not available, digitizing methods are exploited to make the documents processable in the electronic components of the system. Before EDD is accepted by the average patron and hence becomes a viable proposition, inexpensive hardware is needed, with little or no training required; cost must be affordable commensurate with advantages offered and appreciated by users, and the method of billing must be lucid and convenient. Retrospective depth and comprehensive coverage are a must.

10.4 Artificial Intelligence

If making any forecasts in electronic publishing is a precarious undertaking, as stressed above, owing to the instability caused by the ongoing technology shake-up, any thought about possible long-term impact on it of artificial intelligence which itself is an emerging discipline, runs the risk that it will be described as speculation; but even so the prospects of it are fascinating inasmuch as artificial intelligence is introducing into electronic publishing some elements that will initially serve to improve some of its functions while having the potential of radically changing its face as time goes on. Asking for a document in one's language of choice, automatic consultants and publishers, automated referral service and robots employed in highly intellectual or routine mechanical tasks are not so far distant in the future as many of us might be inclined to think. Expert systems are already contending for recognition in the information or knowledge industry. In the online systems area they can revolutionize the human-database interface by adding initially a natural language capability but eventually, they can replace many a system while offering factual answers to queries rather than masses of relevant and not-so-relevant references. Electronic journals, similarly, might be "front-ended" with expert systems which might eventually, in some cases at least, finish them off entirely. If we conceptualize the above examples, it boils down to substituting consulting services for reading media, but if straight answers are not sufficient then a report writer might be added. Other possibilities include the selection and design of publishing systems, failure diagnosis, and others, too numerous even to contemplate. Artificial intelligence and electronic publishing possess a great deal of affinity to each other because electronic publishing is about computer-assisted modes of communication while AI strives to bridge the gap between humans and machines through design of intelligent perceiving and cognitive systems simulating the human mind. The contiguous area of concern are information and knowledge-processing functions both human and machine. This common ground is the reason why both print- and non-print-based electronic publishing inclusive of electronic document delivery all stand to benefit from the anticipated, and already emerging, developments in AI, which may well become the catalyst leading to integrated electronic communication by facilitating use by humans of the new automated computer-based systems in knowledge acquisition, processing, dissemination and final assimilation. It would appear that, whereas traditional publishing systems for centuries were experiencing mostly quantitative changes with minor substantive modifications, what we have lately been witnessing in the field is a major metamorphosis effecting momentous qualitative jumps in the state of the art in which computers/communications may be viewed as the essential physical, corporal infrastructure with artificial intelligence following in their wake to impart an enhanced mind to the nascent construct whose lifeblood is the information and knowledge injected into the system by humans.

After having said a great deal about the potential boons of the electronic prepress era, we hope we may not be accused of undue pessimism if we depart from the conventional optimism and mention briefly a few mementos about risks to both users and society at large stemming from noncritical adoption of the new electronic technology. On the part of users, it is necessary to make informed acquisition decisions. We posit here two extreme cases: some individuals and companies harbor unwarranted expectations as to economic benefits to be realized from new technology, base their decisions on insufficient systems analysis and have serious misconceptions about maintenance, training and operating costs as well as after-the-sale service; on the other side of the spectrum there are those who procrastinate with modernization unduly out of fear that there will be a superior product on the market tomorrow which could render today's acquisition obsolete.

CONCLUSIONS

Both of these approaches are deleterious and should be corrected by study and consultation.

For society, on the other hand, the hazards of precipitous, undiscriminating introduction of unfamiliar technology, motivated solely by its availability, are varied and include displacement of the labor force, disputes between unions and management, problems of training and retraining, economic consequences for large segments of industry groping for solutions to problems such as customer service, financing of new ventures or the shortage of experts in frontier research areas. Stress figures high on the list of woes brought about by abrupt changes in an environment characterized by long-lasting, relative stability now replaced by uncertainty amid stiffening competition; the ironic aspect of this phenomenon is that nobody clamored for this technology and people involved in it have a hard time determining what it could be exploited for and what it all means with regard to them. But the main concern from the societal point of view, and this applies equally to print and nonprint-based modes, should be where it is not readily perceived owing to our preoccupation with the onslaught of gizmos of all kinds: the contents and its quality. Publishing has been traditionally the guardian of our cultural treasures and an effective instrument in recording, evaluating, editing, disseminating, preserving and archiving the continuing progress of our civilization as we know it, and we all have too much at stake not to keep this mechanism alive and well. No matter what technology, this vital role of publishers must continue to function if our cultural heritage is to be preserved.

Let us conclude this study on matters mostly technical in nature by stressing two factors that strongly bear on the technological aspect of electronic communication, namely education and economics. Even though events in electronic publishing, as in other technology areas labeled "high-tech," are conceived by knowledgeable individuals, the evolution of functional and accepted systems has been somewhat spontaneous; droves of potential users try to assess what this awakening beast could do for them, if anything, and wonder if what we have opened is not a Pandora's box. Whereas formerly necessities were the mother of invention, today inventions beget necessities. Our ability to deal with them will depend on the most precious asset there is in electronic publishing as in other fields: the people. We have to realize that communication of any kind begins and ends in the human mind. Successful performance in complex electronic communication systems will be a function of the educational background for any individual. It has already become evident to perceptive observers that electronic publishing requires higher qualifications than its conventional predecessor, and that the requisite knowledge is best secured by a solid general background in liberal arts rather than by a lopsided selection of easy courses purporting to introduce a person into the world of high technology. People with a good general education find it easier to adjust to constant changes and their specialized training can build on a general, broad conceptual base; it takes less time and costs less in the long run to train and retrain them in the varied sophisticated functions outlined throughout this volume. The importance of proper education assumes new dimensions in the context of new communication systems as a result of their enormous productivity, which may serve either to dispense knowledge or spread ignorance depending on who is running the system.

The economics of present and future electronic communication systems will play a prominent role in shaping their public image and hence, affect directly their acceptance. Increasing government intervention involving everybody's tax dollars and the profound impact of new technology in the vertical dimension make it necessary in all technology deliberations to consider the cost of the entire communication cycle rather than the cost incurred by individual links in the chain. The expectations that electronic publishing would bestow on us lower costs have already been proven unwarranted. Whereas some costs are eliminated such as paper and stamps, and other costs are on the decline, as for instance hardware, new costs appear, e.g., transmission and electronic storage, while some continue climbing, e.g., software, maintenance, training, etc. Technology alone will not break the inertia of the past unless other aspects of the progressive future, among them costs and user response, are harnessed. It would appear that the cost picture and, consequently, pricing policies will become more fluid and dynamic and that there will be shifts in revenue and costs from one sphere into another, rather than any dramatic drop of costs across the entire communication cycle. Publishers may seek reducing their own costs and motivate authors to submit papers electronically, authors on their part may make greater use of the corporate equipment, and readers may continue to reduce individual subscriptions while relying more on subsidized information and knowledge stores. Publishers have to recoup some loss of subscriptions to hard copies by promoting their electronic sales much the same as information providers are able to charge users directly. New information and knowledge brokers will enter the scene to enhance and repackage information, thus contributing to the disruption of the established patterns of economics prevailing in publishing. The technology of electronic publishing is extremely involved and so are its economics; ignoring their inexorable logic has already hurt a great many players whether they be corporations or individuals, producers or consumers, on the expanding scene of electronic communication.

References

Alam Mahbub, U., with Arthur D. Little, Inc. Cambridge, Mass. (in the article by Bindra, see below)

Alexander, G.A.; Edwards, S.E.; Stivison, D.S.; Swain, T. (1984). Electronic libraries. *The Seybold Report on Publishing Systems.* Vol. 13, Nos.19/20, pp. 40-43. July 9.

American Printer (1986). Laser technology creates consistent contact screens. *American Printer.* Vol. 196, No. 4, pp. 56. January.

Aveney, B. (1984). Electronic publishing and library technical services. *Library Resources and Technical Services.* Vol. 28, No. 1, pp. 68-75. January-March. Chicago, American Library Association.

Barr, A.; Feigenbaum, E.A. (1982). *The Handbook of Artificial Intelligence.* Kaufman, Los Altos, Calif. Vol. 1, 1981; Vol. 2, 1982.

Bechhoefer, A.S. (1983). Electronic publishing: The new newsletter. *Byte.* Vol. 8, No. 5, pp. 104-130. May.

Bender, E. (1986). CD-ROM to take blinders off users searching data bases. *Computerworld.* Vol. 20, No. 10, pp. 9, March 10.

Bigelow, C.; Day, D. (1983). Digital typography. *Scientific American.* Vol. 249, No. 2, pp. 106-119.

Bindra, A.K. (1984). Flat panels are getting bigger, brighter and better. *Electronics.* Vol. 57, No. 6, pp. 113-123. March 22.

Bivins Noerr, K.T. (1983a). Cable television in the United States and Europe: Part 1. Electronic Publishing Review. Vol. 3, No. 2, pp. 131-143. June.

Bivins Noerr, K.T. (1983b). Cable television in the United States and Europe: Part 3. *Electronic Publishing Review.* Vol. 3, No. 4, pp. 319-325. December.

Blaiwas, D. (1984). Sideline update: Books on cassette. *Publishers Weekly.* Vol. 225, No. 13, pp. 36-40. March 30.

Bonczek, R.H.; Holsapple, C.W.; Whinston, A.B. (1984). Developments in decision support systems. In: Yovits M.C., ed. *Advances in Computers.* Vol. 23, pp. 141-157. New York, Academic Press, Inc.

Boyum, R.R. (1986). Prepress densitometer/dotmeter can reduce reject rates on platemaking and proofing. *American Printer.* Vol. 196, No. 4, pp. 53-54. January.

Broad, W.J. (1982). Journal: Fearing the electronic future. *Science.* Vol. 216, pp. 964-968. May.

Brody, H. (1986). Ultrafast chips at gate. 1986 *High Technology.* Vol. 6, No. 3, pp. 28-35. March.

Brownrigg, E.B.; Lynch, C.A.; Pepper, R.L. (1984). Packet radio for library automation. *Information Technology and Libraries.* Vol. 3, No. 3, pp. 229-244. September.

Bruno, M.H. (1985). Scaling the heights of high technology. *American Printer.* Vol. 136, No. 1, pp. 39-43. October.

Buckland, L.F. (1984). Data Input for Publishers: Techniques for Authors, Editors, Typesetters & Data Base Producers. Littleton, Mass., Inforonics, Inc. 8 pp. March.

Butler, B. (1986). Electronic publishing business: The publisher's goal. *Electronic Publishing Business.* Vol. 4, No. 5, pp. 1. May.

Canzii, G.; Degli Antoni, G.; Lucarella, D.; Pilenga, A. (1984). A scientific document delivery system. *Electronic Publishing Review.* Vol. 4, No. 2, pp. 135-143. June.

Carlisle, W.M. (1986). The videotex alternative. *Datamation.* Vol. 32, No. 7, pp. 30-32. April.

Carney, R. (1985). InfroTrac: An inhouse computer-access system. *Library Hi Tech.* Vol. 3, No. 2, pp. 91-94. Consecutive issue 10.

Carroll, J.M. (1982). Hidden dangers of electronic mail. *Proceedings of the Tenth Annual Canadian Conference on Information Science.* Ottawa, Ontario, May 2-6, 1982. Canadian Association for Information Science. pp. 190-193.

Cercone, N.; McCalla, G. (1984). Artificial intelligence: Underlying assumptions and basic objectives. *Journal of the American Society for Information Science.* Vol. 35, No. 5, pp. 280-290. September.

Chevreau, J. (1986). Voice technology gets vocal. *Canadian Datasystems.* Vol. 18, No. 3, pp. 76-79. March.

Collier, H. (1981). *Electronic Document Delivery*—II. *Proceedings of a Workshop and Exhibition Organized by the Commission of the European Communities.* Directorate General Information Market and Innovation, Luxembourg, December 18-19, 1980. Page, J.R.U., ed. Oxford, England. Medford, N.J., Learned Information.

Conrad, M. (1985). On design principles for a molecular computer. *Communications of the ACM.* Vol. 28, No. 5, pp. 464-480. May.

Cook, P.R. (1984). Electronic encyclopedias. *Byte.* Vol. 9, No. 7, pp. 151-152, 154, 157-158, 160, 162, 164, 168, 170. July.

Criswell, L.B. (1983). Serials on optical disks: A library of congress pilot program. *Library Hi Tech.* Vol. 1, No. 3, pp. 17-21. Winter.

Cuadra Associates, Inc. (1985). *Directory of Online Databases.* A quarterly publication. Santa Monica, Calif., Quadra Associates, Inc.

Cuadra, C.A. (1981). A brief introduction to electronic publishing. *Electronic Publishing Review.* Vol. 1, No. 1, pp. 29-34.

Daniel, M.E.; Gwyn, C.W. (1982). CAD system for IC design. *IEEE Transactions on Computer-Aided Design of Integrated Circuits and Systems.* Vol.CAD-1, No. 1, pp. 2-12. January.

Davis, D.B. (1986). Business turns to in-house publishing. *High Technology.* Vol. 6, No. 4, pp. 18-26. April.

Dawes, A.; Durno, G. (1984). Comparing six current technologies. *Canadian Datasystems.* Vol. 16, No. 3, pp. 30-35.

Dempsey, D.; Parkinson, C.K. (1986). What are the differences between printers? Here's a guide. *Data Communications.* Vol. 15, No. 2, pp. 106-113. February.

Denning, P.J. (1985). The science of computing. Parallel computation. *American Scientist.* Vol. 73, No. 4, pp. 322, 323. July- August.

Desmarais, N. (1986). Laser libraries. *Byte.* Vol. 11, No. 5, pp. 235-246. May.

Di Sante, E. (1986). X*PRESS: The online news machine. *Online.* Vol. 10, No. 2, pp. 110-112. March.

Ditlea, S. (1984). Inside software. First video-book. Laser producer. *Publishers Weekly.* Vol. 226, No. 8, p. 44. August 24.

Donovan, T. (1983). *The ISIL Papers: User Experience with DCF and GML.* San Jose, Calif. IBM Corporation, General Products Division, Santa Teresa Laboratory. June 16.

Dowlin, K.E. (1984). *The Electronic Library: The Promise and the Process.* New York, Neal-Shuman.

Dyson, P.E.; Edwards, S.E.; Seybold, J.W.; Solimeno, W.J. (1986) ANPA '86: Large systems, scanners & output recorders. *The Seybold Report on Publishing Systems.* Vol. 15, No. 23, pp. 3-31. July 21.

Electronic Publishing Business (1986). For immediate release. *Electronic Publishing Business.* Vol. 4, No. 5, pp. 2. May.

Elton, M.C.J. (1982). *Teleconferencing: New Media for Business Meetings.* AMA Management Briefing. New York, American Management Associations.

Enter the robot librarian (1984). *New Scientist.* Vol. 97, No. 1347, p. 586. March 3.

Eres, B.K. (1983). Information technology: Status, trends and implications: Part 1. *Electronic Publishing Review.* Vol. 3, No. 3, pp. 223-243.

Fiteni, A.O. (1986). The new wave. *Canadian Datasystems.* Vol. 18, No. 3, pp. 36-41. March.

Forsyth, R. (1984). Machine Learning Systems. *Aslib Proceedings.* Vol. 36, No. 5, pp. 219-227. May.

Fox, C. (1986). Future generation information systems. *Journal of the American Society for Information Science.* Vol. 37, No. 4, pp. 215-219. July.

Freund, A.L. (1985). A regional bibliographic database on videodisc. *Library Hi Tech.* Vol. 3, No. 2, pp. 7-9. Consecutive issue 10.

Gaffin, H. (1985). A key player in the graphic arts for this century: Film. *American Printer.* Vol. 196, No. 3, pp. 46-48. December.

Gallup Fayen, E. (1983). *The Online Catalog: Improving Public Access to Library Materials.* White Plains, N.Y., Knowledge Industry Publications Inc.

Gates, Y., et al. (1982). *Electronic Document Delivery—A Study of the Relationship Between User Needs and Technology Options.* Vol. 2. Prepared by PIRA (The Research Association for the Paper & Board, Printing & Packaging Industries). Leatherhead, Surrey, England, IEPRC (The International Electronic Publishing Research Centre).

Gevarter, W.B. (1985). *Intelligent Machines: An Introductory Perspective of Artificial Intelligence and Robotics.* Englewood Cliffs, N.J., Prentice-Hall, Inc.

Givens B. (1986). How we got where we are: ECRM. *The Seybold Report on Publishing Systems.* Vol. 15, No. 17, pp. 14. May 19. A chapter in the article: Seybold Seminars '86, Part II, by Seybold, J.; Solimeno, W.J.; Tribute, A.

Guernsey, J. (1982). *Electronic Document Delivery—III Electronic Publishing Trends in the United States and Europe.* A Report by Information

Management Associates for the Commission of European Communities. Learned Information, Oxford, England and Medford, N.J.

Haley, P.; Williams, Ch. (1986). Expert systems development requires knowledge engineering. *Computer Design.* Vol. 25, No. 4, pp. 83- 88. February 16.

Hendley, A.M. (1983). Future optical based document storage and retrieval systems. *Reprographics Quarterly.* Vol. 16, No. 4, pp. 141-149.

Hershey, W.R. (1984). Thinktank. *Byte.* Vol. 9, No. 5, pp. 189-190, 192, 194.

Hills, P.J. (1983). The scholarly communication process. In: Williams, M.E., ed. *Annual Review of Information Science and Technology.* White Plains, N.Y., Knowledge Industry Publications, Inc. Vol. 18, pp. 99-125.

Hindin, H.J. (1986). 32-bit parts and architectures vie for attention. *Computer Design.* Vol. 25, No. 1, pp. 49-61. January.

Holman, D. (1985). Telidon and Manitoba. *The Canadian Journal of Information Science.* Vol. 10, pp. 44-48.

Huntington, D. (1986). Expert systems on micros—a meeting of the minds. *Words (USA).* Vol. 14, No. 4, pp. 36-41, 52. December 1985-January 1986.

Hurwood, B.J. (1984). Publisher presence growing at consumer electronic show. *Publishers Weekly.* Vol. 225, No. 7, pp. 41-44. February 17.

Hwang, K. (1983). Computer architectures for image processing. *Computer.* Vol. 16, No. 1, pp. 10-12. January.

J.C. (1984). Software for rent through new telephone users network. *Publishers Weekly.* Vol. 225, No. 16, pp. 58. April 20.

Johnson, T. (1986). NLP takes off. *Datamation.* Vol. 32, No. 2, pp. 91-93. January.

Jones, C.L. (1984). The impact of technology on users of academic and research libraries. *IFLA Journal.* Vol. 10, No. 1, pp. 49-55.

Jones, K.P. (1984). The effects of expert & allied systems on information handling: some scenarios. *Aslib Proceedings.* Vol. 36, No. 5, pp. 213-217. May.

Judge, P.J. (1984). *The Technology of Document Delivery.* Paper for Library Association of Australia, University and College Section. National Seminar on Collection Management in Academic Libraries. Surfers Paradise, Australia. February 16-17.

Knapp, S.D. (1983). Online searching: Past, present, and future. In: Maloney, J.J., ed. *Online Searching Technique and Management.*

Chicago, Ill., American Library Association, pp.3-15.

Koenig, M. (1984). Fiber optics and library technology. *Library Hi Tech.* Vol. 2, No. 1, pp.9-15.

Krummel, L.L. (1984). Just the way users told us it should be. In: *Seybold Seminars '84: Digital Graphics.* March 7-8, Santa Monica, Calif.

Krummel, L.L. (1983). The Iterative Nature of Technical Publishing. *Computer Graphics World.* Vol. 6, No. 6. June.

Lancaster, F.W. (1984). Implications for library and information science education. *Library Trends.* Vol. 32, No. 3, pp. 337-348. Winter. In Allen, W.C., Auld, L.W.S., eds. Atypical Careers and Innovative Services in Library and Information Science. Champaigne-Urbana, Ill., University of Illinois: Grad School of Library and Information Science.

Lancaster, F.W. (1978). *Toward Paperless Information Systems.* New York, Academic Press, Inc. In: Library and Information Science Series.

Lanham, C.D. (1983). Help on the path to word processing. *Scholarly Publishing.* Vol. 15, No. 1, pp. 82-90. October.

Laub, L. (1986). The evolution of mass storage. *Byte.* Vol. 11, No. 5, pp. 161-172. May.

Lemmons, P. (1984). Beyond the wordprocessor. *Byte.* Vol. 9, No. 1, pp. 53-54, 56. January.

Lerch, I.A. (1983). The movable conference. *Byte.* Vol. 8, No. 5, pp. 104-120. May.

Lerner, R.G. (1978). Electronic publishing. In: Taylor, P.J., ed. *New Trends in Documentation and Information.* Aslib Proceedings of the 39th FID Congress, University of Edinburgh, Sept. 25-28. pp. 111-116.

Lerner, R.G.; Mick, C.K.; Callahan, D. (1980). *Database Searching and Document Delivery Via Communications Satellite.* Final report to the National Science Foundation. New York, American Institute of Physics. AIP80-1. June.

Lerner, R.G.; Metaxas, T.; Scott, J.T.; Adams, P.D.; Judd, P. (1983). Primary publication systems and scientific text processing. In: Williams, M.E., ed. *Annual Review of Information Science and Technology.* White Plains, N.Y., Knowledge Industry Publications, Inc. Vol. 18, pp. 127- 149.

Library Systems (1986). 1.4 million passwords. *Library Systems.* Newsletter by Library Technology Reports. Chicago, Ill., American Library Association. Vol. VI, No. 3, pp. 19. March.

Look, H.E., ed. (1983). *Electronic Publishing—a Snapshot of the Early 1980s.* Oxford, England, and Medford, N.J., Learned Information.

Lu, C. (1986). The state of the micro. *High Technology.* Vol. 6, No. 1, pp.31-35. January.

Markoff, J. (1984). Trends in telecommunications. *Byte.* Vol. 9, No. 7, pp. 341-342, 347, 350, 352, 354, 356. July.

Martin, J. (1982). *Viewdata and the Information Society.* Englewood Cliffs, N.J., Prentice-Hall, Inc.

Martin, J. (1985). *Fourth Generation Languages.* Vol.I, Principles. Englewood Cliffs, N.J., Prentice-Hall, Inc.

Maslin, J.M. (1982). The importance of information in information technology. In: *Trends in Information Transfer* Greenwood Press. Hills, P.J., ed. Westport, Conn.

McCorduck, P. (1983). Introduction to the fifth generation. *Communications of the ACM.* Vol. 26, No. 9, pp. 629-630. September.

McQueen, J.; Boss, R.W. (1983). High-Speed Telefacsimile in Libraries. In: White, H.S., ed. *Library Technology Reports.* Vol. 19, No. 1. January-February. Chicago, Ill., American Library Association.

Monitor (1984a). Another host "resting". *Monitor.* No. 37, pp. 4-6. March.

Monitor (1984b). Online New York. *Monitor.* No. 38, pp. 1-2. April.

Morris, R. (1983). Information and satellite technology. *Aslib Proceedings.* Vol. 35, No. 2, pp. 71-76. February.

Morton, H.C. (1984). A new office to strengthen scholarly communication. *Scholarly Publishing.* Vol. 15, No. 2, pp.99-145. January.

Murphy, B. (1985). CD-ROM and libraries. *Library Hi Tech.* Vol. 3, No. 2, pp. 21-26. Consecutive issue 10.

Naiman, A. (1983). *Word Processing Buyer's Guide.* Peterborough, N.H., Byte/McGraw-Hill. pp. 325.

Neufeld, M.L.; Cornog, M. (1983). Secondary information systems and services. In: Williams, M.E., ed. *Annual Review of Information Science and Technology.* White Plains, N.Y., Knowledge Industry Publications, Inc. Vol. 18., pp. 151-183.

Neufeld, M.L.; Cornog, M. (1986). Database history: From dinosaurs to compact discs. *Journal of the American Society for Information Science.* Vol. 37, No. 4, pp.183-190. July.

Newell, A. (1973). Production systems: Models of control structure. In: Chase, W., ed. *Visual Information Processing.* New York: Academic Press, Inc. pp. 463-526.

Nugent, W.R.; Harding, J.R. (1983). *Pictures and Productivity: How Image Automation Will Amplify the Output of the Knowledge Worker. Productivity in the Information Age. Proceedings of the 46th ASIS Annual Meeting 1983.* Vol. 20. Washington, D.C., October 2-6.Vondran, R.F.; Caputo, A.; Wasserman, C.; Diener, R.A.V., eds. White Plains, N.Y., Knowledge Industry Publications, Inc.

Online Newsletter (1986). Times Mirror and Knight-Ridder end their videotex services. *Online Newsletter.* Vol. 7, No. 4, pp. 2. April.

Painter, J.D. (1983). Bits and pictures—a review of some current ways of capturing graphic data. *Reprographics Quarterly.* Vol. 16, No. 2, pp. 60-65.

Pasricha, S. (1984). InfoColor presentation. In: *Seybold Seminars '84.* March 7-8, Santa Monica, Calif.

Pemberton, J. (1986). Laserdisks ... tidal wave or ripple. *Database.* Vol. 9, No. 1, pp. 6-7. February.

Pezzanite, F.A. (1985). The LC Marc database on video laserdisc: The Mini Marc system. *Library Hi Tech.* Vol. 3, No. 1, pp. 57-60. Consecutive issue 9.

Policy Studies Corporation (1983). Optical digital storage at the Library of Congress. *Technology Watch for the Graphic Arts and Information Industries.* Vol. 3, Nos.7/8, pp. 1-3. May/June.

Pollitt, A.S. (1984). A front-end system: An expert system as an online search intermediary. *Aslib Proceedings.* Vol. 36, No. 5, pp. 229- 234. May.

Psych INFO News (1986). Psych LIT on CD-ROM ready for field testing. *Psych INFO News.* Vol. 6, No. 1, pp. 1. February.

Raitt, D.I. (1985). Information delivery systems. In: Williams, M.E., ed. *Annual Review of Information Science and Technology.* White Plains, N.Y., Knowledge Industry Publications, Inc. Vol. 20, pp. 55-90.

Raitt, D.I. (1985) Look no paper! the Library of tomorrow. *The Electronic Library.* Vol. 3, No. 4, pp. 276-289.

Ramsey, H.R.; Grimes, J.D. (1983). Human factors in interactive computer dialog. In: Williams, M.E. ed. *Annual Review of Information Science and Technology.* White Plains, N.Y., Knowledge Industry Publications Inc. Vol. 18, pp. 29-59.

Rhodes, S.N.; Bamford, E. Jr. (1976). Editoral processing centers: A progress report. *The American Sociologist.* Vol. 11. pp. 153-159. August.

Rivenburgh, J. (1984). CATV opportunities. *Computerworld.* Vol. 18, No. 36A, pp. 39-40. September 5.

Romano, F.J. (1986). Where we've been and where we're going: Automated composition update. *American Printer.* Vol. 197, No. 1, pp. 39- 42. April.

Rothchild, E.S. (1986). An eye on optical disks. *Datamation.* Vol. 31, No. 5, pp. 73-74. March.

Rose, D.A. (1983). Optical disk for digital storage and retrieval systems. *Journal of the American Society for Information Science.* Vol. 34, No. 6, pp. 434-438.

Salmon, J.D. (1984). The handling of integrated pictures and text for page composition, image processing and data transmission. In: *Seybold Seminars '84: Digital Graphics.* March 7-8, Santa Monica, Calif.

Sargent, J. (1986). What's going on here? An in-house market update. *American Printer.* Vol. 197, No. 2, pp. 59-64. May.

Seybold, J. (1985) Comdex: Electronic printers under every tree. 1985. *The Seybold Report on Publishing Systems.* Vol. 15, No. 7, pp. 15-31. December 23.

Seybold, J.; Stivison, D.S. (1984). Interactive page make-up. The *Seybold Report on Publishing Systems.* Vol. 13, No. 14, April 9.

Seybold, J.W. (1984). *The World of Digital Typesetting.* Media, Pa., Seybold Publications, Inc.

Shackel, B. (1983). The BLEND system: Programme for the study of some "electronic journals." *Journal of the American Society for Information Science.* Vol. 34, No. 1, pp. 22-30. January.

Shapiro, E.Y. (1983). The fifth generation project—a trip report. *Communications of the ACM.* Vol. 26, No. 9, pp. 637-641. September.

Simeone, G. (1983). Online news by videotex. *Electronic Publishing Review.* Vol. 3, No. 1, pp. 33-37.

Simkins, M.A. (1983). The impact of new technology on the information profession. *Aslib Proceedings.* Vol. 36, No. 2, pp. 92-98. February.

Sloan, B. (1984). Sharing resources in Illinois: Statewide library computer system. *Wilson Library Bulletin.* Vol. 59, No. 4, pp. 259-261. December.

Snyder, L. (1984). Supercomputers & VLSI: The effect of large-scale integration on computer architecture. In: Yovits, M.C., ed. *Advances in Computers.* Vol. 23, pp. 1-33. New York, Academic Press, Inc.

Solimeno, W. (1984). Hastech presentation. *Seybold Seminars '84: Interactive Page Make-up.* March 5-6; Santa Monica, Calif.

Sommerfeld, A. (1986). Page printers: For speed and volume, now is the time to buy. *Computerworld.* Vol. 20, No. 16, pp. 45-55. April.

Standera, O.L. (1984). Electronic publishing: Some observations evolving from our experience. In: Helal, A.H.; Weiss, J.W., eds. *New Trends in Electronic Publishing and Electronic Libraries.* Essen Symposium August 29- 31, 1983. Essen, Federal Republic of Germany, Essen University Library. pp. 119-148.

Stoate, C. (1984). The case for COM in data processing. *Canadian Datasystems.* Vol. 16, No. 11, pp. 65-69. November.

Strassmann, P.A. (1984). *The Role of Electronic Printing in the Office of the Future.* Executive Presentation II. Xerox Canada Inc. Stamford, Conn. Systems Group, Xerox Corporation.

Summit, R. (1986). Spring meeting summary. *ASIDIC Newsletter.* No. 52, pp. 11-13, Spring. Athens, GA, Association of Information and Dissemination Centers.

Sumner, F.H. (1983). The future of information technology: a personal view. *Aslib Proceedings.* Vol. 35, No. 1, pp. 1-13. January.

Surprenant, T. (1984). Direct broadcast satellites: An interview with Hartford Gunn. *Library Hi Tech.* Vol. 1, No. 4, pp. 7-12. Spring.

Takatoshi, M.; Kenjiro, Y.; Takashi, T.; Morikawa H.; Takahashi, O. (1983). Optical wireless modem for office communication. In: *AFIPS Conference Proceedings.* Calif. Smith, A.N., ed. 1983 National Computer Conference, May 16-19. Anaheim, pp. 721-728.

Terrant, S.W. (1983) *Publishing Scientific Information Today ... and Tomorrow.* Special Report. Washington, D.C., American Chemical Society.

The Seybold Report on Publishing Systems (1986). The latest word. Canon offers still-video camera. *The Seybold Report on Publishing Systems.* Vol. 15, No. 22, pp. 2. July 7.

The Seybold Report on Publishing Systems (1986). The latest word. Texas Instruments desktop laser printers. *The Seybold Report on Publishing Systems.* Vol. 15, No. 24, pp. 44. August 4.

Turoff, M.; Hiltz, S.R. (1982). The electronic journal: A progress report. *Journal of the American Society for Information Science.* Vol. 33, No. 4, pp. 195-202. July.

Vacca, J.R. (1986). Shifting winds of storage. *Computerworld.* Vol. 20, No. 15A, pp. 29-34. April 16.

Valovic, J. (1986). Charting the rocky course of technological change. *Computerworld.* Vol. 20, No. 14, pp. 17. April 7.

Veith, R.H. (1983a). *Television's Teletext.* New York., Elsevier Science Publishing Co., Inc.

Veith, R.H. (1982). Teletext (broadcast videotext) as a selective information distribution facility. In: *Proceedings of the ASIS Annual Meeting.*

Petrarca, E.; Taylor C.I.; Kohn, R.S. eds. White Plains, N.Y., Knowledge Industry Publications, Inc. Vol. 19, pp. 314-315.

Veith, R.H. (1983b). Videotex and teletext. In: Williams, M.E., ed. *Annual Review of Information Science and Technology*. Vol. 18. White Plains, N.Y., Knowledge Industry Publications, Inc.

Vickers, P. (1984). Information management: A practical view. *Aslib Proceedings*. Vol. 36, No. 6, pp. 245-252. June.

Wallace, R. (1984). Broadband in Boston. *Computerworld*. Vol. 18, No. 36A, pp. 35-38. September 5.

Webb, T. (1984). Author as compositor: Word processor to typesetter. *Scholarly Publishing*. Vol. 15, No. 2, pp. 117-190. January.

Whitaker, D.A. (1985) Using cable television for library data transmission. *Library Hi Tech*. Vol. 3, No. 1, pp. 35-38. Consecutive issue 9.

Wiederhold, G.; Beetem, A.; Short, G. (1982). A database approach to communication in VLSI design. *IEEE Transactions on Computer-Aided Design of Integrated Circuits and Systems*. Vol.CAD-1, No. 2, pp. 57-63. April.

Williams, M.E. (1983). *Federal Policy Issues for Electronic Databases and Database Systems*. Presented at National Science Foundation Workshop on Policy Issues for Computers, Communications and Information, March 21-22, Dedham, Mass. pp. 45.

Williams, M.E. (1984). Highlights of the online database field- statistics, pricing and new delivery mechanisms. In: Williams, M.E.: Hogan, T.H. eds. *National Online Meeting, Proceedings 1984*. New York, April 10-12. Medford, N.J., Learned Information, Inc. pp. 1-2.

Williams, M.E. (1986). Transparent information systems through gateways, front-ends, intermediaries and interfaces. *Journal of the American Society for Information Science*. Vol. 37, No. 4, pp. 204-214. July.

Winfield, B. (1984). Document Transfer by Satellite. *Aslib Proceedings*. Vol. 36, No. 4, pp. 177-185. April.

Winsbury, R. (1979). *The Electronic Bookstall (Pushbutton Publishing on Videotex)*. London, International Institute of Communication.

Wood, J.L. (1982). Document delivery: The current status and the near-term future. In: Network Planning Paper, No. 7, *Document Delivery Background Papers*. Washington, D.C., Network Advisory Committee, Library ofCongress.

Working Group on Electronic Publishing. (1983). The impact of electronic publishing. *Electronic Publishing Review*. Vol. 3, No. 4, pp. 281-301.

Yaghmai, N.S.; Maxin, J.A. (1984). Expert systems: A tutorial. *Journal of the American Society for Information Science.* Vol. 35, No. 5, pp. 297-305. September.

Yeates, R. (1986). Videotex in libraries and information centres. *The Electronic Library.* Vol. 4, No. 1, pp. 56-63. February.

Zabel, G. (1982). Experiences of a regional newspaper publisher on Prestel. In: *Videotex—Key to the Information Revolution.* Proceedings of Videotex '82—the International Conference and Exhibition on Videotex 1982, New York. Northwood Hills, U.K. Online Conferences Ltd. pp 59-68.

Appendix

The three sections of this appendix are adaptations of three papers emanating from the project on electronic publishing at the University of Calgary (see the end of Chapter 3):

A.1 Casual Users and the Editorial Process

Adapted from a paper published in the *Journal of the American Society for Information Science* (1985), Vol. 36, No. 4, pp. 230-240, July. New York. Reprinted by permission of John Wiley & Sons, Inc. Copyright © 1985 John Wiley & Sons, Inc.

Introduction. Electronic publishing has become a major topic in world literature in recent years as a result of the convergence of several technologies and subject areas, namely conventional publishing, information science, computer and communications technology, mass media, the automated office and library science. The new communications technology, with respect to the scholarly communication process, has been recently reviewed by Hills (1983). Lerner, Metaxas, Scott, Adams and Judd (1983), in their report on new technological developments with emphasis on scientific publications discuss, among other things, the concept of the automated editorial office as being not dissimilar to the notion of the editorial processing center (EPC) according to the study of Berul, King, and Yates (1974). Turoff and Hiltz (1982) report on their experiences gained during operation of the Electronic Information Exchange System (EIES) offering four forms of electronic journals, and Shackel (1983), and Pullinger (1983) and Singleton and Pullinger (1984) discuss various aspects of the Birmingham and Loughborough Electronic Network Development (BLEND) funded by the British Library Research and Development Department. An electronic alternative to communication through paper-based journals was envisioned by King and Roderer (1978) in a paper based on the study report "Systems Analysis of Scientific and Technical Communication in the United States" completed for the National Science Foundation, and by Senders (1977).

When discussing electronic publishing, it is advisable to define the topic carefully because it may mean different things to different people. Perhaps, most appropriately, electronic publishing is an umbrella term for a wide variety of publishing endeavors in which the material to be published appears at one or more stages entered in, or transformed into, the electronic form to be processed and possibly, but not necessarily, output as such. Without participating in any hair-splitting disputes over definitions, let us state that, in the present discourse, we shall focus on text entry, editing and editorial review with particular emphasis on occasional users, their problems, concerns and their performance. Because user behavior and performance are a function of the technology employed and the overall working environment, a brief description of our project is in order to put the ensuing discussion of the phenomena of the casual user into proper perspective.

A.1.1 University of Calgary Project on Electronic Publishing

In this section we will briefly delineate the scope of our project (Standera 1983a and b), as we conceived it at the outset to suit our financial and other resources. To set the stage for the casual user, let us address the background against which to observe some problems experienced by occasional users: the hardware, software, project team, papers, training, tools and assistance, as well as the mode of paper entry and the editorial process.

This brief account of the relatively modest size of our project will make clear the thus far unrealized potential for setting up one or more electronic journals based on the existing computer communication systems, if and when financial viability can be safeguarded and the computer environment can be made more hospitable to all involved in the scholarly communication process with due regard to the old, proven values of conventional publishing.

Scope of the Project. The objective of the study was to investigate the editorial process of scholarly journal publishing by creating 10 papers (Standera 1983b) to be an issue of a journal in the social sciences and humanities, with all functions being performed electronically. After completing this step, we explored (Standera 1984) the human-machine interface from several aspects: (1) We evaluated the performance; (2) then we examined various phenomena and issues on the human-machine interface as they relate to our project and to electronic publishing in general; (3) we also scrutinized activities taking place on the interface from the perspective of human information processing. Further, (4) we studied reader response to the outputs of our trial and (5) compared costs of the alternative five output formats; finally, (6) we proposed some questions for further study.

Hardware and Software. The hardware we selected for our project was Honeywell model DPS 8/70M (MULTICS operating system) with three processors. At our workplace we had a Lanpar model XT100 video terminal accompanied by an intelligent printer Dataroyal 5321 with bidirectional printing capability; connection to a direct telephone line was via a 212A modem allowing for 1,200-baud operation.

Because we did not have at our disposal any software that was custom-tailored to our specific needs, neither was there any well-trodden path for our project to follow (i.e., both available and affordable). We had to decide which software tools to adopt in order to achieve the projected goals.

We had to bear in mind that people on the project had very little, if any, knowledge of computers (casual users) and therefore, we adopted two guidelines when shaping up the working environment:

1. The set of commands, requests and procedures had to be minimal; authors, reviewers and editors have their own commitments and could not spend much time on the project.
2. The computer procedures had to be straightforward and easy to understand, lest they might discourage the voluntary participants. Obviously, this did impose certain constraints on our selection and enforced some compromises. We employed several software modules on our project:
   A. The first module was Electronic Mail applied for communication among authors, reviewers and editors, other than handling papers themselves.
   B. Another module was the qedx Editor; this is a line-oriented editor designed to assist the users to create, edit and store their own files which may be papers, programs, criticisms, etc.
   C. Once the papers were entered, edited and passed through the review process, they had to be formatted on the Wordpro facility. This program generates an input file of text and formatting commands to define headers and footers, set the line

length and page length, etc., for the typesetter. Because the control language has not been designed for casual users and generic coding is not available, we did not require our users to learn this aspect of the project.
D. The HELP command offers information on more than 500 information "segments" online. If we had a facility tailor-made to our specification, we would demand a much more specific advice in a given circumstance in a more user-friendly form.
E. The commands employed to support channels between authors, referees, editors and eventually readers were especially important for the completion of our project and are critical in any similar undertaking. This is an area that can turn out to be the decisive one for successful implementation of any computerized editorial environment in a publishing system. It presents a real challenge to system designers because it is supposed to serve a variety of people with different background and volume of use: authors, editors, reviewers, typographers, page compositors, management, and, last but not least, readers. Each of these users has a different interest in the system and has a different job to do. More importantly, each class of people must be allowed certain functions and must be prohibited from performing unauthorized functions through different modes of access by means of varying password levels. A generalized computer system will not do for this specialized purpose if a reasonable degree of success is to be expected in terms of user acceptance.

The integrity of files (papers) is of paramount importance throughout the entire process from paper creation to presenting the output version. We used some 26 selected commands in accomplishing the tasks of moving, listing, printing, copying, naming, renaming, creating, deleting papers and directories as well as permitting and disallowing access to individual papers and to the online journal. This called for constant assistance by the technical editor to all participants in this aspect of the operation because the system was too elaborate for the casual user. This obviously is not permissible in real-life systems, but it happened to be an invaluable learning experience. The problem here is the complexity of syntax whereby a command may have to specify the project name, originating file, destination file, paper name, command name, including possible modifiers, etc.; this applies to any system and casual users find it difficult to learn and recall the complex syntax rules involved. The rescue can only come from the new emerging features on the human-machine interface.

APPENDIX 293

Project Team and Papers. All in all, there were six people involved in the project work team, five of them acting as authors, referees and editor, and the sixth person in the capacity of technical editor. Whereas authors, referees and editor functioned as they would in conventional editorial systems (if we disregard for a moment the new technology), the technical editor worked closely with the editor to forge ahead with the project and advised the project team in all matters related to new technology; he acted as the team instructor as well. The technical editor was also one of three project principals in the dual capacity of the technical director.

Members of the project team entered, edited and reviewed altogether 10 papers into our electronic journal titled *Selected Papers from Social Sciences and Humanities.*

Training. Out of the five authors/reviewers, three were beginners and had to be trained, whereas two of them had enough knowledge of the system to be able to enter their papers and review other authors' papers once they had been placed into their home directory.

The aim of the training was to:

Acquaint users with the overall project objectives

Explain basics of the hardware, software and telecommunications employed in the project

Teach users how the software facilities (described above) that were selected achieve the given objectives and also how to communicate with the system as well as among themselves

Learn how to utilize the tools and assistance in their respective pursuits

Training was an ongoing endeavor in that we could not anticipate all the features we would need to the most minute detail. That is why we started with what we could foresee as necessary and added new items as we went along. The three novices on the project had little, if any, previous experience with computers and not much typing experience either. Their attitude may be characterized as positive and they picked up the requisite knowledge and skills as expected. On the average, 4 hours of initial training plus brief periods of updating later on as our work progressed were required.

Because users were volunteers interested in learning new skills and willing to participate in a new venture accounts for their motivation. Entering papers coincided with the end of the fall term and this caused some delay. As a result, they all had to be retrained because they had forgotten the acquired skills while not applying them for 2 weeks.

The process of training was expedited by the fact that trainees were all university teachers. It also called for a correspondingly higher level of training. The subject matter at hand was outlined and then the instructor encouraged each user to try out the learned skills and intervened only when necessary or to answer questions. An important point is that each user was trained individually. This allowed for an intensive interaction in the beginning stages of skill acquisition (both human-machine and instructor-trainee), avoided early frustration, kept up interest in the project and boosted motivation; it also eliminated embarrassment from human failure in the early stages of the human-machine getting acquainted. The extra time spent in the individual training is redeemed by a lower dropout rate.

Tools and Assistance. Training was supplemented by tools that the trainees could utilize during the training itself and subsequently on the real job. It was clear that we could not present our users with the full-fledged instructions as used by computer programmers and advanced users. Therefore, we developed for our users, two kinds of tools:
1. Abridged instructions for editing, which was nothing more than a booklet 15 pages excerpted from relevant MULTICS materials; the materials were digested by the instructor and handed out to users in the first session. It is in keeping with our policy that users must be trained and supported in what they need but nothing more. This steered the project away from the treacherous waters of redundant information and resulted in achieving the project objectives in minimum time and without users being discouraged. This material was designed for an easy "off the work site" reference and for a quick review.
2. Posters were provided on the surrounding walls to aid in performing the project functions. These posters were found much more effective than the so-called "reference cards" or "vest-pocket reference tools." They were handprinted in big contrasting letters and their contents were threefold:
A. Editing commands
B. Electronic mail commands
C. Three concepts that we anticipated would present some difficulties to our users
   a. The buffer concept which demonstrates how buffers may be established and parts of text moved between buffers to achieve the "cut and paste" effect
   b. The storage concept which depicts the way segments may be moved in and out from the working storage
   c. Moving between the command level, edit mode and input mode

APPENDIX

These posters were intended to be used during sessions at the terminal.

Apart from the abridged instructions and posters, we provided two versions of the log-in procedure on the blackboard situated right beside our terminal outlining access procedures both through the front-end processor and the Datapac network.

Besides training and tools, we also made sure that users would find assistance in case of need. The instructor was available on-site in the start-up period, but we did not want the instructor to be consulted on a continuing basis in order to make the conditions look as real as possible. In a real situation the authors/reviewers will have to depend on the built-in HELP functions and/or online instruction and will have to be able to interpret the system error messages and to avail themselves of the tools provided. In addition to this, four telephone numbers on the blackboard directed users to computer services consultants in case of need.

Paper Entry and the Editorial Process. Papers were expected to be keyboarded by authors themselves and not through an intermediary (e.g., secretary, undergraduate, assistant, etc.). We thought that, if papers were entered and subsequently amended by an intermediary, this would deprive the authors of immediate control and make them dependent on a third party. This would represent no improvement to the existing practice in which some authors have their papers typed and corrected. Besides, we wanted to test the feasibility of casual users entering their "compuscripts" electronically. All 10 papers were keyed in by authors themselves. It may be stated that as a rule, the first paper required assistance, second paper required less assistance and the third required no assistance. Hand in hand with error-free performance goes user acceptance of the innovation. When we say error-free performance, we mean a relatively error-free performance with errors occurring not because of user's lack of knowledge (comprehension errors) of the system, but because of fatigue or oversight (random errors). These types of errors will always happen whatever the method of data entry may be (typing, keypunching, etc.). The instructors' role here is crucial; they must recognize early what the nature of the most frequent mistakes is and concentrate on their elimination. In our project there were essentially three kinds of mistakes, which we identified early in the trial, and displayed on the posters mentioned in the subsection on tools and assistance (the buffer concept, the storage concept and command/edit/input moves). Another imperative for the instructor is to identify and emphasize those mistakes that cause irreparable damage. Most of the mistakes are intercepted by the system and signalled to the user for an easy correction. (The better the system, the fewer irreparable mistakes can be committed by any user; the messages should be concise and informative.) We have encountered in our project one pitfall, which on several occasions resulted in authors having their papers or parts thereof lost irrecoverably. In some cases, despite the warnings and posters, this same mistake was committed several times until it generated a strong alert system in the authors themselves. Namely, if one enters the WRITE command while in EDIT, any text that happens to be in the workspace will irrevocably supersede the entire text of the original file (paper). Thus, it is possible that one created line, which is intended to supplement the text, in fact replaces the whole document.

The problems we encountered at this stage may be defined as follows:

1. Users were volunteers and authoring of papers coincided with the end of one and the beginning of the next semester. Nevertheless, users showed interest in the project and recognized that everybody had something to gain from its successful completion.
2. Computer systems, unfortunately, are rarely completely stable. At the time we needed flawless operation, the system was due for an upgrade. There were also several power failures and this was a severe test for the project.
3. There was one central workstation initially. In a real situation authors must have terminals available on their desk top.

The participating authors had no access to one another's papers at the time of creation of their papers. The technical editor and the editor obtained access to keyboarded papers in order to be able to discharge their respective duties. The technical editor copied each paper into the appointed referee's directory.

The editor, who is an author himself, nominated referees from among the authors based on their subject area expertise. The editor could read and print the paper contents of "his" authors and, if he elected so, he could copy the paper and add it to his files. Once they became "his" files, the papers could be edited (in the qedx), formatted (in wordpro), renamed, listed or a name could be added or deleted. The editor and the referee(s) could append their comments to any paper. They would copy a paper into their file directory, enter qedx to "read," print, edit and/or append, then they would save ("write") the paper back into their directory. At this point they would notify the author that his paper was ready and would establish access to the particular paper or, preferably, the technical editor copied the paper back into the author's files. Original papers were preserved for reference and comparison purposes.

APPENDIX

Communication between participants in the project, other than of editorial nature, was conducted by electronic mail. Any party to the project could use mail to communicate with anybody else anytime. Messages were transmitted back and forth using the mail commands. Messages could be edited before being sent as in most other electronic mail systems.

Final Word. In concluding this section it may be stated that paper entry and copy editing could be accomplished quite efficiently under the conditions described above. The system we selected for the project out of necessity did not allow direct control by the user of many desirable functions such as bold characters, italics, footnotes, footers, headers, etc., which would have been possible on some workstations introduced recently on the market. This complication imposed definite constraints on the selection and number of papers. Many of these functions were implemented by means of typographic codes embedded into the text streams later at the formatting stage before final reproduction took place, which presented our journal in five formats for the subsequent reader evaluation. Reviewing papers on the screen has not found much favor with our users inasmuch as reviewers preferred to read any major portion of text in printed form derived from the "purely electronic" form. The screen appeared to be an inadequately small window into the contents of paper under the circumstances of our test; the new workstations allow for making notes on split screens and enable editors and reviewers to move quickly back and forth in the text while scrolling in both directions, thereby emulating much more closely work with familiar paper copies, including annotation.

A.1.2 Casual Users

Having outlined the specific environment on the background of which we examined some issues of occasional usage, we will now discuss the performance of casual users in some more detail; we suggest "actions per error" as the performance measure for three project team members and see how the amount of usage affects user performance. "Abstraction errors" will be singled out next as indicative of potential problems casual users may face in system areas involving abstract concepts. Finally, we will trace in retrospect the progress of a casual user in solving an identical "abstract" task three times within a period of 4 months.

The Notion of Casual Users. In the previous sections we alluded on several occasions to our productive users (authors and reviewers) as casual users. Most often authors in scholarly electronic publishing systems will be occasional users because of the number of papers they publish; certainly one to five papers published yearly is not going to make them professional system users. They may elect not to use computer terminals at all and have their secretary act as an intermediary. Even if they provide the data entry part in their publishing role with the subsequent text editing, they may not get involved in text formatting, which might be looked after by the technical editor or a service bureau (in a University, e.g., within the departments of computer services or printing services).

For our purposes a casual as opposed to a steady user may be defined as an occasional user with no formal computer training, even though he may have previously acquired experience with some other computer system or with some other application within the same system. The essential ingredients of this definition are casual or occasional use and lack of professional computer background. Casual use means either infrequent or low-volume use, but even a user with computer background may become a casual user under certain circumstances.

Needless to say, all the problems encountered by users in general will not only apply to casual users but will be much more exacerbated.

Time intervals between training or working sessions have adverse effects on performance as does an insufficient number of actions within a given period of time (a month in our case). All three users in our project required retraining in the beginning of our trial after not having used the system for 2 weeks. Casual users can afford only limited amount of time to spend on training; the instructor has to strike a compromise between the time available and the amount of knowledge he deems necessary to convey to the trainees.

Casual Use and Performance. As part of our project, we have evaluated the performance of the system and its users. "Performance" in our context is one of different measures of a system which tell us how the system performs in the light of the expectations (demands and objectives) we placed on it when we selected it for our electronic publishing project. The term "system" in the narrower sense denotes the Honeywell MULTICS system including software; in the broader sense it encompasses the working environment, terminal, printer, tools, etc., and the participants themselves as is required by the human-machine interaction concept involved. The source material for our evaluation was the terminal printout whose 4497 human-actions were scrutinized as to the kind of errors and failures that were occasioned in the course of project activities (Standera 1983b).

Human actions in the context of our project represent traceable user actions at the terminal, not including login/logout procedures because these are specified on the blackboard for user reference and are not expected to result in errors. Corrections of typing errors are not accounted for because these are neither productive actions nor errors in our sense. Carriage return is also not included because of its routine nature. Actions in our context are one of the following: (1) MULTICS commands, (2) qx-editor requests, (3) electronic mail commands, (4) answers that initiate further computer action.

For our purposes "errors" have been defined as those actions in the human-machine interface that exceed the computer's capability to perform an intended task in a particular instance. The person at a terminal has an idea of what he/she wants accomplished (albeit an idea not always well defined), and he/she wields human information-processing capabilities plus a more or less complete knowledge of the computer system. The computer, on the other hand, can partake in the cooperative task-solving activity only if certain strict rules are observed; if the human's and machine's capacities do not match, an error results and typically an error message or warning is posted by the computer. Errors are presented by the system to the user but that does not necessarily mean they are the user's fault; in fact, in most cases they attest to the inadequacy of the computer system. In the future when more artificial intelligence will be put to use, we can envision advanced systems where, indeed, it will be the user who will be issuing messages and the computer will do most of the adjusting. In any case, errors are good indicators of mismatches at the human-machine interface, and, if suitably analyzed, may be used to advantage in problem diagnosis and remedy.

The following categories of errors were analyzed:

1. Comprehension errors
2. Random errors
3. Total errors as percent of actions
4. Error interval (minutes per error)
5. Actions per error as performance criterion of individual users
6. Errors caused by abstraction (successful and unsuccessful attempts, number of actions in attempts, cause of failures)

We have discussed errors under categories 1-4 elsewhere (Standera 1983b and 1984); in this paper we take a critical look at actions per error and errors caused by abstraction in the context of casual users.

In our frame of reference, comprehension errors are those resulting from the lack of knowledge of how to achieve a given intended goal through the operation of the system; random errors are those made while the user most likely knew the correct procedure but failed nevertheless to perform properly because of insufficient attention, fatigue, impatience, frustration or slip of memory.

Users A, B and C: Actions per Error. In the performance evaluation of the project, we endeavored to evaluate, among other factors, the perfor-

TABLE 3 User Characteristics

	User		
Criterion	A	B	C
Education/degree	University/Ph.D.	University/Ph.D.	University/Ph.D.
Subject field/ expertise	Social sciences	Humanities	Humanities
Professional orientation	Teaching/research	Teaching/research	Teaching/research
Computer background	None	None	None
Data procesing experience	Minimal	Minimal	Minimal
Motivation	Positive, strongly	Positive, strongly	Positive, moderately
Temperament, disposition	Calm generally, impatient under stress	Calm under stress, patient, systematic	Calm generally, easily frustrated, impatient under stress
Amount and frequency of use	Low, casual	Low, casual	Low, casual

mance of the three novice participants (out of the five) who assumed the roles of author, referee and the editor. Table 3 portrays the three casual system users, giving the main characteristics deemed significant in their behavior during the human-machine interaction under scrutiny. (The remaining two users/referees entered their papers independently and forwarded them to our journal on the same computer system; they are not included in the performance study.)

All three users have similar education (university) and the highest degree earned (Ph.D.), their subject field expertise lies in social sciences and humanities and they all are involved in teaching and research. None of them had any formal computer background and their data processing experience was nil at the beginning of the trial. The only observable differences between the three users are their degree of motivation (users A and B being strongly motivated while user C only moderately so) and their temperaments—user A generally calm but impatient under stress, user B calm under stress, patient and systematic, user C, while generally well composed, tended to be easily frustrated and impatient under stress. All users received the same amount of individual instruction from the same instructor and operated the same equipment.

APPENDIX

We have selected as the quantitative indicator of user performance (*UP*) the average number of actions *A* per error EC+R (both comprehension and random), *UP* = A/EC+R; in other words a higher *UP* means that a user makes errors less frequently or that he completes more actions before an error is statistically predicted.

User B has the highest mean value of *UP* = 11.03 (these values are computed across the entire duration of the trial), which is explained by his positive attitude and patience in dealing with his tasks. Next comes user A with mean value of *UP* = 7.76; this user is generally calm but impatient under the stress of the job if unexpected events do arise. He is positively motivated and he always completed the job. Third is user C who was only moderately motivated and easily frustrated; his *UP* = 3.4 indicates that this user has not attained the degree of proficiency required for this kind of work because of the low number of his actions.

User performance *UP* for individual months is summed up in Table 4 separately for users A, B and C. The same figures are plotted in graphs in Figure 22. The graphs for user A and B show a steady improvement of performance reflecting the growth of comprehension. The graphs also point to the plight of the casual user; with both users A and B we can observe the dramatic improvement as the number of their actions increases (e.g., user A in February over January) in a given month. If, on the contrary, the number of actions is insufficient (user A in October and November) or decreases (user B in February) or is infrequent and low (user C in both November and January), then performance deteriorates into an absolute drop or at least a slower progress. But the graphs also indicate that the amount of use, namely frequency of use and number of human actions, is not the only factor determining the absolute level of performance: user B achieves a higher level of user performance than user A despite the lower number of his human actions (1037 by user B vs. 3313 by user A); this may be explained, given the same degree of motivation, by the more favorable temperament and possibly better aptitude for problem solving in this type of task. It appears that motivation, temperament and aptitude for specific tasks may move the performance up or down in absolute values but the relative progress, or lack of it, of individual performance is affected by the amount of use, i.e., frequency of use and number of actions within a period of time. This demonstrates the need for special treatment of casual users, as opposed to steady users, in terms of a user-friendly interface as well as training, tools and assistance. As a user's amount of action (as defined above) increases, the number of comprehension errors will continue to drop as skill is increased. Random errors (see definition above) cannot be completely eliminated (they fluctuated between 4.5 and 10.5) because their causes are in the uncontrolled cognitive area and/or in the emotional sphere. In our

TABLE 4 Users A, B and C: Actions per Error

Month	User A Actions A	User A Errors E$_{C+R}$	User A A/E$_{C+R}$	User B Actions A	User B Errors E$_{C+R}$	User B A/E$_{C+R}$	User C Actions A	User C Errors E$_{C+R}$	User C A/E$_{C+R}$
October	114	29	3.9	0	0	0	0	0	0
November	155	54	2.9	171	26	6.6	7	2	3.5
December	507	102	5.0	326	33	9.9	0	0	0
January	755	108	7.0	475	31	15.3	140	42	3.3
February	1,782	134	13.3	65	4	16.3	0	0	0
Total	3,313	427	7.76	1,037	94	11.03	147	44	3.34

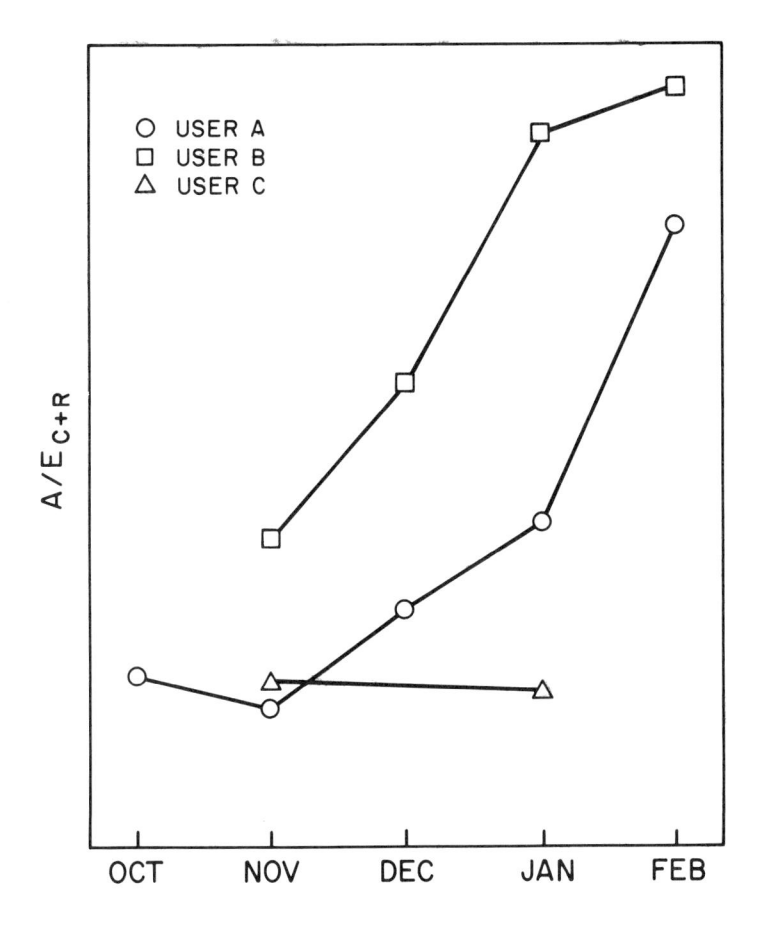

FIGURE 22 User performance ($UP = A/E_{C+R}$).

TABLE 5 Total Errors as Percentage of Actions

	User		
Month	A	B	C
October	25.44	—	—
November	34.84	15.20	28.57
December	20.12	10.12	—
January	14.30	6.52	30.00
February	7.52	6.15	—

study (Standera 1983b), we observed a decline of random errors toward the end of the trial, which indicates that when authors become more acquainted with the system (as demonstrated by comprehension errors approaching zero) they concentrate more on "doing things right" rather than on "how to do it." Because they feel more at ease, their tension, impatience and frustration diminish and random errors decline as a result. Under the conditions of our study, it would appear that, at the level of around 7%, "total errors" (i.e., the sum of comprehension and random errors) do not unduly disconcert users, neither do they present any problem in achieving projected goals (Standera 1983a and 1983b). This was independently confirmed by observing users and querying them. In our present context (Table 5), it is interesting to note that user B achieved this level of performance in January and maintained it in February, whereas user C ended up with a record of 30% total errors. We have concluded that, under the conditions of our project, this level of performance indicates a state of affairs in which casual users attained the proficiency of steady users.

Errors Caused by Abstraction. Abstract thinking in our present argument denotes a user's human information processing, which lacks the physical parameters of concrete objects and requires a great deal of imagination and memory if it is not helped by a suitable (user-friendly) system design.

Unfortunately, computer applications have so far required a considerable degree of abstract thinking on the part of users. Abstraction may refer to both tangible objects (e.g., storage, file, scratchpad, etc.) and intangible concepts (modes, modules, levels, commands, etc.). Computerizing conventional operations has required uninitiated novices and expert users alike to deal with abstract notions existing, on the one hand, in electronic form in the computer sphere and, on the other hand, in the user's mind as abstract constructs built on the basis of whatever documentation there may be. It is up to the user to apply his cognitive system to cope with this problem. Some computer systems are more helpful than others in this respect. The problem arising out of situations involving a great deal of abstraction is that users, instead of being able to concentrate on solving their particular problems, have to devote their human information processing resources to a struggle, rather than cooperation, with the computer interface. In our case "abstract" refers to spatial considerations but the term conceivably can be related to time, logic, operation sequence, etc.

We have defined above three major areas in our projects where users were prone to err very often. All three instances referred to have one thing in common: they work with abstract entities devoid of any physical parameters such as shape, size, weight, color, place in space, etc., and exist only in electronic form and in user's mind. They can be learned even by casual users but they are easily forgotten and they burden the memory, both short-term and long-term, when it is needed most for problem solving and decision making. To eliminate this problem we have to do any or all of six things:

1. Define these abstract concepts and use definitions liberally wherever applicable, if we cannot avoid them altogether
2. Turn the abstract notions into concrete entities by assigning them names familiar to the user
3. Give them some physical appearance, which is easy to draw and easy to recognize, i.e., replace recall by pattern recognition
4. Make these objects mobile so their physical manipulation by the user can assist in the formulation of as many commands as possible, thereby freeing the user's memory for problem solving; in other words, enable the user, by means of some interface features (such as trackball, paddles, joy-stick, mouse) to control objects and events by doing instead of memorizing an elaborate syntax of commands
5. Use color if possible to distinguish between categories of objects or actions
6. Substitute graphics for text where appropriate

To illustrate the problems inherent in features involving abstraction, we singled out the "cut-and-paste" feature and took a closer look at it. We examined its usage by all three users working at the central facility for the 5 months of our trial. A typical successful operation would include the following seven steps, four of which are optional:

1. Move a certain number of lines to another buffer and assign a name to it (the "cut" operation)
2. Option—transfer to the created buffer to verify status
3. Option—make changes to the "cut" portion of the text
4. Option—transfer back to the main buffer
5. Point to where one wants the "paste" done: define the line and select "append," "insert" or "change"
6. "Paste" the "cut" section to the spot defined by moving it back from the created buffer
7. Option—check the result for accuracy

The "cut-and-paste" facility is obviously of considerable utility to any author, referee and editor in entering and editing papers. It was, therefore, with some surprise that we found the very limited usage of this facility despite the special attention we paid to it in our training program, the pictorial posters right close to the workstation, the documentation dispensed to users and the consultation available to users. Out of 4497 human actions undertaken by users within the framework of our project, there were only five attempts involving as few as 100 actions related to "cut-and-paste" (2.22%). User C who did not achieve a satisfactory degree of performance because of the low amount of usage, did not use this feature at all; whereas user B did only once and unsuccessfully; and user A availed himself four times of the "cut-and-paste" feature and each time he eventually succeeded. We monitored the failures that users sustained during their attempts and found invariably that they can be attributed (1) to the lack of spatial orientation where the user loses track of in which buffer he is, and (2) to the improper spatial manipulation of the text involved. In these five reported attempts (both successful and unsuccessful), users employed a total of 100 actions; as outlined above three to seven actions per attempt could have accomplished the desired objective, in other words, 15-35 actions only were required. The case of the "cut-and-paste" feature is yet another proof of the plight of the casual user: user A accomplished his task with nine actions in February, whereas prior to that he needed 25.3 actions on average.

But the main message of the above observation is to show that users, and particularly casual users, shun using system features, which owing to their abstract nature, engage their cognitive resources when they need them in the pursuit of their tasks. Users may try to circumvent these features and replace them with other, simpler ones even though they may be tedious. This is all the more interesting in the light of the fact that our editing system did have a simple command whereby a user could ascertain which buffers are currently in existence and which one is his "active" buffer. Other features can be programmed but users will still struggle with these expedients if their usage of the system is an occasional one.

Abstract Task Solving Traced in Retrospect. In this subsection we demonstrate, by way of examples from the printed log, how human performance improves in time on the same kind of task as users acquire more advice and find the right problem solving strategy. The improved performance is due to (1) better understanding within their short-term memory, (2) deeper encoding in their long-term memory inasmuch as increasing knowledge of other system features allows for better integration of new data and concepts, (3) faster and more precise recall because of point 2, (4) the establishment of more effective procedures through repeated problem solving, (5) greater appreciation and exploitation of external memory (posters, instructions), (6) the perfection of the time-spatial thinking, peculiar to this kind of application. All the above points lead ultimately to freeing human information processing resources for creative purposes in a synergistic manner.

APPENDIX

The protocol below, in lieu of the original computer printout which cannot be reproduced here, documents the behavior at the human-machine interface of the same user during our trial: case A at the beginning, case B later in the project and case C at the conclusion of the trial. All three depict his performance on an identical task, namely the "cut-and-paste" feature common in most editors. The user is a casual user and the task he is contending with involves abstract thinking.

CASE A
1. The user decides to use the cut-and-paste feature. After some conceptual thinking related to a suitable strategy, he looks up the poster. With the intention to move five lines of text to another location, he evaluates the commands as to their suitability. He identifies the suitable command. He determines the range of lines. He chooses the name of the transfer buffer. He assembles the command.
2. He checks the overall strategy, looks up the poster, selects the next command and modifies it for his application.
3. He checks to see if the move has taken place, by printing the rest of the current buffer. He recalls the command.
4. He gets mixed up in space and time. He does not recall the instruction properly and fails to look up the external memory (poster) in an attempt to act independently. He recalls the right command but at a wrong space (in buffer XYZ instead of buffer 0) and in a wrong sequence (command should have been proceeded by a, c, or i).
5. The computer is baffled. It cannot interpret user's intention and considers the information stored in buffer XYZ as a request. It issues an error message accordingly.
6. Even though the user got the message telling him he is in buffer XYZ, he verifies his location by the request X. His information processing system becomes overloaded, and because of lack of practice, he cannot coordinate within his processor and short-term storage (STS) the space, the time and the proper sequence of commands. He panics.
7. User checks a second time the contents of his current buffer.
8. User issues the request to move to the buffer where he is already.
9. In his predicament he checks the contents of the buffer the third time.
10. He persists in his erroneous image of the cut-and-paste operation. He issues the incorrect request second time to transfer the contents where he wants to.
11. He receives the error message once again.
12. Now the user realizes his strategy is wrong, and in his panic he

recalls that an input request must be entered, yet he enters *i* while in the wrong buffer.
13. Since the user does not get any system message acknowledging the receipt, in his flustered state he issues another *i* which is now interpreted as text to be inserted.
14. He checks again on buffer contents.
15. User deletes the erroneous insertion correctly, which proves that the substitute request has become automatic and may be recalled even under stress.
16. The user assumes that the command format was not proper and he enters the wrong transfer command for the third time.
17. He repeats the same mistake the fourth time.
18. He finally leaves the loop, looks up the correct procedure on the poster, leaves the XYZ buffer and returns to buffer 0.
19. He checks the contents of this buffer.
20. He calls up a new current line.
21. He decides to append.
22. He proceeds to transfer the contents of the buffer XYZ back to buffer 0 behind the title line.

CASE B
1. The user determines which line he is currently on.
2. He looks up the strategy in the external memory, identifies the command format, determines the range of line numbers, chooses a name for his buffer and assembles the whole request.
3. He recalls correctly that he must transfer to the new buffer.
4. He checks to see whether text is correctly moved.
5. He transfers back to buffer 0.
6. This time he has failed in the "paste" phase and the subsequent activity indicates some confusion about how to append the "cut" text from the auxiliary buffer.
7. But this time he did know better how to coordinate the external storage (the poster) with his long-term storage and has entered the correct command with less effort than in case A.

CASE C Case C, a February event, demonstrates a flawless coordination of cognitive resources resulting in a smooth operation whereby 7702 characters stored temporarily in buffer "Tim" were appended to the intended destination in a paper of 59,731 characters in buffer 0 and written back into the computer storage.

Cases A, B and C prove that humans are very adaptive and they can adjust even to some unhospitable environments if need be. Casual user A has finally managed to operate an abstract procedure. Our goal, however, should be to free the user's human processing resources for creative purposes and not to exploit them to their capacity and beyond.

We may describe the system we have used (here designated as system I) as one where:

Syntactically involved commands have to be specified

Text being manipulated must be identified by abstract symbols (line numbers)

Spatial orientation must be kept up; changing from one working buffer to another is accomplished by means of commands

Nonspecific messages are offered

Higher on the evolution ladder is a system (system II) where:

The user selects commands from a menu by typing their numeric representations

The user marks the text to be moved by pointing with a cursor controlled by arrows, keys, etc.

Higher yet stands a system (system III) where:

The user selects commands from a menu by means of a mouse or similar pointing devices

The user selects the starting and target position with the help of icons and a mouse

It is obvious that the amount of human information processing required to do a job decreases sharply as we move from system I to systems II and III. It is mainly because: the recall of commands is replaced by pattern recognition; abstract thinking of a spatial nature is replaced by dealing with concrete objects; the sequence of entering commands is more obvious; pattern recognition is facilitated by graphics; pointing saves human processing time and effort compared with typing; and manipulation with mouse is less tiring than keys or arrows. All this applies to any systems user but has a special bearing on casual users if they are to achieve a satisfactory performance as defined above and still accept the system as their preferred working tool.

A.1.3 Conclusions

The objective of this paper has been to point to the peculiar nature of the phenomena of casual use in the course of the computer-assisted editorial process in an electronic scholarly journal. The environment was described in which the examination of the issue took place. The problems specific to casual users were then illustrated against the background of user performance, and the number of actions per error was adopted as a performance indicator for three casual users on the project. It appears that motivation, temperament and aptitude for specific tasks may move the performance up or down in absolute values, but the relative progress, or lack of it, of individual performance is affected by the amount of use, i.e., frequency of use and number of actions within a period of time. Even though the figure may vary contingent on specific circumstances, we have found that at the level of "total errors" around 7% (i.e., the sum of comprehension and random errors), casual users attained the proficiency of steady users. Then we examined the phenomenon of errors caused by abstraction in which users, instead of being able to concentrate on solving their particular problems, have to devote their human information processing resources to coping with a "user-surly" computer interface. Six measures were suggested as helpful in alleviating the problem. Singling out the "cut-and-paste" operation as an example of abstraction-type features, it has been recognized that users, and more particularly casual users, shun using functions, which because of their abstract nature engage their cognitive resources when they need them to deal with their task: out of 4497 actions at the interface investigated, there were only 2.2% cut-and-paste-related actions despite their obvious usefulness to authors, referees and editors. Monitoring the failures revealed that they may invariably be accounted for by lack of spatial orientation and incorrect spatial manipulation. Finally, to document further the plight of casual users, we have traced in retrospect actions of one user in solving an identical task by documenting his progress over the duration of our trial as more support was needed and received to overcome the rigors of an abstraction-laden procedure.

References

Berul, L. H.; King, D.W.; Yates, J. G. (1974). *Editorial Processing Centers: A Study to Determine Economic and Technical Feasibility.* Report for the National Science Foundation. Rockville, Md., Westat, Inc. and Aspen Systems Corp. p. 61.

Hills, P. J. (1983). The scholarly communication process. In: Williams, M. E., ed. *Annual Review of Information Science and Technology.* White Plains, N.Y., Knowledge Industry Publications, Inc. Vol. 18. pp. 99-125.

King, D. W.; Roderer, N. K. (1978). The electronic alternative to communication through paper-based journals. In: Brenner, E.H., ed. *The Information Age in Perspective: Proceedings of the American Society for Information Science 41st Annual Meeting.* November 13-17, 1978, New York. White Plains, N.Y., Knowledge Industry Publications. Vol. 15. pp. 180-182.

Lerner, R. G.; Metaxas, T.; Scott, J. T.; Adams, P. D.; Judd, P. (1983).

Primary publication systems and scientific text processing. In: Williams, M. E., ed. *Annual Review of Information Science and Technology.* White Plains, N.Y.; Knowledge Industry Publications, Inc. Vol. 18. pp. 127-149.

Pullinger, D. J. (1983). Attitudes to traditional journal procedure. *Electronic Publishing Review.* Vol. 3, No. 3, pp.213-222.

Senders, J. W. (1977). An online scientific journal. *Information Scientist.* Vol. 11, No. 1, pp.3-9. March.

Shackel, B. (1983). The BLEND system: Programme for the study of some electronic journals. *Journal of the American Society for Information Science.* (1983). Vol. 34, No. 1, pp.22-30. January.

Singleton, A.; Pullinger, D. J. (1984). Ways of viewing costs of journals: Cost evaluation of the BLEND experiment. *Electronic Publishing Review.* Vol. 4, No. 1, pp.59-71.

Standera, O. L. (1983a). *Electronic Publishing (Pilot Project: Online Scholarly Journals).* Grant No. 446-820001 from Social Sciences and Humanities Research Council. Report No. 2, February 1983. Calgary, Alberta, Canada, The University of Calgary Press; The University of Calgary Libraries.

Standera, O. L. (1983b). *Electronic Publishing (Pilot Project: Online Scholarly Journals).* Grant No. 446-820001 from Social Sciences and Humanities Research Council. Report No. 3, September 1983. Calgary, Alberta, Canada, The University of Calgary Press; The University of Calgary Libraries.

Standera, O. L. (1984). Electronic publishing: Some observations evolving from our experience. In: Helal, A.H.; Weiss, J.W., eds. *New Trends in Electronic Publishing and Electronic Libraries.* Proceedings of the 6th Essen Symposium, August 29-31. 1983. Essen, Federal Republic of Germany, Gesamthochschulbibliothek Essen. pp. 119-148.

Turoff, M.; Hiltz, S. R. (1982). The electronic journal: A progress report. *Journal of the American Society for Information Science.* Vol. 33, No. 4, pp.195-202. July.

A.2 Electronic Publishing: Some Notes on Reader Response and Costs

Adapted from an article published in the journal Scholarly Publishing (1985), Vol. 16, No. 4, pp. 291-305, July. Toronto, Ontario, Canada, University of Toronto Press. Reprinted by permission of the University of Toronto Press.

The term "electronic publishing" has been recently used to describe a wide variety of processes in which the material to be published apears at one or more stages, or at all stages, in electronic form. At the earliest stage, it may be put into electronic form at the moment when the ideas to be conveyed have been conceived, and it may remain in the electronic state all the way to the moment of delivery to the consumer on the screen of a terminal or microcomputer as, for example, in an electronic journal stored in a computer, or as videotex pages presented on a TV monitor. Alternatively, the final product may be delivered to the consumer (reader) as a hard copy (for example, a printout of an online search in a computer-stored database) or as a computer-generated microfilm or microfiche (COM), as a recorded voice, or braille, or videodisk, or diskette, and still other forms. The distributed product need not be the end product: it could be a magnetic computer tape containing an issue of a journal for different uses by different people, either as a revision of a database or as input into typesetting. And there are many ways to obtain a hard copy from the original electronic "copy," including an increased potential for on-demand and synoptic publishing.

Problems of reader acceptance and costs of electronic publishing have been tackled, for example, by Montagnes (1983), who surveyed the relevant literature and concluded that "it is far from clear whether, or to what extent, electronic or microform publication will contribute to...greater cost-effectiveness and greater accessibility of materials embodying the results of scholarly research. More study is required to determine these questions." Venkataraman (1983) reported on an informal survey of reader preference between electronic publications and print on paper. Of the 71 respondents—faculty members of the University of British Columbia, professionals in industry, and school teachers—only 5% accepted electronic publishing without reservations. Another 5% would prefer electronic publishing if a cheap and portable screen were available; 52% required print on paper, although they preferred electronic publishing for browsing; the 38% remaining described print on paper as an unqualified preference.

Although readers may be reluctant to use the new medium, it is becoming easier for authors to do so. Some journals have made it possible for authors to contribute papers in electronic form on some magnetic medium or transmitted directly by communication networks. *The Biophysical Journal* (E. Ackerman, editor) and *Biophysical Discussions* (V.A. Parsegian, editor), for example, accept papers in computer-readable form. The editors of these journals surveyed members of the Biophysical Society and concluded that there appears to be a good potential for increased "compuscript" submission, but electronic journalism must still wait for more receptive readership. On a broader front, to meet the problems of incompatibility, the American Association of Publishers (1983) has sponsored a major study intended to establish industry-wide standards for preparing and processing manuscripts in computer-readable form.

Palmer, Fitzgibbons and Carrier (1983) described in a recent paper the keying of a short, academic publication into a computer file by a scientific user who had had no previous computer-related background. They concluded on the basis of their small-scale study that computerized manuscript preparation is a cost-effective alternative to corresponding operations in traditional publishing: they reported the costs of preparing the 50-page manuscript as camera-ready copy to be $585.25 using computerized methods compared with $680.00 to $860.00 by conventional methods—savings of 25% to 40%. Singleton and Pullinger (1984) have produced an account of the cost evaluation of the BLEND experiment. Problems of pricing have been dealt with by Neufeld and Cornog (1983), albeit in the different context of abstracting and indexing online services. The problems of building a cost model were addressed in 1978 by King and Roderer (1981), who are coauthors of a more recent book dealing with, among other things, economics of journal publishing. Economics and, more particularly, costs were among the issues addressed at a 1980 conference in Europe (Price, Turoff and Hiltz 1980). There are a few other papers in which the problems of reader preference or acceptance and costs receive more or less scanty attention, but costs in particular are difficult to pin down and there is a definite need for more hard data. The subject of electronic publishing is still relatively new.

The study of cost has not been made any easier by a lack of definition of what electronic publishing is meant to be, and by the substantial difference in the impact of costs on authors, publishers, online providers, libraries and readers. Comparisons between systems are further complicated by the diversity of hardware and software which may be exploited to a varying degree of capacity, depending on the size, number, and regularity of runs. The matter is further complicated by the fact that the most valuable resource—the human element—varies as existing personnel are trained, retrained and motivated to cope with change. It would appear, further, that in most research to date more attention is given to technology than to economics.

Modern technology has been affecting traditional publishing in many ways; the impact is noticeable in both primary and secondary journals, in book publishing as well as publication of reports, manuals, brochures and the like. The new technology has affected all of the planning, preprint, production and distribution stages. It is the editorial process in scholarly journal publishing which has been the subject of our investigation at the University of Calgary.

Our Project: A Brief Background Review. The traditional editorial process in scholarly journal publishing involves repetitive processes. Authors prepare manuscripts, have them typed and send them to the editor, who, in turn, sends them to referees—specialists in the respective subject areas. The referees review the papers and propose their acceptance or rejection, or suggest amendments or corrections to the editor, who then communicates with the authors. In an electronic journal, all this can be done more efficiently and more quickly by relying on electronic means of entry, editing and electronic mail. As a part of our project (Standera 1983), we selected a system in which all this could be done, albeit with some inconvenience. We recruited and trained authors and put 10 papers through the editorial process. Five faculty members acted as authors, reviewers and (one of them) editor. The 10 papers constituted an issue of an electronic journal which was then presented to readers in five formats (defined below) under the name *Selected Papers from Social Sciences and Humanities*. The reaction of users was assessed, and the costs of the five manners of publishing examined.

The hardware used in the project was a Honeywell computer system DPS89/70M with three processors. At our workplace we had at our disposal a Lanpar model XT100 (VDT) video terminal and an Dataroyal 5321 intelligent printer with RS-232-C interface. The video terminal was connected to a direct telephone line through a 212A modem providing access into the Datapac network. In software, we used the MULTICS electronic mail module, a line editor (qedx), a formatting module (wordpro) and a number of general commands. These facilities were used by authors, reviewers, the editor and, later on, by readers.

As a spinoff of the editorial process, we gathered the printout of most of the interactions that took place between the computer and the participants, a total of 4497 human-actions. These were subjected to a thorough examination as to the type of errors made; in this manner we obtained some evidence about the performance of participants and the system itself. We also took a critical look at the human-machine interface and arrived at some concrete conclusions about how this should be optimally shaped for scholarly publishing. And we reviewed the editorial process in scholarly publishing from the point of view of human information processing, which must be considered both separately and in conjunction with the computer as a tool. These latter studies have been reported elsewhere (Standera 1984). This section will discuss our findings about user response and costs, and consider the cost-benefit of the five journal formats under the defined conditions. Even though the size of the user (readership) sample is relatively modest, it is well defined so that comparisons can be made with different populations and sample sizes.

Reader Response. The reader's response is the ultimate test of feasibility and viability of any publication system, much as user acceptance is the test of any product developed in industry. We presented readers with a journal in five different formats:

A. Line printer copy, the crudest form of hard copy output, delivered from the computer line printer in dot-matrix characters; this form must be burst before being bound (102 pages of text)
B. Letter-quality copy, much enhanced in legibility through the use of daisy wheel printing and some degree of formatting, including bold characters (101 pages of text)
C. Conventional journal typeset, printed, and bound; it is much more compact because of proportional spacing and back-to-back print (65 pages of text)
D. Computer output microfiche (COM) prepared directly from magnetic tape (122 frames on one fiche)
E. Electronic journal read on a video display terminal; in other words, electronic publishing in its "purest" form

It must be emphasized that all five formats are at least partially electronic. All have common "roots" in that all were captured and edited on the same terminals. But from there their paths diverged, and the readers judged the formats on their merits as they appeared at the moment of reading. The typeset, printed and bound journal, for example, looked "conventional"; the COM was perceived as a microfiche normally would be; and only the VDT rendition was viewed as being "electronic." In computing the costs of the five formats, however, the reader's point of view was omitted and all were evaluated for what they really were.

The contents of the five formats were identical: 10 papers in the social sciences and humanities, written by scholars for scholars. The five formats were presented to 20 readers: 10 were academics from various departments in the social sciences and humanities engaged in teaching and research, 10 were librarians with a nonscience background working at the University of Calgary Library. All the readers were given explanations of the five formats and were briefed about the project, its objectives, and its progress to date so they could understand their role in the entire context. They were instructed to inspect the materials in any way they felt would be useful for their evaluation. Specifically, they were asked, first, to disregard their views as potential authors, referees, editors, librarians, publishers, disseminators, etc., and rank the formats solely as readers of scholarly publications; and, second, to address themselves to the current state of the art without anticipating the potential of the technology.

They were asked to complete three simple forms. On the first they were asked to rank the five journal formats by numbers to indicate their preference. In the final evaluation, the highest score of 5 was assigned to the format most preferred, the score of 4 to the second choice, and so on.

On the second form they were asked to indicate the relative importance of 13 selected factors in their judging of the five formats. This was intended to help them in ranking their choices as well as to provide data for the project evaluator. The 13 factors were to be scored as extremely (5), considerably (4), moderately (3), little (2), or not at all important (1). We could have listed more than 13 criteria but feared that a longer questionnaire might arouse negative attitudes towards the project.

The third form simply solicited overall comments about the readers' attitudes towards the various journal formats.

The 20 readers overall gave the conventional journal first position, with 87 points out of a possible 100 and a mean ranking of 4.35. Second place was occupied by the letter-quality copy with 79 points and a mean ranking of 3.95; third came the electronic journal, far behind with 51 points and a mean ranking of 2.55, closely followed by the line printer copy with 48 points and mean ranking of 2.40. The computer output microfiche received only 35 points and a mean ranking of 1.75 (Table 6).

Ranking by academics and librarians was remarkably similar and bears witness to the homogeneity of the entire sample. All are readers of scholarly publications, all have university education, and all work in similar subject areas. The only discrepancy obtained in their third and fourth choices; academic readers ranked the electronic journal on VDT as third and the line printer as fourth; the librarians were of the opposite opinion.

It is not surprising that there was also a great deal of similarity in the criteria both groups applied in ranking formats (Table 7). Both valued legibility most highly in accepting a journal format. Both also agreed on the three next most important criteria—ease of browsing, availability of indexes and user-friendly procedures—but with some differences in emphasis. Both ranked lowest a reluctance to change one's information-gathering habits, and agreed on the relative unimportance of health concerns (academics 12th, librarians 11th position) and appearance (academics 11th, librarians 10th place). The cost of reading was allotted by both groups the relatively low eighth rank, possibly be-

APPENDIX

TABLE 6 Scores of Format Acceptance: Twenty Academics and Librarians

Identification	Format	Academics	Librarians	Total	Mean	Rank
A	Line printer copy	25	23	48	2.40	Fourth
B	Letter-quality copy	36	43	79	3.95	Second
C	Conventional journal Typeset, printed, bound	43	44	87	4.35	First
D	Computer output microfiche	16	19	35	1.75	Fifth
E	Electronic journal on video display terminal	30	21	51	2.55	Third

Maximum possible score = 100.

cause neither views them as personal costs. Portability was assessed differently, as might be expected: librarians showed less concern for it than academics. The academics, on the other hand, seemed less worried about fatigue than librarians, who probably consider it as one of their occupational hazards. Librarians gave much more importance to timeliness of information, but this might look very different in areas of science and technology. Rather surprisingly, librarians placed much less importance on storage than academics.

These findings send a clear message to the designers of electronic publishing systems: if the preference of readers as shown in Table 7 is to change, the current state of the art must be improved across a number of criteria by which readers (and by implication authors, referees and editors) judge journal formats. Designers must provide improved legibility, easy browsing, more friendly procedures, ready availability of indexes, portability and less fatigue. Inasmuch as both groups placed the availability of hard copy only at the middle of the scale, while at the same time designating the conventional journal as by far their first choice, it appears that they would be ready to change from hard copy if other formats could offer more convenience in reading.

TABLE 7 Significance of Criteria Applied to Acceptance Ranking

		Academics		Librarians	
No.	Criterion	Total (n)	Rank of Significance	Total (n)	Rank of Significance
1	Legibility	46	1	46	1
2	Portability	40	5	32	9
3	Cost	37	8	33	8
4	Hard copy available readily	38	7	35	6, 7
5	Storage considerations	39	6	28	12
6	Appearance	28	11	31	10
7	Timeliness of information	35	10	35	6, 7
8	Easy to browse back forth (random access)	44	2	40	3
9	Availability of indexes (subject, author, etc.)	42	4	43	2
10	Reluctance to change information gathering habits	23	13	24	13
11	Easy, user-friendly procedures of access (log-in, commands, error messages)	43	3	37	4
12	Health concerns (alleged radiation, cramped position)	26	12	29	11
13	Fatigue (increased eyestrain, tension)	36	9	36	5

Comparative Cost Analysis. This section examines costs of the journal as produced in its five formats.

First, we identified the actual costs associated with the production of the various formats in total and per unit for the number of copies actually produced. This is set out in Table 8. In this context, a unit means a copy (formats A, B, C and D) or a reading session (format E). All costs are in Canadian dollars.

The total cost of computing was $195.86, which amounts to $39.17 equally distributed among the five formats. This includes direct costs of entering the manuscripts, editing the journal, refereeing, electronic mail, copyediting, 12-month storage, and some training. All papers were entered by the authors themselves from their manuscripts. The earlier the text is captured in machine-readable form the better: it enables the editor to have effective control of the journal from the beginning, and the advantages of electronic processing come to the fore—easy correction and manipulation which save multiple retyping.

Terminal/printer rental, including delivery and installation, totalled $3551 per year. Considering the overall use of the equipment, it seemed reasonable to charge one-third of the cost to the journal and, as a result, $1183.67 was equally apportioned to all five formats at $236.73. This is an appreciable portion of the total cost and could be reduced by a long-term lease or outright purchase.

Computer line printing has been charged only to the line printer copy (format A). It was done by the Academic Computer Services (ACS) of the University of Calgary.

Formatting was also done by the ACS, which embedded formatting commands and some minor corrections. The total cost of $662.50 has been equally distributed to all five formats ($132.50). This expensive step can be done by the authors themselves if a system with nonprocedural language is available. Generic coding is becoming popular with casual users.

The letter-quality master was duplicated instead of being individually printed on a Multiwriter, at some savings in cost. This was charged only to format B (letter-quality copy).

For COM, the magnetic tape had to be reformatted; the cost of $50.00 was charged to format D. So was the COM output charge of $78.50. It includes a minimum charge of $56.00 (which could have bought up to 50 fiche) plus $22.50 for deliveries.

The typesetting cost of $450.00 was assigned to format C: it breaks down to $6.92 per composed page or $18.00 per journal copy. The cost covers transmission from ACS, some corrections, coding, and page composition. To this format also were charged the specific costs of photoduplication ($94.25 or $1.45 per page or $3.77 a journal copy);

TABLE 8 Actual Costs of Five Journal Formats

Cost Item	A. Line Printer Copy, 12 Copies	B. Letter-quality Copy, 13 Copies	C. Conventional Journal Copy, 25 Copies	D. Computer Output Microfiche, 15 Copies	E. Electronic Journal On Video Display Terminals, 20 Subscribers
Computer cost	$39.17	$39.17	$39.17	$39.17	$39.17
Terminal/printer	236.73	236.73	236.73	236.73	236.73
Computer printing	20.00				
Duplicating		107.43			
Reformatting tape				50.00	
Fiche master and duplicates				78.50	
Formatting	132.50	132.50	132.50	132.50	132.50
Typesetting			450.00		
Photoduplication			94.25		
Cover			26.85		
Binding			16.75		
Total Cost	428.40	515.83	996.25	536.90	408.40
Unit cost	35.70	39.68	39.85	35.79	20.42

APPENDIX 321

cover production comprising stock ($3.60), negative ($7.10), plate ($6.15), and run ($10.00); and binding ($16.75).

For the electronic journal, the cost of one reading session is composed of the production cost, which decreases with increasing patronage, and of the computer connect cost, which may depend on the time of day (prime vs. nonprime time), optional print cost, length of session, and extent of use of computer resources; it contains communication costs as well. Twenty subscribers were assumed for the purpose of our calculation; this was the number of readers acting as preference evaluators.

The costs outlined in Table 8 are those we incurred in the course of our project; to make them more comparable and realistic we calculated the production cost of five journal formats in print runs prorated according to readers' preference (Table 6). The conventional journal (preference score of 87) was selected as the base with a not unreasonable print run of 1500 copies. The number of copies of other formats was set accordingly as 828 for the line printer copy (preference score of 48); 1362 for the letter-quality copy (score 79); 603 for the computer output microfiche (score 35); and 879 for the electronic journal (score 51). The costs were revised in accordance with the extended print runs for the paper and film-based formats; for the electronic journal costs were assessed assuming a connect time of 60 minutes per journal issue, or $1.50, per subscriber (total of $1318.50) in addition to the fixed costs. Costs were assigned as in Table 8 with one exception. In actual practice the five formats would not likely coexist and share facilities. A journal would most likely appear in only one, or at most two, formats. To reflect this reality, the costs shared in the calculations in Table 8 have been fully allocated to each of the formats in Table 9.

Any complete cost model would, of course, have to incorporate additional expenses to reflect the total cost to be applied in consideration of pricing policies. These would include the fee of the journal editor, the salaries of any copy editors and of a technical editor involved in computerization of the publishing process, plus fulfillment, promotion and other overhead costs, which can be significant. Postage and mailing would increase the cost of the paper- and film-based formats. These additional costs would increase the cost per copy (or access) but most likely would not (considerably) affect the cost performance of the five journal formats in their ranking.

Cost-Benefit of Five Journal Formats Under Study. To put both the cost and benefits of the five journal formats in some perspective we have juxtaposed the acceptance ratings from Table 6 and cost rankings as computed in Table 9. The formats ranking first were given 5 points, those that were second 4 points, etc. Finally, the points for acceptance

TABLE 9 Cost of Five Journal Formats (Size of Run as Determined by Reader Preference)

Production Cost Item	A. Line Printer Copy, 828 Copies	B. Letter-quality Copy, 1362 Copies	C. Conventional Journal Copy, 1500 Copies	D. Computer Output Microfiche, 603 Copies	E. Electronic Journal On Video Display Terminal, 879 Subscribers
Computer cost	$195.86	$195.86	$195.86	$195.86	$195.86
Terminal/printer	1183.65	1183.65	1183.65	1183.65	1183.65
Computer printing	3259.00				
Duplicating		2453.29			
Reformatting tape				50.00	
Fiche master and duplicates				175.95	
Formatting	662.50	662.50	662.50	662.50	662.50
Typesetting			450.00		
Photoduplication			1300.40		
Cover			203.25		
Binding			930.00		
Subscriber access					1318.50
Total Cost	3733.01	4495.30	4925.66	2267.96	3360.51
Unit cost	4.51	3.30	3.28	3.76	3.82

and cost were added for individual formats to produce cost-benefit rankings (Table 10).

Needless to say, this cost-benefit evaluation applies to the conditions as set out in this study and may vary even in this well-defined environment—for example, if some additional costs were added or if some additional benefits were to modify the acceptance ratings; also, the least expensive formats could have their cost points marked up with a progressive coefficient in a cost-conscious environment, whereas the same could happen to acceptance points when reader acceptance is the highest priority. This might be advisable if one wanted to enhance the differences among the individual formats' performance.

In the cost-benefit evaluation, the conventional journal has come out on top with 10 points on account of its being rated as first both with respect to acceptance as well as cost. The letter-quality copy finished second and the electronic journal assumed the third overall position; the COM ended up as fourth and the line printer copy received the fifth rank. It must be noted that formats A, B, C and D benefitted in our case study from computer technology which improved their competitive performance with regard to cost; there is nothing very unusual about it in that most publishing systems of the present take advantage of computer technology at some stage in the editorial and production processes albeit to a different degree.

Final Comments. The above costs and acceptance ratings must be viewed in the context of changing technology, and should be studied and periodically adjusted. The expectation that electronic publishing will mean less cost is unrealistic: some costs would be entirely or partially eliminated (paper, stamps, etc.) but other costs will rise (electronic storage, transmission, etc.). The cost of hardware will continue to decrease while costs of software and human services will grow. The cost picture and, consequently, pricing policies will become more fluid, flexible and dynamic as the technology already has. Publishers may require authors to send edited papers electronically for electronic typesetting, thus reducing their own costs; authors for their part may make greater use of their respective organizations' equipment and staff. Readers may not individually subscribe, and information stores (e.g., libraries) may have to pick up the costs of user access. Publishers may recoup some loss of subscriptions to hard copies by selling electronically and information providers can charge users. New information brokers will enter the scene to produce, repackage and enhance information. It will become increasingly necessary to analyze the cost of the entire communication cycle rather than the cost incurred by individual links in the chain.

It would appear that there will likely be shifts in costs from one

TABLE 10 Cost–Benefit of Five Journal Formats Based upon User Acceptance and Journal Cost on a Five-Point Scale

Identification	Format	Acceptance Ranking	Acceptance Points	Cost[a] Ranking	Cost[a] Points	Total Points	Cost–Benefit Rank
A	Line printer copy	Fourth	2	Fifth	1	3	Fifth
B	Letter-quality copy	Second	4	Second	4	8	Second
C	Conventional journal	First	5	First	5	10	First
D	Computer output microfiche	Fifth	1	Third	3	4	Fourth
E	Electronic journal on video display terminal	Third	3	Fourth	2	5	Third

[a] Print run as determined by reader preference.

sphere into another, rather than any dramatic decrease of costs across the entire communications cycle. Technology by itself, although available, will not effect any rapid and deep changes in the status quo of publishing as we know it today, unless solutions are found that will accommodate other aspects of the problem, among them, costs and user response; any solution must be acceptable to all partners involved in the publishing enterprise including (but not limited to) authors, publishers, online suppliers, carriers, information warehouses and readers.

This case study indicates clearly that at this date the typeset, printed, and bound journal is still the first choice of academic readers in the social sciences and humanities, and is thus still the most economical. A ranking of criteria that influence readers points to areas where improvement is needed if electronic publishing on the video screen is to succeed. The lack of enthusiasm for microfiche has surfaced once again.

It may be stated in conclusion that, on the basis of available information and our experience, electronic means of publishing are making significant gains among authors and will have a better chance to be accepted by reviewers and editors with the types of human-machine interface now reaching our markets, but in their "pure" electronic form, still face an uphill battle to win the hearts of our readers. Electronic journals must earn user acceptance and reduce costs if they are to take a major slice of existing market.

References

American Association of Publishers Inc. (1983). Press release. Washington, D.C. July 25.

King, D.W.; Roderer, N.K. (1978). Systems analysis of scientific and technical communication in the United States. Annex 4: The cost model. National Science Foundation Contract NSF-C-DSI76-15515. Rockville, Md: King Research, Inc., 1978. (PB-281851)

King, D.W.; McDonald, D.D.; Roderer, N.K. (1981). *Scientific Journals in the United States: Their Production, Use and Economics.* Stroudsburg, P., Hutchinson Ross.

Montagnes, I. (1983). Electronic and micrographic technologies, cost effectiveness and accessibility. *Canadian Journal of Higher Education.* Vol. 13, No. 2, pp. 1-12.

Neufeld, M.L.; Cornog, M. (1983). Secondary information services. In: Williams, M.E., ed. *Annual Review of Information Science and Technol-*

ogy. White Plains, N.Y., Knowledge Industry Publications, Inc. Vol. 18, pp. 151-183.

Palmer, M.A.; Fitzgibbons, A.A.; Carrier, W.B. (1983). Computerized manuscript processing in a time-sharing environment: An enhancement to productivity in publishing. In: Vondran, R.F.; Caputo, A.; Wasserman, C.; Diener, R.A.V., eds. *Productivity in the Information Age: Proceedings of the 46th ASIS Annual Meeting.* October 2-6, 1983, Washington, D.C. White Plains, N.Y.; Knowledge Industry Publications, Inc. Vol. 20, pp. 280-284.

Price, C.R.; Turoff, M.; Hiltz, S.R. (1980). Electronic mail and teleconferencing: "Information" or "Communication". In: L.J. Anthony, ed. *Eurim 4: a European Conference on Innovation in Primary Publication: Impact on Producers and Users.* London: Aslib. pp. 35-39.

Singleton, A.; Pullinger, D.J. (1984). Ways of viewing costs of journals: Cost evaluation of the BLEND experiment. *Electronic Publishing Review.* Vol. 4, No. 1, pp. 59-71.

Standera, O.L. (1983). *Electronic Publishing (Research Report: Online Scholarly Journal).* Report to the Social Sciences and Humanities Research Council of Canada. Calgary, Alberta, Canada, The University of Calgary; 102 pages plus Appendices.

Standera, O.L. (1984). Electronic publishing: Some observations evolving from our experience. In: Helal, A.H.; Weiss, J.W., eds. *New Trends in Electronic Publishing and Electronic Libraries.* Proceedings of the 6th Essen Symposium; August 29 to 31, 1983. Essen, Federal Republic of Germany, Gesamthochschulbibliothek Essen. pp. 119-148.

Venkataraman, S.R. (1983). New technology and the publishing industry. In: *Proceedings of the Eleventh Annual Conference of CAIS.* May 23-26; Halifax. Ottawa, Ontario, Canada. Canadian Association for Information Science. Vol. 11, pp. 92-107.

A.3 Human Performance and Information Processing in the Context of the Electronic Journal

Adapted from a paper published in Helal, A.H.; Weiss, J.W., eds. New Trends in Electronic Publishing and Electronic Libraries (1984) Vol. 6, pp. 120-148. Essen, Federal Republic of Germany, Essen University Library. Reprinted by permission of the Essen University Library.

Introduction. The recent leaps in technology have not left conventional publishing methods unaffected. Publishers, printers, providers of hardware, software and related services, libraries and scholars in general have begun reassessing their respective positions.

The University of Calgary, through the involvement of the University Press and the University Libraries and with the financial assistance of the Social Sciences and Humanities Research Council of Canada, has launched a research project encompassing two phases over a 1-year period.

Phase I saw creation of an electronic journal of 10 papers in the social sciences and humanities, with the entire editorial process being conducted electronically; this involved five authors with no computer experience, reviewers and editors. The computer system used was Honeywell MULTICS.

In phase II the performance of the editorial system was evaluated in terms of human actions and concomitant errors were examined; In addition to this, the human-machine interface was subjected to scrutiny in some detail. Also, the human information processing aspect of this kind of human activity was investigated. The five various journal formats were subjected to readers' reactions: computer printout; letter-quality printout; computer output microfiche (COM); typeset, printed and bound copy as well as output on the visual display terminal (VDT) screen.

Finally, a brief cost-comparison study was performed to put the viability of the above forms of scholarly publishing into some perspective.

The present section touches upon some component parts of the above project. After defining the notion of electronic publishing, we examine the performance of the tested system and take a closer look at the human information processing involved in the editorial process.

Electronic Publishing: Definition. The term "electronic publishing" has been defined in the introduction to this book and in the previous sections of this appendix.

In the context of this paper, we are concerned with the editorial part of the electronic publishing process, with special emphasis on the process of scholarly publishing activities.

A.3.1 Performance Evaluation

Definitions. Performance in our context is one of different measures of a system which tells us how the system meets the expectations (objectives and demands) we placed on it when we selected if for our project. It is also called effectiveness.

The term "system" in the narrower sense denotes the MULTICS computer system including the software. In the broader sense it encompasses the working environment, terminal, printer, tools, etc., and the participants themselves as is required by the human-machine interaction concept under investigation.

As the source of our evaluation, we used the terminal printout which we gathered throughout the entire trial. All in all 4497 actions were evaluated.

Human actions in the context of our report represent human actions not including login/logout procedures because these are specified on the blackboard for user reference and are not expected to result in errors. Carriage return is not included either because of its routine nature. Actions in our context are one of the following:

1. MULTICS commands
2. Qx-editor requests
3. Electronic mail commands
4. Answers that initiate further computer action

In our interaction processes we are, therefore, concerned with: (1) primary actions, in which a person exercises his initiative, and (2) secondary actions, in which a person reacts to a machine action.

The actions that our users have taken (authors, referees or editor) in this project were effected in the course of:

1. Learning how to operate
2. Improving their skills
3. Writing and editing their papers
4. Refereeing
5. Acting as editor
6. The concomitant messaging

All actions center around the objective of generating an "electronic" journal encompassing 10 papers in the subject areas of social sciences and humanities.

Criteria. We have examined the interface protocol using a number of criteria and in this paper we will report on the following ones:

1. Comprehension and random errors
2. total errors
3. errors caused by abstraction

An analysis of errors and failures has proven to be a useful means in evaluating the performance of a system or in comparing two or more systems (Standera 1974). For our purpose here, we have defined errors as those actions in the human-machine interaction that exceed the computer's tolerance in a particular instance of performing an intended task. Humans, on the one hand, have an idea of what they want accomplished (albeit a not well-defined one at times) and they wield their human information processing capabilities plus a more or less complete knowledge of the computer system. The computer on the other hand, can perform in the cooperative task-solving activity only if certain strict rules are observed; an error results if these two capacities do not match each other and typically an error message or warning is posted by the computer.

A.3.2 Comprehension and Random Errors

Comprehension erors are those owing to the lack of knowledge of how to achieve a given intended goal through the operation of the system; this may be caused by lack of or misunderstanding of instructions or simply because the user has tried unsuccessfully something on his own.

Random errors are those made while the user most likely knew the correct course of action to be taken but failed nevertheless to perform properly because of insufficient attention, fatigue, slip of memory or impatience.

Both comprehension and random errors are unacceptable to the computer (exceed its tolerance for a given error) and as such require corrective person actions to carry on the dialogue. Because they are errors presented by the system to the user, does not necessarily mean they are the user's fault: in fact, in most cases they attest to the inadequacy of the computer system.

Typos that have been discovered and rectified by users themselves are not included. Not included are "hidden" errors which do not result in error messages and do not interrupt the interaction; if they escape the user's attention, the computer is either doing something other than what the user wanted, or the desired function is being done but the results will be erroneous. This kind of error is more difficult to detect in retrospect because it involves conjectures about the user's intentions.

Comprehension errors (CE) have been determined and plotted in Figure 23. The number of comprehension errors shown in October 1982 is 20; in November, 67; in December, 48; in January, 62 and in February, 31. More illuminating than absolute numbers is the graph of comprehension errors as the percentage of actions in all months under investigation: except for October data which are based on a small number of actions, the downward trend is clearly apparent: October, 17.54%; November, 20.12%; December, 5.76%; January, 4.52%; February, 1.68%. These figures, by their nature, state what probability

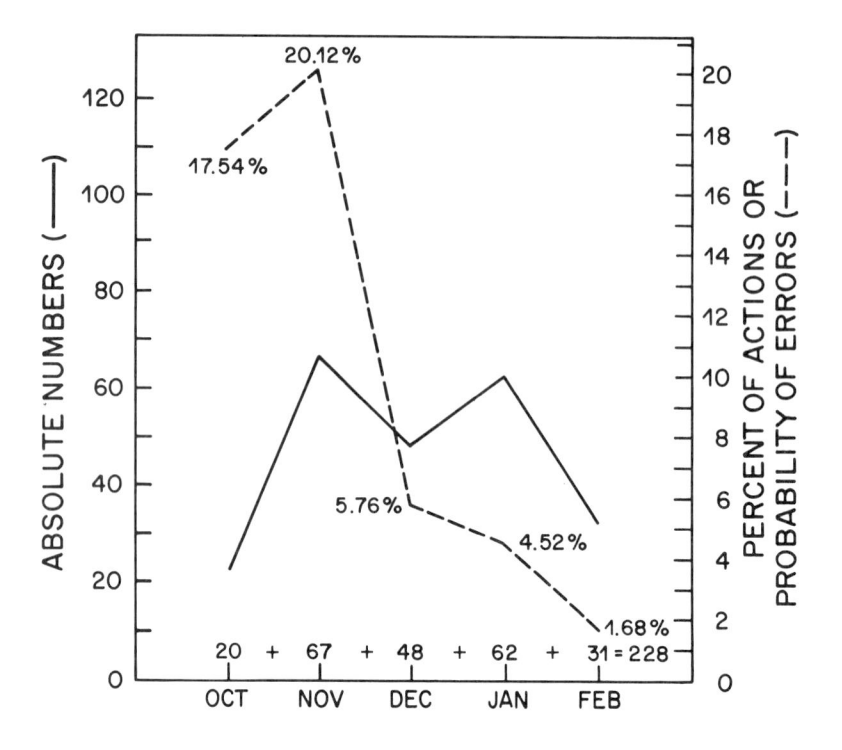

FIGURE 23 Comprehension errors.

of a comprehension error there is when a user takes an action. This graph is indicative of the pace at which participants on the project learned to use the system.

The level of comprehension errors attained by the end of the trial (1.68%) supports a practically flawless operation. There will be always a few comprehension errors attending introduction of new features or trying those which were considered difficult for a beginner.

Random errors (RE) (Figure 24) kept increasing with the growing number of actions up until February when they showed a slight decrease. There were 9 RE's in October, 15 in November, 87 in December, 119 in January and 107 in February. Again, the real situation is better illustrated by expressing RE as the percentage of human actions in the months respective: 7.89% in October, 4.5% in November, 10.44% in December, 8.86% in January, 5.79% in February. These figures also indicate the probability of a RE occurring when undertaking an action. They fluctuate within a relatively narrow margin of 5.94 (4.50 to 10.44%), which demonstrates their relative consistency with a visible downward trend toward the end of the trial. This shows that when

APPENDIX   331

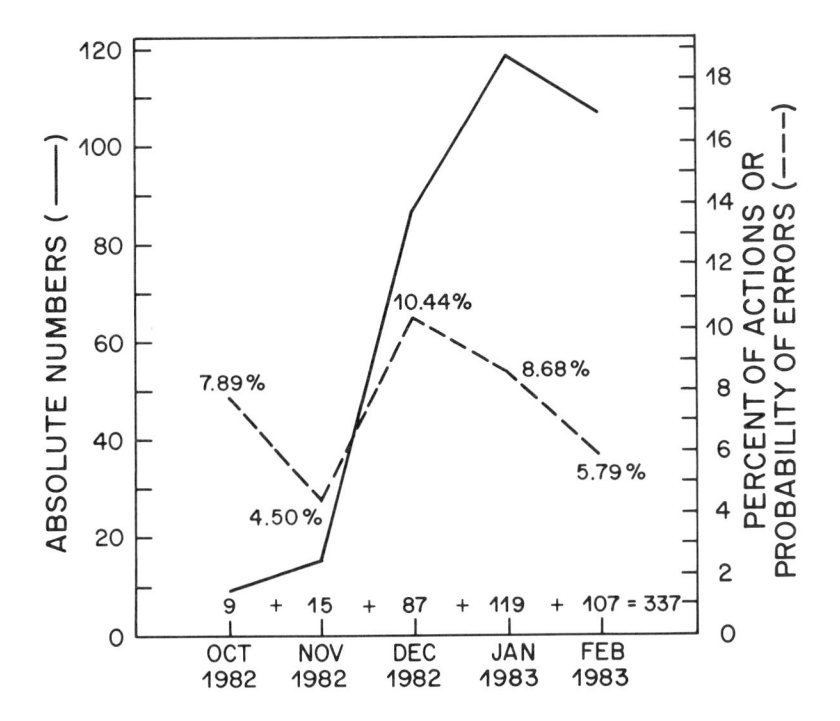

FIGURE 24 Random errors.

authors become more acquainted with the system (as demonstrated on comprehension errors above), they concentrate more on "doing it right" rather than on the "how to do it" aspect; in other words, they feel more at ease, the frustration and impatience is less. At this point, their cognitive resources are freed from the learning aspect and focussed on performing the task.

It appears as a result of this trial that if RE values fluctuate between 4% and 10% on the average, both of these extreme levels signify the difference between a good and bad performance respectively. Random errors cannot be completely eliminated because their causes are in the uncontrolled cognitive or in the emotional sphere, or they are altogether unexplainable; their number can be partly reduced by observing users, offering consulation and removing potential sources on a preventative basis.

A.3.3 Total Errors

Figure 25 summarizes both CE and RE as well as their total and as such it is the most important indicator of performance. It eliminates the inherent element of a certain degree of fuzziness in marking errors as

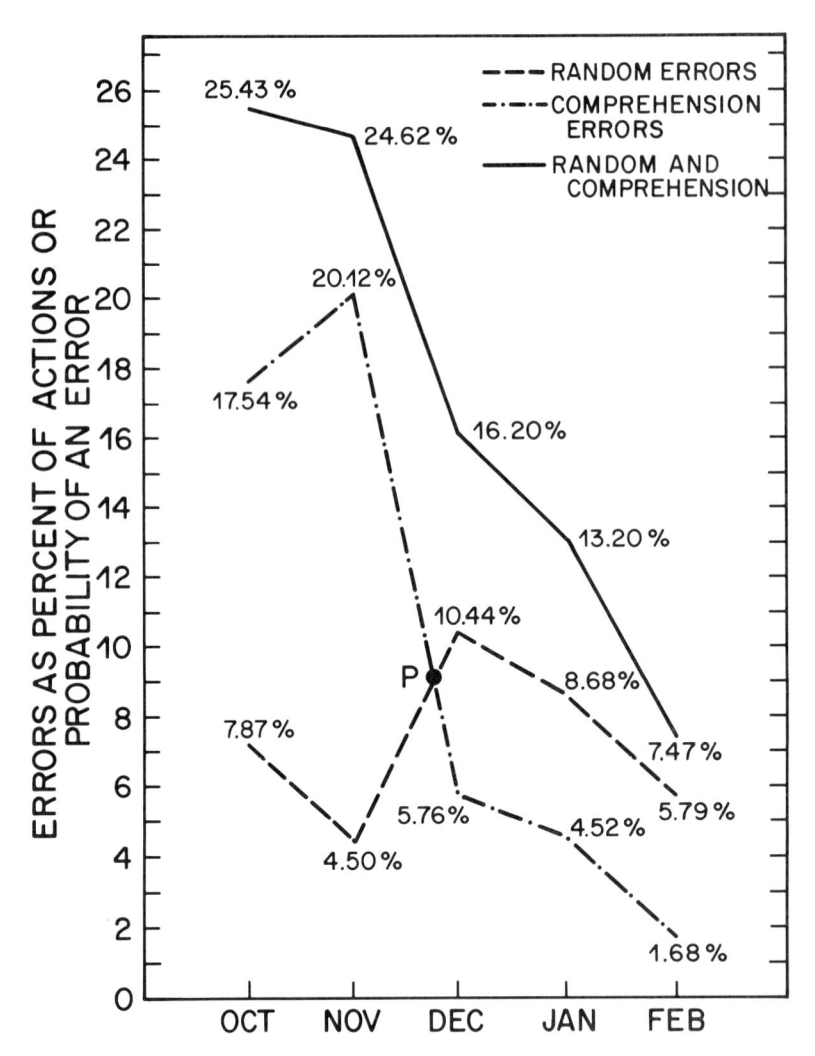

FIGURE 25 Probability of errors.

CE or RE in retrospect. It depicts the general and steady decrease in the number of total errors in the respective months expressed as the percentage of actions, which gives also the probability of an error when an action is taken: October, 25.43%; November, 24.62%; December, 16.20%; January, 13.20% and February, 7.47%. The same figure shows something we may call the "shears effect" exhibited by the CE and RE graphs intersecting at point P, which may be designated as a pivot; because the rate of comprehension errors will be, as a rule, higher in the beginning than that of random errors, a point is bound to come where the CE will cross the more inert RE graph. In our case, this happened in the latter part of November. An ideal shears effect would be represented in a graph which would be flat with CE not far above RE, indicating an easy-to-learn system, one not too high above the abscissa and pointing downward; the smaller the X coordinate of the point of P, the easier it is to learn the system in terms of time required. The shape in detail of the shears may, of course, vary to a large degree in different situations. Easy learning implies also an easy recall in later practical usage.

Our total errors graph displays a very favorable tendency which reflects the progressive improvement in the errors/reactions ratio and indicates that there was no serious problem, at any point, as regards hardware, software or lifeware. It would appear that at the level of around 7%, total errors do not unduly disconcert users, neither do they present any problem in achieving the projected goals; this was confirmed by observing users and querying them. The degree of user satisfaction and acceptance hinges then on user-friendly error messages and simple correction procedures.

A.3.4 Errors Caused by Abstraction

Up to now, computer applications have required a considerable degree of abstract thinking on the part of the users. Abstraction may refer to both tangible objects (e.g., storage, file, scratchpad, etc.) as well as intangible concepts (modes, modules, levels, commands, etc.). Computerizing conventional operations has required uninitiated novices and expert users alike to deal with both tangible objects as well as intangible concepts as abstract notion existing, on the one hand, in electronic form in the computer sphere and, on the other hand, in the user's mind as abstract constructs; it is up to the user to apply his cognitive system to cope with this problem. Some computer systems are more helpful than others in this respect. The problem arising out of situations involving a great deal of abstraction is that users, instead of being able to concentrate on solving their particular problems, have to devote their human information processing resources to the struggle, not cooperation, with the computer interface. "Abstract" refers in our case to spatial considerations but it can conceivably be related to time, logic, operation sequence, etc.

Abstract thinking in our present argument denotes a user's human information processing, which lacks physical parameters of concrete objects and requires a great deal of imagination and memory if it is not helped by a suitable (user-friendly) system design; spatial factors play a major role. We have defined three major areas in our projects where users were prone to err very often:

1. While "reading" and "writing" between the working area and storage
2. While moving between the command level, edit mode and input mode
3. In using the "cut-and-paste" feature involving moves between buffers

All of the above instances have one thing in common: they work with abstract entities devoid of any physical parameters such as shape, size, color, place in space, etc. and exist only in electronic form and in the user's mind. They can be learned even by casual users but they are easily forgotten and they burden the memory, both short and long, when it is needed most for problem solving and decision making. To eliminate this problem, we would have to do three things:

1. To turn the abstract notions into concrete entities by assigning them names which are familiar to the user
2. Give them some physical appearance which is easy to draw and easy to recognize
3. Make these objects mobile so their physical motion can assist in the formulation of as many commands as possible, thereby freeing user's memory for problem solving

We have been missing interface features of some new systems such as mouse and icons in conjunction with menus, and also the split screen with forward and backward scrolling as implemented, e.g., in Xerox's Star and Apple Lisa.

To illustrate the case in point, we singled out the "cut-and-paste" feature and took a closer look at it. We examined its usage by all three users working at the central facility for the five months of our trial (Table 11). A typical successful operation would include the following steps:

1. Move a certain number of lines to another buffer and assign a name to it (the "cut" operation)
2. Option: Transfer to the created buffer to verify status
3. Option: Make changes to the "cut" portion of the text
4. Option: Transfer back to the main buffer
5. Point to where you want the "paste" done: define the line and select "append," "insert" or "change"
6. "Paste" the "cut" section to the spot defined by moving it from the created buffer
7. Option: Check the result for accuracy

APPENDIX 335

TABLE 11 Usage of the "Cut-and-Paste" Feature (Spatial Factors Involved)

Users	Number of Attempts (X + Y)	Month	Successful Attempts (X)	Unsuccessful Attempts (Y)	Number of Actions in Attempts	Failures
User A	4	Oct. 82	1	0	28	a, b
		Jan. 83	1	0	17	b
		Feb. 83	1	0	31	a, b
		Feb. 83	1	0	9	0
User B	1	Nov. 82	0	1	15	a, b
User E	0	—	0	0	0	0
Total	5	—	4	1	100	—

[a] Lack of spatial orientation.
[b] Improper spatial manipulation.

The "cut-and-paste" facility is obviously of considerable importance to any author, referee and editor in entering and editing papers. It was, therefore, with some surprise that we found the very limited usage of this facility despite the special attention we paid to it in our training program, the pictorial posters placed right close to the workstation, the documentation dispensed to users and the consultation available to them. Out of 4497 human actions undertaken by users within the framework of our project, there were only as few as 100 actions related to "cut-and-paste" (2.22%). User E, who did not achieve a satisfactory degree of performance, did not use this feature at all; whereas user B only once and unsuccessfully; user A availed himself four times of the "cut-and-paste," and each time he succeeded eventually.

We monitored the failures which users sustained during their attempts and found invariably that they can be attributed (1) to the lack of spatial orientation where the user loses track of in which buffer he is, and (2) to the improper spatial manipulation of the text involved. In these five reported attempts (both successful and unsuccessful), users employed a total of 100 actions; as outlined above three to seven actions per attempt could have accomplished the desired objective, in other words, 15-35 actions only were required. The case of the "cut-

and-paste" is yet another proof of the plight of the casual user: user A accomplished his task with 9 actions in February whereas prior to that he needed 25.3 actions on average; even if there were any of the above actions expended as part of training or a "warm-up," that would bear witness to the need of an occasional user to spend time practicing these "spatially oriented" features when an occasion for their application arises.

But the main message of the statistics in Table 11 is to show that users, and particularly casual users, shun features which by their abstract nature engage their cognitive resources when they need them most in the pursuit of their tasks. Users try to circumvent these features and replace them with other, simpler ones even though they may be tedious. It is all the more interesting in the light of the fact that our editing system does have a simple command whereby a user can ascertain which buffers are currently in existence and which one is his "active" buffer. Other features can be programmed, but users will still struggle with these expedients if their usage of the system is an occasional one.

A.3.5 Human Information Processing

Introduction. Cognitive factors in human interaction with computers have received more attention lately (see Allen 1982).

Human information processing during the editorial process of scholarly publishing has been subject to drastic changes because the process is becoming more and more computerized. The longhand product has remained intact if we ignore some auxiliary means of providing information such as the author obtaining online information to verify his/her views or receiving statistical analysis from a computer center, etc. Basically, traditional human information processing is applied to prepare a manuscript although authors have additional external (computer) memory and processing at their disposal; the knowledge required for this job has to be stored in their memory and must be recalled from the memory when required.

Our main concern in this section is the human information processing that follows the production of the manuscript. It will take some time before the traditional notepad and pencil will be replaced by electronic equipment of equal convenience even though the technology for this is around the corner.

In this section we will exploit the achievements of cognitive psychology which evolved under the catalysis of the computer science in general, computational linguistics, artificial intelligence, human factors engineering and information theory. We will first describe the model used to explain selected phenomena observed in our trial.

The Model. The model outlined in Figure 26 has been designed to account for the human actions on the human-machine interface in our project although it may be applied to a wide variety of situations; it is only as detailed as requisite for our purpose. Similar models have been proposed in the literature (Rasmussen 1980; Lindsay and Norman 1977; Waite 1982).

According to this model information perceived by human sense organs and stored for a short period of time in the sensory perception storage (SPS) (box 1) is directed by the attention controller (box 2) for high-level processing (involving logic, arithmetic, etc.) to the processor (box 3) with the associated short-term storage (STS) (box 4). For long-term storage it is integrated by integrative processes (box 6) into the database (box 7). The high-level controller (box 5) routes queries to the database and back to the processor. This kind of processing may be characterized as "one-for-one," in other words, one unit of output for

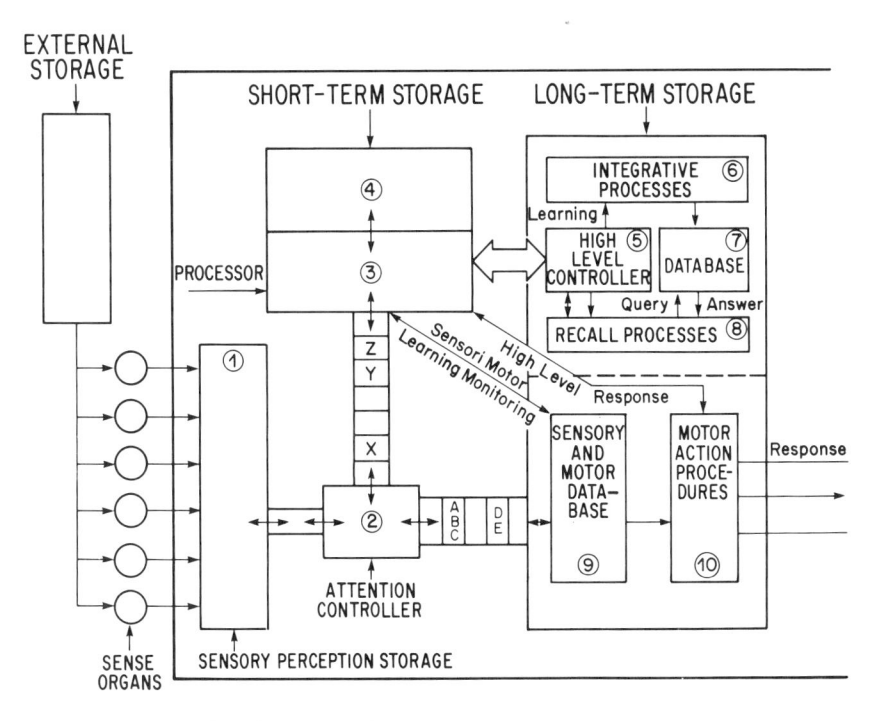

FIGURE 26 Model of human information processing.

one set of input data; it is process-intensive and too much data will have adverse effect on the quality or speed of processing. This is where nonroutine tasks are being solved by conscious operations; multiple or complex tasks will have to be resolved sequentially in that this processor is a serial one where the channel is switched between tasks and partial stored results as needed depending on the capacity of the individuals and their background. It must be stressed that most of the links connecting the above components are two-way channels allowing for simultaneous bidirectional traffic; this enables operations such as learning, retrieval, feedback, evaluation, input, output, monitoring, control, etc. to be combined and/or separated in either or both directions in a kind of "full-duplex" mode.

If a routine task is being performed the low-level processing route is selected which is characterized as "many-for-one" type, denoting an operation in which a number of motor actions may be triggered at the same time in response to one sensory stimulus. Whereas the above described mode involved the intellect, the low-level processing may be designated as automatic. Several actions may be taken as a result of parallel processing: sensory perceptions arriving from the SPS (box 1) and the attention controller (box 2) are passed on to sensory motor database, where they are matched with corresponding images created there by sensorimotor learning (training) and translated into actions in motor actions procedures (box 10).

The above components are described in some more detail below: their interaction and cooperation must be viewed in a highly dynamic manner.

Tools and Procedures. There is a fairly general agreement that at the front-end of our cognitive system is a buffer which is called by different names, e.g., sensory information store (Lindsay and Norman 1977), or very-short-term-memory. (Waite 1982). We call it sensory perception store (SPS). This memory stores information (images and events) as they are received through our sense organs and has very short duration (approximately 250 milliseconds) whereupon it dissipates. In our instance, an author who is editing his paper uses this memory constantly as he watches the VDT screen and/or his manuscript; rarely does his auditory system get engaged as, e.g., through the bell at end of line. The short period of time the information is stored helps the pattern recognition processes to interpret the information at subsequent stages. But first the information must be selected from the redundancy that sensory organs provide; from that follows that there should be always only a limited amount of information presented, especially to an untrained user.

The pattern recognition processes could be aided by some expedients that would help in sorting the perceived information as to categories or priorities and would also assist with learning. For example, warnings of critical nature might be given in voice, graphics could help understanding and color might focus attention. We had in our trial none of these at our disposal but there is no doubt that they will have a secured place in human-machine interfaces of the future. They must be used judiciously though lest the effect might be negative.

In the light of the overwhelming amount of information the user encounters on the screen and elsewhere in the working environment, the effort must be aimed at presenting him with a reasonable amount of information at a time and make the information easy to recognize by pattern recognition processes which bring it to the next stage of the cognitive system. If we tie up too many user's information processing resources at the pattern recognition stage, we are bound to impoverish his other processing aspects.

After the sensory perception storage there is another memory buffer, which has been named short-term memory (STM) or storage (STS). This buffer remembers the interpretation of images or events which were picked out by pattern recognition process from the SPS. The STS has a small capacity (7 2 "chunks" of information) and decay time of 10-30 seconds unless information is rehearsed. In the STS information is interpreted, encoded for permanent storage further down the cognition path. STS is sometimes considered as an independent unit (Waite 1982), or as part of "a higher-level conscious processor" (Rasmussen 1980) or more than one special-purpose processors are regarded as "neglected but more biologically appealing idea" (Monsell 1981); but what matters for our discourse is that its existence has been experimentally proven and it fits into our model. It is important to realize that STS has both the memory (albeit restricted) and processing functions.

The STS can work both in the bottom-up direction (data-driven processing) and top-down direction (conceptually driven processing). An example of the former on our type of interface is a situation where the authors have perceived an error message through their SPS, decode it through pattern recognition processes, and formulate a strategy in the STS; and example of the latter is the decision conceived by the author to send a message which is then translated into practical procedure followed by an action.

Another salient property of the STS is that due to its low holding capacity at any given moment, it can only attend to one task at a time, being able to switch from task to task alternately. The STS with the associated processor is called to task whenever nonroutine processing is being called for. Electronic scholarly publishing is a mixture of routine and skilled routine tasks (with different degree of skill) with intellectual nonroutine tasks. Nonroutine tasks are absolutely prevalent in the actual creation of a unit of scholarly publication where logic manipulation, arithmetic calculation, problem solving and memory interpretation, etc., abound. In the subsequent text entry there are functions that require skill, e.g., editing and formatting, but once the skill has been acquired the cognitive procedures are automated to a degree depending on the amount of skill which, in its turn, is affected by the amount of training and practice. Whenever the routine processing is in trouble as indicated by external data (error message or unfamiliar situation) the nonroutine processing will take over based on the sequential (serial) processor of the STS replacing the routine mode of the sensorimotor system. The interesting point here is that this single-channel operation might effectively result in only replacing one routine (e.g., our author entering text) by another routine selected from the store of various routine procedures (e.g., replacing a character or substituting a word); this in fact, is very often the case in our particular application.

Long-term memory (LTM) or storage (LTS) is the most complex memory system of large capacity (around 100 billion neurons) and long duration: some information is kept for all life depending on the depth of integrative efforts. The LTS is the storehouse of information (or the database in another jargon) and is associated with concepts such as memory, remembrance and thinking. More important than acquiring and storing information is its recall function which is only as efficient as the interpretive processes on the actual database.

From these characteristics of the LTS, it is evident how important training is in the context of the human/machine interface. Retention of the presented material may be helped by a better integration into the existing knowledge: this can be only done by building deep semantic associations. The posters we have used in our training assisted our authors in creating their own mental images (of course, they were also instrumental in the process of understanding which is an STS-related phenomenon).

Using icons in an interface turns process of recall into one of recognition and that makes the process of issuing a command easier. Retrieval should always be facilitated because it frees resources which otherwise would have to be shared with view to the single-channel operation; selecting from a menu has the same recognition/recall effect and a properly designed graphic (icon) representation should have an edge on the textual form of the menu.

We cannot think of problem solving tasks being resolved by a straightforward SPS-STS-LTS action. Rather, there are bursts of interaction between these units moving back and forth. If we take as an example the activity around the "substitute" feature of our editor program, then the SPS presents the text, STS interprets it, the mistake must be detected by checking the LTS database, and the correcting procedure will be loaded by supervisor into the STS which will execute it step by step in close cooperation with both the LTS and SPS.

It is evident that for our model to be functional the LTS must be equipped with a controller (high-level controller) to control the complex operations on a vast database of data and procedures.

Even though not anatomically part of the human information system, the external storage (ES) is an indispensable component of it. As a matter of fact, nothing that can be efficiently kept in the ES should be burdening the LTS. A glaring example are the login/logout procedures which should be kept handy for an easy referral. This is reinforced by the fact that forgetting obsolete information is less manageable than learning amendments and updates.

Sensorimotor control provides the link between the sensory perceptions and actions which result from them. It is a significant part of the LTS but it is not clear how autonomous it is. If we designate information processing taking place in the STS's processor as "high-level," because it involves a great amount of sophisticated processing in response to even a small amount of information from the SPS and possibly very little output, then the sensorimotor control system may be designated as "low-level," implying a small amount of processing with possibly a great deal of output. An example of high-level processing in our instance is working on a relatively unfamiliar task that requires a reviewer to recall information and to employ nonroutine procedures in reviewing a paper. An example of low-level processing is entering one's own text by keying it in where the author is skilled in typing and uses a familiar editor program. It follows that the same activity which is initially unfamiliar and requires nonroutine high-level processing (e.g., electronic mail used to link users with their editor-in-chief) turns gradually into a familiar skilled routine activity entailing low-level processes. Obviously some kind of attention controller as suggested in our model is called for to arrange for immediate switching between these two states, the low-level processing being the default state. Simultaneous high-level and low-level processing can materialize and in fact is often happening as e.g. an author thinking about a subject-matter related problem while entering his paper.

We have not included emotional aspects of human information processing in our model; they are one of the more controversial issues in the cognitive psychology but they seem to be close to the sensorimotor subsystem. We have noticed on several occasions in our project that users baffled by some unforeseen events displayed symptoms of panic, abandoned rational procedures of high-level processing and unsuccessfully used short-cuts in their attempt to solve the problem.

Sensorimotor processing allows humans to increase productivity with less effort than would be otherwise expanded by high-level processing.

A.3.6 General Observations

The notion of fatigue is an important aspect of human information processing much the same as in other areas of human endeavor where economy of a person's effort matters. In the light of the above low-level/high-level processing dichotomy, it may be said that most tiring are operations which involve a great deal of "time-sharing" type of tasks where the single-channel of the serial high-level processor is switched between tasks which have to be attended simultaneously. An example of this situation are authors creating their paper on the screen from a few cursory notes on paper, struggling with an unfamiliar editor program when suddenly a message arriving in real time begins appearing on the VDU, requiring a consultation with the manual. On the other side of the spectrum, the pure sensorimotor operations will consume only a fragment of the energy expanded in the previously cited case.

In a previous section dealing with errors we distinguished between the comprehension errors (CE) and random errors (RE); it is appropriate to state that CEs have their roots in the high-level processing sphere at the stage of learning and are due to improper or inadequate chunking (encoding and integration) in the LTS. In this context the plight of the occasional user is viewed from yet another angle: it is a user who cannot (because of infrequent usage) permanently encode the semantics of a system to a depth that would lend itself to a process of pattern recognition or to that of recall; the rehearsal would only improve understanding but not retention. The RE's stem from lack of attention, fatigue, panic, etc. and these may disrupt processing at either high or low level.

It is imperative that principles of a computer system should be taught first and details later; this is because the integrative learning processes try to accommodate newly acquired concepts into association with the existing ones; if there is nothing with which they could be associated then the process of generalizing would have to be started from the more specific items to the more generic terms; this is more demanding than building associations "top-down" and involves an additional process of induction. The mental model users create of a system (Borgman 1982) may be a wrong one.

It has been also noted that users do not like changing from one medium to another: this can be explained in terms of the processing load associated with such a move. First, there must be an exigency calling for the present activity to be interrupted. The current results must be stored so they do not get lost. Second, the alternative solutions must be brought from LTS into the STS and evaluated as to their suitability. Third, the selected procedure must be loaded from the LTS: this may include a number of subroutines involving hardware and software, which may have to be recalled, reviewed or even learned. Humans instinctively shun complexity and this situation may lead to a near overload; this is a glaring example of a conceptually driven operation. The situation is complicated even more when data start arriving from the environment calling for immediate attention and resulting in more interrupts. It is much easier to be able to obtain assistance on the familiar hardware and software.

A.3.7 Conclusions

On the basis of the description of principles of the human information processing we may conclude that a good ("user-friendly") human-machine interface is one that does not take advantage of the indisputable flexibility and adaptability of the human part in this cooperative arrangement but, on the contrary, exploits the immense capabilities of the computer system to become an extension of human processing.

References

Allen, R.B. (1982). Cognitive factors in human interaction with computers. In: Badre, A., Shneiderman B., ed. *Directions in Human/Computer Interaction.* Norwood, N.J., Ablex Publishing Corporation. 225 pages.

Borgman, C.L. (1982). Mental models: Ways of looking at a system. *Bulletin of the American Society for Information Science.* Vol. 9, No. 2, pp. 38-39.

Lindsay, P.H.; Norman, D.A. (1977). *Human Information Processing: An Introduction to Psychology.* New York, Academic Press, Inc. 777 pages.

Monsell, S. (1981). Representations, processes, memory mechanisms: The basic components of cognition. *Journal of the American Society for Information Science.* Vol. 32, No. 5, pp. 378-390.

Rasmussen, J. (1980). The human as a system component. pp. 67-96. In: Smith, H.T., Green, T.R.G., eds. *Human Interaction with Computers.* London, New York, Academic Press, Inc. 369 pages.

Standera, O.L. (1974). *Comparative Study of Two Online Retrieval Services: CAN/OLE and SDC.* Internal Report, Information Systems, Library. Calgary, Alberta, Canada, The University of Calgary. 31 pages.

Waite, R. (1982). Making information easy to use. *Bulletin of the American Society for Information Science.* Vol. 9, No. 2, pp. 34-37.

Glossary of Terms and Acronyms

The individual items in this Glossary contain terms that have occurred in this volume or may be encountered in subject-related materials. They are intended to be the first introduction to the concept or to refresh the memory and thus assist in reading the text. They cannot, by their nature, be considered as exhaustive definitions.

AAP: Association of American Publishers.

Access time: Time measured from the moment a request is issued to access data up until the moment those data are available. See Seek time.

ACM: Association for Computing Machinery.

Acoustic coupler: A portable modem device used with telephone sets to act as a converter between digital electronic signals of data-processing hardware and analog signals of communications facilities.

Ada: High-level programming language developed by Department of Defense (USA).

Address: An identification of a location where data are stored.

AFIPS: American Federation of Information Processing Societies.

AI: Artificial intelligence.

ALGOL: Algorithmic language.

Alogrithmic language: High-level programming language suited for applications in mathematics.

Alphaphotographic: A method of display by videotex (along with alphanumerics) of high-resolution pictures occupying the entire screen or its part.

Alphageometric: A method of display by videotex (along with alphanumerics) of graphics composed from instructions (called picture description instructions) rather than formed from a limited number of basic building blocks (mosaics). For example, Telidon forms pictures from five elementary geometric shapes in the decoder (point, line, rectangle, arc and polygon).

Alphamosaic: A method of display by videotex (along with alphanumerics) of graphics which are presented as a composite mosaic of small rectangles.

AM: Amplitude modulation.

Amplitude modulation (AM): One of the modes of modulation where the amplitude of the carrier wave varies proportionately to the variations of the modulating signal.

Analog: The mode of representation by continuously varying physical conditions such as voltage, current, pressure or temperature. Input to digital systems has to be converted if analog. Output from digital systems may be analog as in voice synthesizers. Cf. Digital.

Anamorphic: Magnification (enlargement) which is not equal along two axes perpendicular to each other; a capability of some systems designed to manipulate images.

AND: The Boolean connector where the resulting signal is true if all of the input values are true simultaneously.

ANSI: American National Standards Institute.

Antiope: The French standard for videotex/teletext representation of characters and graphics; generic name for systems respective.

Architecture (computer): The physical arrangement of internal functions in a computer.

Architecture (network): The arrangement of layers and protocols in a network.

Area composition: A capability of a typesetting (imagesetting) machine to set type and some graphics in a spatial arrangement (part of a page or entire page) thus eliminating pasteup.

ARPANET: Advanced Research Projects Agency Network. A large packet-switched network developed by the Department of Defense (USA).

Artificial intelligence: A study discipline striving towards machines capable of performing tasks formerly associated with human intelligence, such as the ability to perceive, understand speech, print, think, talk, work, etc.

Ascender: The portion of a lowercase character reaching above the x-height.

ASCII: American Standard Code for Information Interchange eight-level code using 7 binary bits for information and the 8th bit for parity; a communication standard in North America.

ASIS: American Society for Information Science.

Assembler: A programming language (translator type) that converts assembly language statements into the machine code.

Assembly language: A low-level programming language where each statement can be translated by an assembler into one machine word (one-for-one principle) in the machine language. Cf. High-level languages.

Asynchronous transmission: Synonymous to start-stop transmission. Transmission is controlled by start and stop symbols appended to the beginning and end of each character. Cf. Sychronous transmission.

AT&T: American Telephone and Telegraph (one of the telecommunications companies in the United States).

Audio conference: Teleconferencing involving voice only. It may be augmented by any of many means of transmitting static graphics (such as videotex, freeze-frame TV, etc.) short of full-motion video.

Autodialer: A facility to permit a terminal or computer to call one or many phone numbers which are predesignated by the user.

Auxiliary storage: Secondary storage. Cf. Main storage.

Backup file: A copy of a file designed to substitute for the original file in case the latter is destroyed, damaged, lost or stolen; the backup device is selected with storage capacity, cost per bit and transfer rate in mind.

Band: Range of wave frequencies between the lower and upper limits.

Bandwidth: The difference, measured in hertz (Hz), between the lower and upper limits of a band that can be transmitted over a channel.

Barcode: The representation of aphanumeric characters by adjacent strips of varying width.

Bar-code scanner: An optical device that reads barcodes; the amount of light reflected on scanners differs between black and white portions of the code as determined by a photocell. These differences are interpreted as digital information.

Baseband: The frequency band of an originating device before modulating the carrier wave.

BASIC: Beginner's All-purpose Symbolic Instruction Code. An easy-to-use language existing in a number of variations.

Baud: A unit of signaling speed—the speed of data transmission over a communication line. A 2400-baud line means a line supporting transmission of 2400 signal elements per second. If one signal element equals 1 bit (as is usually the case), then it is synonymous with 2400 bits per second.

Batch processing: Processing of input items that can be processed together in one computer job using the same hardware and software.

BCD: Binary-coded decimal.

Benchmark tests, benchmarking: Comparison of performance by testing computer systems under conditions as are expected in the intended use. For instance, a bench mark program may test the CPU, input/output devices, throughput, etc.

BER: Bit error rate.

Bidirectional printer: Device that prints lines alternately left-to-right and right-to-left to achieve higher speed.

Bildschirmtext: The German videotex system.

Binary: Denotes choice between two alternatives only. A binary code makes use of two distinct digits: 0 (zero) and 1 (one).

Binary-coded decimal (BCD): A system of binary number representation in which each decimal is represented by a group of bits. Four bits (16 possible states) are required to express the decimal digits (10 states); more bits are needed for alphanumeric values.

Bit: A contraction of the term "binary digit". Unit of information con-

GLOSSARY OF TERMS AND ACRONYMS

tent—a bit can be either 0 or 1 and is the smallest unit of information.

Bit density: Density of recorded bits in a storage medium as a measure of effectiveness or efficiency of that medium.

Bit error rate: The average number of bits transmitted in error as compared with the number of transmitted bits. The rate of 10-12 means 1 error bit in 1 terabits transmitted over a channel.

Bit map: Each position on a video screen displaying an electronic signal is a picture element (pixel, pel); if every pixel is addressable, then it can be stored and processed at that level. Each pixel may be represented by 1 bit (two states are capable of distinguishing between black and white) or more bits: 8 bits could specify 256 shades of gray or colors. A bit map is the two-dimensional matrix of pixel representation. If more than 1 bit is used per pixel, multiple-plane memories are needed for storage and processing; otherwise, the bit map in the storage holds a picture to be transferred for processing or display.

Bit rate: Bits transmitted per second. If 1 bit constitutes the signal element then bit rate is equal to baud rate.

Black box: An expression used to facilitate understanding and design of systems in which it is not essential to know what processing is taking place inside a device; instead, one is concerned with the input and output only.

BLEND: Birmingham and Loughborough Electronic Network Development.

Board: A card with special circuiting that enhances the existing characteristics of the basic configuration, e.g., communications capabilities, additional language, disk control, memory, etc.

Boolean logic: Encountered in electronic publishing as boolean connectors "AND," "OR," "NOT" in information retrieval. A significant tool in specification of queries because it affects relevance and recall. Named after George Boole, an English mathematician and logician.

Booster: A device strengthening a signal for retransmission.

Boot: In microcomputers, to load the operating system in preparation for computer use.

Bootstrap (bootstrapping, bootstrap loader): A small program-loading routine that initiates loading of another program into the main memory to activate a computer.

Border: Decorative frame around a body of composed text produced by a typesetting machine.

Broadband: A band covering a wide range of frequencies (such as cable, fiber optics, microwaves) exceeding those required for voice communications.

Broadcasting: Delivery of programs to large audiences simultaneously. Cf. Narrowcasting.

BRS: Bibliographic Retrieval Services.

Buffer: A temporary storage area or facility for electronic data in computing and communication.

Bug: Error in software or malfunction of hardware.

Bus: Pathway encompassing one or more conductors for signal transmission within a computer system.

Byte: A group of adjacent bits. Typically, 8 bits would represent one character.

Cable television: A broadcasting and narrowcasting system with two-way capacity; it receives TV signals from over-the-air broadcasts and satellites and retransmits programs to homes via coaxial cables usually for a fee.

Cache memory: Fast storage from which data can be moved into main memory whenever needed, at a rate higher than possible from a disk.

CAD: Computer-aided design.

CAI: Computer-aided/assisted instruction.

CAIS: Canadian Association for Information Science.

CAM: Computer-aided manufacturing.

Camera (electronic): An electronic device converting visual images into an electron flow and then into a transmittable electrical signal.

Canned formats: Format specifications that are computer stored and may be called up at any time to control a word processor or typesetter; used in cases where storage is cheaper and more convenient than reentering format specifications.

CAN/OLE: Canadian Online Inquiry; an online system of the Canada Institute for Scientific and Technical Information.

CAP: Computer-aided publishing.

Capacitance: The capability to store electrically separated charges in an electric field when potential differences exist between the conductors (such as the disk and the reading head in a videodisk system). Unit is called farad.

Captains: Character and Pattern Telephone Access Information Network System, Japanese videotex system.

Cartridge: A convenient, small container for data storage on magnetic tape consisting of a single reel or two reels including reel-to-reel transport.

Cassette: A self-contained case of magnetic tape for recording and replay with minimum handling required; storage medium for data and analog information.

Cathode ray tube: An electronic vacuum tube producing a visual display of information as a result of the focused electron beam impacting the fluorescent screen of the tube; part of such a terminal.

CATV: Community antenna television system; sometimes interpreted as Cable TV.

CAV: Constant angular velocity. See Optical disk, Videodisk.

CB: Citizen band.

CBC: Canadian Broadcasting Corporation.

CCD: Charge-coupled device.

CCITT: Consultative Committee on International Telephony and Telegraphy.

CCTV: Closed-circuit television.

CDAD: Compact digital audio disk.

CED: Capacitance electronic disk.

Ceefax: A teletext service of the British Broadcasting Corporation.

Cellular radio: A mobile phone system in which computer-controlled telephone service is offered to vehicles moving within one or across many cells (geographic areas), each having its own transmitter.

CEPT: Acronym in French for European Post and Telecommunications Administration.

Chain printer: A printer outputting line by line by impact on type slugs as they pass by the place of destination on the respective line.

Slugs are situated on a revolving chain and applied under control by a print controller.

Channel: An electrical transmission path for transmitting electrical signals between two or more stations.

Character: One symbol (digit, letter, special character) or its digital representation coded in bits. Also used in specifying storage capacity, transmission speed, etc.

Character set: All characters that a system can handle.

Charge-coupled device (CCD): A semiconductor element designed to sense and store data (for instance, a bit-by-bit representation of data scanned by a raster scanner, line by line) as an electrical charge corresponding to the amount of light reflected from the scanned line, for subsequent display or recording. Typically, 1000-4000 elements may be used in a strip.

Chip: An integrated microelectronic circuit—one or more electronic circuits on a slice of silicon, or lately, on some other suitable material.

Chrominance: Color (as associated with a pixel in scanning of color images). The chrominance signal carries information about color, i.e., "hue" and "saturation." ("Hue" represents the amount of red, green and blue, respectively, in a colored object.) See also Luminance.

CIM: Computer input microfilm. A technique of computer input that relies on scanning microfilm frames and reading the resulting data into the computer for storage and processing.

CIPS: Canadian Information Processing Society.

CISTI: Canada Institute for Scientific and Technical Information.

Clock: A device in a digital computer or a transmission system generating periodical, accurately timed pulses that synchronize all actions of a synchronous computer.

Closed circuit television: Transmits television signals to a closed user group over a closed circuit.

Closed user group: A group of users using an exclusive service as opposed to a public service.

CLR: Council on Library Resources.

CLV: Constant linear velocity. See Optical disk, videodisk.

Coaxial cable: A transmission line that has a conducting tube with a wire running down its center. The tube and wire are held in place and separated by insulators. Used to transmit high-frequency signals such as TV.

COBOL: Common business oriented language. High-level programming language suited for the business environment.

Codec: A contraction of coder-decoder. A circuit for conversion of an analog waveform into a digital code for transmission and vice versa at the other end. Codec is the inverse of "modem."

Color: See Chrominance, Hue, Luminance.

Color filters: Filters used in a process camera or in a color-separation scanner. The original color copy is photographed four times in a process camera or scanned by a separation scanner. The blue filter yields the yellow printer, the green filter produces the magenta printer, and the yellow filter results in the cyan printer; the combination of the above three filters produces the black printer. All of the above-mentioned printers are black/white negatives used in platemaking. In color-separation scanners the data obtained from scanning are digital signals which may be stored, processed, transmitted and used in subsequent processes. See also Process color.

Color separation: See Color filters, Process color.

Color-separation scanner: A scanner particularly suited for the purpose of color separation; it can produce the printers or the resulting digital data may be stored for further use.

COM: Computer output microfilm. Microfilm output from a computer.

Common carrier: A corporation licenced for provision of communications services to the general public for a fee.

Compatibility: Compatible software can be run on different types of computers; also called portable software. Two compatible systems can work together.

Compiler: A program that produces a machine language equivalent translated from a high-level symbolic program (source program) before execution.

Composition: A term with at least dual meanings at present—(1) a synonym for typesetting; and (2) with the advent of computers and, particularly, microcomputer technology resulting in fluid borderlines between authors, publishers, typesetters and printers, a broader sense has come to include justification, hyphenation, editing, pulling proofs, proofreading, corrections at any stage and page makeup (text only or text plus graphics).

Compunications: Contraction of computers and communications to describe integrated systems composed of both ingredients; same meaning as telematics.

Computer-aided/assisted instruction (CAI): An educational/instructional technique that relies on computers in presentation of instructional material to individual students and emphasizes the individually paced, interactive approach.

Computer architecture: The field of computer science dealing with mutual arrangement and dependencies of individual components in computer systems.

Computer conferencing: Using computers in conducting a meeting (conference, discussion) or exchanging major files on a local system or more frequently, over a network of computers, typically in the asynchronous mode rather than in real time. Computer serves to edit, format, store and deliver messages.

Computer literacy: The beginner's knowledge of how computers work gained in some elementary courses or by self-education enabling students to get started in understanding and eventually using computers.

Computer output microfilm: Microfilm output from a computer.

Configuration: An assembly of compatible hardware and/or software grouped together to form a system.

Connect time: Denotes the time spent by a user in using a computer online; time elapsed between logon and logoff.

Constant angular velocity (CAV): System of storage in which CAV disks store one frame per track. Rotation speed is higher toward the edge of the disk. Freeze-frame is possible as well as random access to each frame. See also Constant linear velocity, Optical disk, Videodisk.

Constant linear velocity (CLV): System of storage in which CLV disks store multiple records per track in the spiral toward the rim of the disk, hence higher storage capability. Speed of disk rotation diminishes toward the edge. No freeze-frame feature, limited random access. See also Constant angular velocity, Optical disk, Videodisk.

Contone: Contraction for continuous tone (image).

GLOSSARY OF TERMS AND ACRONYMS

Converter: (1) A device for reception of all cable TV channels authorized for a particular TV set; 2) device that converts data from one medium into another (e.g., floppy to hard disk,) or from one form to another (e.g.,EBCDIC to ASCII).

CPI: Characters per inch.

CP/M: Control Program for Microprocessors developed by Digital Research Corp., a popular disk operating system for microcomputers. CP/M86 is designed for 16-bit micros. MP/M is a version for multi-user environments.

CPU: Central processing unit; the component of the computer system that processes data by executing instructions and includes an arithmetic-logic unit and a control unit; cooperates closely with the main memory.

CRT: Cathode ray tube.

CRTC: Canadian Radio-Television and Telecommunications Commission.

Cursive: An enhanced italic bearing some semblance to handwriting.

Cursor: Movable spot or symbol on the screen of a VDT whose position may be manipulated by the operator using either a keyboard or some other of many varied means such as a joystick, mouse, trackball or lightpen. It may indicate location of the next character or move around a screen as a specific task may require.

Daisy wheel printer: A letter quality printer where characters are situated on spokes radiating from the center towards the circumference in a daisylike arrangement.

DAMS: Display ad makeup system.

DASD: Direct access storage device (such as magnetic disks) designed for random (direct) access rather than sequential access where the file must be searched until the wanted item is reached. See Random access.

Data: Basic piece of information in various form (analog, digital) capable of computer processing. Different quantities of data have some informational content ascribed to them that constitutes "information." Sometimes used interchangeably with "information."

Data bank: A collection of online data; sometimes synonymous with database but more commonly composed of multiple databases.

Database: A collection of logically interrelated data organized for easy updating, structured for easy retrieval and use and independent of hardware and software applied in handling the database. Reference databases (bibliographic and referral) lead the user to full-text sources. Source databases (such as full-text and numeric) contain the information itself.

Database management system: A software package for creating, updating, storing and maintenance of files, with convenient access and retrieval facilities as well as report writing capability; usually of very general applicability.

Data communications: Electronic transmission of encoded data (analog or digital) over communications lines, synonymous with telecommunications.

Datapac: Canadian packet-switched network.

Data set: See Modem.

Data Vision: The Swedish videotex system.

DBS: Direct broadcast satellite.

DDD: Direct Distance Dialing.

DDP: Distributed data processing.

DCT: Data conversion and transmission unit.

Debugging: Removing bugs. See Bug.

Decoder: A device translating an encoded signal into one readily understood—(1) decoding a videotex signal received over the phone and a data set into human-readable information displayed on a screen, (2) unscrambling TV signals.

Definition: See Resolution.

Density of recording (storage): Number of bits per inch.

Descender: The portion of a lowercase character that reaches below the baseline.

Descramble: To make a scrambled TV signal recognizable again to an authorized TV subscriber; to unscramble.

Direct broadcast satellite (DBS): Satellites broadcasting directly to information consumers (houses or offices) via satellite dishes rather than to intermediaries for retransmission.

GLOSSARY OF TERMS AND ACRONYMS

Dish: An earth satellite station for signal reception and/or transmission.

Desktop computer: A microcomputer.

Dialog: Online retrieval service provided by DIALOG Information Services, Inc.

Didon: The French teletext service based on the Antiope standard.

Digital: The mode of information representation by a code consisting of a set of discrete elements. In character digital encoding, a specified number of ones and zeroes are used to represent characters; in the raster (facsimile) digital mode, ones and zeroes are used to represent white and black (or shades of gray if more than one bit reserved for a picture element). Cf. Analog.

Digital TV: The TV system that encodes TV signals digitally rather than as analog continuous waves in the present system. Although it offers technical advantages, the commercial application is insignificant at present.

Digitize: To convert analog values obtained as a result of scanning, measurement, sensing, etc. into digital, numerical values for further processing, storage, transmission or output.

Digitizing tablet: A flat computer input device resembling a tablet. By means of a stylus the user can draw various geometric shapes which will be transmitted to the computer as digital data for subsequent processing and storage.

Direct access: See Random access.

Direct read after write (DRAW): A method of recording on an optical disk so that the information may be read immediately after writing; access to incorrect data may be blocked by erasing pointers to it and corrected data may be entered; contrasts to replicated disks by the process of pressing.

Disk drive: A device that accommodates disks and a read/write head to write and read information from the disk once the desired location on the rotating disk has been accessed.

Diskette: Synonym for floppy (disk).

Disk operating system (DOS): An operating system in which programs are stored on magnetic disks which thus function as primary online storage. See Operating system.

Disk pack: A set of magnetic disks that can be removed (as opposed to nonremovable disks, e.g., Winchester type) from the disk drive.

Distributed data processing (DDP): A type of computer processing using a centralized database on a central computer facility shared by local sites, but local data entry and processing take place on a distributed network of local computers and terminals. The objective is an optimal distribution of computing tasks while at the same time the produced information is shared by all participants.

DOS: Disk operating system.

Dot matrix or dot-matrix printer: A rectangular matrix of dots within which all characters fit and are formed by selection from these dots. As such they are displayed on a CRT or printed on a dot-matrix printer in which the print head holds a set of selectable pins held in a matrix and applied over a ribbon. The clarity of characters depends on density of pins.

Double density: Diskette holding twice the amount of information of a single-density diskette.

Double-sided diskette: Diskette capable of storing information on both sides.

Downlink: A communications facility for satellite signal reception.

Downloading: Transferring information from a remote computer for local use on one's own computer. The information may be a file or software and the reason is economy or convenience.

DPI: Dots per inch (resolution).

DPMA: Data Processing Management Association.

DRAW: Direct Read After Write.

DRCS: Dynamically redefinable character set. A method of extending the character set in which the shapes of letters and graphics are not predefined, but are downloaded from the database and subsequently used by the terminal.

DSDD: Double-sided, double-density disk.

DSSD: Double-sided, single-density disk.

Dummy: A page layout, or a set of layouts, to give a rough outline of a completed graphic work (newspaper, magazine, book, etc.).

Dvorak keyboard: An alternative to the QWERTY keyboard (q.v.) designed for easier use.

Earth station (dish): The receive (or both send and receive) antenna for satellite communication.

EBCDIC: Extended binary coded decimal interchange code.

EDD: Electronic document delivery.

EDP: Electronic data processing.

EFT: Electronic funds transfer.

EIA: Electronic Industries Association.

EIES: Electronic information exchange system.

Electronic blackboard: A means of transmitting a freehand-drawn picture or text over a distance using voice-grade lines; the signal is generated by the pressure of chalk on one blackboard and converted into an identical picture at the other end.

Electronic document delivery (EDD): A service providing the electronic communications channel through which a client (end-user or intermediary) may obtain the desired document(s); "documents" must be interpreted loosely in the light of the diversity of existing formats. Subcategory of electronic publishing.

Electronic Industries Association (EIA): A consultative group of electronic equipment manufactures involved in preparation of standards for electronic hardware and interfaces in the United States.

Electronic journal: A publishing venture in which all the functions associated formerly with the production of conventional journal are performed on a computer system; output appears on a videodisplay unit rather than on paper. Associated electronic mail takes care of exchanging messages in the editorial process. Data entry takes place using word processing and formatting facilities of the same or another compatible system. Suits well the principle of on-demand publishing.

Electronic mail (EM): Computerized systems providing computer hardware, specialized software and communications for messaging purposes.

Electronic page makeup: The stage of prepress technology following text entry and capture of illustrations whereby all components of a page are gathered and made ready for local or remote output whether it be for display, proof or print media purposes.

Electronic publishing: A wide variety of processes where the material to be published appears at one or more stages, or at all stages, transformed into and processed in the electronic form. In the narrow sense, a mode of publishing with a nonpaper-oriented output such as videotex, teletext, videodisk, electronic journal, etc.

Emulator: Hardware, software or combination of both enabling a program written for a particular computer (imitated system) to be executed on a different computer (imitating system); also, a microcomputer fitted with an appropriate emulator can imitate a particular terminal in communication with another computer.

EM: Electronic mail.

Em: A typeface measurement; an "em space" means a space which, in an X-point type, is X points wide and X points high.

EN: One half of "em."

Encipher: To scramble; to make information unintelligible unless unscrambled.

Encryption: Scrambling, enciphering information; making information unintelligible when unscrambled.

EPC: Editorial processing center.

EPROM: Erasable programmable read-only memory; identical with EROM. ROM that can be repeatedly erased and reprogrammed on a special machine.

Ergonomics: The science aiming at improving the physical aspects of the work place. A possible result is an increased productivity stemming from better health, fitness and job satisfaction of workers.

EROM: Erasable read-only memory.

Euronet: European packet-switching network.

Expert system: A computerized system considered to be a part of the discipline of artificial intelligence capable of providing expert answers to queries in a particular field; the program called "inference engine" operates on a database referred to as knowledge base in which knowledge has been deposited by experts in the field themselves or through knowledge engineers. Expert systems are expected to explain their conclusions, to write reports, to learn, to be able to talk and eventually to extract knowledge automatically.

Extended binary coded decimal interchange code: A coding system used to represent data by means of an 8-bit code; used primarily by IBM.

Facsimile: The process whereby images (such as full pages) can be scanned at one end (at the transmitter) and transmitted to the receiver where they are reconstituted into a reproduction of the original. The working principle may be analog or digital. Systems differ as to resolution and speed.

FAX: Contraction of facsimile.

FCC: Federal Communications Commission.

FDM: Frequency division multiplexing.

Federal Communications Commission (FCC): The administrative agency governing telecommunications in the USA.

FGCS: Fifth-generation computer systems.

Fiber optics: Transmission of information by pulses of a laser beam down optical fibers, i.e., through cables of glass fibers.

Field test: Testing of a technology under conditions resembling the real production with the objective to determine feasibility, marketing aspects and profitability.

Film processor: A machine attached to a phototypesetter or located in a dark room that processes photographic film or paper exposed in the typesetter (developing, fixing, washing and drying).

Firmware: Software permanently stored inside a piece of hardware such as ROM. It is not designed to be changed or modified but rather to perform an unalterable action when activated.

Flat-screen TV: A TV system under development in which picture elements on the screen are not turned on and off by electron guns; instead the light-emitting elements are directly addressed. Now of small size and battery-powered for portability, a flat-screen system could conceivably be made large and thus synonymous with "large-screen TV."

Floppy (disk): Low-cost removable storage for minicomputers and microcomputers. A flexible plastic disk of 8 inches, 5 inches (minifloppy) and 3 inches (microfloppy) in diameter with smaller sizes under consideration. Storage capacity of some 400 Kbytes has lately been increased to 1.2 Mbytes and is still on the rise.

FM: Frequency modulation.

FOIA: Freedom of Information Act.

Folio: A sequential page number.

Font: A set of characters belonging to a typeface (e.g., Helvetica) of a certain style (e.g., italic) and of a given size (point size and set).

Footprint: An area over which a satellite's signal may be received.

FORTRAN: An acronym for formula translator. A high-level language widely used for computing in science and mathematics.

Four-color process: See Process color.

Frame: One frame (complete scanning cycle) in the NTSC standard consists of 525 scanned lines which are formed by two interlaced fields odd and even.

Freeze-frame television: A television system that freezes the individual picture by storing it locally where it has been shot and only then passes it along via a voice-grade channel to the destination screen. In this manner selection of pictures to be "frozen" is done where the action is and when deemed appropriate. Cf., Slow-scan television.

Frame-grabber: The component of the teletext decoder that captures one of the database frames being broadcast in continuous loops, as determined by the user operating his keypad.

Frequency: The number of times an electromagnetic wave (or possibly other periodically recurring phenomenon) repeats a cycle in a unit of time. If the unit of time is 1 second, then the frequency is expressed in hertz (Hz).

Frequency division multiplexing (FDM): Simultaneous transmission of two or more signals in a multiplex system by dividing the transmission frequency range into narrower bands, thus creating separate channels for intelligence conveyance.

Frequency modulation (FM): A mode of modulation in which the frequency of a carrier waveform of constant amplitude is varied proportionately to the instant value of the applied modulating signal.

Front-end processor: Computer interposed between another computer (the main computer) and communication channels with the purpose to spare the main computer of controlling and preprocessing chores, thus freeing it for the main tasks.

Full duplex: A mode of transmission simultaneously in both directions.

GLOSSARY OF TERMS AND ACRONYMS

Full-face typesetter: Typesetter that sets type anywhere on a page and thus makes setting of multiple columns possible without having to resort to reverse loading.

Full-text storage, retrieval and delivery: In contrast to storing and delivery of document surrogates only (titles, abstracts, etc.), this mode implies the content of complete documents.

Galley proof: A printout of draft copy in columns designed for proofreading by editors and authors.

Game paddle: A synonym for joystick.

Gate: An integrated logic circuit with two or several inputs and one output pulse if certain specified conditions on input are met (e.g., Boolean AND, OR, etc.).

Gateway: Communications facility whereby two or more networks (local or wide area) are connected together for user convenience so that one piece of hardware and a simplified access procedure may serve to use all of them (one logon procedure, unified command structure, billing, etc.).

Giga: Metric prefix for 10^9.

Gigabyte (Gbyte): One billion bytes (precisely 1,073,741,824).

Gigahertz (GHz): Frequency of 1 billion hertz.

Glare: The undesirable characteristic of a display screen reflecting light, thus causing operator's discomfort and interference with proper and efficient operation.

Half-duplex: A mode of transmission in either direction of the circuit where only one end may send or receive at any particular time.

Halftone: Continuous-tone images (e.g., photos) cannot be reproduced by printing from a flat surface plate. Such pictures are filtered by a screen and the whole picture is transformed into a grid of dots of various mutual distance, size and shape. The resulting dots can transfer on paper various amounts of ink to generate the impression of white, black and different levels of gray as in the original continuous-tone picture.

Halftone screen: A glass or film screen provided with a fine cross-line mesh; it serves to convert a continuous-tone image into a pattern of tiny dots of different size and density as a result of a photomechanical reproduction. Screening can be done at different angles and the line density varies over a wide range (50-500 lines per inch).

Hard copy: Information printed by any means rather than displayed.

Hardware: The physical aspect of computers and data-processing systems (the mechanical, magnetic, optical, electrical or electronic components) as opposed to software and firmware.

HDTV: High-density TV.

Head-end: A cable TV facility for reception of signals from varied sources for distribution within the network.

Hertz (Hz): A unit of frequency equaling one cycle per second (cps).

High-density TV (HDTV): TV systems with higher than the present picture resolution. (The NTSC standard offers 525 lines.)

High-level language: Any of an increasing number of computer languages in which instructions are specified by the programmer using English language statements that are compiled by the compiler into the machine language understood by a particular computer.

Holography: A method of producing holograms or three-dimensional images which can also be used to store data at high density; the image is created by interference between a laser reference beam and a beam reflected from the object respective. The image is stored on and retrieved from a thermoplastic or similar recording film.

Host computer: The central computer in time-sharing online systems that provides the computer power through its CPU, central files and communications facilities for remote users connected to it through their computers and terminals.

Hue: The redness, greenness or blueness of a scanned colored object.

Huffman code: One of the methods of data compression (compaction).

Hyphenation: A special case of line justification in which a word must be divided between two lines. Hyphenation used to be done manually but in computerized composition systems, word breaks are performed as discretionary by the operator for longer words, without hyphen by spacing words or letters, by computer logic or with the assistance of an exception dictionary in support of logic. Combinations of the above are available in specific systems.

Image scanning (page scanning): A process of examining the entire image or page (paper or film) spot by spot on a line and line by line down the page by an array of photosensors (e.g., CCD elements, photodiodes) and recording the amount of reflected light (from black, white spots and dots on the greyscale) as converted into electrical signals of corresponding intensity. Resulting digital data may be stored or displayed; the image may be processed, modified, transmitted or output on a variety of media (film, plate or paper).

Imposition: The ordering of pages on a printed sheet so that the printed sheet can be folded to 4, 8, 16 and 32 pages and trimmed with the pages arranged in proper order. See also Signature.

Ink-jet printer: A nonimpact printer that forms characters and graphics (also in color) by using a fine jet of ink applied as droplets, under computer control.

Integrated circuit: The entire electronic circuit built on a chip, the chip being inserted into a protective body.

Interactive service: A service that allows some degree of interaction to take place between the user and the system. It may range from "grabbing" a specific frame in teletext to complex interaction in on-line retrieval.

Informatics: Information science to include all aspects of information handling and system design.

Information: The meaningful content ascribed to data; now often used interchangeably with "data."

Interface: A piece of hardware or its combination with software enabling two components of a system to work with each other. Human-machine interface is more complex because it involves human perception and cognition.

Interpretor: A translator-type program for conversion of higher-level instructions into machine code and instantaneous execution.

Inverted file: A file consisting of pointers indicative of the contents of the sequential source file from which the pointers were selected. Pointers may be keywords, subject headings or all significant words occurring in the source records; inverted file is thus a tool in retrieving relevant records from the sequential source file by whatever strategies may be available on a given system.

IP: Information provider.

ISBN: International Standard Book Number.

ISO: International Standards Organization.

ISSN: International Standard Serial Number.

Joystick: An input tool for graphics terminals, videotex input creation, etc., operated by the user, sometimes as an alternative to key functions; used to manipulate the cursor, in generating points, lines, arcs, circles and other geometric primitives.

Jukebox: A computer-controlled device designed to store multiple optical digital disks (up to over 100) and to serve them automatically as required in a particular application.

Justification: Spacing of words or even intercharacter spacing with proportionally spaced characters so that even margins result.

Kanji: The subset of Japanese writing based on Chinese characters.

KBS: Knowledge-based system.

Kerning: Improving the visual effect by reducing the space between two contiguous characters in composition. Kerning pairs may be stored in computer memory for automatic execution by a composition program.

Keypad: A hand-held device to input user's information to a videotex or teletext system.

Keyword: Used interchangeably with term, index term, descriptor, subject heading, etc., to denote words in textual context as characteristic of a document's content; used to retrieve the document in a variety of applicable strategies often via inverted index.

Kilo: Metric prefix for 10^3.

Kilobyte: One thousand bytes (precisely 1024).

Kilohertz: One thousand hertz (1000 cycles per second).

Knowledge base: A database incorporating a mass of expert knowledge in a particular subject area large enough to be able to function in a given computer system (such as an expert system) as a source of expert advice under the control of a program capable of making conclusions (the program is called an inference engine.)

Knowledge-based system (KBS): Synonymous with expert systems.

LAN: Local area network.

Large-screen TV: TV screen of larger than normal size; can be synonymous with "flat-screen TV" or "projection TV."

Laser: Acronym for "Light amplification by stimulated emission of radiation"; a process of generation and source of coherent light with application in scanners, laser disks and electronic laser printers.

Laser disk: See Optical disk.

Laser printer: A page printer (nonimpact) having its own digitized fonts and able to integrate text and graphics by "painting" them from the memory where they have been prepared as an entire page using some page description language. High speeds are possible but there are now also medium- and low-speed printers often of desktop size. High speed is around 20,000 lines per minute and low speed around eight pages per minute depending on complexity. Resolution is improving (standard resolution presently 300 dots per inch) steadily.

Layout: The hand-drawn (formerly) or computer-designed preliminary plan of basic elements (text columns, line graphics, images, etc.), on a page or pages as a guideline for subsequent operations. See also Dummy.

LCD: Liquid crystal display.

Leading: Space left between lines of set type.

Leased line: A communication channel at the sole disposal of a customer leasing it at a fixed cost rather than using a dial-up line based on a different fee structure.

LED: Light-emitting diode.

Ligature: Two or more letters generated as one character.

Light-emitting diode (LED): A semiconductor junction diode that converts electric energy into radiant electromagnetic energy at visible wavelengths. Application in display units and in optical fiber transmission systems.

Light pen: An input device resembling a fountain pen. The points where the light pen touches the screen are picked up by the electronics of the pen and transmitted via cable to the computer as coordinates of the respective points on the screen as intended by the operator. The computer then interprets the data as sketching on the screen, selection of items in a menu, etc.

Line of sight communications: Transmission or broadcast in such a manner that there is a straight line between the transmitter and receiver; beyond that the signal must be retransmitted by a repeater owing to attenuation.

Line printer: Computer printer printing one line at a time.

Liquid crystal display: Visual display in which two glass plates with liquid crystal material in between have segments of characters etched on them; by selectively applying voltage, the arrangement of crystal molecules is changed which results in visibility of characters.

Local area network (LAN): A transmission medium connecting computers of all categories, terminals and varied peripherals (printers, facsimile devices, display units, various storage devices, etc.), confined to a small area (such as rooms, floors, buildings or campuses) with the purpose of better cooperation, more efficient procedures and sharing of resources (hardware, software and data).

Logoff: The process of disconnecting a terminal from a host computer.

Logon: The process necessary to connect a terminal with a host computer.

LPI: Lines per inch (resolution).

LPM: Lines per minute.

LSI: Large-scale integration; refers to density of transistors on a single chip (upward from 200).

Luminance: A level of light (as associated with a pixel in scanning). Often referred to as brightness.

Machine language: Language consisting of ones and zeroes that a computer can interpret and act upon. The program compiled is said to be in object code.

Magnetic disk: A storage media in the shape of a flat, rotating circular plate with magnetizable surface; data are written on and read from the disk by means of a magnetic head in the disk drive. Data are recorded as polarized spots on the surface.

Magnetic tape: Computer storage medium consisting of continuous tape (length most often is 2400 feet) with a magnetic surface where bits are recorded in parallel as bytes for storage and sequential access; handling takes place in a magnetic tape drive. Current common recording densities are 800, 1600 and 6250 cpi.

Main frame: Often used as synonym for central processing unit, but recently (especially as "mainframe") more frequently to denote a large computer as distinct from mini- and microcomputers. It typically involves high-speed, high-volume processing often in remote mode.

Main storage (main memory): Addressable storage controlled by the central processing unit; it stores currently processed data and the program being used. Also internal or primary storage. Cf. Auxiliary storage (secondary storage).

MARC format: Acronym for "machine-readable cataloguing." This format has been designed to facilitate exchange of information nationwide and internationally.

Measure, or line measure: The width of a composed line in picas.

Mega: Metric prefix for 10^6.

Megabyte: One million (precisely 1,048,576) bytes.

Megaflop: One million floating-point operations per second.

Megahertz: Radio frequency of one million cycles per second.

Membrane keyboard: Keyboard for typing information on a flat surface rather than keying it.

Menu: Command or information options from which users of a system can select at a particular junction, leading them possibly through more hierarchical levels. User-friendly interface for a novice, sometimes irritating to the seasoned system user.

Message switching: Concept sometimes synonymously applied to the store-and-forward principle, sometimes to packet switching.

MICR: Magnetic ink character recognition.

Micro: Metric prefix for 10^{-6}.

Microcomputer: A small computer with a microprocessor as its CPU; its capabilities are on such constant rise as to make it hard to differentiate from the minicomputer. Personal computer is a synonymous term even though at times it is used in contrast to business microcomputers.

Microforms: See Micrographics.

Micrographics: The discipline concerned with producing and using microforms for convenient storage—16-, 35- and 105-mm film or microfiche (fiche) with reduction ratio in the range of 18 and 48 and accommodating up to 200 images. Reduction ratio of 150 yields ultrafiche with up to 3000 microimages. Computer-output microform devices store computer-processed data.

Microprocessor: The central processing unit of a microcomputer; also a control device for appliances and many other common use machines, tools, toys, etc. Usually supplied on one chip.

Microsecond: One-millionth of a second.

Microwaves: Electromagnetic waves upward from the 1000 MHz frequency range (wavelength on the order of centimeters).

Mil: A unit of length equal to 0.001 of an inch; used sometimes in determining size of the electron or laser "writing" spot in image-setters.

Milli: Metric prefix for 10^{-3}.

Millisecond: One-thousandth of a second.

Mips: Million instructions per second.

MIS: Management information system. A computerized information system usually composed of several subsystems, whose objective it is to provide all levels of management with information in support of their respective activities in areas such as planning, accounting, budgeting, statistics, personnel, marketing, etc.

Mnemonic Codes: Abbreviations of codes designed to assist the operator in remembering and recall of codes.

Modem: Abbreviation of modulator-demodulator. A hardware device that modulates binary codes (digital information) into tones (analog information) to be transmitted over telephone lines; conversely it demodulates the analog signal into the digital, binary language of computers, etc. Also known as data set.

Modulation: A process of modifying a characteristic of the carrier wave by the modulating wave.

Monitor (video monitor): Basically a television receiver without any channel selection; e.g., for display of videotex pages as generated by a decoder.

Monospacing: Typesetting in which characters are allotted an equal space. Cf. Proportional spacing.

Mouse: A relatively new type of input device gaining popularity as a user-hospitable input tool. When the hand-held device is rolled on a flat surface, the built-in potentiometer causes the cursor to move on the screen in the same direction; provided with one or more buttons for related functions.

MSI: Medium-scale integration (20-200 gates).

MTBF: Mean time between failures.

MTTR: Mean time to repair.

Multiprogramming: Simultaneous execution of more than one program.

Mux (also Mpx): Multiplexor.

Nano: Metric prefix for 10^{-9}.

Nanosecond: One-billionth of a second.

NAPLPS: North American Videotex/Teletext Presentation Level Protocol Syntax.

Narrowcasting: Serving narrower audiences, which may be widely dispersed, with specialized programs to suit their interests. Cf. Broadcasting.

Network: Computer systems and other electronic devices (workstations, terminals, file servers, etc.) mutually interconnected via telecommunications.

Network topology: Way in which nodes are interconnected.

NFAIS: National Federation of Abstracting and Indexing Services.

NLP: Natural language processing.

Node: Junction point in a network where switching is done.

Noise: Unwanted signal caused by circuit components or natural causes associated with use.

Nonvolatile memory: Memory in which data is stored permanently and is not lost when power is turned off.

NOT: Boolean operator used to negate items to which it pertains; e.g., in information retrieval it would cause items designated by certain keywords not to be retrieved if the keywords in a query are negated by the NOT logic.

NTSC: National Television System Committee, the system and standard for television broadcasting in North America. See also SECAM and PAL.

Object code: A program state when compiled into machine language; opposite to Source code.

OCLC: Online Computer Library Center, Inc. (formerly, the Ohio College Library Center); the first bibliographic utility service to libraries.

OCR: Optical character recognition.

OEM: Original equipment manufacturer. An arrangement whereby a company acquires from original manufacturers hardware in bulk without a brand name and assembles it into customized integrated products, thus adding value to the components as well as providing marketing infrastructure to sell the products.

Office automation: New methods aimed at increasing the productivity of office workers and employing new technology based on computers and communications. Often described in conjunction with "office of the future."

Offline: Not in direct communication with the central processing unit of a computer system. Cf. Online.

Offset (lithography): A planographic (as opposed to relief and intaglio) process of printing where both the image and nonimage area are on the same plane; the basic principle of offset printing is that the image area is ink-receptive whereas the background is water-receptive. The plate is inked on a plate cylinder; the printing ink is transferred onto a rubber blanket and finally the image is offset onto a blank page supported by an impression cylinder.

Online: In direct communication with the central processing unit of a computer system; output data are received where input data have been entered. Cf. Offline.

Online information retrieval service: A publishing system in which the end user obtains online the requested information, more often than not, with the assistance of an intermediary usually using a terminal or microcomputer.

OPAC: Online public access catalog. A computerized library catalog for public access within a library or using communications lines, without intervention of an intermediary.

Operating system: A collection of control programs that makes it possible for a computer to manage its own operations—calling in a compiler, utility and user programs, data, controlling the input and output, scheduling of jobs, debugging, accounting, etc.

Optical character recognition (OCR): An information technology that converts human-readable data (typed, printed and handwritten) into machine-readable form through the use of optical (light-sensitive) devices; scanners measure the amount of reflected light (white spots reflect more than black spots) from paper and transform it, using photosensors (CCD elements, photodiodes, etc.), into electrical signals which are subsequently converted into digital form. Patterns as determined by scanning are matched against stored patterns using some recognition logic to reconvert them into human-readable characters.

Optical digital disk: Optical disk 12 or 14 inches in diameter based on optical reflective technology. Data is entered using the DRAW principle but disks may be pressed as well. Disks can be applied in jukeboxes. (See Optical disk)

Optical Disk: Disk serving as information storage medium in which information is encoded by a source of light (most frequently a laser) in a spiral (or concentric rings) as markings (called commonly "pits") with spaces in between (called sometimes "lands"). Zeroes and ones represent either bits as part of bytes (denoting characters) or they are elements in digital image (also called raster or facsimile) coding where 1 bit denotes either "white" or "black" or multiple bits (per pixel) represent shades of gray or colors.

Optical memory: Storage system in which memory writes and reads information by means of light (most often laser).

OR: The Boolean connector in which the resulting signal is true if only one of the input values is true (exclusive OR, also XOR) or if only one or both of the input values are true (inclusive OR).

Oracle: Teletext service offered by the Independent Broadcasting Authority in United Kingdom.

Orbit: An online information retrieval service offered by Systems Development Corporation.

Orphan: The first line of a paragraph by itself at the bottom of preceding page.

Packet switching: The mode of transmission whereby a message is parceled into addressed packets and sent through a network of computer-controlled nodes interconnected by multiple channels. On arrival the message is reassembled from the packets. In packet switching no direct connection is established between the originating and receiving station.

Page: A videotex or teletext unit of information occupying the screen at any particular time; a page carries a menu or constitutes a unit by which information is distributed and often, billed. Also a frame.

Page description language (PDL): Computer software that specifies contents of a complete page, inclusive of text and graphics, in a manner understandable to an imaging device which outputs complete pages.

Page printer: A printer that outputs a full page at one time rather than character by character or line by line. The necessary information is assembled prior to printing and is often formulated in a page description language.

Page scanning: See image scanning.

Pagination (electronic): Same as electronic page makeup or electronic pasteup; also numbering pages.

PAL: Phase alternate line. See also SECAM and NTSC.

Paper size: Letter size, 8.5 inch × 11 inch; legal size, 8.5 inch × 14 inch; ledger size, 10 inch × 14 inch or 11 inch × 17 inch. Common European sizes: A3, 11.7 inch × 16.5 inch; A4, 8.3 inch × 11.7 inch; A5, 5.8 inch × 8.3 inch.

Paper tape: Information carrier 7/16 inch or 1 inch wide with characters encoded into it in binary form as punched holes representing bits. With the proliferation of other more efficient means of storage, its importance has decreased dramatically.

Parallel transmission: A mode of transmission whereby individual bits constituting a byte or word are transmitted concurrently over separate channels. Cf. Serial transmission.

Parity bit: A check bit used in error detection; the bit is added to a group of bits to make the sum of bits either always even (even parity) or always odd (odd parity). The value of the parity bit is 0 or 1.

Parity check: The process to determine whether an error in transmission has occurred based on the total of "one" or "mark" bits received. See Parity bit.

Pascal: A high-level programming language named for the French mathematician credited with the invention of one of the first desk calculators; available on a wide range of computers in a variety of applications.

Pasteup (electronic): Same as electronic page makeup.

Pay-cable (more precise than pay-TV): A cable TV system in which for a flat fee subscribers can receive programming without commercials. (STV is over-the-air subscription TV.)

Pay-per-view: Charging scheme in cable TV whereby subscribers are charged per program viewed rather than a flat fee.

PBX: Private branch exchange.

PCM: Pulse code modulation.

PDL: Page description language.

Pel: Picture element, pixel.

GLOSSARY OF TERMS AND ACRONYMS 375

Penetration (TV): Indicates the marketing success of cable TV as the percentage of subscribing homes out of the total number of households in a given area.

Peripheral device: Equipment attached to a computer by cables and serving primarily auxiliary functions that would be impossible or functionally improper for the computer to perform. (Examples: image scanners, laser printers, file servers and many others).

Personal computer: Sometimes used as a synonym with microcomputer, sometimes used to stress the personal aspect of the term in contrast to use in business applications.

Phase alternate line: One of two European systems of 625-line color television. See also SECAM and NTSC.

Phase modulation: A method of modulation in which the amplitude of the modulated wave is constant and varying in phase with the amplitude of the modulating wave; a variation of frequency modulation.

Photocell: See Photodiode.

Photodiode: A photosensor (photoelectric transducer); a semiconductor used in scanners to transform the light reflected from a spot on the scanned line into electric current. Arrays of photodiodes are used to scan the entire length of a line and produce electrical signals varying in intensity proportionate to the amount of light reflected as they scan white, black and gray spots, also photocell.

Photoelectric transducer: See Photosensor.

Photosensor, photodetector: General term for a device capable of converting light energy into electrical energy as is the case in a scanner (e.g., photodiode, CCD elements, etc.); also photoelectric transducer.

Phototypesetters, first generation: Typesetters that constituted the first departure from the purely mechanical types. They were in their basic design similar to their predecessors, the hot metal and typewriter, but they generated type by photographically exposing it on photomaterial.

Phototypesetters, second generation: Typesetters in which the positive type images are exposed on photosensitive film or paper by selectively directing a beam of light through the respective negative character images stored on a suitable carrier such as film strips, disks or grids.

Pica: Unit of measurement for width and depth of type equal to a 12-point em (0.166 inch).

Pi characters: Characters (letters, symbols) not normally a part of a standard type font but still required in composing a given job.

Pico: Metric prefix for 10^{-12}.

Picosecond: One-trillionth of a second.

Picture element: The smallest individual element that can be depicted on a display screen by illumination. See Pel, Pixel.

Picturephone (R) Meeting Service (PMS): A commercially available two-way, full-motion video conferencing system by American Bell, Inc.

Pixel: Picture element; pel.

Plotter: An output device used in computer graphics to plot graphics under computer control by means of the plotting pen on paper (or optical beam on photosensitive material) spread flat (flat-bed plotter) or moving around a drum (drum plotter).

PMS: Picturephone (R) Meeting Service.

Point: Approximately 1/72 of an inch (0.01383 inch); 12 points constitute 1 pica, 6 picas equal 1 inch (approximately).

Port (input/output): The connection (interface) that links a computer to user communications lines or to peripheral devices.

Portability: A quality of software whereby a program may be run on different computers; also compatibility.

Prepress: Those stages in publishing that precede final printing.

Prestel: The British videotex system.

Printer: An output device printing character by character, one line at a time or page by page.

Private branch exchange (PBX): Telephone exchange of one single organization connected to a public telephone exchange.

Process Camera: Standard equipment for halftone preparation, color separation, etc. in the conventional prepress. Today process camera is being replaced by electronic devices such as electronic scanner, color separation-scanner, etc.

Process color: The process of full, four-color reproduction based on the fact that human eye perceives the tiny dots deposited on paper by the printing process in three basic colors (cyan, magenta, yellow) plus black, as a continuous transition of a multitude of composite color shades. In the process the original color copy is separated by means of filters into four separation negatives (black and white) from which four printing plates are made and printed successively one over the other. Electronic color separation and platemaking are being increasingly adopted.

Programmable read-only memory: Memory purchased blank and programmed by a special device whereupon it becomes "read-only."

Projection TV: An optical system for projection of a large TV picture onto a screen.

PROM: Programmable read-only memory.

Proportional spacing: Typesetting in which space is assigned to individual characters commensurate with their width; thus achieving a better typographic effect. Cf. Monospacing.

Protocol: A set of conventions specifying how electronic devices can communicate with each other in a compatible manner.

Pulse code modulation (PCM): Process consisting of sampling, signal quantization, transmission in digital binary form and recovering of the original signal by a reverse process at the other end.

Quantization: Process in which an input analog signal is divided at time intervals into value ranges, and when it falls within a range, it is allotted a discrete (digital) value corresponding to that range; quantization follows sampling.

QWERTY: The first six letters in the top row of keys on the traditional keyboard.

Ragged; right, left, center: Irregular margins of text right or left. A contrast to justified margins.

RAM: Random access memory, a temporary, volatile type of memory. In contrast to ROM, one can not only read from it but also "write" into it.

Random access storage: Synonymous with direct access storage; in this scheme of storage, any data may be obtained by reference to its physical location on the device in a time independent of the location previously accessed.

Raster: The pattern of television scan lines generated by an electron beam and constituting a frame on the picture tube.

Raster image processor (RIP): Also raster imager, raster image controller, raster image device. A special-purpose computer that functions between a device where a page is finalized and an output device to drive a film, paper or plate imaging unit, an electronic printer, telefacsimile receiver or a video display. RIP is a versatile device potentially with a wide variety of capabilities in addition to feeding page-bits to an output device.

RC paper: Paper that is resin-coated to make it water-resistant during typographic processing and to produce permanent type.

Real time: Computer operations on a physical process performed in such a manner that its results can be used to monitor and modify the physical process (e.g., in manufacturing, production, scanning, etc.). Such processing is said to be taking place in real time.

Reference databases: Records in a database leading the user to full-text original sources. Bibliographic and referral databases are typical reference databases.

Reflective disk: A kind of optical disk in which reflection is measured. Two-sided disks must be turned over for reading the second side. Most optical disks are based on the reflective technology. Cf. Transmissive disk. See Optical disk, videodisk.

Register: Computer hardware in which central processing unit stores small amounts of data (bits, bytes, words), e.g., intermediate results of preceding operations for subsequent further processing.

Relational database: A method of data organization (database management system) in which data are arranged into arrays of rows (representing records) and columns (representing fields). Logical relationships between data are represented by a two-dimensional model.

Reserve leading: Capability of a typesetting machine to set two or more columns of text on the same page resulting from its ability to move photographic material up and down.

Resolution: A term used to define the quality of a display or printing device as related to its ability to reproduce detail. It is determined by the number of picture elements (pixels, pels) per area unit. For example, in TV it is a function of the number of lines, in VDT the number of dots constituting a character, in scanning the number of lines per inch or centimeter. Also called Definition.

Reverse video: Display of text and graphics in black (dark) on white (light) background rather than as usual, vice versa to achieve special effects. The capability of displaying both modes is referred to as reverse display.

RF modulator: Radio frequency modulator; used with microcomputers it enables computer output to be converted into an analog modulated signal displayed on a standard TV.

RGB (red, green, blue) monitor: A method of displaying color video signal on a special monitor which has three electron guns for mixing the three primary hues (red, green, blue) into the resulting color of the triplet (picture element). The amount of each of the three constituent colors is controlled by special electronic circuitry. (Standard television sets are based on composite color video and have only one electron gun.)

Rivers: An undesirable effect in composed text manifested by white spaces (rivers) running down the text. In electronic publishing, this effect calls for recomposition and can be detected on a display unit (soft proof).

RLIN: Research Libraries Information Network.

Robot: A computer-controlled device independently performing specific functions for which it has been programmed (production and service functions) using a special robot-control language.

Robotics: Branch of artificial intelligence specializing in the study and design of robots.

ROM: Read-only memory. A nonvolatile memory device with nonerasable contents for extremely fast access to data it stores. An example would be "booting" in micros wherein the CPU fetches the required software from the ROM when power is turned on.

Routine: Component part of a program usually composed of subroutines; sometimes used as "subprogram," sometimes used interchangeably with "program."

RS 232 C: Current revision of the RS 232 interface standard for connection of computer systems to data communication systems; standard determined by Electronic Industries Association (EIA).

Runaround: Type set so as to leave space for an illustration in any shape.

Run-end: A method of data compression (compaction).

Run-length: A method of data compression (compaction).

Satellite: A device orbiting the earth that relays communication signals across its path.

Scanning, image or page: See Image scanning.

Scrambler: A device used to make a signal unintelligible to unauthorized TV sets which are not equipped with descramblers.

Scrolling: Moving data displayed on a CRT up or down (vertical scrolling) or horizontally (horizontal scrolling).

SDC: Systems Development Corporation.

SDI: Selective dissemination of information.

SECAM: French television system; one of two European systems of 625-line color television. See also PAL and NTSC.

Secondary publishers: Database producers and abstracting and indexing services.

Seek time: Time required in the search for data to position the access mechanism of a direct access device at the data location. A direct access device may be a magnetic disk and the access mechanism may be the read/write head.

Selective dissemination of information (SDI): Periodical dissemination of information to users on the basis of the match between their profiles and the keywords describing a document.

Serial transmission: A mode of transmission whereby individual bits constituting a byte or work are transmitted sequentially, one after another over the same channel. Cf. Parallel transmission.

Serif: A short stroke projecting from the main stroke of a character; typefaces are called "serif" in contrast to "sans serif" typefaces, which do not have this feature.

Sheet size: See Paper size.

Signal: Electrical impulses conveying information, from point to point through electronic or optical means. Information transmitted may be encoded in the analog or digital mode.

Signature: A set of pages printed together and occupying both sides of the same sheet.

Simplex: Transmission in which signals travel only in one direction. Cf. Half-duplex, Full duplex.

Simulation: Application of a system (computer, mathematical model, etc.) to imitate the behavior of another system, e.g., using a computer simulation program for convenience, lower cost, time savings or because the phenomenon under study cannot be examined directly. For instance, a market simulation program can be used in estimating the success of a certain kind of publication in a given market; a flight simulation program can be applied in training prospective pilots. The market and an airplane are the systems being simulated.

Slave typesetter: A typesetter under the control of another unit (front-end).

Slow-scan television: Sending a still video image via a regular voice-grade channel in a trade-off of motion for a lesser bandwidth. Suitable where real-time presentation is not required such as in transmission of printmatter, pictures and slides.

Small-scale integration: Density on a single chip of less than 20 gates.

Soft proof: Proof as displayed on a display screen sometimes obviating the need for a hard proof.

Software: A set of programming instructions to be followed by a computer in completing intended tasks.

Solid setting: Setting of type so as to leave no leading (spacing) between lines.

Source code: Program statements as written by a programmer in a source language (usually a high-level language); requires compiling before execution.

Source databases (original databases): Collections of data containing the substantive information, as opposed to reference data leading the user to the source of information. Source databases are full-text and numeric databases.

Spreadsheet: A type of software recently becoming popular with the microcomputer revolution; it manipulates numbers in rows and columns for purposes of analysis, simulation, modeling, etc.

SSI: Small-scale integration (less than 20 gates).

Stabilization paper: A kind of phototypesetting material in which the developer is incorporated in the photosensitive emulsion on the paper for fast, waterless processing at the expense of type durability.

Store-and-forward: A method of handling messages in messaging systems (data communications) whereby incoming messages are computer-stored until the destination station is free to receive.

Streaming tape: Processing of magnetic tape continuously rather than interrupting the tape transport between data blocks; the resulting higher speed is appreciated for large-volume operations such as back-up storage.

Stripping: An important function in the prepress whereby individual components of a page (such as photographic negatives and positives) are placed in proper position to form a complete page on a carrier (film, paper or glass) for subsequent platemaking; an expensive and time-consuming job, which in electronic publishing is being replaced by electronic page makeup.

STV: Over-the-air broadcast TV on subscription basis; programs require a decoder to unscramble the signal.

Subscript, also inferior (letter): A small-size numeral or letter positioned below the baseline as used in mathematical text and other special applications.

Supercomputer: A computer characterized by large processing power (measured in hundreds of millions of instructions per second), deviation from the standard architecture as devised by von Neumann for sequential processing (such as parallel processing), and size and cost affordable for shared use by multiple organizations.

Supermicrocomputer: Microcomputer using 32-bit words and working at speeds of 1-5 million instructions per second; this category closes the gap between microcomputers and minicomputers.

Superscript, also superior (letter): A small-sized numeral or letter positioned above the X-height and to the side of another character such as in mathematical setting, footnote citation or other special applications.

Super station: A TV station feeding its programs to cable systems over a satellite for further distribution.

Synchronous transmission: A mode of transmission whereby each bit and character is precisely clocked in a fixed time interval. Cf. Asynchronous transmission.

TCTS: Trans-Canada Telephone System.

TDM: Time division multiplexing.

Telecommunications: See Data communications.

Telecommuting: Working from home via a remote workstation (microcomputer, terminal and requisite peripherals) rather than physically commuting, thus substituting telecommunications for travel.

Teleconferencing: A mode of communication between three or more persons at remote locations in real time using a telecommunications system to replace face-to-face meetings, travel and multiple bilateral communications; may involve audio, video, text and data singly or in combination.

Telefacsimile: See Facsimile.

Telematics/telematique: Term coined in France to include both computers and telecommunications.

Telenet: A packet-switched network in the United States.

Teleprocessing: Computer processing of data at one or more remote locations and most often with involvement of information/data users over communication lines.

Teleshopping: Shopping electronically from home including display of merchandise, ordering and paying via videotex or microcomputers.

Telesoftware: Software distributed (downloaded)electronically to where it is needed.

Teletel: French videotex system.

Teletex: An enhanced teletype service (not to be confused with teletext).

Teletext: A one-way, noninteractive electronic publishing system in which information of ephemeral nature is inserted on the vertical blanking interval and broadcast in repeating cycles to consumers who intercept it by keying desired frame numbers by means of handheld keypads for display on TV screens.

Teletypewriter exchange service (TWX): A semiautomatic switching service similar to Telex (q.v.) for connecting teletypewriter stations.

Telex: An automatic dial-up teletypewriter switching service undertaken by a number of common carriers on a worldwide scale.

Telidon: Canadian videotex system.

Telset: Finnish videotex system.

Tera: Metric prefix for 1012.

Terminal: A peripheral device on the human-computer interface where input and output takes place. (Examples: keypads, keyboards, optical character recognition, bar-code readers, image scanners, voice-input devices, visual display terminals, printers, plotters, voice-output devices, etc.).

Text editor: Software for manipulation of electronically stored text including text entry, additions, deletions, transposition, etc., to prepare a final copy.

Thermal printer: Nonimpact printer of dot-matrix type outputting on special thermal paper by means of heated elements.

Three-dimensional television: TV based on any of a number of systems (split-image, polarization, anaglyph, direction selective, etc.), enabling a user to see TV picture in three dimensions; several principles have been demonstrated to be workable but practical application is very limited at present.

Time division multiplexing (TDM): A method of combining two or more channels of information into one link in which each channel is assigned a different time interval for transmission; the information is interleaved on the multiplexed channel and, at the end, the channels are reconstructed from the fast channel.

Time-sharing: A manner of sharing the central processing unit with other users, giving the illusion that each user has the CPU exclusively accessed via a terminal.

Titan: French videotex system.

Touch-sensitive screen: A display screen enabling users to enter input by touching specific areas of choice on the screen, thus removing the need to memorize commands.

Trackball: A device designed to move a cursor around a computer screen. Like the mouse, it too, is based on potentiometers relating movement of the ball to the position of the cursor.

Transborder data flow: Transfers of data across national boundaries in whatever form.

Transceiver: A device with both transmitting and receiving capability, either concurrently or not.

Transducer: A device that receives energy from one system and transforms it into another form of energy (e.g., optical to electronic) in the process of transmitting a signal.

Transfer rate: An indicator of how fast data are moved between a direct-access device and the CPU, measured in kilobits or bytes per second.

Translator: A program translating from one language into another; more general term than "compiler" (Cf. Compiler), which translates from a source language into machine language ("one for many" instructions).

Transmissive disk: Optical disk made of translucent material so that reading the other side does not require the disk to be turned over but rather the laser beam to be refocussed. See Optical disk, Videodisk.

Transparent operations: Physical parts of a system and their functions that are not perceived by the user; a desirable system characteristic leaving users to concentrate on their tasks.

Tree structure: A hierarchical system of data organization in which each item is related to one item only on a higher level. The highest level is called a root. Access to levels is usually by means of menus leading up and down the hierarchy.

TTY: Teletypewriter.

Turnkey system: A computer-based system with specific applications, designed for operation by nonprogrammers and easy implementation, and marketed by highly specialized suppliers.

TWX: Teletypewriter exchange service.

Tymnet: A packet-switched network in the United States.

Typeface: (1) Collective name of a family of type designs (Helvetica, Bookman, Times, etc.), i.e., typeface family; (2) One of the styles in a typeface family, for instance, bold, italic, roman, etc.

Type library: All typefaces collectively available to a system in physical or electronic form.

Typesetters (phototypesetters), third generation: Typesetters that store fonts digitally rather than as font masters on films strips, grids, etc. Type is electronically generated on a CRT tube wherefrom it is transferred (exposed) on a photographic medium.Laser typesetters are included here but sometimes they are referred to as members of the fourth generation.

Typesetting: Setting of type or completely composed pages (image setting) on paper, film or plate.

UHF: Ultrahigh frequency. Frequencies ranging between 300 and 3000 MHz.

ULSI: Ultralarge-scale integration. Density of 100,000 or more transistors on a single chip.

UNIX: A minicomputer operating system developed by Bell Laboratories, also available for some microcomputers.

Uplink: A communications facility for transmitting a signal to a satellite.

Uploading: Transferring information from a user's local computer to a remote computer. Cf. Downloading.

UTLAS: University of Toronto Library Automation System.

Value-added network: A basic communications network enhanced by some additional facilities (e.g., switching centers) to suit specific applications, for instance, packet-switched networks in online information retrieval.

VAN: Value-added network.

VBI: Vertical blanking interval.

VCR: Video cassette recorder.

VDT: Video display terminal, also video display unit (VDU).

VDU: Video display unit, also video display terminal (VDT).

Vertical blanking interval (VBI): When the electron beam moves from the bottom line to the top line of the TV raster to start a new frame, some 22 lines occur during this time; these lines are used not to carry the TV picture but to blank out the previous one. These lines are called the vertical blanking interval and at least some of them that are not yet committed can be used to carry a teletext signal.

VHF: Very high frequency. Frequencies ranging from 30 to 300 MHz.

Video cassette recorder: A device capable of recording and playing back video information.

Video conference, video teleconference: Teleconferencing involving voice as well as full-motion video or freeze-frame TV.

Videodisk: Disk serving as medium of information storage; "pits" (markings) and "lands" are of the different lengths required to represent the FM signal staying above or dropping below the center line of amplitude. From these pits and lands, the continuously changing signal may be recovered as an analog signal (even though pits and lands may be considered as essentially a digital type of recording being a finite set of elements). Videodisk may be either of the optical or nonoptical (capacitance) variety.

Video display terminal, video display unit: Device for display of information in the course of input or output.

Videotex: Umbrella term including both viewdata and teletext as the interactive and the noninteractive, broadcast variants. Cf. Teletext, Viewdata.

Vidicon: A vacuum tube consisting of a target plate, electron gun and deflection coils; part of a video camera.

Viditel: Dutch videotex system.

Viewdata: A two-way, interactive, electronic publishing system drawing on a computer-based databank from which users select information by keypad or keyboard, often from menus, and have it delivered via telephone lines (or by other communications channels) to their TV screens enhanced by decoders. Contents: news, weather, educational matter, games, transactional processes (teleshopping and telebanking), general and community information. Viewdata and teletext are subsumed under the broader term of videotex. Cf. Teletext.

Viewtron: Videotex system for users in Coral Gables, Florida, a joint undertaking of AT & T and Knight-Ridder Newspapers.

Vista: Bell Canada's videotex field trial.

VLSI: Very large scale integration. Density of (between 10,000 and 100,000) transistors on a single chip.

Virtual memory: Procedure in which pages of data or program are moved between the main and secondary storage (magnetic disk) as required by the computer; this creates the appearance of a larger memory.

Voice recognition system (voice data entry): A system that interprets spoken word by digitizing human voice for computer processing. Systems differ as to the vocabulary size, the need for "training" and to separate spoken words; capabilities are being constantly enhanced.

Voice synthesis: Ability of computers to synthesize words from stored phonemes and output them via loudspeakers, thus simulating human speech.

Volatile storage: Data stored that is lost when power is turned off.

Wafer: Thin disk of silicon from which chips are made.

Wand: A handheld, penlike device designed to read bar codes and input data for processing into a computer.

WATS: Wide-Area Telephone Service, an AT & T service for inward and outward calls on the public dial network at a flat monthly charge.

Wideband channel: A channel of wider bandwidth and higher rate of transmission than a voice-grade channel.

Widow: A single word or its part in a line by itself at the end of a paragraph; the last line of a paragraph by itself at the top of next page.

Winchester disk: A type of nonremovable, hard (rigid) magnetic disk enclosed in a sealed dust-free container featuring high storage capacity and fast access.

WLN: Washington Library Network.

Word: A set of bits as a unit that a particular computer can manipulate and transmit. The number of bits is called word length which may be either fixed or variable.

Word processing: Preparation (input, processing and output), and communication of written documents with the aid of computers on either dedicated word processors or general-purpose computers with appropriate software.

WP: Word processing.

WYSIWYG: "What you see is what you get," expression denoting display devices that have the capability built into them to display the true, exact likeness of the pages output by a system.

X-height (capitals, lower case): Height of capital letters or lower-case letters not including ascenders and descenders.

List of Organizations

Manufacturers, suppliers, consultants, publishers, colleges, libraries, and research institutes, either referred to in the text or relevant to the subject.

Adobe Systems, Inc.
1870 Embarcadero Road, Suite 100, Palo Alto, CA. 94303

Agfa - Gevaert N.V.
Septestraat 27, B-2510 Mortsel, Belgium

Aldus Corporation
411 First Avenue South, Suite 200, Seattle, WA. 98104

Alphatype
7711 N. Merrimac Avenue, Niles, IL. 60648

A M Varityper
11 Mount Pleasant Avenue, East Hanover, NJ 07936

Apollo Computer
330 Billerica Road, Chelmsford, MA 01824

American Chemical Society
2540 Olentangy River Road, Columbus, OH 43202

American Institute of Physics
335E 45 Street, New York, NY 10017

American Psychological Association
1400 N. Uhle Street, Arlington, VA 22201

Apple Computer
20325 Mariani Avenue, Cupertino, CA 95014
Arthur D. Little, Inc.
25 Acorn Park, Cambridge, MA 02140
Associated Press
50 Rockefeller Plaza, New York, NY 10020
Association of American Publishers
2005 Massachusetts Avenue N.W., Washington, DC 20036
Atari
P.O. Box 427, Sunnyvale, CA 94086
Atex
32 Wiggins Avenue, Bedford, MA 01730
AT & T
295 N. Maple Avenue, Room 6143F2, Basking Ridge, NJ 07920
Autologic
1050 Rancho Conejo Blvd., Newbury Park, CA 91320
Auto-Trol Technology
P.O. Box 33815, Thornton, CO 80233
Battelle
Columbus Laboratories. 505 King Avenue, Columbus, OH 43201
Bestinfo
1st Penn Building, 130S. State Road, Springfield, PA 19064
BLEND - Birmingham and Loughborough Electronic Network Development
Department of Human Sciences. University of Technology, Loughborough, United Kingdom
British Library
Research and Development Department. 2 Sheraton Street, London, England, WIV 4BH
British Library Lending Division
Boston Spa, Wetherby, West Yorkshire LS23 7BQ
BRS
1200 Route 7, Latham, NY 12110
Burroughs Corporation
Burroughs Place, Detroit, MI 48232
Caddex
18532 142nd Avenue NE, Woodinville, WA 98072
Camex
75 Kneeland Street, Boston, MA 02111

LIST OF ORGANIZATIONS

Canadian Institute for Scientific and Technological Information (CISTI)
National Research Council Canada. Ottawa, Ontario, Canada, K1A 0S2

Canon, Inc.
7 Nishy - Shinauku, 2-Chome Shinjuku-ku, Tokyo 160, Japan

Canon USA, Inc.
One Canon Plaza, Lake Success, Long Island, NY 11042

Chemical Abstracts Service
P.O. Box 3012, Columbus, OH 43210

CNCP Telecommunications
Room 712, 151 Front Street West, Toronto, Ontario, Canada, M5J 1G1

Commodore Business Machines
1200 Wilson Dr., Brandyvine Industrial Park, Westchester, PA 19380

The Commonwealth Scientific and Industrial Research Organization (CSIRO)
Central Information Service, 314 Albert Street, East Melbourne, Victoria, Australia 3002

Communitree Group
Suite 207-3002, 470 Castro Street, San Francisco, CA 94114

Compaq Computer Corporation
2033 FM 149, Houston, TX 77070

Compugraphic
200 Ballardvale Street, Wilmington, MA 01887

Compuserve, Inc.
5400 Arlington Center Blvd., Columbus, OH 43220

Control Data Corporation
P.O. Box O, Minneapolis, MN 55440

Cox Cable Communications Inc.
219 Perimeter Center Parkway, Atlanta, GA 30346

Cromemco Inc.
280 Bernardo Ave, P.O. Box 7400, Mountain View, CA 94039

Crossfield Electronics
Three Cherry Trees Lane, Hemel Hempstead, Great Britain HP2 7RH
65 Harristown Road, Glen Rock, NJ 07452

Crossfield Hastech
670 N. Commercial Street, Manchester, NH 03101

Cuadra Associates, Inc.
2001 Wilshire Blvd., Suite 305, Santa Monica, CA 90403

Datatek
818 NW 63rd Street, Oklahoma City, OK 73116

DIALOG Information Services, Inc.
3460 Hillview Ave., Palo Alto, CA 94304

Digital Equipment Corporation
146 Main Street, Maynard, MA 01654

Digital Equipment of Canada Limited
505 University Ave., Suite 1100, Toronto, Ontario, Canada, M5G 2H2

Digital Information Group
Stamford, CT

Disclosure, Inc.
5161 River Road, Bethesda, MD 20816

Dow Jones & Company, Inc.
P.O. Box 300, Princeton, NJ 08540

Eastman Kodak
343 State Street, Rochester, NY 14650

Easynet Systems, Inc.
4283 Village Centre Court, Mississauga, Ontario, Canada, L4Z 1S2

ECRM, Inc.
554 Clark Road, Tewksbury, MA 01876

EDUNET/EDUCOM
P.O. Box 364, Princeton, NJ 08540

Eikonix Corporation
23 Crosby Drive, Bedford, MA 01730

Electrohome, Ltd.
809 Wellington Street N., Kitchener, Ontario, Canada, N2G 4J6

Electronic Information Exchange System (EIES)
New Jersey Institute of Technology, 323 High Street, Newark, NJ 07102

Elsevier Science Publishing Co., Inc.
52 Vanderbilt Avenue, New York, NY 10017

Encyclopedia Britanica, Inc.
310 S. Michigan Ave., Chicago, IL 60604

Epson America Ltd.
23530 Hawthorne, Torrance, CA 90505

ESA-IRS, European Space Agency
Via Galileo Galilei, 00044 Frascatti, Italy

Evans Research Corporation
Toronto, Ontario, Canada

LIST OF ORGANIZATIONS

Facit Inc.
235 Main Dunstable Road, Nashua, NH 03061
Gerber
83 Gerber Road West, South Windsor, CT 06074
Golden Rule, Inc.
Chicago, IL
Graphic Communications Association
1730 N. Lynn Street, Arlington, VA 22209
Grolier Electronic Publishing, Inc.
95 Madison Ave., New York, NY 10016
Harris Controls & Computer Division
P.O. Box 430, Melbourne, FL 32901
Hastech Inc.
670 North Commercial Street, Manchester, NH 03101
Hell Graphics Systems
Grenzstrasse 1-5, Postfach 6229, D-2300 Kiel 14, Federal Republic of Germany
115 Cutter Mill Road, Great Neck, NY 11022
Hewlett-Packard Co.
19447 Pruneridge Avenue, Cupertino, CA 95014
Honeywell Information Systems Inc.
200 Smith Street, Waltham MA 02154
IBM International Business Machines
900 King Street, Rye, NY 10573
1133 Westchester Avenue, White Plains, NY 10604
Imagen Corporation
2650 San Thomas Express Way, Santa Clara, CA 95052
ImagiTex, Inc.
77 North Eastern Blvd., Nashua, NH 03062
iNET
Computer Communications Group. Room 900, 160 Elgin Street, Ottawa, Ontario, Canada, K1G 3J4
Info Globe
The Globe and Mail. 444 Front Street West, Toronto, Ontario, Canada M5V 2S9
INFOMART
122 St. Patrick Street, Toronto, Ontario, Canada, M5T 2X8
Information Access Company
11 Davis Drive, Belmont, CA 94002

Information International Incorporated (III)
5933 Slauson Avenue, Culver City, CA 90230

Inforonics, Inc.
550 Newtown Road, Littleton, MA 01460

Institute for Graphic Communication
375 Commonwealth Avenue, Boston, MA 02115

Institute for Scientific Information
3501 Market Street, University City Science Centre, Philadelphia, PA 19104

Inter-Consult
Cambridge, MA

Integraph Corporation
1 Madison Industrial Park, Huntsville, AL 35807-4201

Interleaf
1100 Massachusetts Avenue, Cambridge, MA 02138

International Typeface Corporation
New York, NY

I.P. Sharp Associates
Box 418 Exchange Tower, 2 First Canadian Place, Toronto, Ontario, Canada, M5X 1E3

John Wiley & Sons, Inc.
605 Third Avenue, New York, NY 10158

Knight-Ridder
774 National Press Building, 529 14 Street N.W., Washington, DC 20045

Knowledge Industry Publications, Inc.
701 Westchester Avenue, White Plains, NY 10604

Kurzweil
185 Albany Street, Cambridge, MA 02155

Laser Data, Inc.
10 Technology Drive, Lowell, MA 01851

Learned Information (Europe) Ltd.
Bessesleigh Road, Abingdon, Oxford, England, OX136LG

Learned Information Inc.
The Anderson House, Stokes Road, Medford, NJ 08055

Library Corporation
P.O. Box 40035, Washington, DC 20016

Library of Congress
Washington, DC 20541

LIST OF ORGANIZATIONS

Library Systems and Services, Inc. (LSSI)
Rockville, MD 20850

Linotype
Frankfurter Allee 55-75, 6236 Eschborn bei Frankfurt, Federal Republic of Germany
425 Oser Avenue, Hauppauge, NY 17888

Living Videotex
Palo Alto, CA

Lotus Development Corporation
55 Wheeler Street, Cambridge MA 02138

Magna Computer Systems, Inc.
14724 Ventura Blvd., Sherman Oaks, CA 91403

Massachusetts Institute of Technology
Information Processing Services. Cambridge, MA 02139

3M Company
223-2N 3M Center, Saint Paul, MN 55101

Mead Data Central
P.O. Box 933, Dayton, OH 45401

Microsoft
10700 Northrup Way, Bellevue, WA 98004

Microtek Laboratories, Inc.
16901 South Western Avenue, Gardena, CA 90247

Modtek, Inc.
12 South Walker Street, Lowell, MA 01851

Modulation Associates, Inc.
Mountain View, CA

Monotype
Honeycrock Lane, Salfords, Redhill, Surrey, Great Britain, RH1 5JP
in the U.S.:
509 W. Golf Road, Arlington Heights, IL 60005

Motorola, Inc.
3102 North 56 Street, Phoenix, AZ 85018

Muirhead
34 Croydon Road, Beckenham, Kent, BR3 4BE

National Library of Canada
395 Wellington Street, Ottawa, Ontario, Canada, K1A 0N4

National Library of Medicine
8600 Rockville Pike, Bethesda, MD 20209

National Research Council of Canada
   Information Exchange Centre, Ottawa, Ontario, Canada, K1A 0S2
NCR Corporation
   1700 S. Patterson Blvd., Dayton, OH 45479
NEC America, Inc.
   8 Old Sod Farm Rd. Melville, NY 11747
New American Page Planner
   1 Maple Street, East Rutherford, NJ 07073
Norpak
   10 Hearst Way, Kanata, Ontario, Canada, K2L 2P4
Online Computer Library Center, Inc. (OCLC)
   6565 Frantz Road, Dublin, OH 43017
Osborne Computer Corporation
   28538 Dante Ct., Hayward, CA 94545
Page Planner
   see New American Page Planner
Pergamon International Information Corporation
   1340 Old Chain Bridge Road, McLean, VA 22101
Pergamon-Info Line
   12 Vandy Street, London, England EC2A 2DE
Philips Information Systems
   15301 Dallas Parkway, Suite 300, LB35 Dallas, TX 75248
Radio Shack Tandy
   1500 One Tandy Center, Fort Worth, TX 76102
Ramapo Catskill Library System
   Middletown, NY
RCA Service Co.
   Rt. 38, Bldg 204-2, Cherry Hill, NJ 08385
Reference Technology, Inc.
   5700 Flatiron Parkway, Boulder, CO 80301
Ricoh Corporation
   3001 Orchard Park Way, San Jose, CA 95134
   5 Dedrick Place, West Caldwell, NJ 07006
RLIN
   The Research Libraries Group, Inc., Jordan Quadrangle, Stanford, CA 94305
Rogers Cablesystems, Inc.
   26 Floor Commercial Union Tower, P.O. Box 249 Toronto Dominion Center, Toronto, Ontario, Canada, M5K 1J5

LIST OF ORGANIZATIONS

Sanyo Business Systems Corporation
    51 Joseph Street, Moonachie, NY 07074
Satellite Business Systems
    8283 Greensboro Drive, McLean, VA 22102
Scitex
    P.O. Box 330 Herzlia Industrial Park, 46103 Herzlia B, Israel
    8 Oak Park Drive, Bedford, MA 01730
SDC Information Services
    2500 Colorado Avenue, Santa Monica, CA 90406
Seybold Publications, Inc.
    Box 644, Media, PA 19063
Silver Platter Information Services, Inc.
    Wellesley Hills, MA
Social Sciences and Humanities Research Council of Canada (SSHRC)
    255 Albert Street, P.O. Box 1610, Ottawa, Ontario, Canada, K1P 6G4
Sony
    Sony Drive, Park Ridge, NJ 07656
Source Telecomputing Corporation
    1616 Anderson Road, McLean, VA 22102
Studio Software Corporation
    17862-C Fitch, Irvine, CA 92714
Sun Microsystems, Inc.
    2550 Garcia Avenue, Mountain View, CA 94043
Tektronix, Inc.
    5302 Betsy Ross Drive, Santa Clara, CA 95054
Telecom Canada
    410 Laurier Avenue W., Suite 1160, Ottawa, Ontario, Canada, K1P 6H5
Telenet Communications Corporation
    12490 Sunrise Valley Drive, Reston, VA 22096
Texas Instruments, Inc.
    12501 Research Blvd., Austin, TX 78759
Texet Corporation
    37 Broadway, Arlington, MA 02174
Tymshare, Inc.
    20705 Valley Green Drive, Cupertino, CA 95014
University Microfilms International, Inc.
    300 North Zeeb Road, Ann Arbor, MI 48106

UPI
  1400 Eye Street N.W., Washington, DC 20005
UTLAS, Inc.
  80 Bloor Street West, Toronto, Ontario, Canada, M5S 2V1
Ventura Software
  25665 Tierra Grande, Carmel, CA 93923
Vu/Text
  325 Chestnut Street, 1300 Mall Building, Philadelphia, PA 19106
Wang Laboratories Inc.
  1 Industrial Avenue, Lowell, MA 01851
Warner Cable Corporation
  75 Rockefeller Plaza, New York, NY 10019
Washington Library Network (WLN)
  AJ-11, Olympia, WA 98504
Xenotron, Ltd.
  Vines Road, Diss Norfolk, Great Britain, IP22 3HQ
Xenotron, Inc.
  600 West Cummings Park #2500, Woburn, MA 01801
Xerox Corporation
  101 Continental Blvd., El Segundo, CA 90245
Xyvision
  101 Edgewater Drive, Wakefield, MA 01880
X* Press Information Services
  Golden, CO
Zilog Ltd.
  1315 Dell Avenue, Campbell CA 95008
Zylab Corporation
  233 E. Erie, Chicago, IL 60611

INDEX

A

Abstract thinking, of casual users, 307, 333
Acceleration of technology development, 105
Airbrushing, 152, 153
Alphabet, phonetic, 12
Alphageometric videotex, 66
Alphamosaic videotex, 66
Alphaphotographic videotex, 66
Analog encoding, optical memory media, 76
Analog form of information, 34
Analog signal, transmission, 34
Antiope, 66
Archival copies, in electronic publishing, 259
Archival function, optical disk, 21
Artificial intelligence, 217
   definition, 217
   in electronic publishing, 273
   expert systems, 218
   fundamentally changing publishing, 221
   natural language processing, 226
   and online information retrieval, 50
   robotics, 227
   trend toward hybrid, integrated publishing systems, 227
Audioconferencing (including enhanced audioconferencing), 97
Authors, in electronic publishing, 254
Automatic consultants, expert systems, 221

B

Bandwidth compression, codecs, 35
Billboard channels, on cable TV, 70
Bit-map graphics, in microcomputer-based systems, 168
Bit-map technology, 139
Books, "automated," 269
BRS after dark, 53
Bubble memory, 23
Business graphics systems, 154

C

Cable TV, 67, 267
   database services and polling, 68
   digital data transmission, 67, 71
   interactivity and addressability, 68
   library/information center-related services, 70
   and microcomputers, 72
   potential in electronic publishing, 71
   transmission of voice, data, video and facsimile, 72
   upstream communication, 71
CAPTAIN, 67
Cathode-ray tubes, 23
CD-ROM, 21, 80
   versus online information services, 51
Ceefax, 66
Cellular radio, 33
Character coding, 36
Charge-coupled devices (CCD), 23, 42
Chips, 16, 17
Coaxial cable, 29

Codec, as analog-to-digital and digital-to-analog converter, 35, 36
Codes, typographic, 120
Color graphics, hard copy, 27
Color graphics workstation, capabilities and tools, 152
Color illustrations, 269
Color separation, 144, 187
Color systems, prepress digital, 146
  advantages of film, 148
  assets, 146
  general diagram, 148
  production stage, 154
  remote input and transmission, 150
  similarities and differences, 147
Communications server, 140
Compact disk–read-only memory (CD–ROM),
  examples of applications, 82
  makeup and capacity, 80
  premastering and mastering, 81
  present focus of impact, 83
  representation of information, 80
Compaction (compression) of data, 41, 150
Composition, advancing of microcomputers into, 163, 167
Compression (compaction) of data, 41, 150
Compuscripts, 114, 270
Compu Serve 52
Computer, common sense, 28
Computer-aided design (CAD), 155
Computer-aided publishing (CAP). See Print-based electronic publishing
Computer architecture, 17
Computer-assisted editorial office. See Editorial processing center
Computer conferencing, and electronic publishing, 99
Computer-illiterate, and electronic publishing, 263
Computerization, as foundation of electronic publishing, 269
Computer output microform (COM), 26
Computers
  fifth generation, 19
  first generation, 18
  fourth generation, 18
  second generation, 18
  third generation, 18
Constant angular velocity (CAV), 75
Constant linear velocity (CLV), 75
Continuous tone scanning, and microcomputers, 236
Contone, digitized, 144
Convergence, of electronic publishing and office automation, 233
Converging technologies, 16
Conversion, media and data format, 238
Conversion of data representation forms, raster to vector and vector to raster, 161
Conversion software, 28
Converter (analog-to-digital and digital-to-analog). *See* Codec
Corporate publishing, electronic, 154
Cost-benefit, in electronic journal, 321
Cost model, in electronic journal, 321
Cultural gap, between passive media consumers and other information users, 13
Cut and paste
  electronic, 142
  in text entry and editing, 305, 334

D

Data compression (or compaction), 41, 150
  in prepress digital color systems, 150
Data entry/editorial process, 112
  acceptance of electronic methods, 119
  in book publishing, 118
  in computer conferencing systems, 117
  in newspaper publishing, 118
  originators to commerical typesetter, 114
  total electronic environment, 116
  traditional, 113
Database of databases, 192, 195
Databases
  full-text, 48
  in online retrieval, 47
Densitometers, in prepress, 187
Desktop prepress systems, 139
Desktop workstation, 139
Dialog's Knowledge Index, 53
Digital encoding, optical memory media, 76
Digital form of information, 34
Digital graphics, 269
Digitized color pages, in prepress, 150
Digitized contone, 144
Digitized images, transmission of, 173
Digitized separations, 144
Digitizing, 142; *see also* Scanning
Digitizing subsystem, 185
Digitizing tablet, 153
Direct broadcast satellite, 31
Direct-to-film systems, for newspapers, 148
Direct-to-plate systems, 148
  for newspapers, 148
Display ad makeup, 180
Displays, flat-panel, 23
Dow Jones news/retrieval, 53
Downloading, 49

INDEX

DRAW (direct read after write) optical disk. *See* Write-once optical disk
Dynamically redefinable character set (DRCS), 66

E

Easy Net, 53
Editorial process, 112; *see also* Data entry/ editorial process
  human information processing in, 327
  human performance in, 326
  traditional, in scholarly journal, 314
Editorial processing center, 119
Electronic communication, coexistence of diverse modes, 4
Electronic digitizing camera, 40
Electronic document delivery (EDD), 189, 272
  advantages, 199
  archiving function, 212
  background, 191
  centralized and decentralized, 193
  over complex of terrestrial and satellite networks, 204, 205
  definition, 189
  digital optical disk compared with automated microfiche cabinet, 206
  distribution on audio cassettes, 207
  distribution of encyclopedias, 200
  distribution on videodisk, 206
  distribution on videotape, 207
  electronic libraries in newspaper publishing, 201
  electronic upstream and/or downstream, 193
  examples of system, 197
  as filter imposed on information flow, 211
  finding pertinent items, 196
  future of, 212
  impediments, 191
  innovative distribution formats, 206
  of low-circulation scientific books, 204
  via microcomputer-based multi-media workstation, 205
  and microcomputers, 196
  with microform storage, 208
  modes of operation, 193
  through multiple media, 199
  in newspaper publishing, 198
  on-demand, 195
  optical memory media, 90
  output via teletex or as telefacsimile, 203
  in parallel with conventional publishing, 194
  position of publishers in, 191
  problems of present infrastructure, 190
  problems of users, 195
  as product of technology convergence, 198
  reasons of and motivation for, 190
  reporting on ongoing research, 202
  satellite communications, 199
  satellite delivery, 206
  and secondary publications, 191
  as selective dissemination of information, 195
  software distribution, 207
  software to impart intelligence to terminals, 197
  storage on optical digital disk, 203
  to subscribing libraries, 205
  telecommunication cost, 199
  using electronic document management system (EDMS), 208
  using optical digital disks, 200
Electronic Document Management Systems (EDMS)
  combination of microform and optical digital disk, 210
  diagram of a document delivery system, 208
  in electronic document delivery, 208
Electronic journal, 99, 267; *see also* Scholarly journal
  BLEND experiment, 102
  commercial application, 100, 102
  cost-benefit, 321
  costs, 311
  Electronic Information Exchange System (EIES), 101
  electronic publishing project at The University of Calgary, 103, 290, 293
  and expert systems, 222
  and microcomputers, 103
  reader response, 311
  reasons of nonacceptance, 100
Electronic library, characteristics of, 258
Electronic mail
  benefits and hazards, 96
  in broadest sense, 93
  computer-based systems, 93
  direct and indirect, structured and unstructured, 94
  and electronic publishing, 94
  mailbox, 94
  and networks, 96
  point-to-point, store-and-forward, mailbox principle, 93, 94
  shortcomings, 95
Electronic printers. *See* Printers, electronic
Electronic publishing
  advantages, 255
  authors as their own readers, 254
  contents, 275
  definition, 6

Electronic publishing [cont.]
  division of, 6, 11
  as dynamic chain of events, 253
  economics of, 276
  education for, 275
  fee for service, 263
  hazards of precipitous introduction of unfamiliar technology, 275
  human information processing in, 325
  impact on publishers, 255
  implications for authors, 254
  Information elite, information-poor and computer-illiterate, 263
  and libraries, 257
  by libraries, 54
  non-print-based, 266
  position of, 4
  print-based, 105, 267
  print-based versus non-print-based, 265
  problems, 255
  project at The University of Calgary, 290
  publishers of secondary publications, 256
  quality, 254
  role of the intermediary, 259
  as spin-off application, 11
  technology driven, 254
  users of, 262, 289, 298, 306
  vital role of publishers, 275
Electronic publishers, 3
End-user orientation, in online information services, 51
Erasable optical disk, 78
Errors
  in human-machine interface, 299, 330
  caused by abstraction, 304, 333
  comprehension, 299, 329
  random, 299, 329
Expert systems, 218
  automatic consultants and publishers, 221
  characteristics, 218
  and electronic journals, 222
  general diagram, 218
  some implications, 222
  inference engine, 220
  knowledge base, 220
  as machine learning systems, 225
  and online information retrieval, 224
  in publishing system selection, design and monitoring, 224
  in translation, absracting and indexing, 225

F

Facsimile. *See* Telefacsimile
Fatigue in human information processing, 342

File server, 140
Filmless systems, 181
Flat-panel displays, 23
Fonts, digitized, 126
Formatting, 120
Freehand drawing, 152
Front-end (typesetter's), 126
  definition, 128
  example, 132
  microcomputer-based, 130
  with raster image processor, 129
Front-end plus typesetter, working relationship, 130
Front-end versus typesetter, 129
  division of "intelligence," 129
  handling text and graphics, 128
Full-text documents, and libraries, 258

G

Gateways, 33
Generic coding
  benefits, 121
  definition, 121
Graphics
  resolution independent, 168
  digital, 269
  pasteup-to-plate, 181
Graphics systems, business, 154
Gravure cylinders, 151
Gutenberg, contribution to human civilation, 12

H

Halftones. *See* Screening
Holographic memory, 23
Human information gathering habits, 3
Human information processing
  of casual users, 309, 336
  in electronic publishing (in editorial process), 327
  external storage, 341
  fatigue, 342
  high-level, 341
  long-term memory, 340
  low-level, 341
  model of, 337
  pattern recognition processes, 339
  processing load, 343
  recall, 340
  sensorimotor processing, 341
  sensory perception store, 338
  short-term memory, 339
  and training, 340
  user-friendly human-machine interface, 343
Human-machine interaction, in technical publishing, 1567, 158

INDEX

I
Icons, 140
Idea processor, 124
Illustrations, storage and transmission, 146
Image (raster, facsimile) coding, 39
Image setters, 127; *see also* Typesetters
Imaging engine, in page printers, 246
Inference engine in expert systems, 220
Information
   age (era, society), 2, 15
   analog form of, 34
   digital form of, 34
   elite, in electronic publishing, 263
   lifeblood of electronic publishing, 2
Information manager, 261
Information providers, in videotex, 59
Information representation
   in optical memory media, 75
   vector form, 161
Information systems
   growth of, xv
   paperless, 192
   transparent, 49
Information technology, development stages in diagram, 222
In-house publishing systems, electronic, 154
In-plant publishing, electronic, 154
Integrated circuits
   LSI, 16
   outline of trends, 17
   ULSI, 16
   VLSI, 16
Integrated electronic communication, 236, 268
Integrated Services Digital Network (ISDN), 29
Interaction at the cognitive level, 13
Interdisciplinary science, trend toward, 16
Intermediary, changing role of, 259

J
Jukebox (disk changer), 74, 78

K
Keyboarding, electronic, advantages, 120
Knowledge base in expert systems, 220
Knowledge information processing systems, 19

L
Laser disk, applications, 79
Laser printers. *See* Printers, laser; Page printers; Electronic printers
Laser Writer Plus, and microcomputer, 168
Librarians/information specialists
   as communication facilitators, 261
   distributed, 262
   new roles in electronic publishing, 259
Library
   and archival copies in electronic pubishing, 259
   and electronic publishing, 257
   as an institution in electronic publishing, 258
   and the intermediary, 259
   and out-of-print matter in electronic publishing, 259
Library catalogs, 56
Library consortia, public-access services, 57
Library (bibliographic) utilities, 56
Line graphics, on microcomputers, 235
Liquid crystal display (LCD), 24
Lisp, 28
Local area networks, 31
Logic programming, 19

M
Machine learning systems, 225
Machine-readable text, originated by authors, 119
Magnetic disk
   comparisons, 21
   as working storage, 21
Magnetic storage, on microcomputers, 23
Mailbox, electronic mail, 94
Mass storage system, IBM 3850, 22
Microcomputers, 19
   applications in electronic publishing, 164, 229
   combined with scanners, 171
   composing complete pages, 231
   in composition, 163
   compuscripts by authors, 234
   with continuous-tone scanning, 236
   in control of information flow, 232
   conventional vendors, 240
   convergence of electronic publishing and office automation, 233
   and current trends, 232
   driving typesetters, 231
   economics, 237
   in electronic document delivery, 196
   as front-ends, 163
   and human-machine interface, 234
   in information and document retrieval, 230
   in integrated electronic communication, 236
   integration of text and graphics, 233
   as intelligent facsimile devices, 230
   interactive WYSIWYG display, 167
   and Laser Writer Plus, 168
   line graphics and page makeup, 235
   Macintosh Plus, 166

Microcomputers [cont.]
  low-cost data entry, 235
  Macintosh XL and Laser-Writer, 165
  magnetic storage, 23
  marketing aspects, 239
  media and data format conversion, 238
  and output via typesetters, 170
  in paper-based electronic publishing, 162, 230
  in print-based electronic publishing, 230, 162
  in query preparation and negotiation, 231
  for repackaging of packages, 231
  roles in prepress, 162, 235
  in self-service publishing, 168
  shift of activities closer to the author, 232
  shortening the information/ communication cycle, 240
  software explosion, 234
  specialized micro stores, 239
  systems integrators, 240
  in technical publishing, 234
  in total publishing systems, 164
  value-added microstore, 239
  and vanishing borderlines between prepress areas, 233
  versus videotex, 51
  videotexlike features, 230
  plus word processing software, 125
Microelectronics, impact of, 16
Microfilm raster scanner, 210
Microprocessors, 16; see also Integrated circuits
Modem, 35
Moore's law, xv
Mouse, 140
Multiplexing, time-division, 29

N

Narrowcasting, 73
Natural language processing, artificial intelligence, 226
Networks, 31
New media publishing, see also Electronic publishing
Newspaper publishing systems, interactive picture editing, 183
Non-paper-based publishing. See Non-print-based electronic publishing
Non-print-based electronic publishing, 43, 266
  definition, 11
Nontraditional publishing. See Electronic publishing
North American Videotex/Teletext Presentation Level Protocol Syntax (NAPLPS), 67

O

Offline information retrieval, 44
Off-the-shelf-systems, in electronic publishing, 162
On-demand publishing, 258
  involving optical memory media, 91
  prepress systems, 139
Online catalog
  outlook, 58
  user acceptance, 57
Online Computer Library Center (OCLC), 56
Online information retrieval
  definition, 45
  and expert systems, 224
  hybrid system using videodisk, 86
  and microcomputers, 49, 230
  trends, 49
Online information services
  and artifical intelligence, 50
  versus CD-ROM, 51
  end-user oriented, 51
  number of passwords, 52
  vertical integration, 50
  versus Videotex, 50
Online public access catalogue, 54, 257, 266
Online retrieval systems, searching, 47
Optical character readers, working principles, 37
Optical character recognition (OCR), in electronic publishing, 38, Figure 3
Optical digital disk (ODD)
  comparisons, 21
  definition and advantages, 87
  publishing system based on ODD, 88
Optical disk, 74; see also Laser disk
  archival function, 21
  erasable (writable, alterable), 78
Optical disk systems, and microcomputers, 75
Optical fibers, 30
Optical memory media, 73, 267
  analog encoding, 76
  assets, 90
  challenge to online information services, 91
  compatibility, 91
  digital encoding, 76
  in document delivery, 90
  dynamic applications, 92
  hybrid systems, 78
  impact, 92
  in on-demand publishing, 91

INDEX

problems of terminology, 73
representation of information, 75
Oracle, 66
Original equipment manufacturer (OEM), 108
Out-of-print matter, in electronic publishing, 259
Overlays and underlays, 152

P

Packet radio, as part of a local network, 32
Page description languages, Post Script, Interpress, Reprint, DDL, 166, 248
Page design, electronic, 153
Page-design station, 151
Page makeup (pagination), 142, 153, 177
 definition, terminology, 177
 diagram of a conventional and electronic system, 179
 merits, 178
 a newspaper system, 180
 problems, 178
 text and graphics integration, 178
 workstation, 151, 179
Page printers, 244
 features and performance, 246
 as a focus of entire publishing system, 250
 graphics capabilities, 247
 imaging engine, 246
 output, 247
 production speed and average monthly throughput, 246
 representatives, 249
 resolution, 246
Pagination, 177; *see also* Page makeup
Paper-based publishing, 6, 105, 268; *see also* Print-based publishing
Paperless information systems, 192
Paperless society, 26
Pasteup, 177; *see also* Page makeup
Pel. *See* Picture element
Performance, human, in editorial process, 326
Performance of casual users, in text entry and editing, 306, 327
Phonetic alphabet, 12
Picture description instructions, 42
Picture editing, interactive, 183
Picture element (pel, pixel), 40, 68, 150
Picture manipulation, 152
Pipelining, 18
Pixel (pel). *See* Picture element
Point-to-point, electronic mail, 93
Postindustrial society, 2
Prepress, 105, 270
 microcomputers' role, 162

requisite skills and education, 271
vanishing borderlines between sectors of, 271
Prepress digital color systems, 146
 advantages of film, 248
 assets, 146
 data compression, 150
 general diagram, 148
 production storage, 154
 remote input and transmission, 150
 similarities and differences, 147
Prepress subsystems, 171
Prepress systems
 desktop size, 139
 in-house, 139
 for on-demand publishing, 139
 providing short-run presses, 139
Prepress systems, complete trends, 138
Prepress systems
 originator to film
  color, 144
  input into, 142
  monochrome, 141
 originator to film, plate or gravure. *See* Prepress digital color systems
 originator to paper, 138
Prepress technology
 complexity and cost, 108
 division, 108
 new attitudes needed, 110
 rough outline, 106
 streamlining of, 107
Prestel, 66
Print-based electronic publishing, 105, 267; *see also* Prepress technology
 acceleration of technology development, 105
 important segment of industry, 110
 overview, 108
 trends: short-term, intermediate and long-term, 111
Print-based publishing, definition, 11
Print shop, 185
Printers
 daisy wheel, 244
 dot matrix, 243
 electronic, 243
 electrosensitive, 245
 impact, 243
 ink-jet, 244
 laser, 245
 nonimpact, 244
 page, 244
 terminology and division, 243
 thermal, 245
 thermal-transfer, 245
Process colors, 187
Prolog, 28

Proof printer, 142
Proofing, plain paper, attributes and examples, 184
Publication/communication process, inclusion of new forms, 13
Publishers, impact of electronic publishing on, 255
Publishing format, 3

R

Raster (image, facsimile) coding, 39
Raster image processor (RIP)
　capabilities, 175
　definition, 174
　diagram of a RIP-based publishing system, 175
　and fonts: bit map and outline, 175
　and typesetter, 174
Reader response, to electronic journal, 311
Resolution, in image scanning, 41
Retention of presented material, 340
Robotics, 227

S

Satellite, direct broadcast, 31
Satellite communication, 30
Satellite transmission, link between prepress and remote printers, 31
Scanners
　application in prepress, 172
　color-separation, 173
　common technology basis with OCR and fax machines, 174
　data transmission from, 173
　flatbed, 41, 142
　menus and screens, 173
　picture manipulation, 173
　sheet feeding, 41
Scanning
　digitizing art, 40
　text, 37
Scholarly journal, editorial process, 314
Screen-based publishing, 6; *see also* Electronic publishing
Screening, 186
Selective dissemination of information (SDI), 44
Separations, digitized, 144
Short-run presses, 139
Slow-scan television, 98
Software, 27
　conversion, 28
Source, the, 52
Still-video camera, 159
Storage, 20
Storage capacity, 23
Store-and-forward, electronic mail, 94

Subscriptions, reasons for decline in, 255
Supercomputers, 18
Supermicrocomputers, 20
System integrators, 240

T

Talkwriter, 25
Technical publishing systems, electronic, 154
　benefits of, 155
　characteristics of, 155
　distinctions among, 156
　graphics, 158
　input and output, 158, 159
　raster to vector and vector to raster, 160
　special features, 160
　technofobia, 263
　volume and scope of, 154
Telecommunications, 28
　capability per cost, xvii
　convergence with computers, 28
Teleconferencing, 97
　definition, 97
　economic justification, 98
　and electronic publishing, 97
Telefacsimile (also facsimile, fax), 213
　definition and principles, 213
　and electronic publishing, 214
　intelligent, through microcomputers, 230
　receiver, 213
　resolution, 214
　scanner, 213
　standards, 214
　trends, 215
Telematics, 15
Teletext
　on cable, 69
　definition and outline, 61
Television
　live, with two-way audio, 97
　slow-scan, 98
Text, and accountable, reproducible form of information, 13
Text and graphics
　copy fitting, 153
　integration, 233, 270
　on microcomputers, 167
Text input and manipulation, in word processors, 122
Thought organizer, 124
Thresholding, 40
Time-division multiplexing, 29
Tints, 186
Touch screen, 24
Translation, and expert systems, 225
Transmission
　of analog signal, 34

INDEX

digital, advantages of, 35
  of digitized images, 173
Tree-structures, in videotex, 60
Typesetters 126
  digital, 126
    CRT- and laser-based, 133
    speed, 133
  direct-entry (direct-input), 129
  example, 132
  first generation, 126
  fonts, 135
  fourth generation, 126
  front-end dependent, 130
  front-end independent, 130
  full-face (full-page), 130, 143
  output material, 134
  second generation, 126
  third generation, 126
  trends, 127
Typesetting, as office procedure, 136
Typesetting and printing, in publishing cycle, 135
Typewriter, electronic, 124
Typographic codes, 120
Typography, digital, landmark in human communication, 127
TV watcher, habitual, 13

U

Universal information services (UIS), 29
University of Calgary, The
  project EP
    communication, 297
    cost analysis, 319
    paper entry and the editorial process, 295
    problems, 296
    reader response, 315
    scope, 290
    tools and assistance, 294
    training, 293
    working environment, 291
Users, casual
  in editorial process, 289
  in electronic publishing, 262
  performance in electronic publishing, 298, 327

V

Value-added microstore, 239
Value-added networks, 46

Vector form of information representation, advantages and disadvantages, 161
Vector notation, 41
Vector processing, 18
Vertical blanking interval (VBI), 62
Vertical blanket interval, signal ownership, 69
Videoconferencing, 97
Videodisk, 74
  combined with microcomputer, 84
  in hybrid setup, 84
Videotex, 59, 267
  alphageometric, 66
  alphamosaic, 66
  alphaphotographic, 66
  definition, 59
  information providers, 59
  impact on publishers, 63
  versus microcomputers, 51
  national systems, 66
  versus online information services, 50
  present outlook, 64
  terminology, 59
Viewdata
  definition and overall outline, 59
  merits and main thrust, 61
  role and benefits, 61
Voice input, 24
Voice mail, 26
Voice message systems, 93
Voice response, 26
Voice synthesis, 24, 25
Voicewriter, 25

W

Wire services, 183
Word processing, assistance to authors, 123
Word processing software, on microcomputers, 125
Word processors
  characteristics, 121
  dedicated, 121
  special capabilities, 122
  typical capabilities, 122
  typical configuration, 122
Workstation, desktop, 139
Write-once optical disks, 77
Written conferences, 97
WYSIWIG display, 140

SOUTHEASTERN MASSACHUSETTS UNIVERSITY
Z286.E43 S73 1987
The electronic era of publishing

3 2922 00034 113 8

304577